WILLIAM GILPIN

HIS DRAWINGS, TEACHING, AND THEORY OF THE PICTURESQUE

Oxford University Press, Amen House, London E.C.4

GLASGOW NEW YORK TORONTO MELBOURNE WELLINGTON
BOMBAY CALCUTTA MADRAS KARACHI LAHORE DACCA
CAPE TOWN SALISBURY NAIROBI IBADAN ACCRA
KUALA LUMPUR HONG KONG

William Gilpin: Mountain chasm with a group of soldiers

WILLIAM GILPIN

HIS DRAWINGS, TEACHING, AND
THEORY OF THE PICTURESQUE

———

CARL PAUL BARBIER

OXFORD
AT THE CLARENDON PRESS
1963

PRINTED IN GREAT BRITAIN
AT THE UNIVERSITY PRESS, OXFORD
BY VIVIAN RIDLER
PRINTER TO THE UNIVERSITY

TO THE MEMORY OF
PAUL OPPÉ

Contents

Acknowledgements

I FIRST became interested in William Gilpin, when I tried some ten years ago to find out if drawings, in a volume just acquired, were really by the Vicar of Boldre. By the time I realized my supposed originals were only copies after the aquatint illustrations of his picturesque *Tours*, I had become so engrossed by the problem of what was and was not a Gilpin drawing, that I resolved to make a study of his artistic activities. At the outset I was privileged to receive the guidance and friendship of the late Paul Oppé, and shall ever be grateful to him for the hours he spent introducing me to English drawings and water-colours. I am also greatly indebted to Mr. Christopher Hussey, Professor William D. Templeman, and Mr. Iolo A. Williams, not only for their writings on Gilpin and the Picturesque, but also for the loan of drawings in their possession.

This investigation could not have been undertaken without the sustained interest and most generous assistance of Gilpin's numerous descendants, who between them possessed until very recently the bulk of the Vicar of Boldre's papers. For making drawings, letters, and manuscripts available, for answering the innumerable questions of an outsider, I thank Mr. Willoughby L. Benson; his brother, the late Rev. E. G. Benson; Mr. George F. Benson; Mr. Francis Alan G. Benson; his son, Mr. Alan de Gylpyn Benson; Mr. Archibald L. Fawcett; Mrs. E. G. Gilpin-Brown and Dr. John Bernard Gilpin-Brown; Mr. G. Brownlow G. Benson and Miss Ann Gilpin Benson; the late Mrs. F. E. Moore; her sons, Lieut.-Col. Desmond St. Leger Moore and Lieut.-Col. Neville St. Leger Moore; Mr. Edward Percival Gilpin; Mrs. Gwenn C. Mellis; and the late Mrs. Ella M. Scrymsour-Nichol.

I am also indebted to Major J. R. Abbey for making available many papers in his important collection of Gilpiniana.

For information freely afforded, or the loan of documents and drawings, I am grateful to Viscount Barrington, the late D. C. T. Baskett, Mr. Peter Bicknell, Dr. T. S. R. Boase, Messrs. Christie's, Mr. Andrew Clark of Colnaghi's, Dr. G. Chandler, Mr. G. L. Conran, Miss Mary Crake, Mr. Leonard G. Duke, C.B.E., Mr. Gilbert Davis, Mr. Michael Eden of Scaleby Castle, Miss Megan Ellis, Dr. Rowland E. M. Fawcett, Mr. I. R. Fleming-Williams, Mr. Brinsley Ford, Lady Waechter de Grimston, J.P., Mrs. Margaret M. Harvey, Mr. Luke Hermann, Mrs. Herbert M. Howe, Mr. Hesketh Hubbard, Mrs. Donald F. Hyde, Sir Bruce S. Ingram, O.B.E., M.C., Mr. Edward Ingram,

General Sir Henry C. Jackson, K.C.B., Mr. P. Long, Mr. F. R. Meatyard, Mr. Paul Mellon, Washington, Mr. John Morant, Mrs. John Perkins, Bernard Quaritch Ltd., Mr. Brian Reade, the late Michael Sadleir, Mr. Frank Simpson, Mr. Kenneth Smith, Archdeacon Francis H. D. Smythe, Messrs. Sotheby's, Spink & Son Ltd., Mr. Charles Tomrley, Lord Townshend, Mr. Charles Traylen, Mr. Oliver Warner, Mr. P. F. Williams of St. Bees School, the late Harold J. L. Wright.

For facilities accorded I acknowledge the kind assistance of the keepers and curators of many libraries and museums, especially those of the British Museum, the Bodleian Library, the Cambridge University Library, the Fitzwilliam Museum, Tullie House, Carlisle, the Pierpont Morgan Library, New York, the Victoria and Albert Museum, and the Witt Library of the Courtauld Institute of Art.

In addition to several of the above mentioned my thanks go to the Trustees of the British Museum, the Royal Museum of Fine Arts, Copenhagen, the Trustees of the Devonshire Collections, the Hermitage State Museum, Leningrad, Sir Osbert Sitwell, Bart, C.H., Mr. Philip Spencer, and the National Library of Wales, for permission to reproduce drawings, prints or paintings in their possession.

Lastly a word of thanks is due to the Court and Senate of Glasgow University for grants which enabled me to collect material and reproduce many documents and drawings, to my colleagues Professor Alan M. Boase and Mr. R. O. MacKenna for special facilities, and especially to Mr. Andrew McLaren Young, whose specialist knowledge has always been at my disposal, and without whose active encouragement throughout this book would perhaps never have been completed.

C. P. B.

University of Glasgow
1963

List of Plates

I. Introductory

$\mathbf{F}_{\mathrm{AR}}$ from being incisive, 'picturesque' may mean today anything from vivid, colourful, striking, to curious, quaint, odd, even charming and old-fashioned. It can variously be applied to a face, to the coloured jerseys of a rugby scrum, or to a row of half-timbered cottages; and being a graphic adjective, should call up a definite visual image. Rarely does it summon more than a sketchy vignette, unless supplementary information be given, when the adjective itself becomes almost superfluous, at most only predisposing one to visualize the object. Thus when I am told that a face is picturesque, I am ready to see that face, but remain in doubt as to what kind of face I am to visualize, though my hesitations vanish as soon as a qualification like lined, old, or sharply defined is added. Such was not always the case. The time was when it was sufficient to term a face picturesque for one to conjure immediately an old face with marked features. The adjective then rested on a solid foundation, that of the substantive 'Picturesque', which has now gone out of usage. In the eighteenth and early nineteenth centuries, the Picturesque had generally accepted pictorial connotations, with regard to both subject-matter and treatment, and so long as the Picturesque formed part of British taste, the adjective evoked in everyone a clear response. A picturesque landscape called forth in the mind's eye a sublime romantic subject treated according to specific rules of composition which insured varied and broken surfaces and the dramatic use of chiaroscuro. With the demise of the substantive, the adjective retains but a shadow of its former strength. Today our ideas as to what constitutes a picture are so varied that were I to talk of a picturesque landscape in the eighteenth-century sense, I would evoke little or no response save in one whose pictorial conception of nature happened to coincide with mine.

If we accept Sir Kenneth Clark's contention that the eighteenth century in England is not one of the great periods of creative art, but rather a period of luxury art when the ruling classes collected the works of the past not only for reasons of prestige, but also to establish a standard of taste,[1] then we may look upon the Picturesque as that standard of taste mainly concerned with landscape, which gradually gained general acceptance in the second half of the eighteenth century.

A picturesque outlook presupposes a pictorial vision acquired from an appreciation of certain models, and the eighteenth-century man of taste found these, firstly, in his own native

---

[1] Sir Kenneth Clark, 'Art and Society', *The Cornhill Magazine*, Centenary Number, Autumn 1960, pp. 314–15.

landscape tradition, heavily indebted as it was to painters such as Swanevelt, Van Everdingen, Berchem, and Van Diest,[1] and secondly in the works of Salvator Rosa, Gaspar Poussin,
and Claude Lorrain, painters for whom he developed a particular enthusiasm. This vision,
essentially cast in a seventeenth-century mould, was brought to bear on the multifarious
aspects of landscape which interested the man of reason and imagination, with diverse
results: landscape gardening was transformed; natural scenery was enjoyed for its own
sake and its moods recorded in numerous journals and sketches; travel literature was
endowed with descriptive prose; and our heritage, whether in the guise of ruins or noble
gothic churches, was seen with an understanding which had hitherto been absent.

Since Christopher Hussey brought out his pioneer study of *The Picturesque* in 1927, the
subject has received the serious attention of many scholars, notably in the United States of
America. In the wake of Elizabeth W. Manwaring have come the contributions of William
D. Templeman, Walter J. Hipple, and Paul Frankl, who all recognize the special position
which must be accorded to the Rev. William Gilpin (1724–1804) as the 'Master of the
Picturesque', the man who more than anyone else helped to shape the picturesque vision.[2]
These writers, whose interests are literary or philosophical, give us a narrow idea of
Gilpin's contribution, as they rely entirely on his published works. To understand the full
impact of Gilpin's contribution to the picturesque movement one must take into account
not only the public manifestation of his thinking as found in the various *Essays* and *Tours*,
but also the more private and equally effective means he adopted to disseminate his ideas.
We must examine his thousands of drawings which form the natural counterpart of his
theoretical writings, his active role as drawing-master, his unpublished writings (a number
of which were dispersed at sales in 1802 and 1804), and lastly his sustained correspondence
with William Mason, William Lock, Edward Forster, and Mary Hartley, who were all as
enthusiastic as he was in the picturesque experiment, and who contributed in no small
measure to the ideas he elaborated.

The present study of Gilpin's artistic activity seeks to give:

(1) A comprehensive account of his output as an amateur artist. The plates are selected
from a total of approximately 6,000 sketches and drawings examined over the last ten
years, and should provide collectors and dealers with a reliable work of reference. To
avoid confusion none of the countless copies and imitations made between 1780 and 1830
are reproduced.

(2) A survey of his development, as a critic of prints, paintings, and landscape, leading
to an analysis of his theory of the Picturesque. His theory is more varied and complex than
had been imagined, and his personal taste is considerably more austere and uncompromising
than that of many of his contemporaries.

[1] Henry V. S. Ogden and Margaret S. Ogden, *English Taste in Landscape in the Seventeenth Century*, Ann Arbor, 1955.

[2] Elizabeth W. Manwaring, *Italian Landscape in Eighteenth Century England*, New York, 1925; Christopher Hussey, *The Picturesque—Studies in a Point of View*, London, 1927; William D. Templeman, *The Life and Work of William Gilpin*, Urbana, 1939 (abbreviation: *Templeman*). For further bibliography see p. 98, note 1.

(3) An insight into the world of amateur art with which he was acquainted, beginning with his father, Captain John Bernard Gilpin, who was picturesque before the word acquired general currency, and ending with the many amateurs of a later generation who sought Gilpin's advice at Vicar's Hill in the New Forest. Without this cultured society of amateurs, whose ideas so often outstripped their drawing ability, there would have been no Picturesque. They helped to bring it about and they made it their own.

II. John Bernard Gilpin

IN his *Memoirs*, William Gilpin tells us that whatever artistic talent he possessed was inherited from his father, Captain John Bernard Gilpin (1701–76), and from his grandfather, William Gilpin, the Recorder of Carlisle (1657–1724).

The Recorder 'discovered' and for many years patronized the Whitehaven artist, Matthias Read (1669?–1747), who in his turn taught the Recorder drawing and the method of 'mixing colours in a pallet'.[1] Save for an oil-painting of a Holy Family after Carracci in the Scaleby Castle sale of 1904,[2] no other works of his have come to light. A great many of them were certainly landscapes, for his grandson refers to their picturesque qualities, and, indeed, rated the Recorder's skill above that of his own father. However, what is far more important is that here we have the first instance of that combination of patronage and amateurish skill which was to be such a pronounced feature of the artistic interests of the next two generations of Gilpins.

Of Captain John Bernard Gilpin we know much more, thanks to unpublished letters, and to the discovery of some 150 drawings. Born at Scaleby Castle on 24 January 1701, John Bernard chose a military career, and in 1721 was commissioned in the 12th Regiment of Foot. After an early marriage to Matilda Langstaffe on 3 June 1723, he rejoined his regiment in Scotland, where it remained stationed for the next few years. He was at Stirling, at Fort William, and travelled over to Skye. In 1730 his regiment was in Windsor Forest, but by 1733 Lieutenant Gilpin was back in Scotland, employed as before 'in making roads—in guarding the coast from smuglers—and in preventing and quelling riots, to which the country was then not a little addicted'.[3] Once or twice a year he obtained leave of absence to spend a month or two with his rapidly growing family at Scaleby Castle.

On 16 December 1738, thanks to Sir James Lowther, John Bernard was made Captain of an 'Independent Company of Invalids', two of which garrisoned Carlisle. If this appointment put an end to military ambition, it gave him at least a reasonable income and enabled him to settle down to a happy domestic life at the Deanery in Carlisle, which his old friend Dr. Bolton, the Dean, had some years before placed at his disposal.

His son, William, has left in the *Memoirs* a fine portrait of his father's character. Upright,

---

[1] *Memoirs of Dr. Richard Gilpin, of Scaleby Castle in Cumberland; and of his Posterity of the Two Succeeding Generations; . . .* Edited by William Jackson, London, Carlisle, 1879, pp. 17–18 (abbreviation: *Memoirs*).

[2] See Miss Elizabeth A. Fawcett's manuscript 'Notes on Scaleby Castle & the Fawcett Family', vol. i, 1914 (Dr. Rowland Fawcett).

[3] *Memoirs*, p. 54.

kind, and with a sense of fun, he soon became the centre of a literary and artistic circle. He was himself a gifted musician and interested in antiquities; but what is of especial interest to us, he drew, etched, painted, and fostered these accomplishments in others. This pleasant life was interrupted for a time by the 1745 Rebellion. Captain Gilpin did his best to prepare the town's defences, but when Carlisle surrendered he took his family to Whitehaven for safety. The troubles over, he resumed his former life in Carlisle surrounded by such friends as Dr. Bolton (1698–1763), Dr. John Brown (1715–66), the apologist of Shaftesbury, the Rev. James Farish, and Captain Leonard Smelt (c. 1725–1800), the military engineer who was later to become sub-governor to the Prince of Wales.

In 1749 the two garrison companies, no longer required to defend Carlisle, marched south to Plymouth. Captain Gilpin left his family behind, but a year later he retired on full pay, and henceforth lived at Carlisle, except for occasional spells of garrison duty at Plymouth.[1]

Taught drawing by his father and Matthias Read, he at one time seems to have considered the possibility of becoming a professional artist.[2] His military duties, however, gave him few chances for serious painting, and all he could do on active service was to draw with indian ink, 'a little of it rubbed on the back of the left hand, as a pallet, served a whole morning in stipling some part of a drawing'.[3]

Once Captain Gilpin settled in Carlisle he 'had a regular painting room', and tried his hand at most things. He drew with black-lead, chalk, and indian ink, etched, and occasionally coloured his pen and wash drawings. He also painted in oils, at times on a very large canvas, but it is his work on a miniature scale which seems to have been especially prized.

In Carlisle his enthusiasm was not matched by opportunities for self-improvement, for he was an amateur geographically cut off from those artistic contacts that might have given him the technical apparatus and the imaginative stimulus, without which no amateur can hope to become an accomplished artist. True, he seized what chances his journeys offered to visit country houses and centres such as London and Bristol. But since he had little contact with the crop of young painters (of whom Hogarth is the most important) who were beginning to make a name for themselves in London in the 1730's, he was forced to rely chiefly on such good prints as he could find. Although no oil-paintings of Captain Gilpin's have yet been identified, one would do well not to discount entirely William Gilpin's assessment of his father's ability with that medium: 'his pictures were nearly as good as any that were painted in those days in England; and if he was not the best painter, he was probably one of the best gentleman painters of his time'.[4] William Gilpin did not indulge in rash statements. When John Bernard died on 5 March 1776, the *Cumberland Pacquet* stated, in its notice, that 'he was supposed to have paintings of his own execution

---

[1] In 1749 and 1755 he was in charge of the first of the six garrison companies doing duty at Plymouth. George III renewed his commission on 27 Oct. 1760.

[2] Matilda Gilpin to her husband, 26 Apr. [1732] (A. L. Fawcett).

[3] *Memoirs*, p. 64.

[4] Ibid., p. 65.

worth £1,000',[1] and several of his larger canvasses were still to be seen at Scaleby Castle, after the 1904 sale.[2]

We get an idea of John Bernard's preoccupations from Dr. John Brown's letters to the young William Gilpin, then at Oxford: 'The Captain is at present upon a very grand undertaking: he is going to paint the famous story of Alexander & Diogenes: he has actually finished his design, which so far as I can judge is both just and beautiful. He intends to paint it in Crayons.'[3]

As tutor to the Captain's children, Brown had an excellent opportunity to observe at close quarters this society embued with the ideas of Shaftesbury and Hutcheson, where the concepts of Beauty, Truth, and Virtue were constantly under discussion, and where the reflections on poetry and painting by Dufresnoy and the abbé Dubos gave rise to much speculation on the parallels between poetry, painting, and music.[4] He sums up well the kind of conversation that took place in another letter to William, to whom he had promised a dissertation upon the 'three Sister Arts':

What I intended was only a trifling Paralel between Painting and Musick and Poetry, those three Sister Arts, which, altho each of them has something in her Countenance peculiar to herself, yet bear such a mutual Resemblance as demonstrates them to be of the same Parents; & if not Twin-Born, yet as Ovid says

Facies non omnibus una,
Nec diversa tamen; qualem decet esse Sororem.

But which is the Eldest, and which the most beautiful—which has the greatest Share of Merit, and which the largest Fortune—which a wise Man would chuse for a Mistress, and which for a Wife—whose Charms are the most exquisite, and whose the most durable—which most excites the Passions, which charms the Fancy, which improves the Understanding, all these and many other Secrets, I find, Time only and half a dozen Sheets of Paper can possibly discover.[5]

It is in this happy and earnestly cultured atmosphere that both William and his younger brother Sawrey grew up.

When he was stationed at Plymouth the Captain made many sketches of the surrounding district. In particular he was attracted by the coastline with its variety of little creeks and bays. Here, for example, is the account he sent his wife, in May 1755, of a short expedition inland.

Mr. Smelt, Mr. Mudge (a Son of Dr. Mudge) Mr. Dixon (an Engineer) & I went on a party of pleasure last wednesday; we went about 20 Miles into the Country, amongst the Hills, to view some Cascades & romantick Rocks, we were two days out & had a most agreeable jau[n]t, we saw two fine falls, but not to be compared to lowdour, nor is there any thing equal to Keswick I believe

---

[1] 14 Mar. 1776. See *Memoirs*, p. 88 n.

[2] See 'Notes on Scaleby Castle . . .', vol. i.

[3] 3 Dec. 1741 (W. L. Benson).

[4] 21 Feb. 1741/2 (W. L. Benson). Du Fresnoy's *Ut pictura poesis* was translated into English by Dryden (1695), James Wills (1754), and William Mason (1783). Mason's translation into verse appeared with notes by Sir Joshua Reynolds. See W. Folkierski, 'Du Fresnoy en Angleterre', *Revue de Littérature Comparée*, 1953, pp. 385–402. L'abbé Dubos, *Réflexions critiques sur la Poésie et sur la Peinture*, 1719.

[5] 14 Feb. 1742/3 (W. L. Benson).

to be met with any where—Mr. Mudge is an Apothecary, . . . & a great enthusiast in painting & drawing—My business was to make Scetches, by which you may be sure I have gaind vast credit —Mr. Mudge told me he would have given five Guineas a few Months agoe only to have seen the manner of my scrawling—It seems Mr. Smelt had shewn him some drawings of mine before I came hither, which he was much pleasd with—[1]

In his retirement Captain Gilpin was less isolated than he had been in his younger days; William and Sawrey provided much information as to what was going on in the art world. In August 1744 he had received a visit from Samuel Buck, the typographer, who in 1739 had published a prospect of Scaleby Castle;[2] and on 28 May 1772 he was to meet that other great traveller and typographer, Thomas Pennant, and supply him with drawings of local views and Roman antiquities.[3]

He probably knew Samuel Scott, to whom his son Sawrey was apprenticed in 1749, William Marlow, who sketched Scaleby Castle in the early 1770's, and Paul Sandby, a draughtsman to the Highland Survey from 1745 to 1751. There is a pleasant water-colour signed 'J. Gilpin' entitled 'North View of Tyrim Castle in Loch Moydart from a drawing of Mr Paul Sandby'.[4] He was also almost certainly acquainted with the amateur etcher, John Clerk of Eldin (1728–1812), and possessed a number of his views of Scotland.[5]

However, the artist who influenced him most was Alexander Cozens, whose drawings and theories he came to know in the middle 1760's. A number of drawings of ideal landscapes, which follow Cozens's methods, belong to this last period of his life. His oil-painting technique may also have been influenced, as was Sawrey's, by Cozens's 'Method of painting with tacky colours'.

In a letter from Windsor, dated 21 June 1768, Sawrey Gilpin gives his father an account of this method.[6] Since Sawrey apologizes for the delay in supplying the information, it is probable that Captain Gilpin was well aware of Cozens before 1768, and had urged his son to obtain from him details of the method for painting in oils. Sawrey called on Cozens, who acceded to the request on the understanding that the information be considered a professional secret passed on from one painter to another.

Captain Gilpin both practised and taught the art of drawing and painting, though it is only in this last capacity that art historians have considered him. From the time he set up

[1] 30 May 1755 (A. L. Fawcett).

[2] Captain Gilpin to his son William, 20 Aug. 1744 (A. L. Fawcett).

[3] See the reprint of Pennant's *Second Tour to Scotland*, in John Pinkerton, *A General Collection of the best and most interesting Voyages and Travels*, iii (1809), 203 (quoted by *Templeman*, pp. 23–24); also Richard Gough, *British Topography*, London, 1780, ii, 685. Some of Captain Gilpin's drawings may have passed through the Pennant sale at Christie's in 1938. He certainly supplied Pennant with drawings of the Roman antiquities found at Netherby, drawings which Pennant reproduced. Another set of these drawings is in the collection of A. L. Fawcett.

[4] W. L. Benson Collection.

[5] The families were connected through the marriage of Captain Gilpin's niece, Rosemary Dacre, with Sir John Clerk of Pennycuik (d. 1798). For the Clerk etchings which William Gilpin inherited from his father, see William Gilpin to E. Forster, 7 Sept. 1803 (Rev. E. G. Benson—Brisco transcript) and E. Forster to W. G., 13 Sept. 1803 (W. L. Benson). If etchings by John Clerk of Eldin are topographical in character, his later drawings are very picturesque. A large collection of his sketch-books, etchings and drawings, is to be found among the Pennycuik Papers, recently deposited at Register House, Edinburgh.

[6] Rev. E. G. Benson Collection.

a studio-room in Carlisle, 'he had sometimes half a dozen young people, or more, who used occasionally to attend him for instruction'.[1] Yet even when away from home, he continued to foster in his many children an ability to sketch and a love for painting. Thus, in 1749, he makes a drawing of Kentmere Hall, the birthplace of Bernard Gilpin, the Apostle of the North, 'a Copy of which I design to send to Jack that he may imitate his Namesake—'.[2] Another time he writes to his wife: 'Tell Kitty I do not forgett my promise to send her a drawing, I shall be glad to hear from her, & my two young Men, who I hope do not neglect their drawing—'.[3] Later, his Farish grandchildren were encouraged in the same way. John Bernard Farish (1754–c.1773), before he went to Pembroke College, Cambridge, drew landscapes in the manner of his grandfather [2. f] and animals in that of his uncle Sawrey Gilpin. His sister, Sarah Matilda Farish (1759—living 1782), was known for her chalk drawings of flowers.

Outside the family circle, only the names of a few of the young men, who benefited from his instruction, have come down to us. Dr. John Brown was certainly one. They were, for the most part, the sons of small artisans living in or around Carlisle. One was a Mr. Morrison, whip maker, known to us through a letter of John Bernard to his wife, which shows his readiness to make available his drawings and materials to anyone who could profitably use them:

The inclosd is for Mr Morrison the whip maker in answer to a letter he wrote to me about painting—I told him I had desired you to lett him have any pictures he chose to copy, & that he need only apply to you—that you would also lett him have any books of painting which I have— I told him also that he was welcome to my grindstone & muller, till he could provide himself with one—send him word therefore when you send him his Letter, that he is welcome to have them whenever he thinks fitt—You may lett him see the pictures in the painting room, & those in your closet as well as the rest—There is some nut oyl in a pint bottle, I think upon the drawer head in the painting room, which you may lett him have—it will spoil before I have an opportunity of makeing use of it—He is a modest Man & will be a little diffident in asking; You will therefore make the offer of these, or any thing else he wants—[4]

Of those who became professional artists, perhaps the best known is John Warwick Smith (1749–1831), who was to be very fashionable after his return from Italy in 1781. He was born at Irthington in Cumberland; his father was the gardener of Captain Gilpin's eldest sister, Susannah Maria, who was married to Joseph Dacre Appleby. The Captain took charge of his education, sent him to St. Bees, and then 'recommended him as a drawing master to a school near Whitehaven'.[5] In the early 1770's Smith was apprenticed to Sawrey Gilpin, with whom he stayed till he came under the notice of Lord Warwick, who sent him

---

[1] *Memoirs*, p. 65.

[2] Captain Gilpin to his wife, 18 May [1749] (A. L. Fawcett). John Bernard was born in 1743 and died in youth.

[3] 13 May 1755 (A. L. Fawcett). The children referred to were Catherine, the poetess (1739–1811), John Bernard, and Joseph Dacre Appleby, the surgeon, who was to be knighted for his services at Gilbraltar (1745–1834).

[4] 23 May 1755 (A. L. Fawcett).

[5] *Memoirs*, p. 65. This school may very well have been St. Bees. Unfortunately, I am informed by Mr. P. F. Williams, the senior English master, that the school records do not begin till 1811.

to Italy in 1776. Little more need be said of him at this juncture as we shall discuss his work in the early 1770's in a later chapter.

Two other artists, indebted to Captain Gilpin, were Robert Smirke, R.A. (1752–1845), and Guy Head (d.1800). Smirke, a subject painter, book illustrator, and miniaturist, 'always mentioned Capt. Gilpin, as laying the first foundation of his love for painting'. Guy Head was a native of Carlisle, where his father was a house painter. He went to the Royal Academy at Rome and there made copies of the Italian Masters.[1]

We now come to Captain Gilpin's own work. So far, 150 drawings, a few etchings, and perhaps a miniature have come to light—and this represents but a fraction of the whole of his long activity.

The miniature represents a battle scene, no doubt inspired by such engravings as *Twelve of the most remarkable Sieges and Battles in Europe, sold by Carington Bowles*.[2] Done in oils on a stiff card, it expresses 'the passions well', as William Gilpin would have said—two of the soldiers have head-wounds and one of the horses enters so well into the spirit of the occasion that it is shown viciously biting the head of another! The drawing is firm, though faulty in parts, and the attribution is very likely correct.

Other subjects he is known to have treated on this scale are 'Jove visiting Danae in a shower of gold',[3] and a number of portraits including that of his niece Margaret Gilpin in the 1740's.[4]

He seems to have practised etching only during his middle life, from about 1746 to the early 1750's. This period of activity coincides with that of his son William, who learnt to etch in 1744 and kept it up for only a few years: indeed father and son were spurred on by one another's efforts. His most competent work in this medium is the set of eight head-pieces for the first edition of William's *Life of Bernard Gilpin*, 1752.[5] The subjects, usually framed with elaborate rococo strapwork, vary considerably, from a dog barking at the moon to a rocky landscape, a pastoral scene or subjects borrowed from emblem books [1. a]. William Gilpin thought his best etching was 'a head of Moses's mother from Reubens'; another, executed about 1750, reproduces two of the figures in the print after Salvator Rosa of John preaching in the Wilderness.[6] Other etchings are only known through plates

[1] *Memoirs*, p. 65 and note. In 1790 Head returned to England, exhibited at a rented gallery in London, and died suddenly on 16 Dec. 1800. For Head, consult also T. W. Carrick, *History of Wigton (Cumberland): from its origin to the close of the nineteenth century*, C. Thurnam, Carlisle, 1949, p. 47; and the *Cumberland News*, 15 Mar. and 5 Apr. 1952, p. 4 in each case.

[2] The miniature and the set of engravings formed part of the William Gilpin Collection. The former now belongs to W. L. Benson, and the latter to George F. Benson.

[3] John Bernard Gilpin of Halifax, N.S. (1810–92), to Mrs. James Fawcett, 31 Mar. 1882 (A. L. Fawcett).

[4] Mary Hartley to W. G., 4 Oct. 1800 (W. L. Benson).

[5] Most of the original plates are in the collection of George F. Benson. In the second edition of the *Life of Bernard Gilpin*, 1753, only one of Captain Gilpin's etchings was used, and that was transferred to the title-page.

[6] For a general comment on his father's etchings, see W. G. to Mary Hartley, 7 May 1794 (Rev. E. G. Benson—Brisco transcript). William sent a print of the etching after Salvator

which have been preserved. There is a small head with the monogram IG, also two subjects related to the 1752 series of headpieces.[1]

Generally speaking, John Bernard's etchings display the use of a distinctive if limited technique: hatching for planes, inconsistent cross-hatching for contours, and, most characteristic of all, slightly curved lines grouped in sheaves or bunches to convey foliage.

The more numerous drawings can best be discussed by classifying according to subject and treatment. Though few are dated, they are presented as far as possible in chronological order.

I. *Early topographical drawings*

Most of these early topographical drawings, in common with the chalk drawings and etchings of his middle life, bear the IG monogram. Done with lead pencil and grey washes on white paper, they combine painstaking attention to detail with a niggardly technique. Typical examples are an unfinished landscape with a bridge,[2] and the view of a church incorrectly inscribed on the back 'Carlisle Cathedral by Capt.ⁿ G.'[3]

II. *Chalk drawings after Old Masters*

In the A. L. Fawcett Collection there are a few chalk drawings, mostly after prints from seventeenth-century Old Masters. They include a head of the Virgin in black chalk, a bound figure of Christ in sanguine, and a nude figure of a man seated on a rock. In February 1743 Captain Gilpin sent William some of these, among them a 'Grave-digger in Red-Chalk'.[4]

III. *Carlisle folder*

The Jackson Library in Tullie House, Carlisle, possesses a folder of thirty-three rough sketches executed while John Bernard was stationed at Plymouth, 1749–55.[5] These have all the freshness of spontaneous studies. Here the individual components of landscape are studied for their own sake; trees, rocks, and mountains noted down with all the picturesque roughness that was to be the particular delight of William Gilpin. Stratified rocks jut out diagonally to display their jagged edges, tall larch trees incline inward, and twisted boles cross each other.

Rosa to his eldest son John Bernard in America, whose son, John Bernard Gilpin of Halifax, N.S., gave it to Mrs. James Fawcett of Scaleby Castle in 1882, adding this note on the back of the print: 'By Capt Gilpin of Scaleby Castle after John preaching in the Wilderness, S. Rosa. about 1750.—'

[1] One plate belongs to W. L. Benson, the others to George F. Benson.

[2] W. L. Benson Collection.

[3] Alan de G. Benson Collection. A similar but later drawing came up in the Lowther Castle sale in 1947. It bears the inscription, 'A view of Carlisle Cathedral given me by Captain Gilpin who took it on the spot in 1765', and was reproduced by Iolo A. Williams, 'The Artists of the Gilpin Family with special reference to William Sawrey Gilpin', *Old Water Colour Society's Club*, xxix, 1951.

[4] John Brown to W. G., 14 Feb. 1742/3 (W. L. Benson).

[5] This folder ($8\frac{1}{2} \times 10\frac{1}{4}$ in.) contained originally sixty-two sketches, and was given by Susanna Maria Gilpin, second daughter of Sawrey Gilpin. It is entitled on the inside cover: 'Drawings by Capt.ⁿ Gilpin | Father of Sawrey Gilpin.' On the back of sketch no.12 Captain Gilpin wrote out this itinerary on the confines of Devon and Dorset: 'Axminster—8 | Charmouth—4 | Malcoms Leak [i.e. Morecombe lake]—2 | Bridport [crossed out] | Chidi [i.e. Chidcock]'. In my catalogue for the 1959 Kenwood Exhibition, *William Gilpin and the Picturesque* (abbreviation: *Kenwood Exhibition Catalogue*), I wrongly attributed this folder to Sawrey Gilpin.

Captain Gilpin derived a special enjoyment from his tree studies. Freed from the restraint of topographical accuracy he concentrated on those features which are very picturesque though hardly beautiful. He preferred the gnarled and twisted to the elegant and delicate; the ramification of branches is one of sharp angles and sudden turns; and the foliage is treated summarily by the use of three- or four-stroke patterns.

Besides providing the earliest instances of 'picturesque roughness' in the drawings of the Gilpin family, this folder was used by Sawrey Gilpin to make some of his early landscapes. For example, in a lake scene with vessels seen through a screen of trees, Sawrey repeated (c. 1756–7) one of his father's more spiky studies [2. a and b]. Similarly, a group of sketches of jutting rocks provided material for a carefully balanced landscape, in pen and coloured washes, dated 1757. This drawing is attributed to William Gilpin, though I am inclined to see in it the hand of his brother Sawrey [2. c and d].[1]

IV. *Pen and wash drawings c. 1750–70*

The greater part of his work falls into this period. It includes topographical drawings, imaginary landscapes, and copies from prints.

Whether slight like 'Cave near Plimouth',[2] or 'highly finished' like 'S. Maws-castle in Cornwall',[3] his topographical drawings of the Plymouth area are very stiff. Copies of Dutch prints or Italo-Flemish drawings are equally disappointing.

Another group consists of mountainous rocky scenes, watered by a lake or a stream that rushes down a waterfall. In them the features of the landscape are strongly delineated, and if the now prominent pen strokes give at times a harsh and stiff quality to his work, they express fully the personality of the man, in just the same way as the straight parallel strokes of his well-formed handwriting. Several of these landscapes are reminiscent of Allart van Everdingen (c. 1621–75), and it is quite possible that prints of this Dutchman, who was so impressed by the mountainous scenery of Norway, came into his hands. Many of the drawings executed in the last twenty-five years of his life are done on a coarse grey-beige or beige paper. A slight pencil outline is followed by penwork, using dark-brown ink for the foreground and lighter coloured ones as the distance recedes. The drawing is usually finished with a series of grey washes, and finally framed with a line ruled in dark-brown ink. Occasionally he proceeds to water-colour.

This is the case with a rocky fantasy, complete with winding road, waterfall, little bridges, and a massive boulder planted in mid-stream.[4] A purple and orange-red sky hangs over grey-green mountains that turn to grey-blue in the distance; the sparse vegetation is

[1] In support of my attribution of Plates 2. b and d to Sawrey Gilpin, cf. penmanship with that of his drawings of birds in 1756. The first landscape is in a folder entitled 'Captain Gilpin | Landscape drawings'; the second has been attributed to William Gilpin by several hands, who have inscribed it on both recto and verso (see caption to plate).

[2] W. L. Benson Collection. Inscribed by William Gilpin.

[3] Lieut.-Col. N. St. Leger Moore Collection. Coloured drawing inscribed on verso by William Gilpin. Another drawing of the same subject in the hands of A. L. Fawcett.

[4] A. de Gylpyn Benson Collection. The same owner possesses another fantasy which calls to mind the serpentine ramps Robert Adam was to introduce, only a few years later, into his imaginative compositions. In this case a road rises in zigzags up an artificial ramp and then disappears into a cavity of the mountain side.

green and yellow. The nearer stone-coloured rocks are tinged with blue, green, yellow, and pink, while the water is blue-green and grey.

His more usual way of colouring is seen in an unfinished drawing of Ambleside Force.[1] He builds up with overall washes and coloured dabs. The sky is blue on the left, and admits a yellow light from the right; the rocks are treated with pink and yellow wash over a basis of grey for the shadows, and the trees vary between yellow-brown and pale green. In the centre, however, the steel-grey waters of the cascade are confined by purplish grey rocks with here and there touches of blue, while the trees are dull green in colour [1. *b*]. In all these rocky scenes nature is presented in its wild and awe-inspiring state, and where the works of man are introduced, they only serve to enhance the scale, the power, and majesty of nature's elements.

A later and probably transitional group shows a different concern for composition. The vista is wider, the elements more varied, and the skyline moves down nearer the centre of the picture. He also employs a more skilful technique, as pen and wash combine to give receding planes their proper values. We observe new trends: trees are given greater individuality, penwork decreases in importance, the square-towered castle and the conical mountain appear as focal points of interest, and the area next to the foreground becomes a flat surface, whether rift-valley, road, or more frequently river flowing diagonally across the lower part of the composition.

Skies are occasionally welded into the composition, especially when he attempts effects of chiaroscuro in a conflagration, or in a landscape lit by sun or moon.[2]

V. *Last Period—Influence of Alexander Cozens—late 1760's onwards*

It would be difficult to find in the work of any other artist, a group of drawings so evidently derivative from Alexander Cozens's teaching. The contemplation given to Cozens's ideal landscapes in monochrome wash taught Captain Gilpin a lasting lesson, so much so that the drawings of his last years are by far his best.

What he learnt from Cozens was an attitude towards landscape and a method for effecting a proper reconciliation between the initial conception and the means for carrying this out, so that in the end the execution fits the idea. This meant not only a considerable improvement in his technique, which had always lagged behind his sensibility, it also meant paying greater attention to the proper distribution of light and shade, to the integration of contours and planes, to the gradation of values within the restricted range of the monochrome, and to much more if that 'unity of character which is true simplicity' was to be attained.

The drawings which may be said to introduce his last manner, repeat earlier subjects, but the trees, especially in the foreground, are treated in a new way. Take, for example,

---

[1] Subject identified from another drawing taken from the same standpoint, inscribed on the verso by Captain Gilpin, 'View of Ambleside Force' (W. L. Benson Collection).

[2] See in particular a lake scene (A. de Gylpyn Benson), and houses on fire (A. L. Fawcett).

the rocky and wooded landscape in the W. L. Benson Collection [2. *e*]. There is nothing new in the waterfall, the sheet of water, the unsteady rock, or the ungainly figure pointing to that oddity, so beloved of the picturesque school, a tree rooted precariously to the side of a rock—but, a look at this tree and at that other one in the foreground shows they are drawn with some care almost entirely with the brush, that the use of light and shade gives them solidity, and that contour lines are abandoned in favour of the feathery and indeterminate effect of short dabs with a loaded brush. This newly found skill for portraying trees is used to great effect in all his subsequent drawings, and, moreover, the treatment is varied to suit the mood of the scene he wishes to depict—a fairly natural approach for wild scenery, as in this drawing, a graceful one for ideal landscape, or a rough one where the dramatic atmosphere is to be emphasized.

Another characteristic common to all these drawings is the use of a black stump or greasy pencil. This is passed lightly over the surface of the coarse-grained paper so that only the raised parts are blackened. The device has the advantage of giving unity to the area over which it is applied without interfering with the underlying drawing.

Figures occasionally appear in the foreground at all periods—rather stiffly articulated country folk clad in a jacket cut at the back and trousers tucked into stockings or gaiters. They often carry a staff, wear a broad-brimmed hat, and with half-extended arm point to a curious feature of the landscape.

Particularly pleasing are his ideal landscapes where all is serene and quiet. One of these has a river flowing lazily between rocky banks dominated by a projecting ridge. The curve of the foreground is completed by that of the ridge, and thence the eye moves easily to the large tree on the left, which, together with the darker bank beneath, successfully balance the composition. With the greasy pencil he has united the whole foreground and middle distance into a *repoussoir*, without, however, losing the effect of recession.[1]

The influence of Alexander Cozens is not sufficient to explain the invitation to gaze awhile and collect his thoughts which the beholder receives on looking at this peaceful landscape; Captain Gilpin must have been actuated by an inner compulsion to undertake such drawings. The *Memoirs* show him cheerful and very active in old age, but there was another side to his nature. Most of his friends had long ago died or left Carlisle; his children were dispersed; of three sisters that were left of a large family, two died within a week of each other in 1769; and in 1773 he lost his wife. Captain Gilpin was therefore a lonely man, and we can well understand how he would chase away nostalgia by a hard day's fishing and return to the solitude of his studio in a spirit of calm resignation and work upon one of these serene landscapes.

Some of his squarer compositions come very near Alexander Cozens, though I would not call them copies. If they were, Captain Gilpin would have acknowledged the fact as he did in the case of drawings after Paul Sandby.

[1] W. L. Benson Collection.

One of these, a river meandering between steep banks, seen through a screen of trees, is organized into contrasting areas of light and shade that are particularly satisfying [3. *a*].[1] The escarpment on the right carefully balances the inclined tree, which dominates the scene by its size and central position. He makes up for simplicity by the use of strong accents—if the foreground is dark and almost black, the trees are silhouetted against a very light sky (the grey-beige paper not providing light enough for his purpose, white chalk (?) was applied to the lower part of the sky). The greasy black pencil here covers the whole land mass, adding atmospheric density to the scene.

In other drawings Captain Gilpin returns to his favourite mountain streams which cascade down a deep gully or pour down in waterfalls over succeeding ledges. Two of them retain the stark appearance of the Ambleside Force drawings, while a third in which the water ends in a pool, instead of rushing by the observer, is more in keeping with the mood of his ideal landscapes [3. *b*].

In general we have noticed that he alternates between two moods, the contemplative and the dramatic. Though more successful in the former mood, he does occasionally bring off a dramatic effect, where he limits himself to a simple idea. Such is the case in the close-up view of a waterfall and the entrance to a cave [3. *c*]. The drawing of the waterfall derives its force from the violent contrast of the two planes, for, while the dark silhouetted foreground acts as a *repoussoir*, the imagination supplies the unseen chasm into which the waters rush headlong. Note also in the foreground what must be a fairly early example of scraping or scratching.[2] The drawing of the cave is treated in a similar way. The eye moves from the silhouetted trunk of the riven tree to the dark entrance of the cave. The main light falls on the rocks in the centre, and they are surrounded by dark vegetation treated freely with small brush strokes and black greasy pencil. These two subjects were also to appeal to his son William, who from 1780 onwards made them the subject of many sketches.

A word about the various inscriptions found on the back of certain drawings. Many are by Catherine Brisco, who made her home with her half-brother, William Gilpin. Just as she saw to it that posterity should remember William Gilpin by making transcripts of his correspondence, dating his drawings, &c., so she inscribed several drawings by Captain

[1] Cf. with A. Cozens's 'Landscape with large trees' in the City Art Gallery, Birmingham, reproduced as plate 8 in A. P. Oppé, *Alexander & John Robert Cozens*, London, 1952 (abbreviation: *Oppé*).

[2] Alan de Gylpyn Benson Collection. See *Kenwood Exhibition Catalogue*, Item 15.

Many of the devices and techniques so successfully exploited by the English water-colour school at the turn of the nineteenth century are much older than certain authorities would lead us to believe. For example, Mr. David Loshak (*The Art of Thomas Girtin*, London, 1954, p. 6) states that 'stopping out' is said to have been first practised by Francis Nicholson (1753–1844), but when?—that George Robertson (1747–88) was the first to use scraping or scratching, and this device was then employed by Girtin in a drawing of 1794 (quoting C. F. Bell). Mr. Loshak then mentions the following 'technical tricks' as belonging to the early nineteenth century: 'stippling; stippling and scraping in combination; use of body-colour for highlights; mixture of transparent wash and body-colour; use of the split brush; use of prepared grounds and of absorbent, rough, and tinted papers'.

Such an overall picture is entirely misleading, for nearly every one of the devices mentioned above were used by the two artistic families of the Cozenses and Gilpins, and if I were to suggest a period during which a great number of technical devices were first brought into constant use, it would be between 1750 and 1775.

Gilpin in her long and shaky hand, invariably using dark-brown ink. On several she wrote 'JBG | given me by MG', an inscription she later crossed out in favour of 'Captain Gilpin.'[1] Other drawings inscribed by her have 'Capt. Gilpin | The gift of yᵉ revᵈ Samˡ Hey'. Who Samuel Hey was remains a mystery. He was probably a friend of the family, judging from the collection of drawings by several artists which he gave back to the family.

It is now time to turn our attention to William Gilpin. Yet, just as a man's birth is not the beginning of his story, so William's drawings and, in particular, his theory of the Picturesque cannot be fully appreciated without a glance at the amateur art of the previous generation, which Captain Gilpin epitomizes so well. In matters of taste the links between father and son were, as we shall see, more numerous than their different characters and upbringing might suggest. Each drew for pleasure and encouraged this pastime in others, and on retirement became drawing masters. William not only learnt to draw from his father, but adopted his pen and grey-wash technique, his tinted drawing, and even retained some of his more obvious limitations—an inability to draw figures or represent running water. They both shared the same love for wild nature; the country of the Lake District and around Carlisle, with its mountains, lakes, rocks, and streams, forms the central subject of their landscapes, which, as a glance at the plates will confirm, have a great similarity of appeal. Without realizing it John Bernard Gilpin was picturesque 'avant la lettre', William, on the other hand, consciously harnessed his talent to the service of this ideal, thus ensuring the success of ideas he had mulled over and eventually formulated in his writings.

---

[1] 'MG' stands for Captain Gilpin's wife, Matilda. On another drawing C. Brisco wrote 'Given me by Mr. G.', this she later crossed out in favour of 'Captain Gilpin'.

III. Early Days, 1724–1760

THOUGH practically nothing has survived of William Gilpin's early drawings, quite a lot is known about his early interests, which gradually were to lead him to formulate the theory of the Picturesque. As was to be expected from the ambiance in which he was brought up, he started drawing at a very early age, the first reference to this being in a letter his mother wrote to his father, then serving as a lieutenant in Windsor Forest: 'Billy is now standing by me drawing; & begs I will enclose his picture to you; which I have promised, if he takes pains enough with it.'[1] William was then six years old.[2] His father, during spells of home leave, taught him in the next few years to manage pencil and pen, and how to treat his drawing with grey washes. After going to St. Bees, William left his native Cumberland for Queen's College, Oxford, in January 1740, where he obtained his B.A. in November 1744. In 1746 he returned home and in October was ordained curate of Irthington. However, he soon returned to Oxford where he took his M.A. on 14 May 1748. Ordained a priest on 5 June 1748, he spent the next four years in London, holding several curacies and temporary posts before going to Cheam School in 1752.

As an undergraduate he profited little from the uninspired and outmoded forms of teaching then available. An indigent scholar, with a serious turn of mind, he had no time for the frivolous and riotous pastimes of the bucks, and when he felt homesick, it was to the company of certain of his fellow north-countrymen that he turned: William U. Wray, Wilfred Clarke, Thomas Denton (1724–77), and especially George Potter (1720–55). Here also he continued to draw, broadened his taste by visiting collections of pictures around Oxford, learnt the rudiments of etching, and started what was to become a considerable collection of prints. Thanks to some of the letters which passed between Oxford and Carlisle we can reconstruct his awakening interests at this crucial period of his life.

In December 1741 Gilpin did not feel he could yet draw a composition of his own, though John Brown tried to spur him on: 'Your Objection against drawing I think a very foolish one, but it is in your own Power to remove it. I thank you for the drawing you sent me, & do really think you are much improved: But I will not accept of any acknowledgement for the Crayons till you send me back some of them, spread out upon

---

[1] 3 Aug. 1730 (*Memoirs*, p. 104).

[2] Years later Gilpin recalled an incident which dates from this period: 'One of the earliest pleasures of my life (which you may suppose was great from my remembring it seventy years ago) arose from my father's shewing me a drawing, which he told me was one of the best he ever made; & which he took, he said, from one of my scratches.' W. G. to Sir G. Beaumont, 16 June 1802 (Pierpont Morgan Library).

Paper.'[1] In February 1742 Brown returned to the attack, suggesting various subjects he might tackle: 'What think you to a Copy of a surly unbred Fellow sitting at the Entrance of his Tub? Or of a genteel, condescending, goodnatur'd young Gentleman accosting him with such a dignify'd Civilitie as makes the finest Contrast imaginable?' Or, said Brown, he might pick his own theme, provided he turned it into an original composition.[2]

Whether William did choose the subject from Swift or another we do not know; the first composition eventually materialized and was sent to Carlisle in October 1742. In a jocular mood he told his mother of his triumph:

Among the Drawings I have sent, You will observe a very bold Sketch, done in a most masterly Manner, 'tis I assure You an Original of your Son's, the first he ever attempted, this he humbly as his first-Fruits makes a Present of to You; When You have sufficiently admired his great Talant at Design, You may present it to Miss Kitty to fill up an End in her Baby-House; tho' stay, not before You tell me what you take the Story to be, to tell You the Truth I don't believe You have many of You Sagacity enough to find it out—[3]

Other sketches from nature or prints did not present the same difficulty. The earliest known are four views of Scaleby Castle done in 1741 or 1742 in brown pen on the sheets of a small notebook.[4] Although the execution and composition are bad, the subject cannot leave us indifferent. His birthplace and the home of his family for many years past, Scaleby Castle became increasingly dear to him, and in his later imaginary landscapes it appeared as the prototype of the romantic ruin. So it seems appropriate that the earliest drawings of William Gilpin to have survived should be of Scaleby Castle.

Like his father, by 1742 he had acquired the habit of making sketches whenever he went for a walk. With the years the rambles became excursions, and finally tours of various parts of the British Isles. Having no particular inclination for sports, he found both exercise and enjoyment in walking 'a few Miles into the Country; at which Times I always take my Paper & black-lead Pencil with me, and never fail to bring Home something or other, which together with the Pleasure & Benefit of the Walk makes me think my Time not ill spent'.[5]

Unlike his brother Sawrey, to whom drawing came easily and early, William worked hard and long to attain a modicum of competence. As we shall see, it was not till the 1760's, when over forty, that he was able to execute adequately what he wanted to express.

In August 1744 he sent home a batch of drawings, and asked his father for a landscape to copy. The reply came: 'You have made great Improvements in Heads, & I am glad to find all your Features now regularly placed; continue to draw after good Heads—I did

---

[1] 7 Dec. 1741 (W. L. Benson).

[2] 17 Feb. 1741/2 (W. L. Benson).

[3] 10 Oct. 1742 (A. L. Fawcett). Brown congratulated him on his composition: 'You are really and without Compliment a great Proficient in Drawing—in Designing I think I might say, for I assure you the Original you sent gave us abundance of Pleasure.' 14 Feb. 1742/3 (W. L. Benson).

[4] Some time towards the end of the last century the four sheets were torn from a notebook and pasted down in an album, now in the collection of A. L. Fawcett. The attribution and dating are based on the handwriting of William Gilpin on the back of one of the drawings.

[5] W. G. to his mother, 10 Oct. 1742 (A. L. Fawcett).

think you were the most defective in them'. Captain Gilpin was quite willing to send him one of his landscapes, 'but as you desire it as a Model, I must excuse myself, as I should draw you into Errors by copying my Defects—'.[1]

The following extract from a letter to his mother gives a good idea of the constant traffic in drawings between Carlisle and Oxford, and of the nature of the requests with which William plied his father:

I fancy I shall have something in the Way of Drawing by the Carrier: if I have; pray let a Caution be observed, which I once gave, tho' I find it has since been neglected; this Caution is to roll the Drawings on a Staff longer than they are. I have been reading an Account of the Judgment of Hercules in the latter End of Lord Shaftsbury's Writings, which I was much pleased with; it seems that Painting was designed by him, which I never knew before:[2] If my Father would take the Trouble to do me in oyl Colours a Copy of the little Painting he has of Fry's[3] upon that Subject, he would much oblige me: . . . If my Father engages in the Task I wish it might be done upon Canvas, which I think is a much better Foundation for Colours than what the little Piece he sent me lately was painted upon. He would be much pleased I am sure with reading the Notion (as the Author calls it) above mentioned & would paint with much greater Pleasure.[4]

Avid to learn about paintings, he soon exhausted what Oxford offered, and started to look farther afield. Probably in April 1742 he visited Blenheim,[5] and in November ventured as far as Windsor, where the 'Woman who shews the Palace, was extremely civil, for after she had carried me round it once she told me I might walk about it as long as I pleased by myself, accordingly I wandered about in high Delight, at least three Hours, as long as I thought I could stay with any Decency'. During that time he learnt a great deal: 'I studied those Paintings so long that I am sure I can distinguish between the different Manners of several Masters, . . . nothing can be more evident than the Hardness of M. Angelo . . . and the Softness of Titian.'[6] Soon nothing less than visits to London would satisfy his inquiring mind.

In addition to his study of paintings, Gilpin started in 1744 to examine prints with care—this interest was to absorb him for the next ten years, and the critical notes he accumulated became the *Essay on Prints*, not printed till 1768. He was only a boy when he had made his first tentative purchase of prints, among them a Waterlo and a Rembrandt.[7] Now he began to acquire them in a systematic if modest way. He attended auctions in Town, and on one occasion expressed his good fortune at having secured Raphael's 'Transfiguration'

---

[1] 20 Aug. 1744 (A. L. Fawcett).

[2] *A Notion of the Historical Draught or Tablature of the Judgment of Hercules.* Shaftesbury commissioned Paolo de Matteis to paint the original picture, which appeared, engraved by Simon Gribelin, at the head of the English translation of the 'Judgment of Hercules', in the unfinished *Second Characters or the Language of Forms*, 1713.

[3] Thomas Frye (1710–62). Gilpin was to mention his portraits in the *Essay on Prints*: 'Our countryman Fry has left behind him a few very beautiful heads in mezzotinto.'

[4] 13 Sept. 1744 (A. L. Fawcett).

[5] John Brown to W. G., 1 May [1742?] (W. L. Benson).

[6] 1 Dec. 1743 (A. L. Fawcett).

[7] 'I remember, when I was a mere boy, going *first* into a print-shop, where my eye was caught on every side, with the best engravings of the day: but it settled at last on 2 or 3 old etchings, which I bought & still have. One was a landscape by Waterlo—another an etching by Rembrant. At that time, I had neither heard of Waterlo, nor of Rembrant, but something pleased me; & I have since thought it a sign of my having an innate love for the arts.' W. G. to Sir G. Beaumont, 21 July 1802 (Pierpont Morgan Library).

by Nicholas Dorigny for only *3s. 6d.*[1] He also learnt to etch. Here in his own words, is how he was taught the process and made his first attempt:

I was talking two or three Weeks ago with a Painter here in Oxford, and was asking him particularly if he knew any Thing of the Nature of Etching; he told me he understood the Method in which it was done, and described it to me; from which Description I conceived it possible for any Man that could draw, to etch. Accordingly I applied to the only Engraver we have in Town, Mr. Cole, (whose Name probably you may have seen under the Theatre, in the Title Page of Books printed there).[2] This celebrated Artist for two or three Shillings furnished me with a Plate, and taught me how to lay a Ground. I told him my first Attempt should be a Head, but he judged that too desperate an Undertaking at first, & humbly conceived a Coat of Arms would be more proper. I continued resolute; & resolved to do Honour to Mr. Pope. I asked him if he had any general Instructions for me: he told me all I had to do was to copy as exactly as I could every Stroke of the Print before me, which indeed I endeavoured to do at first, but finding that a Work of infinite Labour, I took up a Method of my own, & dashed the Strokes out any how. The enclosed is an Impression, which, as it is my first attempt, pleased me tolerably well: The Hair, the Neck, the Shading upon the Cheek, the Eye-Brow, & the Mouth are indifferent. The Eye, & Shading upon the Nose are shocking, & all the rest but what I have mentioned, very bad. The next Thing I do shall be much better.[3]

At twenty Gilpin is already the man he will be for the rest of his days; a man of strong faith and decided views, a good critic because he is a good self-critic. Having just learnt the rudiments of etching, he turned his critical eye on those of Joseph Goupy (*c.* 1700–63):

Goupy's Manner of Etching I admire very much; it is indeed extremely masterly, but indeed this is all I think that can be said for his Prints, for with Regard to the Drawing they are most intolerably incorrect, and ought never to be set before a Beginner, except particular Passages here & there. To instance only in one of his Prints, his Diana hunting a Stag [4. *a*]:[4] in this I'll take my Oath there is not one good Head: Diana & a Nymph upon the other Side are the best, but neither of them are extraordinary. Diana herself is a bad Figure: Her right Arm is pretty well, but her left looks as if it grew out of her Back: it is very aukward indeed: Part of this Aukwardness is occasioned by the Print's being left-handed, (which is an extreme Disadvantage in any Print, where the right Hands are put to Uses which the left never are employed in, Goupy has judiciously contrived most of his Prints in this unatural Way, which makes some of them extremely aukward, as it does this). Her Drapery is badly managed: it is patched too much with Spots of Light (in some of his Prints tho' the Draperies are vastly free and noble). The Shade upon her right Leg is hard, & the Foot ill-drawn. The Figure beneath the Goddess's Arm is nothing like a young Lady which her Breasts denote her to be. The two Figures behind Diana are very stiff, lifeless, ill-drawn Pieces, except only one Leg which is a very good one. On the other Side, the Nymph who has just shot the Arrow is pretty well, but the young Lady beneath is not quite so right: her Elbow is prodigious bad. The Doe is very good; the Stag has much too large a Head & Neck; The Dogs are well done, except the hinder Leg of one near Diana, & the fore Leg of that which the Nymph is pointing

---

[1] W. G. to his mother, 7 Oct. 1744 (A. L. Fawcett); *The Spectator*, 226, 19 Nov. 1711.

[2] Possibly James Cole, who had worked in London from 1720 to 1743 as a portrait engraver.

[3] W. G. to John Brown, 12 Nov. 1744 (A. L. Fawcett).

[4] See Max Rooses, *L'Oeuvre de P. P. Rubens*, Antwerp, 1890, iii, no. 589. When Goupy made his etching, the painting of 'Diana and nymphs hunting a stag' was in the collection of Sir Robert Walpole.

to the Doe. The Trees are not done in so good a Manner as I have seen some of Goupy's. This is the most incorrect of any Print I have seen of his; they are however a little faulty with Regard to the Drawing. But as to the Manner they are the best Patterns I think an Etcher can set before him; in landskip especially which he does wonderfully well. An Error in drawing cannot there be so easily seen.[1]

In the *Essay on Prints*, twenty-four years later, his estimate of Goupy was contained within a single paragraph, in which the print of Diana hunting a Stag just received a mention.

During 1745 Gilpin etched various subjects[2] and then made another attempt at the head of Pope. Though Brown proclaimed the result a masterpiece,[3] he was far from satisfied. 'If I had suffered the Aqua-fortis to continue on long enough, it had been much better. I intend to do the same Head again, and take a little more Pains with it.' He ended his letter of February 1746 by urging his father to share his new enthusiasm: 'I have a Scheme to propose to my Father to lay out some of his Time upon Etching; I am sure he would succeed. I saw yesterday three Heads which Mr. Richardson etched for Dr. Mead, which I admired prodigiously.[4] I want to hear my Father's Thoughts upon this Scheme.'[5]

This passage makes it clear that Captain Gilpin had not tried etching before 1746. He no doubt learnt the process from his son William when he came home in March of that year.

Gilpin's stay in the north was brief. When he accepted the curacy of Irthington, not far from Carlisle, he was fully 'determined to leave university-honours, and expectations, behind him, and settle in a life of ease, and quiet'.[6] However, a loan from John Brown enabled him to return to Oxford, early in 1747, to complete his residence for his master's degree. From Oxford, during the summer months of that year, he went to preach every Sunday at Buckingham. These visits resulted in two publications, each of which was to be the first of many of its kind. He published in 1747 a sermon he had preached at Buckingham,[7]

[1] W. G. to John Brown, 12 Nov. 1744 (A. L. Fawcett).

[2] He probably etched a design of his father's which John Brown wanted as a frontispiece for one of his poetical works. The design contained a Temple of Fame and a group of four allegorical figures: 'Satire darting her Thunder', Truth, Justice and 'Apollo supplying the Muse with Thunderbolts'. John Brown to W. G., 18 and 20 Feb. 1744/5 (W. L. Benson).

[3] 5 Jan. 1745/6 (W. L. Benson).

[4] Jonathan Richardson (1665–1745). In the *Essay on Prints*, Gilpin's assessment of Richardson was much cooler: 'Richardson hath left us several heads, which he etched for Mr. Pope, and others of his friends. They are slight, but shew the spirit of a master. Mr. Pope's profile is the best.' It was no doubt Richardson's etching of Pope that Gilpin was using as a model.

[5] 8 Feb. 1745/6 (A. L. Fawcett).

[6] *Memoirs*, p. 112. The reasons which determined him to act in this way had been voiced in a letter to Brown of 10 July 1745: 'I do not know how I shall be able to live three Quarters of a Year in Oxford: my Love for Cumberland I find is much

stren[g]thened by my last Visit: Our Fellows I am told out of Policy sometimes suffer a young Fellow to take one Trip into the North, as the best Method to cure him of the Folly of ever desiring to see it again; but I am an Instance that their Prescriptions are not always infallible: I shall begin I am afraid to cry out O Rus before I shall be able to satisfy my Passion for it. Cumberland has now (as I have the Prospect before me of being settled amongst you) more Charms than ever; and Oxford has fewer; for most of the Persons I had any Value for, have either left it or are just upon leaving it; and the mere Love I have for a College is not strong enough to give me the least Desire to continue any longer in it than is absolutely necessary: I find great Difficulty in complying dayly with a thousand Forms, and Ceremonies, which nothing but the servile Veneration we pay our Superiours could save from publick Ridicule' (A. L. Fawcett).

[7] *The bad consequences of Dissention and Party-rage considered. A Sermon Preached at Buckingham on the 5th of July, 1747, the Sunday following the Election*, London, 1747.

and the following year, his first analysis of landscape according to picturesque principles, *A Dialogue upon the Gardens of the Right Honourable the Lord Viscount Cobham, at Stow in Buckinghamshire.*[1] It was through his acquaintance with Mr. Long,[2] the rector of Finmere, that he came to know the famous gardens of Lord Cobham.

As he makes clear in the 'Advertisement' to the *Dialogue,* he is not writing for those who have never visited the gardens—for them an ordinary description would be useful—but for those who are already familiar with the place. To such readers, he endeavours to give a truer appreciation of the landscape they know, or think they know, by means of critical observations, which will appeal to their pictorial consciousness. Using terms and standards of judgement derived from art criticism, he seeks to awaken in his readers an aesthetic pleasure, akin to the one which arises from the contemplation of landscapes painted within the framework of a canvas, and yet of a different order, for, whereas, according to him, before a painting or print, pleasure is enhanced in relation to our understanding of the way a landscape has been transmuted into artistic terms (landscape into art), before a landscape, our contemplation of the scene can be enriched if we make use of the apparatus of art criticism (art into landscape).

The *Dialogue* contains already many of the features of his theory of the Picturesque, and to those we shall return in a later chapter. For the present we must consider the various factors which influenced his aesthetics. Foremost is his deep-rooted love for natural scenery, especially the wild landscape of his native Cumberland, and the consequent rejection of all that is sophisticated, ornate, and regimented. This attitude is reflected in his choice of authors. Of the classics which he studied, Horace and Virgil were his favourites. In one of those common debates of the period centred on the art versus nature theme, he sided with Virgil against Homer. To this Brown replied:

Yes indeed, I think you are entirely right when you prefer our Cumberland Prospects (some of them at least) to your Oxford ones: In doing this you prefer the Beauties of Nature to those of Art; and that is certainly a true Judgment. Now Sr. I wou'd beg leave to transfer this Principle to another Subject. I find you admire Virgil—and I think very justly—but you prefer him to Homer —there I differ from you. Homer's Works I take to be a very transcript of Nature, drawn out with the utmost Beautie and Simplicity: Virgil is majestic, grave, elegant—and correct; but then there is in him an appearance of Art, which is not so pleasing in Poetry; and all his People talk like Courtiers: You see the Stately Pride of a civiliz'd Roman in many of his Characters, tho' the Scene

---

[1] For attribution of this work, which was published anonymously in 1748, 1749, and 1751, see *Templeman,* pp. 34–35 and 117–28. Conclusive proof of Gilpin's authorship of the *Dialogue* is contained in a letter George Potter wrote to W. G.: 'I have read Bigmanstroff's [*sic*] high Dutch translation of your Stow Gardens but he does not do justice to my arguments for a flat full inhabited Country beyond a romantick NORthern one.' 18 Mar. 1748/9 (W. L. Benson). I have failed to trace the German translation or the identity of the translator.

[2] Gilpin has left a kind portrait of this orderly bachelor whose tidy garden was the opposite of the picturesque gardens of Stowe it adjoined: 'Not a weed was to be seen in any of the beds, or seed-plots: his walks were all nicely rolled—his espaliers in perfect order—& his fruit-trees, & vines exactly trained. Two or three seats & pleasant arbours adorned different parts of his garden. With one Mr. G[ilpin] was particularly pleased. It overlooked Ld. Cobham's gardens at Stowe, to which a latin inscription alluded with this sentiment, *All these beautiful views are mine, if I do not covet them.*' 'A short Account of Different people, with whom Mr. G. was more or less intimate in the several periods of his life' (J. B. Gilpin-Brown).

is laid in an Age and in Countries but just emerging from Barbarity, whereas Homer represents his Heroes just as they were—a parcel of brave rough Fellows, without Disguise, Art or Dissimulation; they scruple not to tell you how voraciously they eat, or how desperately they are frighten'd, and expose all their failings without the least Reluctance.[1]

Gilpin claimed he found a greater pictorial sense in Virgil, who was able to convey more graphically his love of nature. To illustrate a striking scene, he was to make frequent use of Virgil, to whom he deferred as 'a great master in landscape'.[2]

Of the English poets, he was particularly fond of Spencer. As he wrote to a young man up at Oxford, whom he had tutored: 'In this author . . . there is as much poetry as in almost any writer of any age. . . . His obsolete language, which is I think your only objection to him, will grow easy to you, take my word for it, after a little use: For my part I am so bigotted to him, that I esteem it a beauty.'[3]

Unlike many of his contemporaries at Queen's, Gilpin read widely outside the prescribed authors. 'I remember in my time half our young fellows used to read scarce any thing besides classic writers, & that only for the sake of their latin & greek. This is a sad way of study.'[4] Addison, Pope, Locke, Shaftesbury, and Hutcheson chiefly moulded his outlook at this time. The influence of Pope as poet, moralist, and guide in matters of taste is apparent in nearly all that Gilpin wrote in the 1740's; not only in his published writings (both the *Sermon* of 1747 and the *Dialogue* are prefaced with quotations from him) but in his letters and such juvenilia as his early poems.

However, the man who had the greatest impact on him was undoubtedly Shaftesbury. Though he rejected the deist, he admired the moralist and aesthetician, to the extent of recommending his works as the first to be read in moral philosophy:

Ld. Shaftesbury I know in Oxford is reckoned an infidel, & though indeed I should be far from subscribing to all his opinions, yet there are some parts of his works which I think it is scarce possible to read without panting after virtue. His *Enquiry* I would particularly recommend to you, where amongst some errors you will meet with much fine morality.[5]

What appealed to Gilpin in the *Inquiry* was the relation between the Good, the True, and the Beautiful. In *The Moralists* Shaftesbury gave a fresh lease of life to aesthetics, by presenting a cosmology which dealt a blow to the mechanistic interpretation of nature. The analogy of God as creator and supreme artist, and the world as the work of art created by Him, gave nature back part of its old magic. Nature could now be contemplated in its own right as a work of art, a symbolic manifestation of the perfect form which was in God's mind, yet infinitely superior to any artistic creation of man's. Yet man, the artist, was not

[1] 12 Feb. 1741/2 (W. L. Benson).
[2] *Wye Tour*, 1782, p. 24. (For full title see p. 71, n. 1.)
[3] Rough draft of ['Three Letters of Advice to an Undergraduate at Oxford'], *c.* 1749, p. 19 (W. L. Benson).
[4] Ibid., p. 18.
[5] Ibid., p. 12. To put his former pupil on guard against Shaftesbury's advocacy of a natural morality, he adds: 'let me give you one caution, which is not to suffer your reason to be carried away by disputes about the *foundation* of morality. Many wise men, in my opinion, have trifled strangely upon this point, & have run much into what is termed *science falsly so called*. Let it be your chief care to examine the nature & extent of particular moral duties, & rest satisfied that they are all the laws of God, which is enough for any man to know.'

left out. As R. L. Brett puts it, 'The artist was felt to be akin to God, working in the same way, even if on a lower plane; and nature was to be regarded as a work of art, giving us on a larger scale the kind of aesthetic pleasure we get in contemplating a human work of art. Furthermore, if art were to be an imitation of nature, it would not just be the mechanical copying of natural phenomena, but had to be an imitation of the whole creative process going on in nature. Art, in other words, was rightly comprehended as creation, not mechanical construction.'[1]

The distinction, made by Shaftesbury, between nature as a work of art and human works of art, finds its counterpart in Gilpin's theory of the Picturesque, where it is clear that his preference lies in natural scenery untouched by the civilizing hand of man.

Just as the *Dialogue upon the Gardens . . . at Stow*, with its two 'enthusiasts' about nature, Polypthon and Callophilus, assuredly stems from *The Moralists*, so perhaps does the 'Dialogue between Eucomio and Philographicus', which Gilpin was writing in 1744.[2] At that time he was reading the 'Judgment of Hercules'. These remarks, originally devised to help Paolo de Matteis in his realization of the picture commissioned by Shaftesbury, are not what could be termed art criticism. Nevertheless, Gilpin found in the treatment of the aesthetic problem of the 'fruitful moment' many suggestions of what to look for in a work of art—for example, how far the individual parts harmonize and are made subordinate to the whole action depicted, and what are the relative pictorial values of the various possible moments which can be chosen to represent an action.

As for Shaftesbury's 'enthusiasm', Gilpin was too well balanced for this notion to bowl him over, as it did several of his friends at college, in particular his intimate, George Potter, who, gifted with a powerful imagination, suddenly became, as Gilpin put it, 'a mere enthusiast in the cause of liberty'.[3]

William Gilpin's four years in London, from 1748 to 1752, were very full. Though we know little about the curacies he held, we do know that he moved about considerably, and was for a time attached to the Charterhouse.[4] Debts were repaid by tutoring and by writing a *Life of Bernard Gilpin* (1752). This biography, undertaken as an act of piety, gave him a taste for historical research, particularly into the Reformation. Over the years he was to write the biographies of Latimer, Wyclif and his disciples, and Thomas Cranmer.

These were the years when he came in contact with the artistic life of London, partly

[1] R. L. Brett, *The Third Earl of Shaftesbury*, London, 1951, p. 67.

[2] 'I am much pleas'd with your Dialogue between Eucomio & Philographicus, and when you have time, I think it would be no disagreeable Amusement to you to finish it—' John B. Gilpin to his son W. G., 20 Aug. 1744 (A. L. Fawcett). The MS. of this dialogue does not seem to have survived.

[3] For Shaftesbury's influence on Potter, see Gilpin's 'Account of Mr. George Potter', pp. 8–12 (Rev. E. G. Benson).

[4] As far as may be gathered from the few letters that have survived, covering the period 1748–52, here are Gilpin's movements: St. Pancras, July 1748; Kentish Town, November 1748; Winchester, January to March 1749; Princess Street near the Royal Exchange, April 1749; ordained priest at Winchester House, Chelsea, 5 June 1749; preached University Sermon, Oxford, mid-August 1749; curate at Battersea, June 1749 to February 1750; the Temple, March to December 1750 and for probably longer; the Charterhouse, July 1752.

through his own interests and partly through his brother Sawrey, who, as a lad of fifteen, was apprenticed in 1749 to Samuel Scott, the marine painter and English follower of Canaletto. He was able to keep an eye on Sawrey and report on his progress.[1] From the first he took a deep interest in his brother's painting, and theirs was to be a close and enduring friendship.

Through Scott he was probably introduced to the work of van de Velde the Younger, of whom he possessed two drawings.[2] With William Hogarth he was in communication on perhaps two occasions. The first in 1746, when he wrote a Satirical Epistle to him;[3] the second in 1748, when he criticized the painting of 'Paul before Felix'. He recalled this incident to his friend, William Lock, many years later:

When Hogarth painted his picture of Paul & Felix, for the chappel, I believe, of Lincoln's-inn, he represented a scroll falling from the hand of Felix, to mark his trepidation. I was so offended at seeing this thing hang in mid air, that I ventured, tho a very young man, to write Hogarth an anonymous letter on the subject; & he was so candid as to alter his picture, as I afterwards heard, on what I said; tho, as I remember, he did it but awkwardly at last.[4]

Gilpin's objection to the scroll showed that he had not forgotten the lessons to be drawn from the 'Judgment of Hercules'.

Other artists with whose work he was acquainted at this period were Allan Ramsay, Richard Wilson, and Gainsborough, of whom he had a drawing.[5]

By 1752 he had acquired a considerable number of prints, which had cost him little, for his means were meagre indeed. His usual practice was to mount them on sheets of white paper, previously treated with a beige or yellow wash to remove glare. Then on the part of the mount covered by the print he wrote a few significant remarks, for example on the drawing, composition, or quality of the impression. When he obtained sets of prints, as he did of Berchem, Hondius, and Karel Dujardin, these were inserted in folders, and each print given a full and comparative comment. All this critical material, gathered not only from his own prints but from an examination of private collections, he précied to a few succinct remarks about each artist. Only nine prints and the set of the 'Rake's Progress' were given a full and individual analysis in the *Essay on Prints*. From the point

---

[1] 'I received a Letter from your Son [William] here, he tells me Sawrey makes great Improvements.' John B. Gilpin to his wife, Exeter, 11 June 1749 (A. L. Fawcett).

[2] George F. Benson Collection.

[3] 'Now when I recollect I must mention your Epistle to Howgarth; I like the Thought very well, & think it a good form to throw a Satire into.' John Brown to W. G., 5 Jan. 1745/6 (W. L. Benson).

[4] 13 Sept. 1781 (Rev. E. G. Benson). Gilpin probably saw this history-piece before it was sent to Lincoln's Inn in 1748. The Pierpont Morgan Library possesses a red chalk drawing related to this painting of Paul before Felix, before Hogarth made his alteration; it shows Felix, in his astonishment, dropping the paper from his right hand. A. P. Oppé dated the

drawing 1748–52 and considered the falling scroll 'a refinement which does not occur in either of the prints [the two 1752 engravings by Hogarth and Sullivan], and suggests a later stage'. Gilpin's testimony makes it clear that this drawing must be earlier than 1748. See A. P. Oppé, *The Drawings of William Hogarth*, London, 1948, no. 69.

[5] This woodland scene, with two donkeys beside a dead oak, is in the collection of G. F. Benson. 'I have seen some of Gainsborough's painting. I have one of his drawing; but none I have thought excellent. Yet from what I have heard, I believe all that you say of him.—I have seen only his early works.' W. G. to Edward Forster, 19 May 1789 (Rev. E. G. Benson—Brisco transcript).

of view of the history of art criticism, an interesting little volume could be formed by gathering together his unpublished remarks on prints and paintings.

For example, here is his comment on the first of seven etchings by Abraham Hondius, the one depicting hunters and their dogs [4. b]:

This print, which Hondius makes his frontispiece, is equal to any of those, which follow, except the 2ᵈ [The hunted wolf] The principal group of the man & dogs is well-composed. The parts also are good. The figure with a spear over his shoulder (tho good in itself) injures the form of the group. Nor has it much connection with the sitting figure, which seems totally uninterested in the object of pursuit. The light is ill-distributed. It would have been better, if all the removed parts had been in slight shadow; and the light had fallen full on the head, & shoulders of the sitting figure, fading gradually away towards his feet. The gun also, & dog under it should be in shadow.

And here are his remarks on the fifth print of the hunted bear which include a comparison with Ridinger:

A bear, no doubt is an awkward animal; & this has all the awkwardness, which we should dislike in any animal, as well as a bear—that of standing on two legs without being poised. Where this attitude is given to an animal, that frequently uses it, as a horse; & where it is well-balanced, it is often beautiful: but, in general, it should be sparingly used. A bear raised on his hams is proper: that attitude is both natural, & well-balanced. Thus Ridinger would have raised him; who was a greater master of nature, than Hondius; tho he had not his free, & masterly execution. In dogs only Hondius excelled him; whose form & nature he seems perfectly to have understood. Of this, the print before us gives us an instance. We have the heads of two dogs pursuing the bear; a grey-hound, & a sort of mastiff. The latter has his mouth open; the former shut: Hondius well knowing, that the grey-hound never barks, when he pursues his game.—If the sky about the trees, & the trees themselves, had been darker, the effect of light had been better.[1]

When finally published in 1768, the *Essay on Prints* achieved a lasting success as the first standard guide on print collecting in this country, reaching a fifth edition in 1802. On the Continent its influence was even greater, through German, French, and Dutch translations.[2]

In the *Essay* Gilpin formulated the principles which guided him when examining prints.

[1] Gilpin's folder of Hondius prints is in the collection of George F. Benson. The comments on the second (The hunted wolf) and seventh (Hart and hind startled by Huntsmen) etchings were reproduced in the *Kenwood Exhibition Catalogue*, pp. 45–46. The same collector also possesses Gilpin's Ridinger prints. In particular twelve prints of hunting dogs (1728), and *A New Drawing Book of Dogs Heads, . . . 1748* by Darly after Ridinger.

[2] For detailed bibliographical information, see *Templeman*, chap. v. However, Professor Templeman states wrongly that the first English edition bore the title *An Essay upon Prints*: only the second edition (1768) did, and all the subsequent ones were entitled *An Essay on Prints*. After dedicating the third edition (1781) to Horace Walpole, Gilpin gave Edward Forster an amusing account of his hesitations between the two prepositions: 'on and upon. These two words have given me more plague than any two words in the language. When I first printed my essay *on* prints. My bookseller told me, that Lord Hillsborough taking it up, in his shop, had remarked that *upon*, was more proper than *on*. I accordingly thinking, that a secretary of state . . . knew better than I; changed it in the next edition, into an Essay *upon* prints.' Later Gilpin consulted William Mitford, who considered the two propositions might 'be used at option. So I troubled my head no further either *on*, or *upon* the subject.' Then he discussed the question with Lord Warwick. He 'thought, *upon* should never be used, but where something was raised, lifted, or laid *upon* another. This was the first time I received any *light* on the subject; . . . I was then just printing another edition of my Essay, and accordingly wrote it *on prints*—' 2 Feb. 1782 (Rev. E. G. Benson—Brisco transcript).

As may be gathered from the title of the first chapter, 'The Principles of Painting considered, so far as they relate to prints', the standards which he applied to a painting were in some cases identical with those he used for examining a print. He stated his rules as follows: 'To make a print agreeable as a *whole*, a just observance of those rules is necessary, which relate to *design, disposition, keeping*, and the *distribution of light*: to make it agreeable in its *parts*, of those which relate to *drawing, expression, grace* and *perspective*' (p. 2), and proceeded at length to explain each of the terms italicized. For example, under 'Design', he considered '*proper time, proper characters*, the most *affecting manner of introducing those characters*, and *proper appendages*', and, when dealing with the most effective moment to choose in a particular story, echoed Shaftesbury:

With regard to a *proper time*, the painter is assisted by good old dramatic rules; which inform him, that *one* point of time only should be taken—the most affecting in the action; and that no other part of the story should interfere with it. Thus *in* [the Raphael cartoon of] *the death of Ananias*, if the instant of his falling down be chosen, no anachronism should be introduced; every part of the piece should correspond; each character should be under the strangest impression of astonishment, and horror; those passions being yet unallayed by any cooler passions succeeding (pp. 3–4).

Gilpin aimed at giving the laymen a certain equipment to assess the value of prints as works of art, and he did so by explaining to them the rules which formed part of the training of any professional artist. The average Englishman with any pretension to taste, who wished to acquire prints with discernment, was given these criteria, organized in a convincing manner. Gilpin's originality lay not so much in the individual statements he made, as in the general attitude he adopted, in which art and nature were indissolubly linked. So that, while in the *Essay* artistic problems were constantly explained by references to nature, in the *Dialogue* it was nature which had been examined by artistic standards. This ambivalent attitude was to remain unchanged, and when he embarked on his 'picturesque tours' he quite naturally transferred to natural scenery the critical apparatus he had perfected for examining prints.

In that section of the *Essay* where he discussed his 'criterion of distant magnitude', he drew both on his knowledge of Claude paintings and on his own experience as a countryman to show that when representing distance, prints must accept certain limitations which do not apply to painting:

The idea . . . of *distant magnitude*, the print gives only very imperfectly. It is expressed chiefly by colour. Air, which is naturally blue, is the medium through which we see; and every object participates of this blueness. When the distance is small, the tinge is imperceptible; as it increases, the tinge grows stronger; and when the object is very remote, it entirely loses its natural colour, and becomes blue. And indeed this is so familiar a criterion of distance, at least with those who live in mountainous countries, that if the object be visible at all, after it has received the full *ether-tinge*, if I may so speak, the sight immediately judges it to be very large. The eye ranging over the plains of Egypt, and catching the blue point of a pyramid, from the colour concludes the distance; and is struck with the magnitude of an object, which, through such a space, can exhibit form.—Here the print fails: this criterion of distant magnitude, it is unable to give (pp. 39–40).

For him nature should be the constant yardstick, 'the standard of imitation; and every object should be executed, as nearly as possible in *her manner*. Thus SALVATOR's figures, DU JARDIN's animals, and WATERLO's landskips, are all strongly impressed with the character of nature' (p. 30).

———

In 1752, through his acquaintance with the Sanxay family, Gilpin was invited to take over Cheam School from the Rev. James Sanxay. After considerable hesitation, he accepted. For the next few years his energies were completely absorbed in trying to put this establishment on a sound footing. This is the period when he evolved his own conception of what a boarding school for boys between the ages of eight and fifteen should be. Against the general trend of his day, he instituted a broad pattern of general education with a thorough grounding in basic subjects, that was to make Cheam famous for the next fifty years.[1] However, at first success was a long way off. With the help of his first cousin and childhood friend, Margaret Gilpin, whom he married in 1752, he faced difficulties that would have deterred many a young man of twenty-eight. The school he took over could hardly be described as a going concern; it lacked funds and equipment, and in the first year of his mastership the number of boys fell to fifteen. It is only very slowly and gradually, through careful management, that the numbers increased. To judge from the entries in the 'Cheam Promise Book',[2] there were still only twenty boys in 1759. The numbers, however, rose rapidly in the 1760's: 31 boys in 1762, 59 in 1764, 61 in 1765, and 66 in 1766.

Cheam School severely curtailed Gilpin's other activities. His study of prints was laid aside, etching ceased, never to be taken up again, and even drawing was rarely practised. But he managed to keep in touch with the world of art through Sawrey, who was not far away at Twickenham, where Samuel Scott had moved out in the 1750's. Through him, he probably met William Marlow (1740–1813), and John Skelton (d. 1759) who did a drawing of Cheam Church in 1757, and gave Sawrey the sobriquet of 'honest Gilpin', for sticking to Samuel Scott till 1758, two years beyond his apprenticeship.[3]

His interest in his brother's development is shown by the number of sketches he acquired and often dated. This habit of preserving a record of Sawrey's drawings, sometimes adding a title as well as a date, though it makes it difficult to identify certain of his own drawings which are treated in the same way, gives us valuable information about Sawrey's activities between 1755 and 1764. It is said that the Duke of Cumberland took

[1] See *Memoirs*, pp. 123–35; *Templeman*, chap. iv; and my articles in the *Glasgow Herald* (14 Sept. 1957) and *The Times Educ. Suppl.* (17 Jan. 1958).

[2] Major J. R. Abbey Collection.

[3] See R. Pierce's article on Skelton in the *Walpole Society* journal, vol. 36.

him under his patronage in 1761, and that it was in the Duke's stud that he first devoted himself to horse-painting.[1] The fact is, Sawrey Gilpin forsook marine subjects[2] for horses very early in his career. His earliest animal drawings are after James Seymour (1702–52) and John Wooton (d. 1756), and from the number of Seymour sketches which both he and William possessed, it may just be possible that they knew him. Mr. George F. Benson possesses a folder containing signed sketches by Seymour together with Sawrey's copies of them—some of Seymour's and many of Sawrey's sketches bear titles or indications by William Gilpin [4. c].[3] Sawrey Gilpin's earliest dated animal drawing, a water-colour of a chestnut horse, 1755, followed by several small sketch-books of 1757 and 1758, drawings such as 'Gentil, a horse belonging to the King. 1757', 'The back-sign of the White-horse at Hocliffe, near Dunstable. 1758', 'Nutmeg, a horse belonging to the duke of Cumberland 1759', '*Chirk*, a chestnut-horse, belonging to Watkin Wynn esq^re.' 1761, '*Cade*, a coach-horse, belonging to Sir James Lowther', 1761, and finally the 1760–1 series of etchings of various kinds of horses, such as 'The Cart Horse', 'The Road Horse', and 'The Dray Horse', all show that Sawrey was interested in horses for many years before the Duke of Cumberland extended his patronage to him.[4] Even so, he may very well have attracted the Duke's notice before 1761 (see drawing of 1759 above).[5] And, despite opinion to the contrary, it seems clear he provides the natural link between the older generation of sporting painters, such as Wooton, Tillemans, and Seymour, and the generation of Stubbs.[6]

In the 1750's Sawrey tried his hand at many other subjects. Besides the market studies which attracted the Duke's attention, he did in 1756 lively drawings of birds which possess a decorative charm—they are birds of prey, exotic birds, and fowls of the barn-yard. He also turned his hand to landscape, and for a time was employed as a medical artist, as can be seen from the misshapen foetus he drew for William Hunter in 1760.[7]

The only drawing of this period to have survived, attributed to William Gilpin, is a carefully balanced ideal landscape, in pen and coloured washes [2. d]. Up to now, a few landscapes of this period, which might be by either William or Sawrey Gilpin, have come to light. The difficulty is to tell them apart, so similar is their technique and source of inspiration. This is so in the case of the above drawing of 1757, whose inclined rocks and

---

[1] E. K. Waterhouse, *Painting in Britain 1530–1790*, London, 1953, p. 220; B. Taylor, *Animal Painting in England*, Penguin Books, 1955, p. 58.

[2] The few slight drawings of ships and marine subjects by Sawrey Gilpin that I have come across are early and executed in the manner of van de Velde the Younger. One dated 1750 is in the collection of Lieut.-Col. N. St. Leger Moore.

[3] Another drawing in the George F. Benson Collection points to Sawrey Gilpin's early interest in James Seymour. Underneath the drawing of a horse sectioned is written: 'This analysis proposeth a method to assist ye judgment in discerning ye beauties & faults of a horse. By considering him, as if taken to pieces & judging of each part separately, you cannot so easily be imposed upon as when you view ye parts in gross.

This outline is taken f^m a drawing of Seymour, & when anilysed shews a just arrangement of parts—copy.' The handwriting remains unidentified.

[4] All these drawings and prints are in the George F. Benson Collection.

[5] The Duke of Cumberland retired from the army in 1757, and it was no doubt through his contact with Captain John B. Gilpin in the 1745 Rebellion that he took an interest in his son.

[6] Cf. E. K. Waterhouse's statement: 'Between this first generation and the generation of Stubbs and Sawrey Gilpin there is no connecting link.' *Painting in Britain 1530–1790*, p. 216.

[7] Hunterian Library, Glasgow University.

crossed fir-trees derive from Captain Gilpin's Carlisle folder (*c.* 1755). If this competent drawing is by William, and there is some evidence to support the attribution,[1] then Gilpin had made considerable progress since his tentative representations of Scaleby Castle of 1741–2.

[1] This drawing in the W. D. Templeman Collection is dated '1757' on the verso in William Gilpin's own hand; also on the verso in the right-hand top corner is the inscription 'WG—Lymᵹ | 1757' (drawing may have been presented after William took up residence at Boldre in 1778); the drawing is inscribed boldly on the front 'W. Gilpin' in a hand that may be connected with W. Thomson, who acquired many of Gilpin's sketches in the 1780's (William as far as we know never signed or initialled a drawing on the face). In our catalogue to the Kenwood Exhibition we ascribed it to Sawrey Gilpin.

IV. Various Manners, 1761–1768

As Cheam School flourished, Gilpin increasingly devoted himself to his favourite pastime. From 1761 onwards drawings have survived in considerable numbers, so that we can almost follow his yearly progress. For the period 1761–8 this is particularly easy, as many of the drawings are dated down to the month and even to the day. Gilpin draws all the year round. In the summer he makes series of sketches from nature, and during the rest of the year employs his moments of leisure to make more finished drawings. Landscape is the only subject which interests him, and this he treats in the most varied ways. Using at times just plain washes over a simple pencil outline, at others detailed penwork and almost full water-colour, he experiments and tries to convey his feeling for texture and atmosphere. The results vary considerably, ranging from drawings treated in a broad, loose, and almost impressionistic manner to neat and tidy drawings where each stroke conveys a particular meaning. As yet his concern for composition is subsidiary to his interest in particular features of the landscape. His predilections are his father's, boulders, craggy, stratified, and precipitous rocks, curving paths and undermined banks, the ruin, and the contrasting flat sheet of water.

The first drawing, dated 'July 16. 1761', showing a clump of shaggy trees on a bank, is treated with broad washes of beige and light brown.[1] The next, dated 'Nov. 22. 1762' in grey pen and wash, might almost be a lunar landscape rather than an earthly one, were it not for the presence of ruined buildings and trees.[2]

In 1763 varied subjects were treated in water-colour, from a barge moored beside a timber wharf[3] to a lake scene with round tower and viaduct.[2] The round tower and the high arches, derived from Claude Lorrain, were to be used frequently by Gilpin in his later imaginary compositions. A characteristic feature of the drawings of 1762–3 is the use of small strokes or dabs with pen or brush to indicate foliage, and large squiggles to fill shaded areas. The colour scheme is the same as his father's, a narrow range of tints applied to a drawing already defined by grey washes: pale blue or grey for sky; pink to brick colour for buildings and ruins; grey-green, olive green, and yellow for trees and vegetation; earth colours for soil and sand-banks; red, brown, and greys for tree-trunks and the shade of buildings; various greys for water and distant mountains. Gilpin did little work in water-colour; he stopped after 1765 and returned to it again for only a brief period in the 1780's.

[1] A. L. Fawcett Collection.   [2] W. L. Benson Collection.   [3] Alan de G. Benson Collection.

During the summer holidays he made short excursions from Cheam and, whenever he could, made the journey to Carlisle and Whitehaven to see his family and relations. Of the many notebooks he filled on his travels, a few have survived. One, called 'Views between Lancaster, and Coventry 1763',[1] contains seven rough sketches, bearing such titles as 'Lancaster-sands', 'An encampment of the Lancashire Militia on Preston-moor June 9. 1763.', 'Garstang-castle in Lancashire.', and 'Mouth of the Eden, below Rowcliff in Cumberland . . .'. These hasty sketches are little more than memoranda. With pencil, pen, and brush, devices were worked out to convey primarily the texture of ground, tree, and ruin, and these devices increasingly conveyed those qualities of roughness and ruggedness which form such an essential part of Gilpin's idea of picturesque beauty.

With the brush he treats the whole area with broad blotches of grey wash. Where pen is used, the colour and strength of the ink varies with the planes: dark brown in the foreground and grey in the middle distance. Loose, looped strokes indicate foliage, but for texture or accident he uses series of undulating and scalloped lines.

Another notebook, entitled 'Views between Penrith and Shap',[1] was filled with similar panoramas and sketches on a return journey from Carlisle. Here we have an early instance of what was to be a common feature of his writing: the description of landscape enlivened by anecdotes. The subjects are chosen as much for their own sake as for their association with certain events. Thus to a wide panorama he added the following note: 'A view of *Penrith Fell*. Near the Beacon, in the year 1715, Ld. Lonsdale drew up the Posse comitatus of Cumberland to oppose the rebels who took that rout into the south. But the sight of the rebels, who were described marching round the hill (a) imediately put them to flight.'[2]

Going by the vertical treatment of foliage, characteristic of his 1763 work, that summer Gilpin must have filled another little notebook, 'Views of difft parts of Cockermouth-castle'.[1] These rapid monochrome sketches have a spontaneity which his more finished compositions often lack [4. *d*]. Cockermouth Castle was a familiar sight to him. He returned to it in 1766, as can be seen from the more finished drawing of it in the Victoria and Albert Museum,[3] and again in 1772, on his return journey from Scotland.[4]

In September 1763 he did a set of grey-wash drawings reminiscent of his loose manner of 1761. These landscapes all have a ruined castle with square towers placed on an eminence, and the composition is framed in the foreground by thick shaggy trees.[1]

From October 1763 to January 1764 Gilpin did more finished drawings tinted with water-colour. These reflect his interest in rock formations and winding paths through mountainous scenery. A particularly agreeable study of a crag, dated 'Jan. 1764', heralds a period of three or four years, during which he produced his best precise compositions, and these drawings alone are sufficient to assure him a place among our minor accomplished

[1] W. L. Benson Collection.

[2] Event recalled in the *Tour of the Lakes*, 3rd ed., 1792, chap. xix. (For full title see p. 75, n. 2.)

[3] E.491–1947. Bequeathed by Dr. Annette M. Benson through the National Art-Collections Fund.

[4] *Scottish Tour*, 2nd ed., 1792, ii, 148–51. (For full title see p. 77, n. 2.)

draughtsmen. For example, in a rocky landscape of August 1764, by the simple use of pencil, grey wash, and, what is unusual for him, black greasy pencil, he captured effectively the contrasting surfaces of ground, boulders, and vertical rock formation [4. *e*].

We know of two short excursions in 1764. One, in the spring, down the River Thames with his brother Sawrey; the other, probably in the summer, to his old friend, Mr. Long, at Finmere, where among several sketches, there is one treating foliage in the new way— the foliage being conveyed by long digitated strokes of the pen radiating from a centre like the spokes of a wheel.[1] To my knowledge, he only employed this device from 1764 to 1766.

At times he resorted to very simple compositions. One of these, dated 'March 1765', is a peninsula or strip of land, complete with ruined castle and foliage, advancing into a calm sheet of water.[1] The accidented silhouette of castle and trees is not only repeated in the outline of the background screen of distant mountains, but also reflected on the smooth surface of water. His large expanses of water are invariably like glass serving as contrast for the land masses. It is the only water surface he achieves successfully; whenever he attempts a running stream, or a waterfall, he is as clumsy as his father.

In the summer of 1765 he executed finished landscapes in which figures and birds animate the scene for the first time. A mountain and lake scene of June 1765—one of his best coloured drawings—has two soldiers in the foreground which might be straight from Salvator Rosa.[2] These figures are the forerunners of the more simplified banditti silhouettes, which appeared so regularly, in groups of two or three, in his later work. They are never more than accessories, pointing a finger to an object of interest either outside our field of view or within the landscape represented. Thus in the large open landscape of August 1765, the finger points to the striking feature—two trees treated in a rough and bold manner [4. *f*].

In 1766 he provided some of his largest drawings. The subjects vary considerably, from a landscape with a ruined church beside a lake,[3] to an unusual composition with three tall pillars.[1] In the first of these note, in particular, the hatching, usual between 1765 and 1767, and also the technique employed for rendering a tree-trunk: vertical squiggles, dots, and pointed strokes for the rotted stumps of the lower side branches. The second drawing, possibly his largest ($19\frac{5}{16} \times 12\frac{15}{16}$ in.) is unfinished. One wonders where he got the row of strange menhir-like shapes. Perhaps he drew on one of Piranesi's fantastic compositions, or exaggerated the size of 'The Three Arrows' near Boroughbridge. The other feature of interest is the tall foreground tree, which dominates everything and fills half the space. We shall meet it again in his upright compositions, though never again treated with the same delicacy—here, dabs of grey wash and very thin penwork combine to give us Gilpin's nearest approach to a detailed representation of foliage.

[1] W. L. Benson Collection.

[2] A. L. Fawcett Collection.

[3] W. L. Benson Collection. Reproduced in *Kenwood Exhibition Catalogue*, Item 24. On the back of the drawing is written:

'Mr G.VH | The gift of ye reved Saml Hey'. Samuel Hey had a number of drawings by William Gilpin which he gave to Gilpin's descendants. There are quite a few in the collections of the Benson family.

He continued to use thin penwork throughout 1767. Thereafter the treatment of trunk, branch, and foliage became increasingly stereotyped, though the technique varied slightly with the years.

In 1767 Gilpin made a journey which took him to the centre of the Isle of Wight. There, among several subjects that interested him, he made an airy sketch, full of atmosphere, of the town and castle of Carisbrooke, and also a drawing of Ashey Down.[1] Several sketches of the River Tees and its banks done in the same manner suggest that he was also in the north-east of England in 1767. One in particular, 'Banks of the Tees', has two features we shall meet with increasing frequency: the two little figures, summarily indicated, walking along a winding road, and the fir tree with its drooping branches.[2]

From the middle 1760's the wild landscapes of Salvator Rosa had an increasing influence on Gilpin's imaginary compositions, as opposed to the sketches made on his journeys, which were necessarily largely topographical. Though Salvator's paintings were not readily accessible, and it cannot be said his popularity in England at the time was anything like Claude's, Gilpin had known his work for some years largely through the engravings of Joseph Goupy, John Brown (1719–90), and Lady Augusta Louisa Greville. His natural inclination for the sublime drew him to these savage landscapes with their blasted trees and rocks of great proportion. If his subsequent appreciation was to cool a little,[3] his enthusiasm was at its peak in 1768 when he published the *Essay on Prints*.

In *design*, and generally in *composition*, SALVATOR is very great [he proclaimed]. His figures which he drew in exquisite taste, are graceful and nobly expressive, beautifully grouped, and varied into the most agreable attitudes. . . . His style is grand; every object that he introduces is of the heroic kind. . . . We are told, he spent the early part of his life in a troop of banditti: and that the rocky and desolate scenes, in which he was accustomed to take refuge, furnished him with those romantic ideas in landskip, of which he is so exceedingly fond; and in the description of which he so greatly excels. His *Robbers*, as his detached figures are commonly called, are supposed also to have been taken from the life (pp. 80–82).

Here, in his own words, we have the source and justification for the banditti figures which he included in his own landscapes from 1765 onwards. For Gilpin these figures are the only natural inhabitants of sublime landscape. Another extract from the *Essay* shows his reaction to the landscape in the print of Salvator's 'Death of Polycrates': 'The scenery is inimitable. The rock broken, and covered with shrubs at the top; and afterwards spreading into one grand, and simple shade, is in itself a pleasing object; and affords an excellent back-ground to the figures' (pp. 184–5).

[1] W. L. Benson Collection.

[2] W. L. Benson Collection. Another drawing, in the possession of George F. Benson, bears the puzzling title: 'On the banks of the Tees in Northumberland'.

[3] 'An amusing bit of evidence of his waning appreciation appears in the changes made by him in a paragraph of his *Essay on Prints*. In 1768 Salvator is "very great" in composition, draws his "nobly expressive" figures in "exquisite taste", groups them "beautifully", and has a manner "wonderfully pleasing". The later edition softens these respectively to: "often happy", "expressive", "good taste", "well", and "pleasing".' Elizabeth W. Manwaring, *Italian Landscape in Eighteenth Century England*, New York, 1925, p. 52.

The effect of this enthusiasm is very marked in his own large compositions, which are all vertical. The few that have so far come to light show him no longer content with the study of the textures of rock and ground for their own sakes, the more rugged and accidented parts of the landscape are now made to clash and combine, often within a more confined space, to give the whole a greater density and emotional content.

The first drawing, probably done in 1767, is of a rocky landscape with a bridge spanning a gorge.[1] The bridge with the neat masonry of its stilted arches is dwarfed into insignificance by the majesty of nature's own architecture, as from on high, enormous broken rocks tilt diagonally across the picture to the abyss below. The eye takes in with delight the cascade of fragmented surfaces, plumed here and there by scraggy stunted shrubs. Save for the occasional use of pen, the technique of this grey and white composition is largely impressionistic—the areas left in white combine with the grey washes to create by juxtaposition the thousand facets of the weathered and broken strata.

A little later (*c.* 1769–70) he returned to the same subject with a group of soldiers guarding the entrance to a yawning chasm [*frontispiece*]. The elements of the landscape may be the same, but they are handled in a very different manner. The accent has shifted from structural detail to the atmosphere which pervades the whole, as if Gilpin's imaginative powers had been given a new twist. The overhanging cliffs and tilted rocks come down in clashing diagonals to create a deep gorge that remains largely unseen. An impressive sense of structure and a brooding atmosphere, where all is dark, forbidding, and ill defined, combine to give the whole picture a high pitch of visual drama. Such detail as there is is placed at the corners of the composition. Whether you look up at the blasted tree or at the shrub precariously placed on the edge of the cliff, or down at the group of soldiers, these features all lead the eye inwards and throw it towards the centre—a centre hemmed in and held captive by the shadows.[2]

Something of the same intensity permeates the large and dark forest scene of 1771 [5.]. In the foreground a shattered tree crosses its bole with another that rises diagonally across the composition in all the glory of its foliage, while beyond, two little figures stride across the shady glade.[3]

These drawings in their different ways emphasize his debt to Salvator Rosa, while the last two mark a new departure. From now on he is mainly concerned with the total effect created, with composition and light and shade. Hand in hand with this changed outlook goes a new and looser technique. In addition to grey washes he uses beige, brown, sepia, and even red-brown, and the whole drawing is unified by an overall of beige, light-brown or yellow wash. Occasionally, dark shadows are gummed to obtain depth, as is the case in the dark forest scene.

[1] W. L. Benson Collection.

[2] Gilpin's wife wrote on the back of this drawing: 'Mr Gilpin gave this drawing to me Feby 1798 | Margt Gilpin'. It then became the property of her eldest son, John Bernard, in America.

[3] The drawing is stuck to a grey-wash mount, on the back of which is written in pencil by an unknown hand: 'Done in 1771'.

Before moving on to examine the many drawings which he did from 1768 onwards, as he toured the country in search of picturesque beauty, we must pause a little to consider his contacts with his brother during the 1760's. They were many and fruitful.

Perhaps the most interesting project, in which William and Sawrey collaborated, was an early effort to produce a picturesque tour by sailing down the whole length of the River Thames. The scheme got no farther than a day's sailing in 1764, which was written up as 'A Fragment, containing a description of the Thames, Between Windsor and London: Accompanied with 37 Sketches, by Mr. Sawrey Gilpin'.[1] In the 'Advertisement' of this manuscript, written many years later, Gilpin recalled his original intentions. First they were 'to *navigate the river*, & fix the principal points on it's banks. These would remain as a kind of landmarks, from which the appearance of the river from the land might afterwards be examined; & any thing remarkable in its neighbourhood might be brought within a picturesque survey.' William would do the writing and Sawrey the sketches. 'These sketches were afterwards to be turned into finished drawings; & the whole, when compleated, was to be formed into a volume of Thames-scenery.'

In the unpublished fragment, such as it is, Gilpin scans the banks of the Thames for pictorial effects; unfortunately the scenery becomes progressively unrewarding as he approaches the metropolis. He concludes with observations on barges and swans as picturesque objects in themselves and as useful adjuncts to river scenes.

All his life he maintained a lively interest in natural history, and in the 1760's began to set down his observations of birds, animals, and insects in books, which were amended and filled out over the years and illustrated by Sawrey. These works, reflecting as much curiosity in his own poultry-yard as in his brother's pursuits, were later tidied up and given to his grandson William in 1803. They consisted, at first, of 'Observations on horses', 'Observations on domestic poultry', to which were added 'Observations on Turkies Ducks and Bees', and a short account of '*Dingo*, a dog from Botany-bay'.[2]

As might be suspected, aesthetic judgements are scattered among his more general remarks. To select one among many: in the 'Observations on domestic poultry' he devoted

---

[1] Bound in half-calf and blue boards. MS. text followed by mounted drawings. Realized £44. 2s. 0d. at 1802 sale (lot 138). Acquired by L. Y. B. Procter of Harley Street and sold at Christie's as part of his estate (lot 110) to a Mr. Hunter for 26 guineas on 30 Apr. 1804. A. P. Oppé noted its purchase by Edwards (lot 99A) for £4. 18s. 0d. at the sale of Captain Norcliffe Gilpin, deceased, on 20 Apr. 1915. After being in the J. P. Heseltine Collection, it was bought by the Victoria and Albert Museum in 1949 (abbreviation: *Thames Tour*).

[2] These works were gathered into two volumes. The first, in the possession of Miss Ann Gilpin Benson, bears the general title, 'Observations on Horses, and Domestic fowls', and is dedicated by William Gilpin: 'Vicar's hill August 16. 1803 | These two volumes on natural history, belong to my grandson, William Gilpin of Cheam.' The volume, illustrated with fourteen drawings by Sawrey Gilpin, contains the 'Observations on horses' and 'Observations on domestic poultry', for the most part written in the late 1760's, and a very short account of '*Dingo*, a dog from Botany-bay', dating from the end of the century. Gilpin's introduction to the 'Observations on domestic poultry' is dated: 'Vicars hill | Ap. 21.1790.'

The second volume, in the collection of W. L. Benson, entitled 'Observations on Turkies Ducks and Bees', is dedicated in the same way as the first volume, except for the date, 'Aug.18.1803'.

Major J. R. Abbey has another manuscript of the 'Observations on domestic poultry' written by Catherine Brisco and illustrated with sketches by Sawrey Gilpin. The introduction is dated: 'Vicar's Hill April. 29.1790'.

much space to the game-cock, 'the only fowl, I ever took much pleasure in breeding', and at one point justifies on aesthetic grounds, and with some difficulty, the practice of cutting the comb and wattles of the cock-bird. Coming from one who holds cock-fighting in utter contempt, the confession of weakness makes amusing reading:

Yet there is one practice even among cock-fighters, which much as I contemn them, I cannot help owning I prefer in a picturesque light; & that is the practice of cutting off the comb, & wattles of a cock. I am ashamed to own, that depriving an animal of any natural ornament appears to me a beauty. I am more ashamed to coincide with a cock-fighter in any of his professional points. In fact, I conceive that my eye is, in this matter, debauched by a prejudice. As I admire the game-cock, & as this mutilation is one of his specific characteristics; I have, through an association of ideas, contracted a partiality to it. The comb gives the bird more the idea of the dung-hill breed; & the deprivation of it adds that smartness to him, which accords with his nature.—Perhaps indeed I may have—I would persuade myself I have—a better reason for depriving him of this ornament. In severe winters it is apt to be frost-bitten. I have had many birds injured, in point of beauty by this accident. I remember particularly, in the december of the year 1767, when the frost was intense, I had the beauty of a very fine bird injured in this way. Two or three of the highest spiracles of his comb were seized, & all the projection behind. The infected parts turned into a pale yellow; & seemed to be in a state of decay. In about six weeks however this appearance went off; & the comb in a degree recovered its colour; but never its beauty. It lost that rich frosted work, with which it was overspread, & took only the smooth polish of a piece of coral. It lost, also its form—those beautiful points, which became rounded, & shapeless.—If however I coincide with the cock-fighter in this mutilation, I agree with him in nothing else. A cock trimmed for the pit, is one of the most grotesque appearances in nature.[1]

Brief mention must also be made of two other little works. About 1760 he seems to have written an explanatory text to his brother's set of eight etchings of horses (1760–1), but whether the manuscript, entitled 'On the characters of Horses', was ever published I am not certain.[2] The other manuscript, 'On the character, & Expression of Animals', was started in the last years of his life, and remained unfinished.[3] He was probably stimulated to undertake this work because, at that time, Sawrey was becoming very interested in such wild animals as bears, lions, and tigers. The plan was ambitious: he intended to consider 'various kinds of animals, wild, tame, foreign and domestick', but only completed the sections on the lion and lioness. An extract will give some idea of what this work, in the manner of Buffon, would have been. He is describing the eyebrow of the lion:

The eye-brow is that feature, which of all others, marks intuition, and thought. In the noble portrait, which Homer gives us of Jupiter, he marks the eye-brow with particular strength. Some

---

[1] Pp. 32–36 (Miss Ann Gilpin Benson).

[2] Small notebook in the collection of W. L. Benson. The text, written by another hand and corrected by William Gilpin, begins: 'In the following plates it is proposed to distinguish horses into their several classes, as to give an idea of each . . . .' The original scheme is outlined in a letter of Mrs. Elizabeth Gilpin (*née* Langstaffe) to her sister, Matilda Gilpin: '[Sawrey Gilpin] is upon a scheme of printing by subscrip-

tion six horses, a Racer, Hunter, Road horse, Coach horse, Dray H and Cart H. He eitches the plate & Mr. G. his brother writes the characters of each Horse which will be printed with them. The subscription is not yet fix'd, as soon as it is we will Sub[s]cribe for a set . . . .' 1 Jan. 1760 (A. L. Fawcett).

[3] Rev. E. G. Benson Collection. MS. in the hand of Catherine Brisco, with corrections and additions by W. G.

animals have no pretentions to this feature. In some it is slightly touched; but in the lion it is distinctly marked. It is true, the eye-brow of the lion has not that precision, which we find in the human countenance. It consists of a great muscular fullness, assisted by a small annular turn of the hair. In this grand muscle resides that power of contraction, which we shall see, when we speak of *expression*, greatly contributes to cloath his head with terrour. Here, in a *quiescent state*, is placed that thoughtful severity, which is so characteristic in him. This may arise in part from his brows being horizontal; which is perhaps peculiar to the human race, and that tribe, of which the lion is the principal. I remember an old she lion in the Tower, which had this thoughtful cast in a great degree. But when you approached her, her eye-brow began to swell, and the thoughtful cast of her eye was changed into a savage squint.

Another activity which united the two brothers in the 1760's was the teaching of drawing at Cheam School. Fortunately letters have survived which give us a glimpse of the sort of tuition the boys received. Thomas Grimston (1753–1821) was at Cheam from 1762 to 1769 before going to Harrow. In May 1763 he reported to his father, 'I have had two Lessons in drawing since I saw you last'. The loose drawings were posted home, but in September 1766 he explained, 'I shall not have many Drawings to send you because we have a Drawing Book with a blue cover, so I will bring it home with me at Christmas Holidays'. During those holidays his father promised him some paints. However, by February 1767 they had not come: 'I have not yet got my paints from Mr. Couzens but hope I shal have them soon. I believe when you come up you will see the map of Europe drawn by me, for Mr. Gilpin has got us a book to draw maps in. I am afraid you will not see my Drawing Book filled with objects from nature for we do not draw any thing from nature but all from drawings of Mr. Saurey Gilpin's.' After repeated inquiries, the paints from Alexander Cozens eventually arrived, and with the warmer spring weather, he was able to draw outside. On 22 May 1767 he wrote: 'I went into the Town at Cheam this morning to draw some Houses or any thing that I liked, with some more of my fellow Schoolboys. They tyed one of Mr. Robt. Sanxay's Horses up and d[rew] it but they finding it to hard to do all leaft of but one and they drew a barn an a house. I drew Mr. Sanxay's house and Mr. Sorey Gilpin said it was very well done.' With increasing proficiency Thomas Grimston filled many books in the course of that year and the next. In September 1767 he wrote home: 'I have finished another drawing book and have drawn three Pictures in the next one of which is Cheam Church from Nature and the two others from Pictures of Mr. Saury Gilpin's dooing.' And again in November 1768 it is very much the same pattern: 'According to your desire I got a large drawing book and have drawn ten pictures in it some out of doors and some from Mr. Sawrys. there is but two more leaves to draw upon, so if you happen to come here in Xmas holydays it will be ready for you.'[1]

Lastly, William Gilpin, like his father, gained an insight into Alexander Cozens's

---

[1] Thomas Grimston's letters to his father are in the possession of Lady Waechter de Grimston.

various methods and techniques, largely through Sawrey's contacts with Cozens in the late 1760's. They lived very near to one another, Sawrey Gilpin at Windsor while Cozens taught at Eton.[1] Both exhibited at the Society of Artists. Sawrey Gilpin after the death of his patron, the Duke of Cumberland, in 1765, seems to have stayed on at Windsor for some years. He was certainly there in 1768 and 1769, engaged on history pieces in the Grand Manner, in an effort to raise his own status and that of horse-painting generally. Of the several pictures illustrating Gulliver's travels to the land of the Houyhnhnms, the one which was exhibited at the Society of Artists in 1768, on his own testimony, owed something of the success it brought him to Cozens's 'Method of painting with tacky colours'.[2] The two men must have been very good friends, for Cozens confided his professional secrets, and allowed Sawrey to pass these on to his father, and probably also to William. Thus we hear of another 'system' which would have rejoiced the heart of Paul Oppé, that dedicated scholar of Alexander Cozens: it is the 'Method of painting skies', described by Sawrey Gilpin in the manuscript 'Essay on colouring landscape' (c. 1768), which he probably also sent to his father.[3]

As to William, when did he meet Cozens? He could have done so in his London days, when Cozens was drawing-master at Christ's Hospital, but a more likely time would be shortly before 1769, on a visit to his brother at Windsor. Anyhow, on 26 May 1769, Thomas Whately,[4] his friend and occasional neighbour at Nonsuch, inquired after Cozens in a manner which leaves little doubt that by then Gilpin knew Cozens:

What were the particular Observations which Mr Cozens has thought it worth his while to remember, I do not recollect; but if at any time that he comes this way he will do me the favour to call upon me, I shall be very glad to see him: or perhaps it may be more convenient in London in the Winter. Is he a Painter, or only a Drawing Master? I thought him clever, & wrapt up in his Art: what Effect his Principles may have on his Works I do not know: my Opinion of all the Principles of all the Arts is the same: they will prevent faults; but to produce Beauties Genius is

[1] The generally accepted date for Cozens's appointment as drawing-master at Eton is 1763 (see *Oppé*, p. 26). He was certainly there in 1764. Robert Grimston, a boy about to leave Eton for Cambridge, writes to a much older cousin, John Grimston of Kilnwick: 'Eaton May. the 7 1764. Sir. Hearing from Mr. Cozens that you was arrived in Town; I think it my Duty to congratulate you upon your safe arrival, Hoping that you have had an agreeable Journey from the North . . .' (Lady Waechter de Grimston).

[2] Iolo A. Williams possesses a rough annotated sketch by William Gilpin of one of the 'Gulliver and the Houyhnhnms' compositions.

[3] W. L. Benson Collection.

[4] Thomas Whately (d. 1772), literary critic and politician, chiefly remembered for his *Observations on Modern Gardening*, 1770. From early days at Cheam, Gilpin was acquainted with the two brothers Thomas and Joseph Whately, who lived at Nonsuch Park, only half a mile from the school. In his biographical sketch of Thomas he said: 'He laid out Mr. G.'s garden at Cheam; & made it very beautiful; tho Mr. G. sometimes thought, (as the house was large) a square court, with the gates in front, as it was before, was more *adapted to it*; tho in *itself*, the present scene is much more beautiful.—He did a great deal also, & in very good taste, in the gardens at Nonsuch: particularly he changed a chalk-pit, containing about an acre, from a deformity into a beauty. He was very systematic in all his ideas—perhaps more so, than the truth would bear. He planted shrubs, for instance, in such a manner, as to make a harmony among their tints, the darker or lighter to retire, or advance, as he thought the scene required. But an attempt of this kind cannot well succeed. Foliage is such changeable colouring, that it can never be depended on. All harmony therefore from this source must be left to chance. You may happen to see in the forest a very beautiful effect of this kind: but you must look for it merely in the capriciousness of nature; & probably will not find it the next day.' 'A short Account of Different people . . .' (J. B. Gilpin-Brown).

necessary, & Principles too closely adhered to now & then restrains Genius: they are very useful, but a little dangerous.[1]

The 'Principles' referred to are probably the *Principles of Beauty relative to the Human Head*, not published till 1778.[2] Gilpin was interested not so much in Cozens's 'systems' as in his drawings and the methods employed to obtain his effects. He possessed himself one of the 'blots', a small monochrome composition, treated with characteristic broad strokes of the brush.[3] The 'blot' technique would appeal to him for its affinity with his own practice of the rough sketch. I have, on occasion, come across a drawing of Gilpin's bearing the inscription 'a blot',[4] but Gilpin's sketches of imaginary landscapes are not true 'blots', since they lack that accidental and irrational element which Cozens calls into play to fix the original idea upon paper. Nevertheless, the points of departure for Gilpin's and Cozens's imaginary compositions are very similar. For the blot as for the rough sketch certain prerequisites are desirable if the end product is to be successful: namely inventive powers and ready execution—both these are needed to translate and give a rapid form to the initial idea. Also, once the idea has taken form, both men rely on memory for its subsequent elaboration into a more finished drawing.

Gilpin remained interested in Cozens's activities in the 1770's. He knew his book of *Trees* (1771),[5] discussed his use of black ink with William Mason in 1772,[6] and figured, together with his brother and several of his friends, among the subscribers to the *Principles*.[7]

It is interesting to note how many of the members of the Carlisle Group came into contact with Alexander Cozens. Dr. John Brown, as full of literary schemes as Cozens was

---

[1] W. L. Benson Collection.

[2] For the publication of *Principles*, see *Oppé*, pp. 29–30. Subscriptions were asked for early in 1776. Lady Waechter de Grimston possesses what must be a rare specimen of the printed subscription form, which Cozens sent receipted to John Grimston of Kilnwick (1725–80). Here is the text, with the part in Cozens's hand shown in italics: 'February 21, 1776. | PROPOSALS | For publishing by Subscription, | PRINCIPLES of BEAUTY, | Relative to the Female Human Head. | Illustrated by Examples, in Outline in Profile as large as Life. | By ALEXANDER COZENS, | in Leicester-Street, Leicester-Fields. | The Engravings will be executed by Mr. Bartolozzi. | CONDITIONS. | The Work will be printed in Folio, on Imperial Paper. | The Price to each Subscriber, one Guinea; one half on subscribing, and the | remainder on Delivery of the Book, which will be early in the ensuing Year, | 1777. After the Subscription is closed, the Price will be one Pound five Shillings. | Subscriptions taken in at Mr. Dodsley's, in Pall-Mall; | Mr. Boydell's, near King Street, Cheapside; and at the Author's House | as above-mentioned; at all which places Specimens may be seen. | *Aug. 1.* 1776 | Received of *John Grimston Esq*. Half *a* Guinea for *one* | Copy of the above-mentioned Work, which will be delivered, when completed, on | Payment of the remainder of the Subscription. | *Alex*ʳ *Cozens'*.

The volume appeared with the text in English and French.

The English title-page was dated 1778 and the French one 1777. Dr. William Hunter's copy (Glasgow University) has seventeen plates, which with one exception are all inscribed: 'Publish'd 10. April 1777 by Alexʳ Cozens, Leicester Street, Leicester Fields, London. F. Bartolozzi sculp.' Plate No. 13 bears the same inscription but for the date '10 March 1777'.

[3] George F. Benson Collection.

[4] One such drawing, inscribed on the back 'A Blot Dᵒ—' is in the possession of I. A. Williams (see his *Early English Water-Colours*, London, 1952, p. 235); another in the Courtauld Institute of Art (Witt Collection 4380) is inscribed on verso 'A blot by Gilpin | Master of Cheam School'.

[5] At the period when he was gathering information on trees for his *Remarks on Forest Scenery*, Edward Forster drew his attention to the book. Gilpin replied: 'I have seen the trees by Cozens, which you mention. The pollard-oak—the cypress—the Willow, the cedar and a few others are characteristic: the rest I thought less so.' 30 Dec. 1779 (Rev. E. G. Benson-Brisco transcript).

[6] See p. 51, n. 1.

[7] To mention but a few of the subscribers, whom Gilpin knew well at the time or with whom he was to be closely associated: Sir George Beaumont, Mrs. Delany, William Fraser, John Grimston, Mary Hartley, William Lock, William Mason, William Mitford, The Duchess Dowager of Portland, Leonard Smelt, Richard Stonehewer, and the Earl of Warwick.

of artistic ones, gave Cozens one of the best definitions of the blot, in the guise of a comparison between art and poetry—a definition which he incorporated in his last work, *A New Method of assisting the Invention in Drawing Original Compositions of Landscapes*.[1] Brown's relations with Cozens may have extended beyond purely artistic matters. When, shortly before his suicide in 1766, he was invited to St. Petersburg by the Empress Catherine, to assist with educational reforms, it would have been natural for him to consult Cozens, who had family connexions there in the English colony.[2]

Leonard Smelt, after his peregrinations as a military engineer, was appointed in 1771 sub-governor to the Prince of Wales and the Duke of York. Lastly, the young John Warwick Smith, then apprenticed to Sawrey Gilpin, visited Eton on 13 January 1773 and reacted before Cozens's more finished work much as William Gilpin would have done: 'The finished drawings of Cozens much inferior to his sketches. His designs generally want simplicity, & his method very different from what one would expect from the masterly manner of his sketches.'[3]

---

[1] Reproduced in *Oppé*, p. 170.

[2] John Brown is a figure who might well deserve a special study. As the author of essays on Shaftesbury, and of a description of the Vale of Keswick, he played a not inconsiderable role in forming British taste. Were we able to study his drawings, they would no doubt reflect the same enthusiasm for nature to be found in his writings. Unfortunately we have so far been unable to find a single drawing of his. Some will no doubt turn up, for he drew for much of his life. The *Memoirs* (p. 76 n.) just say he 'was skilled in painting, especially in portraiture, and his likeness, painted by himself but much faded, is still preserved in the Vicarage of Wigton'. Shortly after his death we find two references to the fate of his drawings. Thomas Grimston, writing from Cheam School, tells his father on 31 July 1767: 'I have not spoke to Mr. Gilpin about the drawing of Dr. Brown's of Rose Castle but I design to do it soon.' And again on 23 Aug. 1767: 'O dear I have forgot to speak to Mr. Gilpin about Rose Castle and the rest of Dr. Brown's Pictures, but I will do it soon' (Lady Waechter de Grimston).

[3] On a sheet from a notebook. A. L. Fawcett Collection.

V. Years of Travel, 1768–1776

HAVING learnt a great deal from his smaller excursions, Gilpin embarked on more ambitious and systematic projects. During his longer journeys to the north he had hitherto been content mainly to make sketches of what interested him, appending to them little remarks in the nature of precisions. Conversely, when he projected the *Thames Tour*, he confined himself to writing up the journey, leaving the illustrations to his more gifted brother. However, from 1768 onwards he resolved to combine both these activities—to describe the country through which he travelled and to illustrate his particular view-point with his own sketches. The result was to inaugurate a new kind of travel literature: the picturesque tour, in which writing and illustrations complement one another to sing the praises of nature. Gilpin's drawings were illustrations, not in a topographical sense, but in an aesthetic one; his drawings were generalized ideas of specific views, illustrating the quest after picturesque beauty. On the day he sailed down the Thames in 1764, the scenery had proved rather unrewarding, with the result that his account was somewhat thin in content. Now, as he travelled among landscape much more congenial to his taste, his writing filled out and acquired greater density.

With the possible exception of the year 1771, he set out from Cheam nearly always in the summer, for periods which varied from a week to a month. His main travels consisted of a trip round Kent in 1768, a journey into Essex, Suffolk, and Norfolk in 1769, for the particular purpose of examining Lord Orford's pictures at Houghton, journeys down the River Wye and through parts of South Wales in 1770, into Cumberland and Westmorland to see the Lakes in 1772, into North Wales in 1773, along the south coast of England in 1774, into the west of England in 1775, and into the Highlands of Scotland in 1776.

On his travels he recorded his impressions in little notebooks, many of which have survived. For the biographer, interested in Gilpin's original reactions, these notebooks in which he jotted his 'rough thoughts' together with early drafts of the *Tours* provide invaluable material. They contain many 'off the record' impressions which years later were carefully excised or attenuated before publication. We hear of his personal adventures as he travelled on horseback, of the inns he stayed at, coupled with the hazards of a night's lodging. At Charing, for example, the house was so old and oddly constructed that he found his horses stabled just behind the bed. 'By what mode of architecture they came there,

I forgot to examine in the morning; but I heard them, all night, grinding their hay.' In Canterbury he was almost in financial difficulties: 'I wanted to remit my purse. But my credit was so poor there, I mean the character of an honest man was so illwritten on my face, that none of the tradesmen . . . would give me money for my draughts; and I know not what I should have done, if I had not met, in the street, an officer of Conway's dragoons, who knew me, and lent me five guineas.' On another occasion he gatecrashed into the Chatham dockyard, and had walked some distance before he realized the irregularity of his situation. Rather than seek the proper authorization, which meant returning all the way to the porter at the gate, he obtained an escort from the captain of the guard.

When the corporal returned me to the gate, I gave him a shilling to drink his captain's health; which the porter seeing, muttered insolently as he opened the door, that if ever I came there again without complying with the rules of the yard, I should be stopped at the gate. He lost a shilling by it. I heard afterwards, that a jealousy subsists between this great civil magistrate, & the military, who have but lately been introduced into this yard.[1]

In the early drafts we also meet the picturesque writer, the frank and at times caustic critic of other people's 'improvements'. Witness his uncomplimentary remarks about General Henry Seymour Conway's landscape gardening near Henley:

The disposition of the grounds, which contain about 150 acres, is a lawn surrounded by a wood, & that wood again by another lawn. The first lawn, which is the principal one, is a pleasant chearful area, tho there is no play in the ground: but the woody out-line is good. The beech-grove too is pleasant. From this thicket with a profusion of chalk-ruins at one end; & a bridge at the other. The chalk-ruins are disagreeable enough, bearing the marks neither of design, nor of composition. They resemble the ruins of nothing: & the very idea of bringing such a glare of chalk above ground, in a country, which is discovering it in every crevice, is disgusting.

From these ruins we descended along the valley, which, without break or variation, is a mere blanket held at the 4 corners. The farther end of it is graced by a bridge running *parallel* with the Thames, which flows a few yards from it. It was necessary, it seems, to carry a road across this part of the garden: but a bridge, so near a great river, with which it has no connection, is the last species of architecture one would have chosen. Through the arch of the bridge we were carried to see a piece of *rock-scenery*, consisting of half a dozen large stones brought together. Nothing can be more absurd. They neither give any idea of what they were intended to represent; nor are they suited to the country, in which they are introduced. They are heterogenious ornaments. In our attempts to improve, if we do more than just adorn what nature has done, by planting & giving a little play to the ground, we err. To turn a level country into a mountainous one, or a smooth scene into a rocky one, is absurd. . . .

Water indeed, even in a grand style, may be introduced with propriety; because water is an element, which we may command: but to attempt a mountain, or a valley, or a rock, or any of the

---

[1] W. L. Benson Collection. The notebooks record his movements fairly closely. The night of 31 May was spent at Dartford, that of 1 June at Feversham. On 2 June he went through Canterbury and stayed the night at Dover. On 3 June he reached Margate, on 4 June Charing. On 5 June he moved on to Leeds Castle. The length of his journey is confirmed by a letter, written from Dover on 'thursday night June 1., 1768' (1 June was a Wednesday) in which Gilpin told his wife he expected to be home on Monday or Tuesday (6 or 7 June) (Major J. R. Abbey).

immensities of nature, is ludicrous. And yet this piece of rock-scenery was probably the most expensive part of the garden; as the carriage of these stones from countries, where they are produced (for they are not natives) must have been considerable.

From the rocks we were carryed into a walk, which runs shelving along the side of the hill; above the Thames. This walk is rather fatiguing through a want of variety.

But even if the greatest taste had been shewn in ornamenting these gardens, nothing very beautiful could have been effected. The soil is forbidding, the verdure is soon burnt; the plants poor and stunted; & a *chalkiness* (which in painting is the most disgusting of all *hues*, except *sootiness*) prevails over the whole.

Nor is this poverty much compensated by the views into the country. Tho the offskip is adorned with a noble river, & great plenty of wood, yet the objects are broken into too many parts to be very beautiful. . . .

It may be added, (as Mr. Conway seems to have a particular affection for the cypress) that this tree, when stuck about, is formal, & offensive: that its chief beauty arises from contrast; & that it's effect is seldom fine, except when it is connected with a building, or seen towering behind the shrubs of a plantation. *Here* it is commonly introduced single.[1]

Needless to say such strictures were never printed, and Gilpin, finding he could say little that was complimentary, made no reference to Conway or his residence when he finally published the *Tour of the Lakes*. Yet it is likely that General Conway heard of these criticisms, as the account is found in the final manuscript version which received such a wide reading in court circles.

If there are considerable differences between the manuscripts of the *Tours* and the texts as printed, the disparity is even more pronounced when the rough sketches are compared with either the finished drawings or the aquatint illustrations. For the sake of clarity we shall first examine the rough sketches and then the finished drawings. The rough sketches are easily dated and can be presented as a running sequence; not so with the more worked-up drawings, which were done in the manuscript volumes of the *Tours* or inserted into them at very different times, sometimes many years after the journey had been completed. Therefore to avoid confusion we shall consider them separately. Even if we were to attempt to trace every step from primary sketch to finished drawing in the case of every *Tour*, the result would not be sufficiently rewarding. What is more, the rough sketches that have come down to us are so different in spirit from the finished ones and indeed from anything else that Gilpin did that they are worthy of being examined on their own. Quite unknown to the public, as nearly all of them still are in the hands of his descendants, they display a great freedom of treatment, which gives them a freshness and lightness of texture that quite disappear when Gilpin rehandles the subject for insertion into the manuscript volumes of his *Tours*.

---

[1] MS. of the *Tour of the Lakes*, i, 3–10 (Charles Traylen). See also pp. 35–37 for strictures on the Priory at Warwick, then owned by Mr. Wise.

(a) THE ROUGH SKETCHES, 1768–1776

> A few scratches, like a short-hand scrawl of our own, legible at least to ourselves, will serve to raise in our minds the remembrance of the beauties they humbly represent; and recal to our memory even the splendid colouring, and force of light, which existed in the real scene. *Three Essays* (1792), p. 51.

The first systematic journey undertaken seems to have been that into Kent. On 31 May 1768 he set out for a tour round that county and was back home eight days later. Our information comes from three small notebooks, the first of which is entitled 'To | Dover &c | 1768 | I'.[1] In the *Southern Tour*, which was not published till 1804, Gilpin used the the material he had gathered on this expedition and amalgamated it with the south coast tour of Hampshire, Sussex and Kent of 1774. That the journey of 1768 should have escaped previous biographers is not surprising as the *Southern Tour* makes no mention of it and only bears the title of *Observations on the Coasts of Hampshire, Sussex and Kent, . . . made in the summer of the year 1774.*

The notebooks contain some fourteen pen and grey wash drawings, which are much in keeping with what we have already seen of his manner in 1767 and 1768. He disposes his light and shade to effect strong contrasts and the pen moves with increasing freedom. Particularly in the second notebook, 'To Dover &c. | 2', the whole area of the sketch is generally covered over with a light wash except for the flat surfaces in the focal area which are left white, as, for example, the cliffs of Boulogne. In these two-plane compositions the dark foreground is drawn in with real gusto using twisted shrubs, logs, fences, or a framing tree. Gilpin also showed that year a predilection for stilted arches and round towers. The most pleasing sketch of that tour is one that combines the castle with the cathedral at Rochester.[2]

Three other drawings with their accompanying notes must, from their treatment, have been done that same summer.[1] Their titles suggest that Gilpin made another small excursion in 1768, this time to Stonehenge *via* Basingstoke, thus familiarizing himself with some of the ground he was to cover in his *Western Tour* (1775)—the material was incorporated at the beginning and end of the account of that tour. One of the drawings, entitled 'The ruins of Basing-house', is the earliest we have come across to be covered with an overall yellow wash, a device we commonly associate with the finished sketches of the 1770's.

Several imaginary compositions were also done that year, and they are probably the last drawings that he dated. Generally, Gilpin adopted a three-plane technique: foreground, middle-distance, and background; but in one group of drawings he explored the possibilities of using only two very sharply contrasted planes: an area of rock and foliage forming an L-shaped *foreground*, darkened and defined by grey blotches and brown penwork,

---

[1] W. L. Benson Collection.
[2] W. L. Benson Collection. Reproduced in *Kenwood Exhibition Catalogue*, item 32.

and a *background* in light grey consisting usually of a sheet of water and beyond it a screen of cliffs or mountains closing the composition. Mr. A. de Gylpyn Benson possesses such a composition, dated '1768'; it portrays one of Gilpin's favourite subjects—the conclusion of a lake set amidst mountainous scenery. Another is of a waterfall encased by vertical banks.[1] Here Gilpin has not succeeded in overcoming some of the obvious disadvantages of the two-plane composition, and we are left with the impression of flatness and lack of depth we associate with a stage set. Despite the perspective recession is not achieved. At the same time, through the absence of a focal point, the eye returns to the foreground and fixes on its accidented surface, which, due to the light background, takes on the qualities of a silhouette. Also, by placing a sudden drop and an expanse of water immediately behind this foreground, he gives the feeling that quite a void separates the two planes, that quite an area of ground or water lies hidden from view.

In another group of sketches he treats very freely landscapes with a ruin as the central subject. Several have an affinity with the work of Richard Wilson.

At present all we know of the drawings he did in the spring of 1769, when he journeyed into the eastern counties, are the few aquatint illustrations made from them, when the *Eastern Tour* was published posthumously in 1809. However, the chief interest in the two journeys of 1768 and 1769 lies not so much in the description of scenery as in his remarks concerning collections he visited. At this juncture perhaps I may be allowed a digression to consider his attitude to paintings before returning to the rough sketches.

───────

In these early *Tours*, he reveals himself a competent critic of paintings, though his standards of judgement remain those expressed in the *Essay on Prints*. He extends his knowledge of artists of all schools, and when he comes across paintings by an artist whom he chiefly knows from prints, he compares print with painting. Thus Claude, who in his judgement often fails in composition, is ill served by prints: 'I have thought few masters are less indebted to the engraver, than he is. The print gives us the *composition* chiefly of the master, which is what we least value in Claude. But it can give us no idea of that lovely colouring, in which alone his works excell all others.' He finds the same quality in another Claude, a seaport at Houghton: 'If the most vivid effusions of light, and the most harmonious touches of nature can make a good landscape, this undoubtedly is one.'[2]

Sometimes the painting fails to answer his expectations. In the *Essay on Prints* he had praised Bolswert's landscapes after Rubens, and singled out the print called 'The Waggon' as deserving admiration (p. 148). But when confronted with the painting of 'The Waggon' at Houghton, the colouring disappointed him: 'There is little of the hue of nature in this landscape; and as little of the effect of harmony. The hills are green, the sky is blue; and

---

[1] W. L. Benson Collection. [2] *Eastern Tour*, p. 65. (For full title see p. 83, n. 3.)

the rest of the objects of a brownish tint. In all this there is discord. It is called a moonlight: but there is nothing of the shadowy dusk of evening in it; nor of the lunar splendor.—In the *composition*, there is much nature; but it is rather too unadorned.'[1]

As he examined Sir George Young's pictures at Foot's-Cray, or those at Raynham and Houghton, he looked for freedom and spirited execution, and rejected formalism which 'disgusts', and anything that appeared strained and unnatural. Each picture that attracted his attention was carefully examined in detail and then considered as a whole from the points of view of composition, expression, light and shade, and harmonious colouring. As might be expected Rubens, Rembrandt, and Salvator Rosa are approved of, while others like Carlo Maratta do not fare so well under his critical eye.

His enthusiasm for Salvator, already plain in the *Essay on Prints*, continued to grow as his knowledge of his paintings increased. His attitude, however, remained critical. Of the two Salvators he saw at Foot's-Cray in 1768, the 'Diogenes' illicited little praise, whereas of the other he wrote:

Democritus by Salvator is a large and capital picture . . . [6. *a*]. Salvator, in his etching from this picture, inscribed it thus, *Democritus, omnium derisor, in finem omnium defigitur*.[2] Notwithstanding the merriment he had always indulged about human affairs, the painter supposes him at last brought to serious contemplation. The moral is good, and the tale well told. The variety of objects about him which are subject to the decay of time; the contemplative figure of the philosopher; the dark and gloomy tint which prevails over the picture, in short the whole solemnity of the scene, and every part of it, contribute to strike that awe, which the painter intended. The only part of the picture which does not join in harmony with the rest, is the ramification of the trees, which are too much in vigour to agree with the other decayed parts of nature. A ruin perhaps might have had a better effect, and would have joined more solemnly in the composition, than the trees of any kind. The scathed trunk of an oak might perhaps have been added.[3]

The next year he called at Raynham, particularly to see the 'Belisarius', owned by Lord Townshend, and found it 'a very noble picture of which the print gives but an inadequate idea' [6. *d*].

The unfortunate chief stands resting against a wall. He occupies almost the whole piece; leaving room only for two or three soldiers, who make a distant group. The story, tho told in this simple manner, can hardly be mistaken. A blind figure, squalid, tho dressed in rich armour—discovering great dignity of character, both in his own appearance, and from the distant respect shewn him by the spectators—leads the memory easily to recollect Bellisarius.—The *composition* is as pleasing as the *design*. All the objects of the piece are so contrived, as to form a good *whole*.—*The harmony of the colouring* too is excellent. An agreeable sober tint runs through the picture. Scarce a touch is out of tune. If any, it is a streak of light in the sky, on the left. Bellisarius's drapery is rich in the highest degree; and yet harmonious. His mantle is yellow: his sash of a white, silvery hue; and his armour, steel.—The light also is well disposed. In *expression* there is the most deficiency. Salvator

---

[1] *Eastern Tour*, pp. 61–62. The picture now in the Hermitage is usually called 'Landscape with carrier's cart on stony ground' or 'la Charette embourbée'.

[2] The etching actually bears this inscription: 'Democritus omnium derisor in omnium fine defigitur.'

[3] *Southern Tour*, pp. 122–3. (For full title see p. 83, n. 2.)

has thrown over the hero's face a quantity of squalid hair; and the spectator must, in a great measure, make out the expression from his own imagination. I speak only of the face, which wants something of the *dignity* of wretchedness; in the *action* and *character*, greatness, and misery are well united.[1]

And in a comparison with what was then considered to be Van Dyck's well-known painting on the same subject, in Lord Burlington's gallery at Chiswick [6. *b*], Gilpin gave the palm to Salvator:

With regard to *design*, Vandyck's accompanying figures engage the eye too much; and confound the story. It is better imagined also to represent the old chief, as Salvator has done, in his military habit; than dressed in a civil garment. The story so told is better told; and the mind is more interested. In point of *composition* also we give the preference to Salvator. Vandyck's detached figures are no groups. Nor is there that *harmony of colouring*, and agreeable mass of light in his picture, which strikes us in the other. *Expression* is the only part, in which Vandyck enters into contest with Salvator. There is a union of great *dignity*, and *wretchedness* in every part of his principal figure; and the expression of the soldier is inimitable. He is certainly however too interesting for a secondary figure; at the same time his expression is an index to the spectator and refers him to Bellisarius, as the object of concern. After all, perhaps there may be as much *expression* in the wonder mixed with pity, and the respectful distance of Salvator's soldiers, as in the melancholy dejection of Vandyck's. Such a mode of expression certainly gives an air of grandeur to the fallen chief, which Vandyck has lost by mixing him with low characters.[2]

He liked the freedom and spirit Rubens showed both in his oil sketches and in his larger canvasses. And although he sometimes found the figures awkward, when a particular canvas was not entirely to his taste, as the 'Venus and Adonis' at Foot's-Cray, he qualified his criticism with the statement: 'Among the innumerable pictures by Rubens we do not often find a bad one.'[3] The 'Mary de Medicis' at Raynham he thought an 'admirable portrait'.[4] At Houghton, he noticed a 'Bacchanalian . . . painted in his best style of colouring. The *composition, light*, and *expression*, are all admirable. With regard to *particulars*, the woman, and the sucking satyrines are particularly beautiful.'[5] He reserved his encomiums for the large picture of 'Mary Magdalen washing the feet of Christ' [6. *c*]:

This picture is one of the noblest monuments of the genius of Reubens, that is to be seen in England. It contains fourteen figures, as large as life. We seldom see, in one piece, so numerous a collection of expressive heads.—The point of time seems to be taken, just after Christ had said, *Thy sins be forgiven thee*. An air of disgust runs through the whole table. The expression in Simon's face is admirable. With whatever view he invited his divine guest, it is very evident he was disappointed. The whole picture indeed is an excellent comment upon St. Luke. Our Saviour's face has great sweetness, grace, and dignity. All the other characters are fine; the two full faces, especially, which are nearest our Saviour. The attendants are all good figures; particularly the girl carrying the dish. The Magdalen is the worst figure in the picture. She is rather awkward and clumsy: but her passion is well expressed. A penitential sorrow, beyond the sense of anything but it's own unworthyness, has taken possession of her. Her eyes are finely coloured with high-swoln grief.

[1] *Eastern Tour*, pp. 34-35.
[2] Ibid., pp. 35-37.
[3] *Southern Tour*, p. 121.
[4] *Eastern Tour*, p. 37.
[5] Ibid., pp. 44-45.

Among deceptions, we seldom see a better, than the watery hue of that tear which is nearest the eye. Our Saviour's hands are bad.

We are *inclined* to dwell more on the *parts* of this picture than on the *whole*. And yet the *composition*, tho not perfect, is far from being disagreeable. It's chief want, as a *whole*, is a balance of *shade*. Reubens is often, I think, faulty in this particular.[1]

Lastly Rembrandt. His smaller pictures attracted him for their disposition of light and shade and for their sense of colouring. In 'Abraham and Hagar' at Foot's-Cray, 'the light is wonderfully fine; and the clearness of the colouring pleasing. It is by chance only that Rembrandt conceives so elegant a form, as he has given to Hagar. She is mounted on an ass, and just taking her departure.'[2] In the 'Presentation of Christ in the temple . . . the composition is good; and there is an artificial effect of light. We are at a loss indeed to know from whence it comes; but I am never much distressed with that circumstance, if the light is good.'[3] In Rembrandt's portrait of his wife, at Houghton, 'are united all the beauties of the master; his strong colouring—his management of light, and the spirit of his touches.'[4] And of the 'Sacrifice of Isaac' [7. *a*], in the same collection, he wrote:

We seldom see a picture of this master in so good a style. We have here something like Italian elegance. Abraham's head is finely painted; and full of every expression, which the subject could inspire. Isaac's body is a fine piece of anatomy, and colouring. The angel is a bad figure, and injures the whole. The falling knife is an unpleasant circumstance so near the eye. *Bodies in motion* should never be brought close to the sight.—There is a peculiar delicacy in Abraham's covering his son's face with his hand—a delicacy which one should least have looked for in this master.[5]

———

On his return to Cheam, Gilpin conveyed the first vivid impressions of the *Eastern Tour* to his friend, Thomas Whately. Whately's reply, dated 26 May 1769, is of the utmost interest. It contains an early testimony of Gilpin's capacity for vivid description. Long before the *Tours* were published in the 1780's, privileged friends like Whately, William Mitford, and Richard Glover the poet, appreciated the evocative qualities of his descriptive prose. Furthermore, Whately shared many of Gilpin's interests, was stimulated by his remarks, but refused to be bowled over by his enthusiasm for Salvator Rosa:

I was thinking of writing to you to ask how you liked your Norfolk Tour, when I was favoured with your Account of it: I am much obliged to you for the Letter: I could not expect a Description of Houghton: you shall tell me what struck you there when I see you, for I can understand your Descriptions; most people are so general in their Expressions, that they give me no particular Ideas: the slight Sketch you have now favoured me with of Places I do not know is yet an Introduction to some Acquaintance with them. Of those which I do know, I think you hardly do justice to King's College Chapel: side Isles would give it space, & be an Improvement; but did you ever see one Isle so perfect? so light without being broken into parts? so rich, without depending on its

---

[1] *Eastern Tour*, pp. 46–47.
[2] *Southern Tour*, pp. 118–19.
[3] Ibid., p. 121.
[4] Ibid., p. 62.
[5] *Eastern Tour*, p. 45.

Ornaments for its Beauty? so vast, so stupendous, yet not bulky? so fit to depress & humilitate a superstitious Mind with Wonder & Awe? . . .[1] I know no more of the picture at Raynham than the Print informs me: but I can easily conceive it to be superior to those at Foots-Cray, which you know I do not value much higher than the Etchings of them: Two of the same at Sr R. Lytteltons in London I put at the same rate, & yet they too are call'd Original Salvators. As to the Comparison between his & Vandyke's Belisarius, you tell me you have much to say upon it, & when I have heard what you have to say: I may probably be a Convert: as yet I keep to my own Faith, & I give you notice before hand, that I will not enter into the Merits of *technical* Composition, of Light and Shade, & pyramidal forms, in all which I know the Picture of Vandyke is defective: but in Character, in Expression, & in what I call poetical or historical Composition, I do think it admirable. I am happy your idea of Carlo Moratt is so exactly the same as mine; he has an Elegance but an Effeminacy in his Taste: or else there is a Barbarity in mine; for he seems to me to have no Energy, no Enthusiasm, & he therefore raises no Raptures.[2]

Throughout his life Gilpin remained interested in art and nature, explaining one in terms of the other by means of a set of criteria evolved in the 1740's. However, it is broadly true to say that his interests gradually shifted from art to nature, from prints to paintings and other works of art, and finally from these to natural scenery in all its infinite variety. In 1768 and 1769 his interests were equally divided between collections of paintings and the country through which he travelled, and it was only in the following year that the critic of landscape took command. Having drawn attention to Gilpin, critic of paintings, a side of his activity that has so far received but scant attention, we return to the sketches.

At the beginning of June 1770 he embarked on his first truly picturesque tour, sailing down the Wye from Ross to Chepstow, and then exploring several of the valleys of South Wales, returning home *via* Bristol, which he reached on 10 June. On this occasion he deliberately sought 'to criticize the face of a country correctly', and many of the sketches have a didactic intention. Sailing down the Wye proved a very different experience from the tame journey down the Thames: the ruined castles and mountains of Wales were indeed exciting after the flat countryside of eastern and south-eastern England. The north countryman was again in his element—here was landscape that called for description, that matched his conceptions of beauty and grandeur. William Mitford was one to whom he confided his excitement, as soon as he got home:

[1] Gilpin took notice of Whately's remarks, yet retained an unfavourable opinion of the Chapel: 'King's college chappel gives us on the *outside*, a very beautiful form: *within*, tho it is an immense, and noble aisle, presenting the adjunct idea of lightness; and solemnity; yet its disproportion disgusts. Such height, and such length, united by such straitened parallels, hurt the eye. You feel immured. Henry the Sixth, we are told, spent twelve hundred pounds in adorning the roof. It is a pity he had not spent it in widening the walls. We should then have had a better form, and should have been relieved from the tedious repetition of roses and portcullisses; which are at best but heavy, and unpleasing ornaments.' *Eastern Tour*, p. 11.

[2] W. L. Benson Collection. Of the paintings at Houghton by Carlo Maratta and his school, Gilpin said in the *Eastern Tour*: 'I can see in them many fine heads, great sweetness in the Madonnas, broad folds of drapery, elegant attitudes, and pleasing expression: but still they are unpleasant pictures. There seems to be a deficiency both in the *colouring*, and in the *execution*.' As to their execution, he explained: 'There is so much effeminate softness, and want of spirit in it, that you do not think you are surveying the work of a great master; but rather of some pupil, copying with fear, and exactness. It is not necessary for a painter to execute with the fire of Bourgognone, but without some degree of freedom, and spirit, his *execution* will never please' (pp. 48–49).

If you have never navigated the Wye, you have seen nothing. Besides three or four capital views upon it, the whole is such a display of picturesque scenery, that it is beyond any commendation. Not that I prefer it to the grand beauties of the North. I should ill-deserve to be a native of that noble country, if I did: but thus far I must acknowledge that the beauties are more ornamented, and more finished; and more correct. Indeed very little more is necessary than to transfer them upon canvas, and they are pictures. In the wild beauties of the North, there is more room for the imagination, and judgment to work: Here nature herself composes. . . . The materials I present to your imagination, and if it combine them in the most beautiful manner, it cannot go beyond the original. —But I saw scenery still beyond all this.—From the bottom of Battus-mountain, in Carmarthenshire, to Neath, and from Neath to Margam every thing is—in short beyond description! When I returned into England and looked into two or three pieces of ground [it] made my gorge rise at the pimping ideas of men![1]

The early draft of the *Wye Tour* contains fifty-six touched-up sketches. This is the manuscript which Thomas Gray saw and praised shortly before his death in July 1771.[2] The drawings themselves conform exactly to the directions for a rough sketch which Gilpin sent to William Mason in April 1772:

The first touches need only be extremely slight. It is a great error, I think, to do too much. In the transient view of a country, all that appears needful, or rather, all that can be done is to mark the *shapes*, & *nature* of objects; & their *relative distances*. By the *nature* of an object, I mean only the rock, or wood, or broken ground, of which it consists. The *shapes* & *nature* of an object are easily marked; the distance is more difficult. As a wash (which marks a distance the best) is incommodious both to carry, & to manage, we are obliged to substitute lines. Few views, at least few good views, consist of more than a foreground, & 2 distances; all which should be carried off with great distinctness, or the spirit of the view will be infallibly lost. I have practiced 2 ways to prevent a confusion of distance. The foreground may be marked with a pen; & the 2 distances with black-lead; only the nearer distance may be touched with more strength. Or, the foreground may be marked with red-chalk; the nearer distance with a mixture of red-chalk, & black lead; & the 2d with pure blacklead. In washing your sketch afterwards, the warmth of the red is not injurious to the foreground; & the coldness of the blacklead is the proper hue for distances. A sketch, I think, should be retouched, & washed, as soon as possible, after it is taken; while the air of the view remains upon the memory. In retouching, I have found pale ink to have a good effect in the distance: & in washing, burnt umbre mixed with black on the foreground; & a slight tinge from the black alone in the sky & distance. I think you told me, that Cozens had left off the use of his own black. I wonder at it; for I find two great advantages in it, beyond Indian ink—it is stronger—& with a bit of moist spunge may be erased.

I have sometimes tryed another method of washing a sketch, which has a grand effect: the foreground with some brown tinge, smartly touched here & there in the lights with some warm lively colour—the distances with grey, tinged, in the slightest manner with purple or blue—the

---

[1] 3 July 1770 (Rev. E. G. Benson—Brisco transcript). For fuller quotation see C. P. Barbier, *Samuel Rogers and William Gilpin*, London, 1959, p. 6.

[2] 'Observations upon the River *Wye*, and some parts of *S. Wales*, relative chiefly to picturesque beauty; made in the year 1770.' Volume bound in rough brown calf ($8 \times 4\frac{15}{16}$ in.), labelled 'S. Wales' on the spine, bears inscription (heavily cancelled): 'This little tome which is the first work of the kind the author was engaged in: fell accidentally into the hands of the late Mr Gray, [two or three words illegible] month before he dyed.' Text written out by John Warwick Smith, with later corrections and additions by W. G. Belonged to Margaret Farish (1762–1842), sister(?) of W. G.'s wife. A. L. Fawcett Collection.

sky with the same tinge. But a sketch washed in this manner must be done upon white paper.[1]

The *Wye Tour* sketches are washed and tinted in this last manner. Some deal with the compositional possibilities of river scenery, such as the various combinations of side and front screens, whether they be high or low, simple or complex; others represent ruined castles and abbeys or simply the stratified rocks which fascinated him so much at this period. The penwork is neat and restrained, whereas the washes are freely brushed in or dabbed in—the result is that these simple sketches are very lively [7. *b* and 9. *c*]. Of particular interest is a group built up entirely by means of an impressionistic technique of superimposed and juxtaposed washes [7. *e*].

We know of no journey undertaken in 1771. The following year he set out in June on his tour to the lakes of Cumberland and Westmorland. Back home he told Mason:

I have brought back with me a variety of remarks & sketches, which lye at present in great disorder. If I ever should have leisure to methodize & transcribe them (for most of them are written in short hand) they shall, at any time, do their best to amuse you. I have a great curiosity to see Mr. Grey's account of the north; which I suppose you will print: if not, I hope you will contrive some way to let me see it. He did not, I find, penetrate into some of the wildest parts of that rough scenery. I heard of him through Dr. Brownrigg,[2] an ingenious, & hospitable physician in those parts; whom Mr. G., I believe, visited. I spent 5 days among the lakes & mountains; & could with equal pleasure have spent 50.[3]

As was to be expected, he did full justice to this region, so familiar to him and so close to his conception of picturesque beauty. The result was a lavishly illustrated manuscript of the most ambitious *Tour* he ever composed. The rough sketches[4] in the original notebooks are among his least interesting. Done on the spot with great speed, these graphic notes were used each evening to make more intelligible sketches before the day's impressions were lost. The penwork goes into wide loops and the grey and brown washes are dashed in. A characteristic device, which will stay with him, is the series of blotches and dabs to convey foliage.

In addition to his annual tours, Gilpin continued to make local excursions. Six weeks after his return from the Lakes, he visited Pain's Hill and filled a small notebook entitled 'Mr. Hamilton's gardens at Painshill near Cobham Aug. 14. 1772'.[5] It contains a sketchy

[1] 25 Apr. 1772 (W. L. Benson). On 17 May 1772 Mason acknowledged receipt of the sketches and directions, and said: 'I am convinced that in my attempts of this kind the aim at doing too much, has constantly misled me, & consequently made me do much Less, with all my pains, than you are able to do with a single stroke. But as your Directions are full & plain & accompanied too with such examples, I do not dispair of profiting by them & shall make an experiment the first Leisure moment I have.' Gilpin had evidently misunderstood him on the subject of Cozens's use of black ink, for he added a postscript to his letter: 'I did not tell you that Cozens had left off his ink, it was, I believe, the brown. for he now finishes all his paper drawings with Ink only & that of his own Composition' (Rev. E. G. Benson).

[2] William Brownrigg (1712–1800), M.D., F.R.S., a pioneer of modern chemistry. When he lived in Whitehaven, he was a member of the Carlisle circle. He retired early to Ormathwaite, near Keswick, where he continued his scientific experiments.

[3] 18 July 1772 (W. L. Benson).

[4] One small notebook filled with sketches is in the possession of W. L. Benson.   [5] G. F. Benson Collection.

description of his walk round the gardens which, according to Mitford, Charles Hamilton had planned 'from the pictures of Poussin and the Italian Masters',[1] together with nine rough sketches and a plan of the grounds and artificial ruins. He noted the abbey, the hermitage, the Roman arch, the temple of Bacchus, and of the grotto he said: 'of Gloucestershire stone—a whimsical effect—the terrace bad—& the stone too much detachd, & in unatural shapes'.

On 24 May 1773 he set out from Manchester for a tour of North Wales, and was back at Cheam on 19 June. Some five small notebooks contain ninety-one rough sketches, mostly executed in grey wash over slight pencil outlines.[2] Their distinguishing features are: the loose technique, the amount of drawing done entirely with the brush, and the textural effect reminiscent of the blots of Alexander Cozens.

Possibly the same year he completed a set of twelve sketches of a trip on the lakes of Killarney.[3] As Gilpin never went to Ireland, though he had an opportunity to go there in May 1775, the sketches were probably copied from someone else's drawings.[4]

In June 1774 he undertook a south coast tour of Hampshire, Sussex, and Kent. This time he seems only to have taken very brief notes, and the sketches also are quite rudimentary. Three notebooks survive; they contain twenty-seven rough sketches mostly indicated by penwork over a slight pencil outline.[3] Their interest lies in the minimum technique employed for jotting down the essential features of a subject. His pen conveys buildings by means of dots, strokes, and squiggles—the following year he was to render buildings in the same way, but this time with the brush. As to the foreground, where he bothers to indicate it, the effect is very rough indeed.

The next tour proved a more ambitious undertaking. From 31 May to 23 June 1775 he explored the western parts of England, and again favoured Mason with a lengthy uninhibited account of his journey. In general he was more impressed by the buildings and ruins than by the face of the countryside. The ruins of Glastonbury Abbey were 'divine'.

Our guide lamented much, that a parallel wall had been pulled down in the year 1714, to build a Presbyterian meeting-house. But the honest man's zeal misled him. The wicked Presbyterians, whatever they intended, have in reality done good; & I think it may be esteemed among the

[1] E. W. Manwaring, *Italian Landscape in Eighteenth Century England*, p. 155.

[2] The first three are in the possession of W. L. Benson, the other two in that of Rev. E. G. Benson.

[3] W. L. Benson Collection.

[4] 'I am at this time however under a great temptation. I have long wished to see the lake of Killarney. I have dreamt of it, & seen it a thousand times in visionary exhibition. And at this time a most desirable opportunity falls out of seeing it. Mr. Herbert, the proprietor of the best part of it, a gentleman with whom I have had long connection & acquaintance, is now going over, just as our vacation begins. His son, an ingenious young fellow, once a pupil of mine, & now a fellow-commoner of St. John's, in Cambridge; who knows every nook of it, has promised, that I shall ride admiral of all those waters, & he will be my pilot. Can any thing be more tempting? But here is a little woman, whom I dare not take with me; & who dare not let me go without her. Can you say anything to persuade her, (I am sure *I* cannot,) that between Holyhead, & Dublin, there is a less space of water than between England & the East Indies.' W. G. to William Mason, 6 May 1775 (W. L. Benson). While the dream of Killarney was to remain unfulfilled, Gilpin continued to receive news of its splendour. See, for example, A. Yorke to W. G., 12 Nov. 1781 (W. L. Benson).

advantages of the present age, that the ruins of Glastenbury abbey, are, at this time, in high perfection. Oh! these ruins! I could live, & dye among them.

Within two or three miles of the falls of Lidford he stopped several times in an effort to 'hear them, but without success; and no wonder, for when I came upon the spot, there was scarce a drop of water. I was informed however, that the millar would let some down presently: which indeed he did: but his allowance was so scanty, that I could not help suspecting, this hoary river-god had acted in character, & had discharged the stream from his own urn.'

From Launceston he pushed as far as Bodmin, 'through wilds, naked, & barren of every idea of beauty', before returning by way of Liskeard, Plymouth and Exeter. A twelve-mile detour to see Powderam Castle proved unrewarding, 'when we got there, we found it not worth a half-penny'. At Ford Abbey, the beautiful ruins were defaced, turned as they were 'into an awkward house'; and 'the simplicity of a monkish valley . . . deformed by statues, & canals, & other trumpery'. After such disappointments he met his reward on skirting the New Forest,

where we found some of the most inchanting sylvan scenery, that the pencil of nature ever drew. Such Dryads! extending their taper arms to each other, sometimes in elegant mazes along the plain; sometimes in single figures; & sometimes combined! What would I have given to be able to trace all their beauteous forms on paper! Alass! my art failed me. I could only sketch: and a sketch amounts to no more, than, N.B. Here stands a tree.

He crossed over to the Isle of Wight which was 'as barren of beauty, as it is fertile in corn', and returned to the mainland to visit Netley Abbey, totally overgrown with ivy. 'In twenty years you may look for Netly-abbey in vain. The shepherd may point to the spot, & tell you it lies there: but you will see nothing, but one vast ivy-bush, surrounded every where, and imbowered by wood.' He reached home *via* Southampton and Winchester, and concluded his letter to Mason with these words: 'Thus I have given you a bill of fare: if I ever cook it into a collation, you shall dine with me, if you please.'[1]

The promise was kept. Mason received in 1777 the fair copy of the *Western Tour*, containing the finished drawings, and it was not till after Mason's death in 1797 that Gilpin published the work. The rough sketches,[2] numbering more than eighty, may amount to no more than 'N.B. here stands a tree', to use Gilpin's phrase, yet they, like the account just quoted, enable us to recapture something of the original atmosphere of the journey. Also, on the *Western Tour*, he seized his impressions with far greater delicacy than heretofore. The sketches, which cannot have taken more than a few minutes to execute, have about them a lyrical quality; some shimmer with air and sunlight, others have a Japanese flavour, as pen and brush run riot to provide a contrasting foreground [7.*f*], in others again, the brush alone, by washes, lines and squiggles and dots, provides an adequate and satisfying statement.

[1] 12 July 1775 (W. L. Benson).   [2] W. L. Benson Collection.

Gilpin kept beside him a working copy of this *Tour*, and into it he made from the note-books a second set of rough sketches, which differ very little in spirit from the first. This manuscript contains seventy-eight (originally eighty) sketches and plans.[1]

Early in 1776 he planned a journey into the Highlands of Scotland, and thinking he would take the east-coast route, consulted Mason's local knowledge. Mason, who shared Gilpin's views on picturesque travel, replied on 29 January in his dry categorical vein which is not without humour:

The eastern coast of Yorkshire, if you mean to visit that next summer I can tell you will never answer your trouble. it is the most unpicturesque spot in the kingdom. and I can speak of this with the greater confidence, because all my little temporal matters lye disperst in it; and I have often been obligd to visit it lately, but was always tird even when I rode over my own ground. I have eight or nine different farms there, all in different townships & I will venture to bet you the annual rent of any of them that you dont make a landscape out of them all. The town cliffs & Castle of Scarbro with the vale of Hakeness & another where I think there is an iron forge are the only things in that circuit worth your notice. Castle Howard is Blenheim, as to the House, & Versailes, as to the garden, in Duodecimo. I am told there is a fine ruin of an Abbey at Whitby but situated on a bare bleak cliff. So much for the East [,] the North & the west riding have too many beauties to enumerate.[2]

On 17 May Gilpin set out with his wife and younger son, William, for the Highlands, on what was to be his last systematic tour. He stayed a day or two with Mason at Aston, not far from Worksop, and proceeded through the West Riding, along the Appleby road to Carlisle, and so north to Edinburgh by the Langholm road. Back in Carlisle on 13 June he informed Mason:

I have got safe from my Scotch expedition; which I feared indeed, when I left you, I should not have had time to execute. I have been much entertained indeed, & saw a face of country wholly new. I carryed my little woman no farther than Edinburgh, from whence I sent her to this place with a friend; & went on to Sterling—Loch-Leven—Perth—Killicrankie—Dunkeld—Blair of Athol—Inverary—Loch-Lomond, & twenty other Lochs. I shall not enter into any particulars. In the moment of hurry it would be debasing my subject.[3]

Only two notebooks of rough sketches, covering the first stage of the journey, have so far come to light.[2] The fifty-one sketches therein are poor compared with those of the previous year. A few are treated with his usual brown pen and grey wash, the rest have in addition a strong sepia wash in the foreground. Use of sepia and red-brown is a characteristic of his work in the 1770's. Perhaps the best sketches of this tour are those of the Bridge at Hawick (an aquatint of this subject illustrated the work when it was printed), the Bridge at Dunkeld, and the approach at Sterling Castle.

In the spring of 1777 Gilpin was offered the living of Boldre in Hampshire, by William

[1] 'Remarks on the Western parts of England; relative chiefly to picturesque beauty; made in the year 1775.' Volume bound in stiff marbled paper. 8⅝ × 5¼ in. Text written out by his eldest son, John Bernard Gilpin, with later cancellations and additions by W. G. Major J. R. Abbey Collection.

[2] Rev. E. G. Benson Collection.

[3] W. L. Benson Collection.

Mitford. As the intimation coincided with the Easter Holidays, he set out with his wife to see the place.

Our road led us through the heart of the new forest—such scenes of wood, as I had never beheld. I had often before skirted the new-forest; but never penetrated its depths. For more than a dozen miles we rode past thousands & thousands of ancient oaks, with every one of which a man would wish to form an intimacy; & continued among them, till we knew, by our skill in geography, together with the intimation of mile-stones, that we were within 2 or 3 miles of the place we aimed at. 'My dear, said I, turning from the trees to my wife, I am perfectly satisfyed, & will give the postilion orders to turn back, if you please. To be within the distance of a walk of such scenery as this, is all I desire.' But my wife rather wished to see the house & conveniences, . . . so we trudged on to *Vicar's-hill*; which is the name of the place which will probably be our future abode. It is, I assure you, a sweet spot; & there is a view from the parlour-windows, enough to make a man jump out of them. If I have time, I will annex a sketch of it.

Set on retirement, it is not without a note of regret that he added, in his letter to Mason:

Thus you see me converted, (that is, I suppose, I shall be speedily) into a country-vicar. But this business will make no change in my plan; except that of ordering the postilion, when I leave Cheam, to drive South-ward, instead of north-ward. . . . I always had a predilection for the north of England; & wished to lay my bones under a mountain: but I shall submit to fate. I assure you I had no hand in this business myself: for I knew so little of Mr. Mitford's affairs, that I did not so much as know, he had the living of Boldre in his gift.[1]

By August 1778 he had removed to Vicar's Hill, after handing over the school to his son, William, and was soon engrossed in tackling the many pressing problems of his extensive parish. He continued enchanted with his new domain, and sang its praises to Mason, hoping thereby to tempt the landscape gardener to come down and advise on the laying-out of the grounds of Vicar's Hill:

I will venture to promise you the sight of a country finer than any garden, you ever saw. For woodland-scenery, it is infinitely beyond any thing I have found in England. Narley-wood, which is a corner of new-forest, & lies within a walk (about 2 miles) from my house, is a delightful scene: and if I penetrate deeper into the recesses of the forest, the grandeur of the scenery rises upon me. These woody-scenes are relieved by vast tracts of heath; in which the ground is often beautifully broken; the horizon skirted with wood; or adorned with islands, or peninsulas of forest-scenery shooting into them. It is a delightful contrast. And I must tell you, that in winter, I think, these scenes are finer than in summer. I have long been of opinion, that a leafless forest is an object of great beauty. Then, on the other side, we have sea-views, which in their way are likewise fine; the isle of Wight forming a good background to them all. Then again the inhabitants are a very pleasant set of people to live amongst. They have nothing of that sharpness, which you Yorkshire-men possess; but in its room great plainness, & simplicity of manners. . . . As an instance of the simplicity of the people, I'll tell you a fact. It happened at Lymington last week. A jocky from the north came hither to purchase some wild forest-horses; which, it seems, are become very fashion-able in carriages. He lost a £20 bank-bill; which was cryed on the market day. Nobody knew any

[1] 19 Apr. 1777 (W. L. Benson).

thing about it. At last, some one wiser than ordinary, going into the house of one of the inhabitants, found the bill in miserable plight. The woman who had found it, had cut out the Britannia, & I believe the flourish, which she had pasted up in her house as pictures. The rest of the bill I believe was destroyed. However enough was left to identify it; & she gave it up with all readiness; but had not the conscience to claim the reward, till she was put upon it.[1]

Among the many sketches of the New Forest which he did soon after his arrival at Vicar's Hill, is a group of nine, depicting its eastern fringe.[2] They are very free, and washed-in with brown and red-brown. He also embarked straightaway on a systematic study of the Forest, with its trees, animals and lore, though at first there was little time for this fresh pursuit; his parish was large, and he had no wish to be thought an idle pastor.[1]

(b) THE FINISHED SKETCHES

The years of travel are interesting for the way in which Gilpin obtained the collaboration of Sawrey and of the young John Smith. These two provided, between them, 110 finished sketches for the *Tour of the Lakes*. Smith, from about 1770 till he went to Italy in 1776, was apprenticed to Sawrey Gilpin and under his guidance developed his rather topographical representation of landscape. The basis of his early colouring technique was probably derived from Sawrey's 'Essay on Colouring Landscape', for Mr. A. L. Fawcett possesses a partial copy of this essay in Smith's own hand. What is not generally realized is that during this same period Smith was also employed by William Gilpin and received tuition at his hands. For this we have not only Gilpin's testimony but quite a few early sketches by Smith done around Carlisle and the Lake District and executed in Gilpin's manner. It is from these very sketches, most of which are still in the hands of the Vicar of Boldre's descendants, that Smith made many of the oval drawings that illustrate the manuscript of the *Tour of the Lakes*. He may very well have accompanied Gilpin on his *Wye Tour*. Anyhow, he copied out the manuscript of it which was shown to Thomas Gray. From him he learnt to jot down his impressions in notebooks and how to make a rapid sketch—this is borne out by two sheets of a notebook,[3] the first of which contains three brief sketches of Welsh castles under the general heading 'Mnemosyne. 1773.'. The composition of these three castles corresponds exactly to three drawings of Gilpin's in the *Wye Tour* manuscript just mentioned [7. c]. There exists also a small drawing-book filled with sketches by both Sawrey Gilpin and John Smith. Several of Smith's are done from William Gilpin's rough sketches of the *Western Tour* of 1775.[4] From their manner, Smith must have completed these before his departure for Italy in 1776. He does not seem to have resumed relations with Gilpin till about 1784, when the latter considered him as an illustrator for the *Tour of the Lakes*. Though in the 1780's relations between the two became very strained, as Gilpin found

---

[1] W. G. to William Mason, 3 Sept. 1778 (W. L. Benson).
[2] W. L. Benson Collection.
[3] A. L. Fawcett Collection.
[4] See *infra*, p. 65.

Smith increasingly unreliable, in the early 1770's harmony reigned between them—Smith was diligent and adaptable to the point that in the manuscript of the *Tour of the Lakes*, he modelled himself so closely on Gilpin that their drawings are almost indistinguishable.

Now for an account of the finished sketches. Gilpin wrote up his tours according to a fairly set pattern. As he stated in the preface to the *Tour of the Lakes*, 'the following observations . . . were at first thrown together, warm from the subject, each evening, after the scene of the day had been presented; and in a moment of more leisure, were corrected, and put into form'.[1] Travelling during the day, he jotted in little notebooks what he called 'Rough thoughts', and these were interspersed with the sketches we have just examined. At the end of each day the impressions were strung together into a narrative and the sketches were sometimes touched up and strengthened. On returning to Cheam, he devoted the autumn and winter months to writing up, before setting out on a fresh excursion the following year. However, the finished drawings which illustrate the manuscripts were not completed so systematically. The finished or 'adorned sketch' required more time to prepare, and in several instances only pressure from friends, eager to acquaint themselves with the novelty of picturesque travel, spurred Gilpin to illustrate the fair copy of his *Tours*. Apart from the drawings of the *Eastern Tour* and the *Southern Tour*, which have so far eluded us,[2] the finished drawings of the *Tours* were done in this sequence: those of the *Tour of the Lakes* (1772) were completed in 1774, followed by those of the *Western Tour* (1775) in 1777, the *Scottish Tour* (1776) c. 1778, the *Wye Tour* (1770) c. 1779, and those of the *North Wales Tour* (1773) c. 1790. Except for the drawings of the *Scottish Tour*, which were bound in with the letterpress of the first edition in 1792,[3] the other drawings all illustrated manuscript copies of the *Tours*, which, since Gilpin's day, have fared very differently according to the vicissitudes of ownership.

We shall now examine in detail the fortunes and drawings of the manuscript which first brought Gilpin to the notice of a wider public, and which he had every reason to consider as his *opus magnum*, the *Tour of the Lakes*.

When Gilpin visited the Lake District, he was encouraged by Mason, who had been unable to join him at Ambleside, to treat his subject as he had done in the *Wye Tour*:

I am rejoicd however that hitherto you must have had favorable weather & I hope to profit by it sometime or other by reading your description and viewing your sketches, for I take for granted this tour will produce both, & united as you unite them I assure you I think they give the most satisfactory Idea that can be, whereas verbal ones only are never sufficient for me, insomuch that

---

[1] *Tour of the Lakes*, chap. ix.

[2] Their presence was last recorded by A. P. Oppé in a catalogue of the sale of Captain Norcliffe Gilpin, deceased, on 20 Apr. 1915. He noted that lot 9 contained among other items 'Gilpin Norfolk original drawings poor', and that in the eight volumes of Gilpin's *Tours*, which made up lot 83, were the 'orig. of So. Tour'.

[3] 'Blamire bound me up all the original drawings of the Scotch tour, with the 4to. letter-press in 2 4to. volumes; for which a gentleman in his shop offered him 50 guineas; which Blamire treated with disdain; saying, he would give that himself to make profit of them.' W. G. to W. Mason, 25 Feb. 1792 (W. L. Benson).

tho I have Mr Grays acct of this very tour by me at present, I find a constant want of accompanying sketches.[1]

It is precisely this combination of description and illustration that was to give the work its immediate appeal. By mid-1774 the manuscript was ready; it consisted of no less than 830 pages, which were eventually bound in eight volumes, and bore the title of 'A tour through *England*; more particularly the mountainous parts of *Cumberland*, and *Westmorland*: with a view chiefly to illustrate the principles of picturesque beauty in landscape'.[2] The work was first shown to an old friend, the poet Richard Glover, whose literary strictures were taken into account. Then, wishing for the opinion of one better versed in picturesque matters, Gilpin dispatched the manuscript to Mason in several parcels between August and the end of the year. On 13 August he informed Mason that four volumes were now ready:

For the sake of the drawings they may be worth your inspection. I have no execution myself; & got 2 or 3 ingenious painters of my acquaintance to adorn them from my sketches; & many of the drawings are very beautiful. It is unnecessary to tell you, that those only, which are unmarked, are mine.

On my own account also I should wish to put those papers into your hands; if you will be so good as to give them a few strictures. And you need be under no restraint; as I have not the most distant idea of printing them. I wish it merely for the improvement of my own taste.[3]

In his answer, Mason echoed Whately in paying tribute to Gilpin's descriptive powers: 'Do not think I flatter you when I say that your mode of description is the only one that is to me in any sort satisfactory because it is the only one which gives me precise & peculiar Ideas.'[4] When he received the volumes, he was so impressed that he held up the publication of Gray's works to insert, with Gilpin's permission, the following footnote to Gray's account of the Lake District:

Without the pencil nothing indeed is to be described with precision; and even then that pencil ought to be in the very hand of the writer, ready to supply with outlines every thing that his pen cannot express by words. As far as language can describe, Mr. Gray has, I think, pushed its powers: For rejecting, as I before hinted, every general unmeaning and hyperbolical phrase, he has selected . . . the plainest, simplest, and most direct terms: yet notwithstanding his judicious care, in the use of these, I must own I feel them defective. . . . I have seen one piece of verbal description which compleately satisfies me, because it is throughout assisted by masterly delineation. It is composed by the Rev. Mr. Gilpin, of Cheam in Surry, and contains, amongst other places, an account of the very scenes which, in this tour, our author [Gray] visited. This Gentleman, possessing the conjoined talent of a writer and a designer, has employed them in this manuscript to every purpose of picturesque beauty, in the description of which a correct eye, a practised pencil, and an eloquent pen could assist him. He has, consequently, produced a work *unique* in its kind at once. But I have

---

[1] 13 June 1772 (Rev. E. G. Benson).

[2] The eight volumes are dispersed in three collections: I (Charles Traylen); II, III, IV, and VI (W. L. Benson); V, VII, and VIII (Major J. R. Abbey).

[3] W. L. Benson Collection.

[4] 23 Aug. 1774 (Rev. E. G. Benson).

said it is in manuscript, and, I am afraid, likely to continue so; for would his modesty permit him to print it, the great expence of plates would make its publication almost impracticable.[1]

This note served to whet the appetite of many who sought to catch a glimpse of the manuscript. It was, however, probably on its way to court circles before Mason's edition became generally available. Besides Mason, who was one of the chaplains in ordinary to the King, Gilpin had several friends at court, in particular Leonard Smelt, who, though he was to resign his office of sub-governor to the Princes in 1776, remained to the end of his days a courtier and a close friend of George III.

The great work was sent to Smelt in March 1775,[2] and soon was seen by the Prince of Wales, Lady C. Finch, the Bishop of Chester and Lady Mary Montague. In the summer Lord Dartmouth, who had then three of his sons at Cheam, took it down with him to Staffordshire and read it twice over.[3] Through him the papers were eventually brought to the notice of George III. What the King thought of them is unknown, but for a while, Gilpin feared they might find their way into the royal collection, never to be heard of again; or as Mason put it: 'if they are got into certain great hands they will be laid up with the papers of Leonardo da Vinci, for from that Den there is never any trace of returning Footsteps.'[4]

Towards the end of 1775, thanks again to the Earl of Dartmouth, Lord Strafford and Lord Warwick became acquainted with the *Tour of the Lakes*.[5] As the manuscript continued to circulate Gilpin acquired in the next few years a large circle of new friends, who offered praise and criticism, urged him to publish the work, and helped him over the major stumbling-block hinted at by Mason—finding a suitable method of reproducing the drawings that would not prove too expensive. There was Mrs. Delany, the Duchess of Portland, who had it twice, Lord Harcourt, Horace Walpole, to say nothing of Gilpin's closer friends such as Henry B. Cay, Edward Forster, William Mitford, and William Lock. Gilpin was particularly moved when Queen Charlotte asked to see the work a second time in 1781, and it was to her that he finally dedicated it on publication in 1786.

The eight volumes of the *Tour of the Lakes* contain in all 249 sketches, of which 208 are drawings and the remainder sketch maps and panoramas. This total represents the combined

---

[1] *The Poems of Mr. Gray. To which are prefixed Memoirs of his Life and Writings by W. Mason, M.A.*, York, 1775, pp. 376 n.–377 n. Gilpin's assent to the inclusion of this note is characteristic of the innate modesty of the man: 'if I had not been assured of your sincerity, I should almost have feared you had been playing upon me. I had indeed the vanity to hope, I should amuse *you* a *little*; as your ideas always seemed to me so very picturesque: but my vanity never soared near the height, to which you would raise it. Perhaps I should have pasted your letter to the first leaf; to give the grandfather, in some future time, a little consequence in the memory of his grandson: but I had not the least conception of being carryed *per ora virûm*. What can I say to your kind partiality? What is a man to do, when honours are *offered*, which he feels he does not merit? I believe I must shelter my modesty under the example of my betters, & answer you in the sincerity of a *nolo episcopari*. You offer me such a flattering idea of fame, that it is impossible to resist it. You put it beyond the power of criticism to hurt me: *post clypeum lateo*: while you leave it to the imagination to conceive my merit to be ten times greater than it is. To my other reasons against printing this little business, you have added two more: the first is, to save your credit; & the 2d., to secure my own.' W. G. to Mason, 30 Nov. 1774 (W. L. Benson).

[2] W. G. to W. Mason, 6 May 1775 (W. L. Benson).

[3] W. G. to W. Mason, 11 Sept. 1775 (W. L. Benson).

[4] W. Mason to W. G., 31 July 1775 (Rev. E. G. Benson).

[5] W. G. to W. Mason, 6 Jan. 1776 (W. L. Benson).

efforts of seven, perhaps eight artists, who drew to Gilpin's specifications and thus gave a definite unity to the whole set of illustrations.

Most of the drawings are oval compositions executed in pen and wash on paper tinted all over in either yellow, light-brown, or beige. The penwork is usually brown or grey, and sometimes both colours are used in the same drawing. The predominant wash is grey-brown, though grey is often used for all planes, and brown or sepia added to strengthen the foreground.

The team consisted of William Gilpin, John Warwick Smith, Sawrey Gilpin, Nicholas Thomas Dall, William Marlow, A. C., B., and perhaps another unknown artist. It is not easy to determine William Gilpin's exact contribution, as his pronouncements on the subject are rather vague. Besides the information given to Mason on 13 August 1774, we have the preface to the manuscript (different and much shorter than the printed preface) in which he tells us:

With regard to the *plans*, and *drawings*, which are very numerous, and of course hastily, & inaccurately taken, in a tour of scarce 5 weeks, the author by no means wishes them to be considered as *exact portraits*, but rather as *general ideas*; & illustrations of the description.

So small a scale indeed admits of little more. To have finished every drawing upon a large scale, with all the accuracy, & force, which the grandeur or beauty of the scenes in general demand, would have been an infinite work. Rude however as the sketches are, from which the drawings were taken, many of the drawings themselves are executed in a masterly manner, by able hands, whose marks they bear. For such as are unmarked, the author is answerable himself.[1]

In the light of these two statements it would seem that William Gilpin executed the ninety-five unsigned drawings. Yet not all of them are by him, one or two are certainly by Sawrey, and others come so close to the work of Smith as to suggest that Smith had at least a hand in touching them up.

The 113 signed drawings are distributed as follows: Sawrey Gilpin 55, Smith 45, Dall 5, A. C. 4, William Marlow and B. 2 each. Despite Gilpin's suggestion that these signed drawings were taken from his sketches, I feel quite certain that in the majority each artist worked from his own sketches, though they may very well have had William Gilpin's rough sketches before them to give them an idea of what was required.

William Gilpin's drawings vary greatly in quality. He was in a better position than anyone else to illustrate the meaning of his text, and as we know, was particularly interested in showing the face of nature under all its varied aspects, yet those sketches which seek to convey the atmosphere of a particular passage are among the least successful, as, for example, when he tried to give 'An idea of the clouds sweeping over the precipices of Gatesgarth-dale'. He did better when illustrating this passage:

The evening, which grew more tempestuous, began to close upon us, and we left the more beautiful parts of the vale of Lorton . . . amid the obscurity, which now overspread the landscape,

---

[1] MS. of the *Tour of the Lakes*, i, pp. iii–iv (Charles Traylen).

the imagination was left at large; and painted many images, which perhaps did not really exist, upon the dead colouring of nature. Every great and pleasing form, whether clear, or obscure, which we had seen during the day, now played, in strong imagery before the fancy: as when the grand chorus ceases, ideal music vibrates in the ear.

In one part, a view pleased us much; tho perhaps, in stronger light, it might have escaped notice. The road made a sudden dip into a little, winding valley; which being too abrupt for a carriage, was eased by a bridge: and the form of the arch was what we commonly find in Roman aqueducts. At least such it appeared to us. The winding road; the wooden valley, and broken ground below; the mountain beyond; the form of the bridge, which gave a classic air to the scene; and the obscurity, which melted the whole into one harmonious mass; made all together a very pleasing view.[1]

This passage and its companion drawing would have pleased Gray, and we may be sure that those in court circles who handled the manuscript saw in the drawing, with its grey overall tint conveying the 'dead colouring of nature', the atmosphere of the situation which allowed their imagination to play over that scene.

In contrast with these rather coarse and muddy sketches, Gilpin produced some of his finest and daintiest work on a small scale. Such is the 'view in the vale of Lanercost' with its delicate use of brush and pen to convey light and shade [8. *d*]. Similar restraint is used in more topographical drawings like the view up river near Corby Castle, a favourite subject of Captain Gilpin's,[2] and the winding River Esk. In these drawings the characteristic sickle-shaped strokes for secondary branches are well established. He also took particular care of his buildings, even when their function is only to provide a focal point in the composition; in representing them he avoided a harsh outline and favoured the use of straight strokes to convey the structure of an arch or the surface of masonry.

'Brugh-castle' treated in this manner provides also an early instance of body-colour and gummed shadows.[3] Against a sky which changes from blue-grey to red as the eye moves to the right, the grey ruin of the castle is defined with dark-brown ink heightened with white-body colour, while the greys and browns of the foreground are strengthened with gum in the shadows. Gilpin used gum in this way on several occasions, and the result is particularly successful in his larger compositions; body-colour, however, occurred very infrequently and usually in the form of a prepared ground. He may well have introduced Smith to the possibilities of the medium, for it became a common practice for the latter to use body-colour after his sojourn in Italy.

Gilpin's remaining sketches are similar to those that illustrate his other tours, except for a woodland walk, which anticipates his studies of forest scenery.

The next largest contributor is Sawrey Gilpin, who showed himself equally at home with landscapes as with animal drawings. Of the 55 sketches which he initialled 42 are landscapes (at least 2 of which were to be subjects for aquatints when the *Tour* was published, though

---

[1] *Tour of the Lakes*, ii, 19–20.
[2] A large sketch of this subject by Captain Gilpin is in the hands of W. L. Benson. Corby Castle is situated 5 miles east of Carlisle.   [3] Major J. R. Abbey Collection.

this remained unacknowledged), and the remaining 13 are mainly concerned with animal subjects: horses, cows, and sheep.

Sawrey's talent was here very much at the disposal of his brother, who asked him to illustrate such varied subjects as the results arising from the opposition of light and shade, the stratification of rocks or the 'effect produced by a storm, when the objects are uninteresting'.[1]

Whereas in his animal figures the line is sure, firm and sometimes graceful, Sawrey allowed himself much greater freedom in the landscapes. His interest in landscape was of long standing, yet it was never more than a relaxation from the more serious business of animal painting. Like the other main illustrators of the manuscript, he varied his technique with every batch of drawings. At times he favoured a dark foreground and yellow-tinted paper, as in the 'vale of Lorton' drawings, at others a much lighter effect was achieved by tinting the area surrounding the oval. There is a distinct echo of the rapid brushwork of Alexander Cozens in the Levens sketches [7. *d*]; here, vigour and freshness are conveyed by a loose treatment at every stage of the building-up process, from the pencil contours through the grey and brown washes to the final application of almost dry black. Other sketches are drawn mainly with a thin pen; this is the case with the 'Entrance of Warwick-castle' where the masses are conveyed with light-grey and warm-brown washes.[2] Using the stock-in-trade of his brother's compositions, he entered fully into the spirit of the undertaking—thus, he introduced cattle to furnish a foreground or replaced the unsightly mills at Taplow with an imaginary castle.[3]

In his picturesque undertakings William Gilpin made constant use of Sawrey's gifts to complement his own. While William sought to explain the principles of picturesque composition as applied to landscape, Sawrey taught the characteristics of domestic animals and how animals and human figures could agreeably be grouped in landscape.[4] In the manuscript of the *Tour of the Lakes*, in particular, he grouped horses, cattle, and sheep, and he also brought out the salient features of cow, bull, and horse either by comparison, or by making several studies of the same animal.

John Warwick Smith's contribution, interesting as evidence of his debt to the various members of the Gilpin family, already displays that combination of slight stiffness and lack of imagination which was to characterize his work after his return from Italy. His forty-five drawings, signed with the IS monogram, consist of landscapes, views of Carlisle, and sets depicting Kenilworth Castle, and the Abbeys of Fountains and Furness.[5] Some

---

[1] W. L. Benson Collection.

[2] From Sawrey's inscription to the side of this drawing (in the possession of Mr. Charles Traylen) it seems likely that a drawing by John Smith was used for the plate of Warwick Castle in the printed version of the *Tour of the Lakes*.

[3] In the possession of Mr. Charles Traylen.

[4] Besides demonstrations by means of sketches, Sawrey Gilpin's only remarks on landscape figures were published by

his brother at the end of the *Two Essays*, which accompanied the 1802 sale catalogue of his drawings. The footnote, which William Gilpin then inserted, suggests that some unfinished manuscript of Sawrey's may still exist.

[5] Unable to see Furness Abbey on the way from Ambleside to Keswick, 'the loss was in a great manner made up; and our curiosity in a good degree satisfyed by the accounts and drawings of Mr. John Smith, an ingenious young painter, who

of the many preliminary sketches executed for these drawings are in the collections of George F. Benson and Willoughby L. Benson. They range from prospects of Carlisle in the seventeenth-century manner,[1] done perhaps before 1770, to large sketches of the Lake District drawn in the early 1770's, under the guidance of Sawrey Gilpin. A large drawing of the Fratry at Carlisle, in sepia on bright chrome-yellow-tinted paper, lost much of its effect when reduced to the small and somewhat stiff oval which illustrated the *Tour*.[2] On the other hand, the prospects of Carlisle form a pleasing set—here the claims of topographical accuracy and picturesque composition are happily reconciled. For the 'view of Carlisle from the Race-ground', we have Smith's original panoramic sketch, and can see how the strip was adapted to the requirements of the oval [8. *a* and *b*]. For the view of Carlisle from Etterby Scar, he certainly referred to Gilpin's original rough sketch.[3]

His landscapes vary greatly in execution, from the dainty to the slapdash, and this may very well be due to his zeal to reproduce William Gilpin's manners. Compare 'Rose-castle' with Gilpin's 'view in the vale of Lanercost' [8. *d* and *e*]. Where the trees retain some individual character, the drawings have a lightness, a gentleness that is most pleasing. At other times his drawings are coarse, with some of that fussy and untidy treatment one associates with the work of Joseph Barber.

Nicholas Thomas Dall (d. 1776) contributed five landscapes worked in grey-brown washes over pencil—they are of Middleton dale, and of the castles at Castleton and Appleby; another showing 'Part of eastern screen' of Lake Keswick is strengthened in the foreground with penwork.

William Marlow (1740–1813) no doubt came in contact with Gilpin through his brother Sawrey, for he was also a pupil of Samuel Scott's. He did two views of Scaleby Castle in grey pen and water-colour [8. *c*].

Gilpin must have known more of Dall and Marlow than their contribution to this *Tour* might suggest, for he had in his collection seventeen drawings of various subjects by Dall, and six etchings of Italian views by Marlow.[4]

There are two further contributors, known only by their initials. A. C. did a sketch of Haddon Hall and three of scenery at Matlock. B. subscribed two views of the grounds at Blenheim. Their work is very inferior.

Several conclusions arise from this survey of the drawings of the *Tour of the Lakes*. First and foremost, the collaboration of William Gilpin, Sawrey Gilpin, and John Smith went

---

had been studying the ruins upon the spot; and communicated to us his drawings and observations.' MS. of the *Tour of the Lakes*, iii, p. 252. A similar acknowledgement occurs on the back of the plan that precedes Smith's seven views of Furness Abbey. The fourth view was used for plate 10 in the printed *Tour*, and Gilpin added to his description of that plate: 'I had this very pleasing drawing from Mr. Smith.' As far as I am aware, this is the only printed reference to him in any of Gilpin's picturesque works.

[1] Similar to the drawings of the amateur William Lodge

(1649–89), in the grangerized copy of Thoresby's *Ducatus Leodiensis* (Leeds Public Library).

[2] Large drawing in the hands of Rev. E. G. Benson, and small oval in W. L. Benson Collection.

[3] Both in W. L. Benson Collection.

[4] Folder entitled 'Drawings by Dahl' (Rev. E. G. Benson); Marlow prints (George F. Benson). For Dall and Marlow as water-colourists, see I. A. Williams, *Early English Water-Colours*, pp. 71–74; for Marlow as a painter, see E. K. Waterhouse, *Painting in Britain 1530–1790*, p. 178.

much beyond Gilpin's statement to Mason that he 'got 2 or 3 ingenious painters' of his acquaintance to adorn them from his sketches. It would be truer to say they pooled their information and each used the other's sketches whenever the occasion demanded it. As far as landscape compositions are concerned, Sawrey Gilpin and Smith certainly used William Gilpin's rough sketches, but for their speciality, be it animals or architectural drawings, they resorted to their own material,[1] while William Gilpin occasionally drew on the other two's sketches.[2]

Another outcome of this joint effort was the tinted oval illustration, which adorned so many of the *Tours*, in their manuscript and printed forms. It is difficult to say which of the three was the first to use the oval and the most effective yellow wash, but there are several indications that Gilpin's experiments were leading that way. He knew of Dutch engravers who occasionally resorted to the oval, a shape frequently used in miniatures and cameos; although he did not have much use for it, he knew the Claude Lorrain glass, and how, by a judicious arrangement of colours, you obtained a 'mellow tinge';[3] and lastly, he tells us how the idea of the tinted drawing came to him when he browned a sketch by the fire to take the glare off the white paper.[4]

A further instance of collaboration is worth mentioning at this juncture—it is the sketch-book, already referred to, which William Gilpin gave in 1800 to his favourite grandson, William, then only eleven years old yet already showing unmistakable signs that he had inherited the family's gift for drawing.[5]

The book contains fifty-two sketches executed towards the end of 1775, and these make up a course of instruction in landscape composition. John Warwick Smith, who drew the first thirty-eight, dealt in turn with waterfalls, rivers flowing between steep banks, cascading water, ruins, woodland, trees, foregrounds, and the road curving amongst rocky scenery—all elements of a picturesque landscape. The last fourteen sketches are by Sawrey

---

[1] William Gilpin and Smith often treated the same subjects, and Smith, when he saw fit quite naturally worked from his more accurate recordings. Mr. George F. Benson possesses a small book entitled 'Sketches by Smith', which contains a number of views around Ambleside, Ullswater and Helvellyn. It shows not only that Smith covered much the same ground as Gilpin, but also to what extent Gilpin made use of Smith's material. Only seven oval sketches remain, and on the back of five of them Gilpin wrote: 'A view from the top of Kirkstone in the wood from Ambleside to Ullswater'; 'Part of Stribray-cragg, near the head of Ullswater'; 'Martindale fell'; 'Near Stybray-cragg on Ullswater'; 'Yew-cragg on Ullswater'. In the same collection there are further sketches by Smith of the Lake District done in the same period, with rubrics in Smith's own hand.

[2] For example, William Gilpin's drawing of 'Great Torr' (facing p. 749 of MS.) has written beside it: 'from a drawing of Mr. S. Gilpin'; and for the five elevations of Lanercost Abbey, Gilpin probably used material supplied by Smith in preference to any sketches of the place he might have made.

See drawing by Smith in the collection of G. F. Benson, which corresponds to Gilpin's fourth view of Lanercost (facing p. 597 of MS.).

[3] *Scottish Tour*, i, 124.

[4] 'I well remember, . . . when a boy I used to make little drawings, I was never pleased with them till I have given them a brownish tint. And, as I knew no other method, I used to hold them over smoke till they had assumed such a tint as satisfied my eye.' *Five Essays*, p. 152. (For full title see p. 84, n. 3.)

[5] Inscribed as follows by Gilpin, on the inside cover: 'William Gilpin of Vicars hill gives this common-place book of sketches to his grandson, William Gilpin of Cheam, hoping he will encourage in himself, what his grandfather thinks he possesses, a taste for drawing; which in whatever way of life he proceeds, may be a very *useful*, as well as pleasing amusement to him. | Vicar's-hill | April 19, 1800'. Gilpin added on the fly-leaf: 'NB | all the landscape part of these sketches are by Mr. Smith—the figures by Mr. Sawrey Gilpin'. W. L. Benson Collection.

Gilpin, who concerned himself with the grouping of animals and figures. Much suggests that the sketch-book was composed to William Gilpin's specifications: certainly the choice of subjects does, and the treatment and composition of many of the landscapes done by Smith. In fact, we know the six drawings of ruins were done from Gilpin's rough sketches of Glastonbury (*Western Tour*, summer 1775). Plates 9. *a* and *b* show that Smith took into account such indications as 'Light', 'join' and 'all ivy'.

Occasionally, Smith struck an effect of his own, as in a woodland scene, which only lacks an interesting foreground. On the whole he was content to follow directives, so that his manner in this sketch-book was much the same as in the drawings of the *Tour of the Lakes*. He retained Captain Gilpin's fondness for the jutting strata of rock and for the boulder that breaks the line of a waterfall, but was far more successful than either Captain or William Gilpin in managing running water or the meanderings of a river.

Now for a brief survey of the finished drawings of the other tours. As we saw earlier, Gilpin sent Mason in 1777 a fair copy of the *Western Tour*, which contained eighty drawings and two plans.[1] Today this manuscript has only two citron-tinted rectangular drawings. The pen and wash colours vary from grey in the distance to brown and sepia in the foreground, with touches of varnish in the shadows to add luminosity.[2]

The drawings of the *Scottish Tour* remained divorced from any manuscript account of the journey. Together with a few maps and plans, over a hundred of them were bound in with a large paper copy of the first edition of the *Tour*, the two volumes of which are now in the H. C. Green Collection.[3] In treatment, size, and format these drawings are similar to the ones of the *Western Tour*.

The thirty-four drawings of the *Wye Tour* mark a return to the oval shape. Formerly part of a fair draft of the *Tour*, they were cut out by Gilpin *c*. 1785, and mounted on stiff grey sheets of paper to form an extra-illustrated first edition of the *Wye Tour*.[4] The

---

[1] 'I will present you with my west country tour, which is handsomely transcribed; tho not by me; elegantly bound, the drawings amended, & the text corrected, tho not by you. You shall have & hold it, during your natural life; & then leave it to one of my children, who will value it after you. You shall also give me leave to print it; if I find my income scanty; & shall be so inclined, which at present I am not.' W. G. to William Mason, 14 Aug. 1777 (W. L. Benson).

Manuscript of the *Western Tour*. 2 vols. bound in rough calf, $8\frac{7}{8} \times 5\frac{9}{16}$ in. Contained originally eighty drawings and two plans. On Mason's death in 1797, it reverted to Gilpin, who later inserted this dedication on the fly leaf of Vol. I: 'Mr. Gilpin of Vicar's-hill, gave these two MS. Volumes, some years agoe, to his wife; and she, thinking them of more value, than they really are, gave them, as a singular mark of her affection, to her nephew, Mr. J[ohn] Gilpin., *Decemb*.7.1802.' Dr. J. B. Gilpin-Brown Collection.

[2] One drawing was reproduced as plate 6, in *Samuel Rogers and William Gilpin*, facing p. 50.

[3] See Iolo A. Williams, 'The Artists of the Gilpin Family with special reference to William Sawrey Gilpin', *Old Water Colour Society's Club*, xxix, 1951, pp. 19–20 and plates 7 and 8.

Prior to the general sale of his drawings, Gilpin tested their market value by offering at White's for sixty guineas the two volumes in 4to of this extra-illustrated copy of the *Scottish Tour*, handsomely bound in blue morocco and gilt. It was immediately purchased on 11 June 1801 by Edward Forster of Walthamstow, who then informed Gilpin on 4 Aug. 1801 (W. L. Benson).

[4] For an analysis of the sketches see Megan Ellis, 'Drawings by William Gilpin', *The National Library of Wales Journal*, iii, summer 1953, no. i, pp. 104–8.

'I believe I shall get your Wye-prints finished sooner than I told you. When I undertake a piece of business, I generally

manuscript may originally have had thirty-six drawings, if we accept the Rev. Michael Tyson's statement, in a letter to R. Gough, dated 4 December 1779, that 'Forster has tempted us over to Walthamstow, to see *36* Welsh views of Gilpin's tomorrow'.[1] Among these *Wye Tour* drawings are some of the most accomplished and dainty ovals he ever produced [*9. d*].

Similar in delicacy are the thirty-three (originally thirty-six) ovals illustrating the manuscript of the *North Wales Tour*.[2] Done much later, probably *c.* 1790, they are his finest set of water-colours, executed in a very fluid manner. In the sky and distances tender blues and greys predominate, and where red is introduced it is a pale pink area to one side of the sky near the horizon. In the foreground there are no muddy colours, only transparent greys, browns, and greens.

make it a task; and am not easy, till I get it out of my hands. I have done about 8 or 9 of them; & have pleased myself pretty well. I shall perhaps send them by Mr. Holden, who is obliged to be in London, about the middle of this month, But I would not have you to give them to Blamire to put into a book. He has spoiled your Aunt Kitty's [Catherine Gilpin, 1739–1811] (tho I would not tell her so) by pasting them in before the book was bound; & likewise by putting them in so as to face the wrong way. Let him bind you a book, with blank leaves of the same colour as your aunt Kitty's, with guards; & let them all face one way, as I originally told him;

and when you, & I meet, I will place the drawings in the book.' W. G. to his son William at Cheam, *5* Oct. 1785 (Major J. R. Abbey).

[1] Quoted by *Templeman*, p. *229*.

[2] 'Observations on several parts of North Wales; with regard chiefly to picturesque beauty; made in the year 1773'. Bound in rough calf, $8\frac{3}{8} \times 6\frac{3}{8}$ in. Text written out by his eldest son, John Bernard, with numerous additions and corrections by W. G. Contained originally *36* (now *33*) water-colour drawings mounted on black paper, and 8 sketches or maps. Major J. R. Abbey Collection.

VI. Illustrations for the Printed Tours

WITH the increasing popularity of the manuscript *Tours*, Gilpin was gradually forced to envisage their publication. The main difficulty lay with the numerous drawings, which formed such an essential feature of the works. Where was he to find a method of reproduction that would do justice to the quality of the washes of water-colour? Neither ordinary etching nor engraving seemed satisfactory. Perhaps the new process of aquatint would serve his purpose?

Aquatint had been successfully developed in France, where it was usually referred to as 'gravure au lavis' or 'gravure au pinceau'. Jean Charles François (1717–69) first used it in 1758; he was followed by François Philippe Charpentier (1737–1817) in 1765, and Jean Baptiste Le Prince (1734–81), who from 1768 onwards employed it in his scenes of Russian life.

In Britain professional and amateur artists soon tried out the new process. P. P. Burdett, who worked at Liverpool (1700–74), is credited with the earliest aquatint in England (1771); John Clerk of Eldin tried to pierce Le Prince's secret in 1775; and that same year Paul Sandby issued his first series of Welsh views, which showed that he had completely mastered the new medium.

Early in 1775 Mason suggested to Gilpin he should 'call on Paul Sandby in St Georges Row out of Oxford road', as his 'new method of Etching . . . would suit your Sketches admirably'.[1] Sandby quite naturally refused to part with his secret. He was still working out the possibilities of the process, which Charles Greville had bought from Le Prince and given to him, and had not yet issued his first attempts.[2] Gilpin remained undeterred, and for the next few years seized what opportunities came his way to learn what he could of the various methods used in the aquatint process. In August 1776 he told Mason:

I met with a gentleman, the other day, very curious about the *aqua tinta*, (as they call it) which you first mentioned to me. You may remember I told you that Sandby said, it was a secret. This gentleman thinks he has discovered it. The outline, he says, is etched; & when this is done, the

---

[1] 2 Feb. 1775 (Rev. E. G. Benson).

[2] Generally speaking the traditional picture of uneasy relations between professional and amateur artists in the eighteenth century needs some revision. There was considerable fellow-feeling among all artists. Drawing-masters quite sensibly guarded their most precious and useful secrets for as long as they could, from amateurs as well as their professional rivals. Yet Alexander Cozens passed on much information to the amateurs of the Gilpin family. Similarly, Paul Sandby did not hesitate to give his friend, John Clerk of Eldin, not only the method for soft-ground etching but also an aquatint process which he no longer used (see *The Print Collector's Quarterly*, XX (1933), 363–4). Where their living was not likely to be affected, Cozens and Sandby made their knowledge readily available to those amateurs genuinely interested, who might be trusted not to pass on the information.

plate is cleared of its varnish; & the copper washed with a pencil, dipped in aquafortis, over the shades, which it bites in what proportion you please; & leaves the impression.[1]

A little later he actually met one who shared Sandby's secret. Lord Warwick had written to him in 1777 to say that, following hints thrown out in the *Tour of the Lakes* manuscript, he had decided to make alterations to Warwick Castle.[2] They became acquainted the following year when Lord Warwick and his family took a house in Lymington for the summer. Gilpin found in the young nobleman a kindred spirit. His taste 'is wholly of the sublime kind, formed upon the mountains & lakes of Switzerland, & Cumberland', the projected changes at Warwick Castle 'will out-Brown any thing that is done there', as to the 'secret, which he had bought in Italy',[3] Warwick assured him

he hated secrets; & would wish to communicate it: but his brother Charles, who was equally concerned in it, had given it to P. Sandby, with a kind of promise, that he should have the monopoly of it. He must first therefore write to his brother about it; & if the thing can be adjusted, he will let me have it. If I get this secret, & find it as easy as I have heard (tho L[ord] W[arwick] tells me he does not think the operation quicker than the common mode of etching) I believe, I shall print those 3 essays.[4]

Lord Warwick was unfortunately unable to help, and so Gilpin, for the time being, gave up the idea of printing his picturesque writings. Matters took a new turn in 1781. Horace Walpole, to whom he had dedicated the third edition of the *Essay on Prints*, encouraged him to print the *Tour of the Lakes*, and offered, in conjunction with the Dowager Duchess of Portland, to promote its publication if he could but suggest a method. Gilpin told Walpole of his fruitless search for Sandby's process, though he 'had since heard the secret had gotten into other hands'.[5] Lord Harcourt also pressed him to publish this manuscript, and, by way of inducement, sent him a method of etching obtained from a Mr. Taylor of Bath[6] with full permission to use it as he saw fit.[7]

Mason, informed of these latest developments, drew his attention to yet another method, that of the Frenchman Stapart:[8]

the method seems tolerably easy, for what you would first draw on Paper with a Pen & Common

---

[1] 19 Aug. 1776 (W. L. Benson). Putting nitric acid straight on to the plate with a brush was in fact a method which Sandby had discarded.

[2] W. G. to W. Mason, 24 Feb. 1777 (W. L. Benson).

[3] France? Elsewhere, Gilpin stated that 'Mr. Greville had brought from France' this 'new and ready method of etching'. W. G. to Mason, 19 Feb. 1781 (W. L. Benson).

[4] W. G. to W. Mason, 3 Sept. 1777 (W. L. Benson).

[5] W. G. to W. Mason, 19 Feb. 1781 (W. L. Benson).

[6] Probably John Taylor of Bath (c. 1745–1806).

[7] W. G. to W. Mason, 17 Mar. 1781 (W. L. Benson). William Lock may have helped to obtain this aquatint process. William Gilpin II wrote from Cheam to his father at Vicar's Hill: 'As you told me I was to get the receipt for the Aq: Tin: transcribed by one of my young folks, I have pressed my little friend [Lock's son William] into that service: if he should tell his father, he will make a shrewed [*sic*] surmise; indeed when I shewed him (the boy) the specimen he observed, that method would do extreemly well for Mr. Gilpin's drawings: and I suspect that Lord Harcourt has been induced to send you this account of the A. Tinta thro' the means of Mr. Lock; for I believe he was the only person who had any idea that you was in search of the secret to which notion I might have helped him, in speaking one day of the difficulties that would attend the publication of such a work as yours.' 16 Mar. 1781 (Major J. R. Abbey).

[8] *L'Art de graver au pinceau, nouvelle méthode . . . mise au jour par M. Stapart*, Paris, l'auteur, 1773, 8vo, 96 pp. (Bibliothèque Nationale V.24439. No copy in B.M.)

ink, you draw on varnishd Copper with a point in the manner of common Etching. the Aqua fortis having done its office you take the 1st varnish off & wash in the sky & distances with a pencil dipt in weak spirit of nitre. the whole is afterwards coverd with a transparent varnish, over which (while it is in a fluid state) you sift very fine pulverizd Salt. which sinks into it till it reaches the Copper. when cold, you dip it in Water. the salt melts, and leaves innumerable little holes in the varnish. these you stop up where the lights & demitints are to remain. And another application of Aqua fortis produces thro the other holes the dark shades. which he says may be made as dark as the deepest parts of Metzatinta Pray is Taylors method any thing like this?[1]

Gilpin replied that Taylor's method was not the same as Stapart's.[2] It was probably similar to Sandby's, which involved the use of a *spirit-ground*. That is to say, after the outlines of the sketch are obtained by ordinary etching, the plate is covered evenly with a solution of resin dissolved in spirits of wine. As the spirit evaporates, the resin is left as a grain on the surface. The acid can then bite through this porous coating, which partially protects the plate, giving a tone or tint effect.

Publication now seemed a feasible proposition. The next question to be settled was which *Tour* to publish. Rather cautious by nature, and unwilling to rely on subscriptions, he concurred with Mason's advice, to leave aside the *Tour of the Lakes*, for which many clamoured, in favour of the smaller *Wye Tour*, which could be used to test the reaction of the public.[3] If this tentative succeeded, he might be induced to publish his larger works.

Over practical matters, Mason asked him some pointed questions:

1st   Is Mr Taylors method of aquatinta such that you can yourself finish the plates? If you can. then the expence of Copper plates & working them off is only to be calculated. but if you are to employ an artist then

2dly   What will an Artist do them for per Plate?

3dly   How many *good* impressions are likely to come off? for I have been told that the great imperfection of Aqua tinta is, that the plates done in that manner give fewer good impressions than even Metzatinta.[4]

Answering in the same vein, Gilpin replied to two of the questions:

1st.   As to etching the plates myself, I should never think of it. I have neither abilities, nor time, nor eyes, nor inclination.

[1] W. Mason to W. G., 24 March 1781 (Rev. E. G. Benson).

[2] W. G. to W. Mason, 28 March 1781 (W. L. Benson).

[3] This change of plan involved him in a delicate situation with the Dowager Duchess of Portland, who still thought he was considering subscriptions for the *Tour of the Lakes*. 'I was puzzled lately with a piece of great generosity. It was a letter from the Duchess of Portland, in which she tells me, how much pleased she was with hearing I intended to print my tour (my large work) by su[b]scription; & desired early to put her name down. In this letter she inclosed a bill of an hundred pounds. What was I to do? I'll tell you however what I did do. In the first place, I was quite hurt with such a noble instance of her generosity. In the 2d. place, I devised as handsome, & respectful a letter as I could, in which I told her grace, that I

had had such an intention; but that I was so fully convinced by your arguments of the impracticability of it, that I had laid aside my intention—that I hoped her Grace therefore would not take amiss my returning the bill; as under the circumstances, I thought I could not accept it—that as the generosity convinced me of her Grace's partiality, I hoped she would allow me, if I ever did publish it, to place her name before it; & that not from any lucrative view; but from pure gratitude, & respect for her grace's character.' W. G. to W. Mason, 8 Nov. 1781 (W. L. Benson).

The Duchess died before the *Tour of the Lakes* was published, so it was to the Queen that Gilpin finally dedicated it in 1786.

[4] 24 March 1781 (Rev. E. G. Benson).

3d.   Very few good impressions, it is true, can be taken from the aquatinta plate (probably an 100) but I am assured, it may be so easily repaired, that it is of little consequence.[1]

For a while the second question remained unanswered. Allan Ramsay, when consulted, advised him to send his drawings to Paris to be etched there.[2] Finally, in July 1781, he decided to entrust the task to his young nephew, William Sawrey Gilpin, the son of Sawrey Gilpin, who at the age of twenty was embarking on an artistic career.[3] As Gilpin said to Edward Forster, 'I am persuaded . . . that an inferior artist under my own inspection will execute my ideas better, than a superior one at a distance.—I think I told you I have a nephew, who is making an essay.'[4]

At first all went well. W. S. Gilpin etched several plates by the end of 1781, and Mason, who had all along felt some doubts about aquatints, expressed his satisfaction with the proofs he received: 'The specimens of the Plates which you have sent me please me extreamly, and if they are able to print a sufficient number of impressions which they certainly will as far as the Etching goes, must answer your purpose compleatly, provided that the Aqua tinta part is repaired easily. I heartily wish your Engraver all possible success.'[5]

In August the letterpress was completed, but the plates were slow in forthcoming. In September Mason received the text of the *Wye Tour*, together with a proof set of the illustrations, 'which are much better executed than I thought was possible, & which if they will print off a sufficient number of good impressions are very much what they should be and therefore you have done rather ill in underating your relations abilitys.'[6]

Mason's secret fears were soon justified, and Gilpin had to confess the book was delayed, 'because some of the plates were etched on soft copper, which would not endure press-working; & they must be etched again on harder metal'.[7] Eventually the *Wye Tour* was

---

[1] 28 March 1781 (W. L. Benson).

[2] W. G. to Edward Forster, 24 July 1781 and 18 May 1789 (Rev. E. G. Benson—Brisco transcripts).

[3] The possibility of employing William Sawrey Gilpin (or even John Warwick Smith) was entertained as early as March 1781, as may be gathered by this extract of a letter from William Gilpin II to his father: 'I think I see thro' the meaning of what you have written . . . you would not I suppose have him [Sawrey Gilpin] build upon your employing his son to etch the plates for you: & it is true, tho' it were a pity he should be deprived of the profits arising from this part of your work, yet it were a 1000 pities the plates should not be well executed—If his son should not be found sufficient (tho' I hope he will) I should think the best person you could employ would be Smith should he come from abroad in time, as he has been partly under your direction before; but even he either could not or would not do them so well as you could do them yourself; but the office is every way unfit for you. Indeed I know not whether it would not be better policy to have some *artist of name* to do them; tho' I think not, for you could not

get him to follow instructions.' 16 March 1781 (Major J. R. Abbey).

[4] 24 July 1781 (Rev. E. G. Benson—Brisco transcript).

[5] W. Mason to W. G., 5 Jan. 1782 (Rev. E. G. Benson).

[6] W. Mason to W. G., 28 Sept. 1782 (Rev. E. G. Benson).

[7] W. G. to W. Mason, 9 Oct. 1782 (W. L. Benson). By December Gilpin was none too pleased: 'I suppose you wonder that you hear nothing of the Wye.—It was printed several months ago; but I understand there have been, and still are, great difficulties on account of the plates. Some were injured in working; and others were wrought on cop[p]er, which was too soft to bear the roller. When it will appear in its glory, I know not.—I have however desired Mr B[lamire], to send Mr Cay and you each a copy in it's present state.' W. G. to Edward Forster, 4 Dec. 1782 (Rev. E. G. Benson—Brisco transcript). Without examining a large number of copies of the first edition of the *Wye Tour*, it is difficult to say exactly how many of the illustrations required to be etched a second time. Certainly, two different plates were used to run off the 700 copies of illustrations 9 and 15.

published in the summer of 1783 (though dated 1782 on the title-page).[1] In it the reference made to W. S. Gilpin barely concealed Gilpin's disappointment with the aquatints: 'They were etched by a young man, a relation of mine, who had not yet had experience enough to execute the several details, with that masterly freedom, which I could wish: but his endeavours, I hope, have been tolerably successful in giving, what is more essential, the effect of the whole' (p. vi).

The whole affair had given Gilpin more trouble than he had anticipated; his nephew may have lacked experience but certainly not assiduity, and surely his willingness to etch fifteen plates, which were retouched many, many times, as Mason had predicted, before the 700 copies of the *Wye Tour* were ready, deserved a better reward than the faint praise Gilpin managed to summon. The plates were perhaps a little fussy for his taste—he would have preferred a more unified effect with fewer tonal values, yet W. S. Gilpin conveyed the spirit of his uncle's sketches better than anyone else in subsequent editions of the *Wye Tour*. Each plate represented a considerable amount of work in the way of etching, aquatint, and hand-coloured washes. The needle with thin lines in the distances and thicker ones in the foreground rendered very closely Gilpin's free strokes of the pen. Considerable variety of light, shade, and texture was conveyed by the aquatint, in some cases using as many as five tones on one plate. Lastly, when the plate was printed, it was given an overall wash and occasionally strengthened in the foreground with grey or light-brown [9. *e*].

When Gilpin published the *Wye Tour*, he did not make it sufficiently clear that the plates were illustrations of picturesque ideas and were certainly not to be taken as topographical drawings. On the whole the public was puzzled, and for years afterwards Gilpin had to explain over and over again exactly what his illustrations were meant to represent. Mason himself was among the perplexed, and his exchanges with Gilpin illustrate well the general misunderstanding.

As a drawer of existing scenes you are held as the greatest of *infidels*. If a Voyager down the river Wye takes out your Book, his very Boatman crys out, 'nay Sr you may look in vain there. no body can find one Picture in it the least like.' Sr Harry Inglef[i]eld (a man of great Virtù whom I know not) went thither on purpose to examine you, & found you outrageously deficient in point of verity. indeed if what he says be true you cannot even on your own principles defend yourself. But pray how did the Book sell? and how did the Plates wear? of the last I augure very ill from many copies I have seen.[2]

To which Gilpin replied:

you ask me about the Wye, whether it sells? Surprizingly: and it is very much admired. At least Blamire tells me so. He lets me know, what Lords, & Ladies, and bishops, & critics say of it: & sends me down reviews, & scraps of newspapers, & every thing to raise my vanity.[3] He wanted,

[1] *Observations on the River Wye, and several parts of South Wales, &c. relative chiefly to Picturesque Beauty; made In the Summer of the Year 1770 . . . .* London, R. Blamire, 1782 (abbreviation: *Wye Tour*).

[2] W. Mason to W. G., 8 Jan. 1784 (Rev. E. G. Benson).

[3] A result of his publishing the *Wye Tour* was a visit from Thomas Johnes (1784–1816), the translator of Froissart who lived at Hafod. Gilpin recounted the incident to Mason: 'last

3 months ago, to have undertaken another edition: but as the plates cannot supply the edition we have; & all, or a great part of our work would be to begin over-again, I opposed it. In the mean time, I beg you will present my compliments to sir Harry Inglefield, when you see him, & tell him, that he cannot think more contemptibly of my drawings, than I do myself. And you may tell him moreover that I never should have put them into my book (for I myself hate *pictured books*) if my friend Mr. Mason, & my friend Mr. this, & Mr. t'other, had not told me contrary to what I believed myself, that they were very fine. As I was obliged therefore to put them in, I did all I could to make people believe they were *general ideas*, or *illustrations*, or any thing, but, what they would have them to be, exact portraits; which I had neither time to make, nor opportunity, nor perhaps ability; for I am so attached to my picturesque rules, that if nature gets wrong, I cannot help putting her right.—Now I beg you will not go, & tell that silly speech to any body; but keep it to yourself.[1]

Mason was not one to take this banter lightly. He had been deceived as to the real nature of the drawings:

tho I do not know Sr H. I. by sight and have heard he is a great Coxcomb, yet I shrewdly suspect he is right in his Criticisms, because many other Persons agree with him in the same point. I remember several years when you insisted to me, 'that a taker of any real scene had a right to invent a foreground,' you said this to me (as I then beleivd & do still beleive [*sic*]) in defence of your own Practice. but then I never conceivd you claimd more, or that you might invent a second distance or an Offskip. If you do this. if you pay no regard to the shape of a principal Building, place it to the left instead of the right, or vicê versâ; If you give your distant Mountains a totally different shape &c &c I do not see how a drawing thus licentious can either be *illustrative* or give evn *a general Idea of a scene.* Now all these crimes are laid to your charge, & I think myself that the defence you make is not a sufficient one. Nevertheless, I shall never be ashamed of recommending your Tours as I did to the world, because I certainly recommended to them good descriptions as well as good Drawings. & if the latter were not what I beleivd them to be (for I had not seen the places where they were taken) I can be accus'd hardly of Ignorance.[2]

How pedestrian and patronizing he could be! Gilpin, for his part, took the earliest opportunity to explain his drawings, at some length, in the preface of the *Tour of the Lakes* (1786). The skirmishes with Mason on matters of taste help to illustrate two very different attitudes to nature which coexisted through much of the eighteenth century. Mason's Picturesque is confined within his *English Garden*, where art keeps nature within bounds. All therein is prim and tidy, and even disorder is organized. As a landscape gardener he remains influenced by the formalism of the classical garden. Gilpin's Picturesque is of the

week he paid me a visit; & brought with him a large port-folio, full of paintings (on paper) of a variety of views around his house. They were done by [Thomas] Jones, a pupil of Wilson. On the whole, they were not amiss, considering he is one of your *religious copyists*. But tho I could have criticized the paintings, I very much admired the views; which were both great & beautiful; & as far as I could judge from pictures, well managed. When I paid him some compliment on that head, he told me he had nothing to say to them. The walks & lawns were laid out by Mr. Mason; whose English garden he took in his hand; & wanted no other direction. So if you want to see an exact translation of your book into good Welsh, you must go to Mr. Johnes's seat in Cardiganshire. If I will go, he has promised; that his carriage shall meet me, where I please: so if you will go, you had better come hither, & we will go together.' 23 Apr. 1787 (W. L. Benson).

[1] W. G. to W. Mason, 12 Feb. 1784 (W. L. Benson).
[2] W. Mason to W. G., 13 March 1784 (Rev. E. G. Benson).

sublime kind. For him nature is also confined by the rules of art, but he works on the scale of nature herself and is really interested in her characteristic features.

The two men were to clash again over the contents of Gilpin's next publication, the *Tour of the Lakes*. When Gilpin confided that 'these prints are the very plague of my life',[1] Mason advised him to do without them and also strongly recommended that everything that could possibly offend should be excised from the text. This time, however, he exceeded his mandate; misplaced flattery was nullified by blunt and rude language which could not have been better calculated to wound Gilpin's self-esteem:

as to your Tour, I am still more persuaded than I was before that you should print only that part of it which relates to scenes, not to places, & particularly not to Houses. on this account I would wish the first volume almost totally omitted. The 2nd the 3d and as far as the Lakes go are amongst the very best, if not in themselves the very best, of your writings in this way, & tho you have been forstalld by numerous publications written since yours was of the scenes in question, yet what you say, you say so well, that it will totally eclipse all they have said, & you will be the only writer that will be read on the subject of the Lakes, Gray himself hardly excepted. After such a Compliment and that given from the heart, or rather from the Taste, I may surely venture to pronounce much of the rest of your Tour to be unequal to this, & to what you say of Dove dale, Matlock, & Solway Moss. As to your descriptions of Seats & Gardens Blenheim only excepted, they are often imperfect frequently *flippant*, & sometimes false. Could I shew you the very place from whence I write this [Nuneham], I am sure you would own you had committed all these three faults together when you described it. You certainly never saw either the Grecian Church, or the Terras leading from it towards the River. the Pictures you could not have examind, & indeed as to all your descriptions of Pictures I suspect your Judgment to be very cursory. Let me therefore persuade you to print only such parts of your work as relate 1st to natural Scenery, 2d Abbey Ruins, & 3d general views of the Country thro which you passt. these latter are necessary to the work as a Tour, & for proper Connection. If I give you leave to deviate it is only to Blenheim & Mr. Grahams, the latter for the sake of the singular event of the breaking of the Moss. As to Rokeby you are as imperfect there as at Nuneham, you take no notice of the Junction of the Tees & the Greata, which, tho not a beautiful thing in itself (except in a great flood) has many beautiful accompaniments. Be advised therefore from a friend to your Fame, as well as your Peace of mind; and do not print any thing that will either hurt or offend the Owners of Places, when in so doing, you will bring upon you much, & I fear, some well-deserved Criticism from Real Connoisseurs.'[2]

So Gilpin was no connoisseur! This was too much, and Mason got the answer he deserved:

I am mightily obliged to you for all your corrections, & illustrations of my travels. As far as I find, they might all lye with Homer in a nutshell, & not croud him. As for your wise advice about leaving out houses, & places—You are too late. That is, I was determined to cut short all those matters, long before I had your advice. In the first place, I would not wish, in a work meant to please, to give uneasiness; & in the 2d., I am as conscious, as you are, how very crude, & hasty, & inaccurate, many of those remarks are. In the place, where you are at present [Nuneham], I happened particularly to be caught by rain; & saw nothing but the house.—But now give me leave

---

[1] W. G. to W. Mason, 12 Feb. 1784 (W. L. Benson).   [2] W. Mason to W. G., 8 June 1784 (Rev. E. G. Benson).

to tell you, that I differ very much from you in thinking *my judgment cursory, with regard to pictures.* To tell you the real truth, I have as good an opinion of it, as the judgment of any person I know: but then, (as your Scotchman premised, that he liked his grapes sour, before he asserted, that he had eaten them in the highest perfection in Scotland;) I must tell you, that I form my judgment very differently from the judgment of the generality of people. I hold cheap, masters; & hands; & first manners; & second manners; & this mode of colouring; & that. I judge merely by my own ideas of composition, effect, harmony, character, & expression.—I assert, moreover, my own competency in judging even from a slight view: for it is one of my rules, that if a picture does not strike the eye at once, it is defective.—I must add however, before I leave the subject of houses, & places, that I look on you, as a very prejudiced man. Because you have written well on the subject, you think you have a right to set up art in competition with the great Goddess she should imitate. I see much of that spirit lurking about in the notes you wrote on my Forest-scenery.[1] If I could see the furniture of your heart, I have not the least doubt, but I should see pretty lawns, & flowering shrubs, & winding paths, & temples, hanging up in gold frames; while mountains, & rocks, & lakes, & forests, were thrown by in garrets. I often wish I had been acquainted with your friend Gray. I think he & I should have agreed wonderfully in our ideas of these things.'[2]

Gilpin had far more in common with Gray than with Mason. With the latter he remained on friendly terms and continued mistakenly to defer to his poetical judgement. As a serious critic, on the other hand, Mason was gradually ousted by the more reasonable voices of Forster, Mitford, Lock, and Mary Hartley. It was to William Lock that he turned when looking for artists to prepare the illustrations for the *Tour of the Lakes*. W. S. Gilpin, with his other engagements, could hardly be expected to etch all the plates which this larger work required.

But if he, & 2 or 3 more clever young fellows, would each undertake 8 or 10 plates, I think the

[1] As a sample, here are Mason's recommendations after reading the first book of the MS. of the *Remarks on Forest Scenery*: 'Having read this book over carefully and weighd it well not only in parts but as a whole I come with my desperate Hook or rather Scythe and sweep away without Mercy above 50 pages entirely. viz from the last paragraph p.153 to the end. Tis a trite exhausted subject. Pliny & Evelyn had each of them a huge Quantity of the Old Woman in their composition [and so for that matter has Mason!]. of the latters ... [*Sylva*, Dr. Andrew Hunter] a Scotch Physician at York printed [in 1776] a pompous & very expensive edition by subscription which you seem never to have seen & which I do not advise you to buy. in his notes there are measurements of more large Trees but like *more dying woods* they have little more importance. Keep to your Picturesque train of writing, and you are New Original & Entertaining, when you deviate from this, you write like an evryday writer. Dixi.'—'Remarks on *Trees* and their several *combinations*; (relative *chiefly* to Picturesque beauty;) illustrated by the *Scenes of New-forest* in Hampshire in three books', vol. i (W. L. Benson).

One of Mason's less-endearing traits was his hatred of everything Scottish, it even affected his picturesque ideas. In the same MS., Gilpin, speaking of the colour of the yew, made this observation on '*colour in general*': 'I think I speak the language of painting, when I assert, that the picturesque eye makes no great distinction in this matter. It has little, or no attachment to one colour in preference to another: but considers the beauty of all colouring, as resulting almost entirely from harmony. So that as the yew-tree is supported, combined, or stationed, it forms a beautiful umbrage, or a murky spot.' Mason could not agree: 'The Picturesque Eye expects that the foliage of a Tree should be *green*, it may be so dark as to approach even to Black, & it is not offended but sometimes highly pleasd, as in the yew & it may be light as the Willow or Aspin. but it must ever be disgusted with the Scotch fir which is the colour of dirt, muddy, and unlike evry other hue in foliation.'

[2] W. G. to W. Mason, 25 June 1784 (W. L. Benson). A sidelight on Gilpin's retort to Mason is provided by his answer to Edward Forster who had also been asked to make comments on the MS. of the *Remarks on Forest Scenery*: 'I have now looked over, all your criticisms . . . and I am much obliged to you for them, I think there are not above 3 or 4 of them, that I have not taken. You call yourself a sawcy remarker. I think you are a civil gentleman.—In comparison with Mason, you are polite.' 13 Sept. 1788 (Rev. E. G. Benson—Brisco transcript).

thing might be managed. If you should see my brother, I should be much obliged to you, dear sir, if you would talk the matter over with him; which can be much better done, than in a letter. When you see the drawings, you will be a better judge.[1]

The name of John Warwick Smith was suggested, and Gilpin was delighted:

If Smith would undertake a few of the drawings they cannot certainly be in better hands; & I should think, if the whole should be printed in 2 volumes, 9 or 10 drawings, in each volume, would be fully sufficient. To say the truth, I am rather desirous to print these papers. There has been so much said about them, that it looks like affectation to keep them longer.[2]

By the spring of 1784 it was decided that William Sawrey Gilpin and Smith should share the aquatints between them,[3] and Sawrey Gilpin would add six etchings of animals. Whereas for the *Wye Tour* the finished drawings seem to have been used as models for the plates, in the case of the *Tour of the Lakes* Gilpin made copies of such of those finished drawings as he wanted his artists to illustrate in aquatint, and these copies were of the same size as the desired etchings. Fortunately, one of these copies has survived, one of several sent to Smith. On the back of it he wrote directions which show how little importance he attached to exact reproduction, provided the artist conveyed his general intention:

This is a view on Ullswater towards Patterdale. On the left Martindale-fell falls with an abrupt step into the water. On the right two woody promontories pursue each other.—But as the view is meant rather to explain the country, than to give an exact portrait of it, Mr. Smith need not be closely confined to my lines. But it should be etched so as to present the same parts to the right, and left which in the 2 first drawings that were sent is not material.[4]

The *Tour* made its appearance at the end of 1786.[5] For a year Gilpin had again been delayed by the plates,[6] and this time Smith seems to have been the chief culprit. In October 1786 two plates remained to be completed. However, he reassured Mason that as soon as the *Tour of the Lakes* was ready,

it means to pay it's first compliments to you—you, who took it under your protection, when it was a poor sniveling vagabond—introduced it into good company; & gave it the little consequence it had.—In the course of my work I found reason to be dissatisfyed with Smith; & towards the conclusion of it, I met with a Mr. Alkin[7] [*sic*], who has pleased me much. He has done only 2 plates;

[1] W. G. to William Lock, 12 Dec. 1783 (Rev. E. G. Benson).

[2] W. G. to William Lock, 28 Feb. 1784 (Rev. E. G. Benson).

[3] W. G. to W. Mason, 22 Apr. 1784 (W. L. Benson).

[4] Iolo A. Williams Collection. Drawing and directions reproduced in I. A. Williams, 'The Reverend William Gilpin', *The Bookman*, 1933, pp. 120–1.

[5] *Observations, relative chiefly to Picturesque Beauty, Made in the Year 1772, On several Parts of England; particularly the Mountains, and Lakes of Cumberland, and Westmoreland . . . .* London, R. Blamire, 1786, 2 vols. (abbreviation: *Tour of the*

Lakes). Major J. R. Abbey wrongly attributes the plates to William Gilpin (*Scenery of Great Britain and Ireland in Aquatint and Lithography 1770–1860*, London, 1952, item 183). Four of Sawrey Gilpin's plates were ovals. In subsequent editions, his six animal plates filled the whole page.

[6] 'My book is printed: but when it will be published, I know not. I am delayed by artists.' W. G. to W. Mason, 2 Dec. 1785 (W. L. Benson). See also W. G. to Mary Hartley, 1 March 1786 (Rev. E. G. Benson—Brisco transcript).

[7] Samuel Alken (*c.* 1750—*c.* 1825), aquatint engraver who did much of his early work for Gilpin. In 1796 he gave his address as Nº 2, Francis Street East, Bedford Square. Consult

but there is great softness in his manner,[1] which, tho not so pleasing to my eye as the free scratches of a rough etching, is yet much better accommodated, I should suppose, to the publick.[2]

At the beginning of December Gilpin plunged into fresh arrangements:

When I was in London, I concluded with Blamire about a 2d. edition of the Wye. He had often been talking with me about it: but as we must have new plates, I did not care to engage in the trouble. However it was brought about thus. You have probably heard me say, I was not quite satisfyed with Smith, one of my artists. I thought he rather slighted my work. I believe he was himself rather conscious of it; for when I was in London, he called upon me with a large folio full of drawings, which he had made last summer on the banks of the Wye; & in different parts of S. Wales. They were only sketches: but masterly. Some of these he was to etch; which I was to pick out. In short we concluded on this scheme; that he was to etch, (in the manner of Both; not in aqua-tinta) a few plates of illustrations, (no portraits), for a 2d. edition of the Wye; & in the preface, I promised to refer to, & recommend his larger etchings, as portraits, appending to the work. I should hope, he will make both my plates, & his own very clever.—I called also upon . . . Mr. Alkin, who . . . engages to do 30 plates in 2 years, on any work I shall set him. I think of my Scotch expedition.[3]

The scheme, whereby Smith was to etch illustrations to Gilpin's text and provide eight to twelve large aquatint 'portraits', fell through by September 1787.[4] Instead of reprinting the *Wye Tour* Gilpin concentrated on bringing out the *Scottish Tour* and a second edition of the *Tour of the Lakes*. The young Samuel Alken, unlike Smith, proved a most reliable artist, who endeavoured to adapt his manner to suit Gilpin's wishes. He was to have a long career as a prolific aquatintist.

By January 1788 Alken had completed nine or ten plates for the *Scottish Tour*.[5] Gilpin found some of them 'admirable', though he confided to Forster: 'I am quite of your opinion about the neatness of the etching in the Scotch tour, and if I could have them done more roughly, I should like it better: but the world, which Blamire thinks the most intelligent judge, is of a different opinion: so such unfashionable folks as you, and I must submit.'[6]

As few shared his predilection for the rougher method of etching, Gilpin bowed to public taste, which from the King downwards preferred smooth, neat, and tidy drawings.[7] This

Major J. R. Abbey's *Life in England, in Aquatint and Lithography, 1770–1860*, London, 1953, and *Scenery of Great Britain and Ireland.*

[1] 'He tints them without any etched line, which gives them great softness.' W. G. to E. Forster, 23 Dec. 1786 (Rev. E. G. Benson—Brisco transcript).

[2] W. G. to W. Mason, 19 Oct. 1786 (W. L. Benson).

[3] W. G. to W. Mason, 25 Dec. 1786 (W. L. Benson).

[4] W. G. to E. Forster, 23 Dec. 1786 (Rev. E. G. Benson—Brisco transcript); W. G. to W. Mason, 25 Oct. 1787 (W. L. Benson).

[5] W. G. to E. Forster, 14 Jan. 1788 (Rev. E. G. Benson—Brisco transcript). Two of the plates were of Inveraray Castle and the hill of Doniquoich.

[6] W. G. to E. Forster, 13 Sept. 1788 (Rev. E. G. Benson—Brisco transcript).

[7] 'The poor king, who had seen several of my drawings, was speaking of them lately to a friend of mine, only a little time before he was taken ill; Well, he said, I must confess, I like to see something more neat: & I believe nine in ten are of his Majesty's opinion.' W. G. to Mary Hartley, 19 Dec. 1788 (W. L. Benson).

Mary Hartley, in her reply, endorsed public opinion, and refused to be considered as much of a 'rough genius' as Gilpin tended to assume she was: 'I am very glad that the young man who is etching the plates for your Highland Tour, is doing them in a neat manner; for it is true indeed that all the world is of the King's opinion, they all desire to see something neat.

did not prevent him making experiments. In October 1788 Alken came down to Vicar's Hill, to settle final arrangements about the *Scottish Tour*. Their meeting also had this result, as Gilpin reported to Mason: 'we had some conversation about a rougher method; & he has taken 2 drawings of mine to town, to try them in a method, I have prescribed—tho not for this work [*Scottish Tour*]. Alkin is a very good sort of man; & a very ingenious man too; for he assures me my drawings are superior to any he knows for producing an effect on copper.'[1]

The *Scottish Tour* appeared in the spring of 1789.[2] Alken also did the plates for the second edition (1792), making greater use of the etching needle.[3] By then Gilpin felt the public would accept a rougher effect.

The *Tour of the Lakes* had proved such a success that a second edition was quickly rushed through. As regards the prints, Gilpin's plan was:

every artist takes his own, & does them over again: but I do not recollect any new prints, except one of Warwick-castle, & another of Dovedale.[4] My brother has done his six here; & I think greatly better than the old six. He has done them, not in ovals; but the full size of the plate. They have no aqua tinta on them, which he could not manage: but I think they are admirable.[5]

Sawrey Gilpin's soft-ground etchings were made on a prepared ground of bee's wax and lard; the process was explained to Forster:

The mode of etching on *soft-ground* is this: You make your drawing; giving it its effect: if you make it only with black-lead, it is enough. You then trace the out-lines, through a window, on soft silky paper. When this is done, you take your cop[p]er-plate, with soft-ground upon it, and fold your paper with traced out-lines tight over the plate. Placing your drawing before you, you then with a sharp black-lead pencil, make a copy of it upon the traced line. The point of the pencil licks off the soft-ground from the plate at every stroke: so that on your silky paper you have a black-lead drawing on one side; and on the reverse a drawing, stroke for stroke the same. On your plate

---

Ignorant people know of no other merit; & I have had many battles with such persons, about your last plates [*Tour of the Lakes*]. they said they were nothing but blots, & they cou'd copy them in a moment. So they did; but without the spirit, without the genius, without the effect—no force of light & shade—no keeping between the fore-grounds & the different distances—nothing in tune! *So copied* they were indeed blots; yet Papas & Mamas wou'd say, that "Miss had copied them exactly like the originals, you cou'd not know the difference." —But indeed I do not think that I am myself quite so fond of the rough stile as you are. I like to see the objects a little made out; tho I wou'd not, for the sake of that, abate one jot of spirit & genius, nor lose the least effect of light & shade; indeed I am so very eager after that, that in my own drawings I frequently blot out whole groups of trees or objects of any kind, that I have taken the greatest pains about, to cover them all with one dark shade that hides almost every touch, in case it appears to me that such an alteration wou'd give a better effect of light & shade.' 3 Jan. 1789 (W. L. Benson).

[1] 29 Oct. 1788 (W. L. Benson). One of the early professional aquatintists, Alken inspired confidence by his thorough-

ness: 'The prints of the Highland tour, Blamire tells me, will be all equally good: for Mr. Alkin, who etches them, takes them off also himself; & will retouch each plate, as he observes it begins to wear.' W. G. to M. Hartley, 29 Feb. 1789 (W. L. Benson).

[2] *Observations, relative chiefly to Picturesque Beauty, Made in the Year 1776, on Several Parts of Great Britain; particularly the High-Lands of Scotland . . . .* London, R. Blamire, 1789, 2 vols. (abbreviation: *Scottish Tour*).

[3] W. G. to W. Mason, 16 Feb. 1792 (W. L. Benson), and W. G. to his brother Sawrey, c. September 1791 (Rev. E. G. Benson—Brisco transcript). To the *Scottish Tour* Sawrey contributed a soft-ground etching of 'The head of a Lancashire cow'.

[4] New plates were necessary because of considerable alterations to Warwick Castle and changes in the appearance of Dovedale. See W. G. to E. Forster, 28 Jan. 1788 (Rev. E. G. Benson—Brisco transcript) and letters of W. U. Wray to W. G. in 1787 (W. L. Benson).

[5] W. G. to W. Mason, 25 Oct. 1787 (W. L. Benson).

of course the cop[p]er is laid bare, stroke for stroke, like them both. Round this you make your hedge of wax; and bite it in the common way with aqua-fortis: only your aquafortis must be well diluted, or in its rage it would tear up a ground, so little fitted to resist it.[1]

Of the original team of artists employed on the first edition of the *Tour of the Lakes*, someone defaulted: it may have been Smith or William Sawrey Gilpin. Anyhow, when the second edition was published in the spring of 1788, it contained several plates by a new young aquatintist, Francis Jukes.[2]

Mason, as the original patron of the *Tour*, received an early copy. He managed to praise Sawrey Gilpin's soft-ground etchings and reserved his venom for the contents. The basis of his discontent, this time, was that Gilpin had listened to his picturesque critics to say nothing of such '*Cattle*' as reviewers, and so altered the text of the *Tour of the Lakes* as to make it unrecognizable. Mason failed to realize the considerable development that was taking place in Gilpin's descriptive powers of the phenomena of nature in the 1780's, which made him constantly revise and expand the manuscripts of his *Tours*. Here is the little altercation between the two. Mason, in misogynist mood, writes first:

Some ten Years ago when you had given me your western Tour. I shewed it to a Person eminent both in Learning & taste. He read it with avidity. he declared it to be a model for descriptive writing. so strong and withal so simple, no strained metaphors, no forced expressions, no affectation of fine writing, but purity of Language itself &c &c. I saw him again a month after your last Lake tour was published, when he accosted me thus Verbatim. 'I am sorry for your friend Mr. Gilpin[.] You know how much I admired that Manuscript of his which you shewed me. Poor Man, his style is quite spoild! I cannot account for it but in one way (You can tell me whether I am right) Has he not of late been much flatterd by the Women? He writes as if he had.' I told him I hoped you had more sense; it was true you lived near a public watering Place—'Aye there it is, your she Coxcombs always are to be met with at such places in Summer. Tis a great pity! I think you told me he never lived much in the world when he was younger. they have imposed upon the unwary simplicity of his temper; I hope it will do him no further harm; but as a writer they have effectually undone him.' Now as all this actually past in our conversation, & as you tell me that you are revising & correcting all your tours, which I construe into making them fit for the perusal of the Ladies, I think I shall do well to keep my Copy of the Western tour as an Estate in fee, not as I now hold it for Life only, in order that Posterity may learn that you could once write like a Man.[3]

Had he lived, Mason would certainly have found it difficult to recognize the *Western Tour*, as it was published in 1798. In his reply Gilpin kept up the banter and gave him back some of his own medicine—he had now got his measure:

I was much mortifyed with what you said about my book; as people commonly are, when they are disappointed in those they esteem. I thought you had been a man of true, picturesque taste: but

---

[1] W. G. to E. Forster, 28 Jan. 1788 (Rev. E. G. Benson—Brisco transcript).

[2] For Francis Jukes (1746–1812), painter and aquatint engraver, consult the article in Thieme–Becker, *Allgemeines Lexikon der bildenden Künstler,* and Major J. R. Abbey's *Life in* *England in Aquatint and Lithography,* and *Scenery of Great Britain and Ireland.* Jukes gave his address in 1789 as 10 Howland Street, and in 1797 as 57 John St., Fitzroy Square.

[3] 25 June 1788 (Rev. E. G. Benson).

I find you know nothing of the matter. My book is a test. It is impossible, that any body, who does not relish those animated descriptions—that glow of colouring—those brilliant touches, which are striking in every part of it; can have any just conceptions of the beauties of Nature; or of the imitations of her disciple.—Get you along—get you along, you & your friend, out of the precincts of taste. Go, cultivate some clod of earth. In the regions of landscape—of lights, & shades, & glowing tints, you have nothing to do.—I write for ladies!—No, sir,—nor for such critics as you, & your cold, unanimated friend. I write merely, & solely for people of picturesque genius—whether gentlemen, or ladies, I reck not. From them I look for praise; & I have it in ample measure.[1]

It was Mason's turn to feel hurt, so Gilpin began his next letter:

As I find I have dreadfully offended you by turning you out of Nature's garden, (you may walk about an English garden as much as you please) I begin to relent; & shall make interest with the head-gardener to get you admittance again: only you must learn not to be abusive, & swear at any of Nature's under-gardeners; for they are generally men of spirit, & cannot brook ill-usage.[2]

In the summer of 1788 Gilpin set about reprinting the *Wye Tour*, delayed through Smith's defection. Though Smith voluntarily offered again, he was firmly turned down and the illustrations were entrusted to Jukes, who 'etched some of our best plates in the 2d. edition of the Lakes'. As far as we know, this was the last time Gilpin had any dealings with John Warwick Smith. The second edition, published in April 1789, contained two more plates than the first. Whereas W. S. Gilpin had made considerable use of etching, Francis Jukes relied entirely on aquatint, drawing directly on the prepared ground with washes of aqua fortis. The result was not very satisfactory [9. *f*]. As Mary Hartley rightly observed:

I can not say myself that I like the present method of working with the aqua tinta *only*, so well as I did the mixture of that & the etching needle. I have just seen the last edition of the tour to the Wye, with the new prints; but tho they have a stronger opposition of the light, (& in *some parts* I cou'd almost think *too* strong) yet I do not think there is so much spirit in the drawing, nor such good forms in many of the objects, as there was in the prints of the first edition.[3]

The next work to be printed was *Remarks on Forest Scenery*. One day in July 1790 Blamire came down to Vicar's Hill determined to secure the manuscript. Gilpin's reluctance to part with a work he felt could be further improved, was finally overcome when Mrs. Gilpin sided with Blamire, who 'carried it off in triumph'.[4] Though hurried with the text, the prints had been prepared some years earlier and were ready. In 1787 Sawrey stayed with him three weeks 'making characters of bucks & stags, & does & hinds, & new forest horses, & asses; & horse's tails',[5] and in the middle of November 1789 he came again to

---

[1] 3 July 1788 (W. L. Benson). Later, he confided to Forster, after saying that he still possessed all his teeth: 'Mason tells me has lost all his: but he snarls, and bites as much as ever. But I mind neither him, nor Cay.— You are a quiet man; and so is your affectionate Will Gilpin' 24 July 1793 (Rev. E. G. Benson—Brisco transcript).

[2] W. G. to W. Mason, 19 Aug. 1788 (W. L. Benson).
[3] M. Hartley to W. G., 23 Oct. 1789 (W. L. Benson).
[4] W. G. to Mary Hartley, 18 Sept. 1790 (Rev. E. G. Benson—Brisco transcript).
[5] W. G. to W. Mason, 17 Sept. 1787 (W. L. Benson).

complete his set of nine soft-ground etchings.[1] Published in the summer of 1791,[2] the *Remarks on Forest Scenery* also contained aquatints by Alken—with these Gilpin was very pleased, as Alken had succeeded in conveying the rougher method advocated in October 1788. Sawrey Gilpin and Alken repeated their plates for the second edition of 1794.[3]

Mason received his copy of *Remarks on Forest Scenery* in June 1791. This gave him an opportunity to air another grievance:

I find nothing that much offends me, save your Panegyric on Scotch firs, which as it brings to remembrance the tiresome walk which you made me once take to *admire* a group of those swine of the vegitable race, I cannot bear with Patience. Were you now with me I would out of revenge carry you to Worsop manner, where about forty years ago Lord Peter a great Clumper scatterd thousands of them on the side of Sherwood forest in various Patches. the better taste of the Dutchess of Norfolk employd Brown some fifteen years after to cloth all the shelving Hill, which these wretches had not occupied, so as to form one large connected Wood, with Oaks Elms &c &c The Idea was a good one, & Browns plantations are now as tall & flourishing as Lord Peter's. But so discordant an effect no Plantation surely did ever produce This I do not say to convince you, because I know you will not be convinced. I say it merely to assert my own opinion, that Scotch firs accord with no other Tree in the creation.[4]

As might be expected Gilpin stood his ground on picturesque principles. His answer was conciliatory:

as to your other assertion, that *fir-trees will harmonize with no other trees in the creation*, it is equally founded in want of picturesque knowledge. That you should dislike the *mode of growth* in a Scotch-fir *at hand*, I could easily reconcile to myself. But that you should object to a *distant* mass of Scotch-firs, which are dark, mixed with ever-greens, which are lighter, is to me the same as objecting to the power of light & shade. That Lord Peter's woods, (of which I have heard, tho I never saw them) should be disgusting, I can readily believe: but it is not because Scotch-firs, & deciduous trees are *mixed*: but because they are mixed in *patches*, instead of *masses*. *I say not this however to*

[1] W. G. to Mary Hartley, 16 Nov. 1789 (W. L. Benson). When Gilpin sent Mason a print of 'The ass, and the mule compared', the latter replied: 'tho no body holds your brother in his own peculiar art higher than I do. yet I am not so much an elegans spectator formarum animalium as to enter into the merits of his mule & ass. I took his mule for a horse with a bad tail & his Ass for a decent kind of an ordinary mule. so too did my Curate who returns his compliments if after such a confession you will accept them. But a clergyman who visited me & who was once my curate, & who also understands a Horse, as they say, perfectly admired the two etchings so much & thought them so highly *characteristic* that he was highly pleased when I made him a present of them. if your brother ever etches a common Ass, on a road side, mumbling a thistle, with large flapping ears, over a large sapient rugged forehead, send me a copy and I will thank you. let me have an Ass with a skull large enough to contain that quantity of brains with which genuine Asses seem always over weighted & which with me marks the *character* of the species. His is a Lady Coventry sort of Ass, who was remarkable for a small head.' N.d., after 18 May 1790 (Rev. E. G. Benson).

[2] *Remarks on Forest Scenery, and other Woodland Views, (relative chiefly to Picturesque Beauty) illustrated by the Scenes of New-Forest in Hampshire* . . . . London, R. Blamire, 1791, 2 vols. (abbreviation: *Remarks on Forest Scenery*).

[3] Major J. R. Abbey wrongly attributes the plates of the second edition of 1794 to William Gilpin (*Scenery of Great Britain and Ireland*, item 149 and plate 6). Two of the oval aquatints by Samuel Alken are described as 'Two soft ground etchings by William Gilpin'! Towards the end of the 'Catalogue of Prints', Gilpin identified his artists: 'Of these drawings all the landscape part, which I hope the public will think with me is very masterly, was executed by Mr. Alkin. The animals if I am not prejudiced in favor of the artist [Sawrey Gilpin], who etched them, are excellent.' The last of the soft-ground etchings is signed 'S. Gilpin'.

[4] W. Mason to W. G., 15 June 1791 (Rev. E. G. Benson).

convince you, because I know you will not be convinced. And yet the thing being so palpably plain, it will give me an opinion of your candour, if you will own yourself for once in a mistake. I allow you, you see, to object to the *shape* of the fir-tree—I allow you also to object to the *colour* of it, if you please, *when at hand*: but when distance removes it's *bluish tint*, & nothing but *dark green* appears, you may as well, as I observed before, object to the value of shade. I have at this instant before my eye a *clump* (I beg pardon) a *tuft*, composed of Scotch firs & elms, at the distance of about half a quarter of a mile; & I am sure you could not—at least I cannot—perceive there is a Scotch fir in it: but the effect is good.[1]

As soon as the *Remarks on Forest Scenery* was finished, he turned his attention to the *Three Essays*. The plates, which were to be the same size as the full page, were commissioned, by September 1790, from an artist whom he does not name.[2] It was perhaps Jukes, for the plates are done entirely in aquatint in a manner similar to those of the *Wye Tour* second edition of 1789. The *Three Essays*, together with a *Poem on Landscape Painting*, were published early in 1792.[3] There had been some delay, for Gilpin wanted one of the plates hand coloured to illustrate his method of tinting. This tedious task was entrusted to his nephew, W. S. Gilpin.[4] The full-page aquatints did not please Gilpin very much; as he confided to Mason, they 'are not so good as Alkin would have made them; but this to yourself'.[5] Alken, as we have seen, had at this time as much work as he could cope with. Besides providing plates for the *Remarks on Forest Scenery* and the *Scottish Tour*, he was also doing the aquatints for the third edition of the *Tour of the Lakes* (1792), to which Sawrey Gilpin contributed six signed soft-ground etchings.

For some time Gilpin had noticed that his plates were stained very unevenly. He advocated the use of a pale overall wash, 'to take off the glaring rawness of white paper; and to harmonize by a mellow tint, the unpleasant opposition of black and white'.[6] A few aquatints had been so glaringly stained that readers thought he was trying to reproduce a natural effect. This was never his intention. Even where colouring was attempted he thought it should always be chaste, for to attempt natural colouring 'generally turns what may be a good print, or a good drawing, into a glaring daub'. This he made clear in the *Three Essays* and in a manuscript 'Advertisement' to the only set of prints he tinted himself.[7]

---

[1] W. G. to W. Mason, 29 June 1791 (W. L. Benson). Mason's answer brought his anti-Scottish feeling to a climax: 'Now for your second Letter. out of which I expunge all that relates to Scotch firs as unworthy of answer; Lady B[ute, whose stewardship Gilpin's former curate, R. Holden, had failed to secure] not more so, who I verily believe would not have acted as she did, had she not been married to a Scotchman. & as you allow that they do best at a distance (I mean the trees) so do I *opine* of evry thing that is scotch. At the remotest distance then let us cast evry scotch subject in our future correspondence.' 5 Aug. 1791 (Rev. E. G. Benson).

[2] W. G. to W. Mason, 3 Sept. 1790 (W. L. Benson).

[3] *Three Essays: on Picturesque Beauty; on Picturesque Travel; and on Sketching Landscape: to which is added a poem, on Landscape Painting . . . .* London, R. Blamire, 1792 (abbreviations:

Three Essays and *Poem on Landscape Painting*).

[4] In the 'Explanation of the Print', Gilpin acknowledged his nephew's assistance: 'It [i.e. print facing p. 79] was coloured by a relation of mine; Mr. Gilpin, drawing-master at Paddington-green; who in all the copies I have seen, has illustrated my ideas very satisfactorily; and who, as far as the recommendation of a partial kinsman may go, deserves mine.'

[5] 16 Feb. 1792 (W. L. Benson).

[6] *Remarks on Forest Scenery*, 2nd ed., 1794, ii, 'A Catalogue of Prints'.

[7] See the four-page instructions on tinting prints or black and white drawings, inserted in a copy of the *Wye Tour* (3rd ed., 1792). This volume, purchased by Samuel Rogers at the 1802 sale (lot 122) for £2. 12s. 6d., is now in the possession of Mr. Charles Tomrley.

A third edition of the *Wye Tour* also appeared in 1792 to complete a most intensive year.

A second edition of the *Three Essays* was soon called for, and this time Gilpin secured the services of Alken. He was very pleased with the result.[1] The plates were ready by the autumn of 1792, and the edition appeared in 1794.

Probably towards the end of 1793 Samuel Alken, on one of his periodic visits to Gilpin, secured from him six drawings, from which he made large tinted aquatints (full plate $7\frac{13}{16} \times 11\frac{1}{4}$ in.). These he sold to R. Blamire who published the *Six Landscapes* in February 1794.[2] They were the first prints after Gilpin which Alken signed. The unsold stock was taken over by Darling & Thompson, and T. Simpson, and reissued by them on 1 January 1799.[3]

In 1796 Gilpin, to his regret, lost Blamire, who went bankrupt. After some negotiations, he changed over to Cadell & Davies, who acquired the unsold stock of the *Tours*, and agreed to meet Blamire's debts. By now Gilpin had decided not to print any further picturesque works; his executors would be free to publish whatever remained at his death, for the benefit of the school he had established at Boldre. Nevertheless, he was persuaded in the summer of 1797 to print the last of his major works, the *Western Tour*.[4] For this Alken had already made the plates, which he sold to Gilpin for £70.[5] The book was published in the summer of 1798.[6]

[1] 'Alkin has made a new & excellent set of plates for them, and I will bribe you with them, if you will do me any bribe-worthy service.' W. G. to W. Mason, 25 Oct. 1792 (W. L. Benson).

[2] *Six Landscapes, from Drawings By the Reverend Mr. Gilpin, engraved By S. Alken. Printed for R. Blamire, No. 5, Strand.* (original blue wrapper). Each plate is signed: 'Drawn by the Rev.d Mr. Gilpin | Engraved by S. Alken', and bears the imprint: 'London. Pub. Feb.y 1.st 1794. by R. Blamire No. 5. Strand.', with minor variations of punctuation. A complete set is in the collection of Major J. R. Abbey (JA 2926).

[3] *Six Landscapes, from Drawings By the Reverend Mr. Gilpin; Engraved By S. Alken. London:—Published, January 1, 1799, by Darling and Thompson, Great Newport Street; and T. Simpson, St. Paul's Church-Yard* (original grey wrapper). Each plate is signed: 'Drawn by the Rev.d Mr. Gilpin | Engraved by S. Alken', and bears the imprint: 'London Published Nov.r 1. 1798. by Darling & Thompson, G.t Newport Street, and T. Simpson, S.t Paul's Church Yard.', with minor variants of punctuation. A complete set is in the collection of Mrs. John Perkins.

Templeman (op. cit., pp. 213 and 232) wrongly attributes to Gilpin five aquatint 'illustrations of scenery on the South Coast of England, &c.', 1794. This is due to an incorrect entry in the Hornby catalogue. Dr. G. Chandler, the Liverpool City Librarian, kindly explained to me that the composite volume in question contains five of Gilpin's *Six Landscapes*, engraved by S. Alken in 1794; and that these are preceded by five prints by Peter Pindar (John Wolcott), also engraved by S. Alken,

which are similar in character and represent scenes on the south coast of Cornwall.

[4] See *Samuel Rogers and William Gilpin*, pp. 41–43, for role played by Samuel Rogers and Richard Sharp in persuading Gilpin to publish the *Western Tour*.

'I am going to print the *improved* copy of that book, so perhaps you will hardly think the other worth seeing [Mason's copy].—So many of my friends have told me (you I think among the rest) that I shall make more of it as a *school-fund* by printing it now, than by defering it to my death, that I am comed to a resolution about it.—I think it will not make more than one good volume in 8vo:—I wrot to Cadell about it, who I think, has treated me very liberally. He said he did not believe the plates would take off more, than 750 impressions, (nor indeed will they, without retouching) and for an edition of that number, together with the plates, he offers me £250, that is at 180 for the letter-press, and £70 for the plates. I told him I thought he had offered very handsomely, so far as an impression of 750 copies: but that I was persuaded, the plates with retouching, would do more: so we understood one another, that he is to have the copy-right, as soon as he can ascertain the value of it.' W. G. to E. Forster, 13 Nov. 1797 (Rev. E. G. Benson—Brisco transcript).

[5] W. G. to E. Forster, 14 June 1797 (Rev. E. G. Benson—Brisco transcript).

[6] *Observations on the Western Parts of England, relative chiefly to Picturesque Beauty. To which are added, A Few Remarks on the Picturesque Beauties of the Isle of Wight.* London, Cadell & Davies, 1798 (abbreviation: *Western Tour*).

It remains for me to mention briefly the remaining editions of his picturesque works. Of the artists who were concerned we know nothing, except that Sawrey redid his plates. The *Wye Tour* reached a fifth edition in 1800; earlier that year it was issued as a pocket volume without plates.[1] The *Southern Tour* appeared in 1804,[2] the year of Gilpin's death; the *Eastern Tour* and the *North Wales Tour* in 1809, together in one volume.[3] Lastly, Cadell & Davies issued in 1808 editions of the *Tour of the Lakes*, the *Scottish Tour*, the *Western Tour*, and the *Remarks on Forest Scenery*.

Sawrey Gilpin assisted his brother in one more undertaking. As an additional means of raising funds for his school, Gilpin conceived, in 1798, the idea of adding to the sale catalogue of his drawings an explanatory essay of the 'Principles, on which the drawings are executed':

I have a design, [he told Mary Hartley,] if he will suffer me, to do credit to his art in drawing small figures, in which he particularly excells. I have ordered a catalogue, which is already made, to be printed before the sale; & at the end of this catalogue I give an acco[u]nt (a modest one you will suppose) of my own drawings, & the principles on which they are made. In this little essay, which will swell my catalogue to the value at least of ½ a crown, I speak of the ornament of figures: & have gotten from him some very good remarks on this subject, which I mean to introduce as his, together with an explanatory plate, which I shall get him to etch for me.[4]

By the time the essay came out in 1802, it was illustrated with three plates of figures, etched by Sawrey Gilpin.[5] After the Christie sale of drawings, Gilpin found that

[1] The small pocket-size fourth edition of the *Wye Tour* (1800), contained this 'Advertisement': 'As the plates which adorned the former impressions of this little work are much worn, it seemed better to give a new edition without any prints, than with such as the plates could now furnish.—And as the plates are out of the question, a more portable size seemed more convenient to such travellers as think it worth their while to take these observations along with them.' Later, that same year, a fifth edition appeared, complete with seventeen plates as before. This time the 'Advertisement' read: 'As this little work is still thought worth the notice of the public, a new edition of it in large octavo hath been printed, with a set of new etchings, as the old plates were too much worn to be of further use.'

[2] *Observations on the coasts of Hampshire, Sussex, and Kent, relative chiefly to Picturesque Beauty: made in the summer of the year 1774* . . . . London, Cadell & Davies, 1804 (abbreviation: *Southern Tour*). Some copies have on the title-page the additional information: 'Published by his Trustees, for the benefit of his school at Boldre.'

[3] *Observations on several parts of the Counties of Cambridge, Norfolk, Suffolk, and Essex. Also on several parts of North Wales; relative chiefly to Picturesque Beauty, in Two Tours, the former made in the year 1769. The latter in the year 1773.* . . . London, Cadell & Davies, 1809 (abbreviations: *Eastern Tour* and *North Wales Tour*).

[4] 9 Aug. 1798 (W. L. Benson).

[5] *A Catalogue of Drawings, and Books of Drawings, to be sold (On Thursday the 6th May 1802) for the Endowment of a Parish-School, at Boldre, near Lymington, in Hampshire. To this Catalogue is added the Author's Account of the Drawings contained in it; and of the Principles, on which they are executed* . . . . London, Cadell & Davies, 1802.

William Gilpin had asked his brother in September 1798 to draw four figures on a sheet. On finding to his dismay that his specific instructions had been disregarded, he sent Sawrey this brotherly letter: 'My dear Sawrey—I have received your letter, and figures, and return you many thanks. You are a very good man, and an excellent painter—you practice all the duties of your religion, and can touch a small figure with more spirit than any man I know. But notwithstanding you so beautifully mix your religion, and your profession together, (for which I love, and admire you) you are in the language of the vulgar a little *pig-headed*: at the same time taking far more pains (which was always your infirmity) than you needed to have done. I remember once seeing some ladies in a play, dance to a piece of musick, which began, *Double, double toil and trouble*; which I assure you has more than once put me in mind of you. Now by way of instance to this charge, which notwithstanding my gratitude to you, I cannot help producing, you will be pleased to remember, that I begged of you once, twice, if not three, or four times, to take a piece of paper, of which I gave you demensions, and a reason at the same time, that it fitted in size the place it was designed for. On which piece of paper I begged you would sketch me four figures, which also I pointed out. All this seemed very plain: but instead of executing it,

300–400 copies of the catalogue remained unsold. He determined to make good use of them. The catalogue part would be replaced by a fifteen-page account of his school.[1]

Finally he printed another essay, 'On the mode of executing rough sketches', which was bound together with the remaining stock of the other essay; the two were published in 1804 as the *Two Essays*.[2] The essay 'On the mode of executing rough sketches' was illustrated with four full-page aquatints. The *Two Essays* were reprinted in 1808, and added to the third edition of the *Three Essays* under the general half-title of *Five Essays on Picturesque Subjects; with a Poem on Landscape Painting*.[3]

This chapter comes to an end with a few remarks on *Gilpin's Day*, a publication which testifies to Gilpin's popularity for some years after his death. At the 1802 sale, James Forbes, F.R.S., had purchased a number of lots, among them an album of twenty-four landscapes, entitled 'Morning, Noon and Evening', and six other landscapes; from these thirty drawings J. Hamble and M. Dubourg[4] made large oblong aquatints, which were published by Edward Orme, in 1810, as *The Last Work published by the Rev. William Gilpin . . .; representing the effect of a Morning, a Noon Tide, and an Evening Sun*, usually called *Gilpin's Day* from its half-title. Some uncoloured sets of these aquatints, printed in buff and stone colour, were issued in 1811.[5] At the same time, John Heaviside Clark, the author of *A Practical Essay on the Art of Colouring and Painting Landscapes in Water Colours* (1807), took the same plates to demonstrate his own colouring technique, and produced a sumptuous volume, *A Practical Illustration of Gilpin's Day*, issued in 1811 and again in 1824.[6] Clark considerably altered the original character of *Gilpin's Day*. The

we have, over and again, the tune of *Double, double toil and trouble*. A piece of paper is taken nearly twice the size of that I had prescribed; and instead of four figures, you give me six; pretending you knew better my intention, than I knew it myself. I readily allow, that if you had yourself finished this little business, you would have made it a much better thing, than I could: yet as my work only required only a small part, I was perhaps the best judge of the dimensions of that part.—You are a good man, and I love you dearly, and beg pardon for thus thwarting you, and abuseing you; especially as you have added those remarks on sketching figures, which I thought excellent: and as to the large paper, I think I can contrive to bring it within bounds.' 15 Jan. 1799 (Rev. E. G. Benson—Brisco transcript).

[1] W. G. to E. Forster, 7 Sept. 1803 (Rev. E. G. Benson—Brisco transcript).

[2] *Two Essays: One, On the Author's Mode of Executing Rough Sketches; The Other, On the Principles on Which They Are Composed. To these are added three plates of figures, by Sawrey Gilpin, Esq. R.A. These Essays are introduced by an Account of the Parish-School at Boldre, near Lymington, for the Endowment of which the Essays and Drawings are sold. . . .* London, Cadell & Davies, 1804.

[3] *Three Essays: on Picturesque Beauty; on Picturesque Travel; and on Sketching Landscape: with a Poem, on Landscape Paint-*

ing. *To these are added Two Essays, giving an account of the principles and mode in which the author executed his own drawings.* . . . Third Edition, London, Cadell & Davies, 1808 (abbreviation: *Five Essays*).

[4] J. Hamble, active as an engraver from 1790, worked in collaboration with J. H. Clark between 1805 and 1810. He is probably the same person as J. R. Hamble who exhibited occasionally at the Royal Academy from 1803 to 1824, and aquatinted scenes by A. Pugin in Papworth's *Select Views of London*, 1816.

M. Dubourg, active 1786–1838. As a painter he exhibited miniature portraits at the Royal Academy in 1786 and 1787. As an aquatint engraver he collaborated with J. H. Clark between 1810 and 1815. Consult article in Thieme–Becker.

For J. Hamble and M. Dubourg see also Major J. R. Abbey's *Life in England in Aquatint and Lithography* and *Scenery of Great Britain and Ireland*.

[5] See J. R. Abbey, *Life in England in Aquatint and Lithography*, item 131.

[6] *A Practical Illustration of Gilpin's Day, representing the various Effects on Landscape Scenery from Morning till Night, in Thirty Designs from Nature; by the Rev. Wm. Gilpin . . . . With Instructions in, and Explanation of, the improved Method of Colouring, and Painting in Water Colours; by John Heaviside Clark . . . .* London, Edward Orme, 1811.

aquatints remained the same, but he rearranged them in a different order, and removed signatures and imprint.[1] Instead of receiving a slight coloration, each impression was fully painted in water-colour; particular attention being paid to the relatively blank space of the sky. Here Clark added in a most effective manner, according to the subject, a crescent moon or a ruddy sun, flashes of lightning or a double rainbow. Gilpin, who had carefully avoided the direct representation of such natural phenomena, would not have approved of this attempt to bring his drawings in line with popular taste.[2]

[1] The following table shows to what extent J. H. Clark changed the order of the drawings of *Morning, Noon and Evening*. *Gilpin's Day* had retained the original sequence with interpolations.

	Morning, Noon and Evening	Six other drawings
	1 2 3 4 5 6 7 8 9 10 11 12 13 14 15 16 17 18 19 20 21 22 23 24	.. ..
Gilpin's Day	1 2 3 4 6 7 9 10 11 12 14 15 16 17 19 20 21 24 25 26 27 28 29 30	5 8 13 18 22 23
Clark's *Practical Illustration*	1 5 3 21 4 24 8 2 17 29 7 14 28 12 26 11 25 16 9 18 19 22 30 23	6 15 10 13 20 27

[2] For detailed comparison of plates between *Gilpin's Day* and Clark's *A Practical Illustration*, see W. D. Templeman, 'An 1811 publication of drawings by William Gilpin', *Notes & Queries*, clxxxiv (1943), 39–40.

VII. Drawings, 1778-1804

GILPIN'S output during the last twenty-five years of his life is considerable. A conservative estimate would be in the region of 4,000 drawings. Half of these were sold for charitable purposes in 1802 and 1804, and bear the familiar WG blind stamp. As works of art they have no great merit, and Gilpin himself was the first to say so. They are repetitive, offering a set of variations within a fairly narrow range and half a dozen of them should be enough for any discriminating collector. With few exceptions dealers and collectors have endorsed his pronouncement on the value of his own drawings, and these, though not so cheap as a few years ago, are not expensive to buy. I would certainly not endorse the attitude of a certain person who, over the years, systematically threw them away, whenever they turned up in the mixed lots he purchased![1]

In this chapter I shall confine myself to a general account of his artistic activity, for to embark on a detailed analysis of the material would be unrewarding. These drawings, for the most part imaginary, embody Gilpin's conception of the Picturesque, and as such can best be appreciated by looking at the selection of plates in conjunction with the theory of the Picturesque, which forms the subject of the next chapter.

During his first years at Boldre his manner of drawing remained much the same. The features of his technique is dainty penwork, use of light-grey, or more particularly red-brown ink, to mark distant features, a general citron or chrome-yellow wash, and gummed shadows in the foreground.

Among the sketches which combine these characteristics are several repeat drawings of the *Tour of the Lakes* and the *Scottish Tour*, which were destined for members of the family.[2] Sir Bruce Ingram possesses two mountainous lake scenes, in which the general yellow wash combines most effectively with the grey washes of the receding hills to give unity to the atmospheric distance [10. *a*].[3]

[1] Only a few of the drawings of the last period are here illustrated, as they are already well known through reproductions. There are good examples in the *Kenwood Exhibition Catalogue* (items 85, 88, 106, and 119), the *Daily Telegraph*, 5 June 1959, and *The Times*, 8 June 1959. See also Richard Cammell, 'The Master of the Picturesque', *The Connoisseur*, Aug. 1940, pp. 60–63; and Luke Herrmann, 'William Gilpin—A Parson and the Picturesque', *The Connoisseur*, June 1959, pp. 43–45.

[2] Several of the *Tour of the Lakes* went to his Farish sister at Carlisle (now with A. L. Fawcett). Others of the *Scottish Tour* went to his two sons. See in particular: 'Castle & town of Edinburgh; Arthur's-seat, and Craig-miller,' reproduced as plate 3 in *Samuel Rogers and William Gilpin*; and 'Dunkeld-abbey' (G. F. Benson), inscribed on verso by another hand 'Augst 5th 1778 | Odd 1', which suggests that it was extra to those finished drawings of the *Scottish Tour* which were bound in with the letter-press.

[3] Sir Bruce Ingram's other drawing is reproduced in *Kenwood Exhibition Catalogue*, item 61. Other sketches which belong to this period include two oval compositions in the collection of Mr. Peter Bicknell, and another in that of Archdeacon F. H. D. Smythe (reproduced in *Kenwood Exhibition Catalogue*, item 62).

In about 1780 the predominant yellow wash of the 1770's is gradually discarded in favour of brown monochrome landscapes, ranging from sepia in the dark foreground through umber and bistre to pale beige in the distances and light areas. Even the paper used contributed to the general effect; it is coarse and of a grey or grey-brown colour.[1] Gilpin thus explained to E. Forster his liking for this paper: 'You are very right in supposing that one of the chief advantages of the rough paper, arises from the appearance it accidentally form[s] of distant objects. It also gives an agreable roughness to near objects. *Lastly it is accommodated to my stile of drawing.*'[2]

At this time he is particularly fond of a central vista over a sheet of water, be it an enclosed bay, a broad river or a meandering stream, and across it a stone or rustic bridge to focus attention. The hills are capped with ruins which often resemble Martello towers.[3]

The year 1781 was a busy one. He guided the first of his *Tours* through the press, and completed the draft of the *Remarks on Forest Scenery*, which he illustrated with rather inferior sketches.[4] He also found time to have his likeness painted by Henry Walton (1746–1813), a gentleman painter, who had produced some charming genre pieces in the manner of Greuze.[5]

The next year he made one of his sporadic attempts to master water-colours. This one lasted till 1784. Stimulated by one of the many women amateurs who sought his advice, he resolved to experiment with the new water-colours put out by Reeves. 'I have tryed these colours and find them of such excellent temper, that they almost paint of themselves. For the present at least, I have relinquished my stained paper'; and he proceeded

---

[1] '. . . apply to Mr Blamire, for that kind of rough paper, which he gets for me to draw upon.—It is a foreign paper, but I cannot say the importer.'—W. G. to E. Forster, 6 Apr. 1780 (Rev. E. G. Benson—Brisco transcript).

[2] 3 Nov. 1780 (Rev. E. G. Benson—Brisco transcript).

[3] See in particular *Kenwood Exhibition Catalogue*, items 63 and 65.

[4] 'Remarks on *Trees*; and their several *combinations*; (relative chiefly to Picturesque beauty;) illustrated by the *Scenes of New-forest* in Hampshire in three books'. Vol. I, containing twenty-three drawings and small sketches. W. L. Benson Collection. The present whereabouts of Vols. II (book 2), III and IV (book 3) are unknown. For later drawings connected with this work, see the two printed volumes of *Remarks on Forest Scenery* (1794) in the collection of Mr. Peter Bicknell. They contain thirty-two drawings by William and Sawrey Gilpin.

[5] The last known owner of the portrait was Edwin Bernard Benson; since his death in 1940 it has disappeared. A faded photograph can be seen at Tullie House, Carlisle. This museum was given in 1952, by E. Percival Gilpin, a small copy, in oil on panel, reproduced as frontispiece to *Samuel Rogers and William Gilpin*, 1959.

The Walton portrait has been used for several likenesses of William Gilpin. In 1783(?) or 1785 William Sherlock did

a miniature on ivory (George F. Benson Collection), and this miniature in turn was copied several times by Mrs. R. de Gylpyn Benson (*c.* 1900) for members of the family. Examples are in the hands of Mr. Alan de Gylpyn Benson, Mr. Edward Percival Gilpin, and Mrs. Gwen C. Mellis.

After Gilpin's death George Clint issued on 1 Jan. 1805 a good engraving after the original portrait, then in the hands of W. G.'s widow. Another engraving, this time an inferior affair by George Measom, appeared as a frontispiece to W. H. Grove's *A Memoir of the late Rev. William Gilpin*, Lymington, 1851.

Templeman (pp. 218–19) refers to two further representations of Gilpin: another portrait 'in crayons, hanging in Walhampton Park, a house which he often frequented' (Patricius Walker, *Rambles*, 1873, p. 34) and 'a very good bust of Mr. Gilpin by Garrard.' (*Monthly Mag.* xx (1805), 361). I have been unable to find either of these. There is nothing at Walhampton. As to George Garrard, he executed busts of several members of the Gilpin family; in particular that of his father-in-law, Sawrey Gilpin, of which the plaster (1803) belongs to the Marquess of Exeter, and the marble to Major Simon Whitbread at Southill. He also did a small bronze bust of the Rev. John Gilpin (1825) now in the possession of Dr. J. B. Gilpin-Brown.

to tell Mason how, instead of writing with the pen the words *wood, water, meadow*, he was now able with 'a single dash of colour' to indicate such features. Highly delighted, he compared his new box of colours with the water-colours hitherto available: 'We procured them of colour-men, tempered, some in one way, and some in another. They never mixed harmoniously. Some were glazed: others sank into the paper. There was no unity among them. But now you have all the colours you want, tempered exactly in the same way; and working with the greatest ease.'[1]

Mason also acquired a box of Reeves's water-colours, and asked to see some sketches 'that I may know what you mean by your dashes of Colour'.[2] Gilpin sent the following directions which show how amateurs pursuing their hobbies seized and adapted to their ends every fresh idea that might prove useful:

A receipt for making a *large* coloured sketch.

Take a vial of spirit of turpentine. Saturate it with gum-espaltum. Take half a sheet, or a sheet, of strong-textured, rough cartridge paper; & with a pen, which has lost its acuteness, & elasticity by transcribing a couple of sermons, trace the forms of trees, rocks, & broken ground, with a free hand. If your stroke delays, the turpentine blurrs. Leave the backgrounds in their black-lead lines. Then with a free pencil, dipt in colour, dash in the skies, distances, & foregrounds in order. A 2d. touching breaks your general forms, into parts. A third, but it must be conveyed by a sweeping brush, gives them all the harmony that is required in a sketch.[3]

Mason carried out the instructions and found them unsatisfactory for the ink ran. So Gilpin added:

I believe, if you saturate it *sufficiently* with the gum espaltum it will not blur. But *I* do not like it the worse for blurring. It certainly prevents it's being of use in *little* drawings: but I have been lately making some sesquipedalian drawings; in which a little blur signifies nothing: & this species of ink flows freer from the pen, than any I have yet met with. Miss Hartl[e]y (now for a sneer upon my lady-acquaintances) promised me, that she would endeavour to set her brother's chemical powers at work to invent a brown, indelible wash.[4]

Whether David Hartley[5] succeeded we do not know. There was no difficulty in using a brown ink which did not blur, such an ink, however, turned black in time. The problem was to find an ink which stayed brown and at the same time did not blur when washes were applied to the drawing.[6]

Gilpin obtained some success with natural colours, when working on small-scale drawings. Mary Hartley, in London at the beginning of 1783, recovering from a paralytic stroke which had taken away the use of her right hand, was shown some of these by

[1] W. G. to W. Mason, 26 Aug. 1782 (W. L. Benson).
[2] W. Mason to W. G., 29 Oct. 1782 (Rev. E. G. Benson).
[3] W. G. to W. Mason, 2 Dec. 1782 (W. L. Benson).
[4] W. G. to W. Mason, 4 Jan. 1783 (W. L. Benson).
[5] David Hartley (1732–1813), statesman and scientific inventor, son of David Hartley the philosopher, and half-

brother of Mary Hartley. Opponent of the American War and the African slave trade, he was British plenipotentiary at the Paris treaty of 1783. In his last years he studied chemistry and mechanics, and carried out experiments to make buildings fire-proof.
[6] M. Hartley to W. G., 16 Dec. 1781 (W. L. Benson).

W. S. Gilpin at Knightsbridge, and greatly admired 'that gentle tint of different colours, that just serves to separate objects, & to carry off distances'. Like Gilpin she detested 'the tawdry effect of what is called a coloured drawing', and asked him to supply her with directives, adding, 'you cannot imagine how much it wou'd oblige, & how much it wou'd contribute to my entertainment in almost the only amusement that my health now allows me to take'.[1] In answer to this call from a kindred spirit, he sent several water-colours together with details of his usual practice, itemized as follows:

No. 1. with a little red orpiment,[2] (which Re[e]ves calls orange) or lake, or vermilion, or a mixture of one or two, I first tint the light parts of the horizon; & generally rub the same tint over the distances, which helps to harmonize them.

No. 2. the darker parts of the sky thrown in, composed of blue; or of blue & black mixed, or Indian ink alone; or the white paper may be left, in parts, to represent the fleeciness of clouds.

No. 3. the distances rubbed in, composed of blue & black.

No. 4 The whole finished in an attempt at sober colouring.

This last operation, you know, is by far the most difficult. For my own part indeed, I generally please myself most (& that is but little) with my slightest sketches. If I use green, I generally dash it with black, as I do indeed all my colours. A touch of raw gambodge has often a good effect on ground—a touch of terra de Sienna on foliage. I have tryed experiments with tinting slightly my paper *all over* with the first sky-tint—& likewise with drawing on cartridge-paper.[3]

Gilpin's experiments with water-colours did not last very long, and by the end of 1784 he gave up. 'I must leave colours to you heaven-born geniuses', he admitted to Mason. 'I think I can form some judgment of the harmony of colouring when I see it in a picture . . . but how to make reds, & greens, & greys dance into that harmony myself, I am utterly ignorant.'[4]

Small water-colours of this period are not very numerous. A particularly charming example is in the L. G. Duke Collection,[5] and the British Museum possesses two others.[6] Of his larger 'sesquipedalian' drawings 'in which a little blur signifies nothing', Lieut.-Col. D. St. Leger Moore, a direct descendant of Gilpin, has a set of large ovals, where the prevailing hue is a blue sky tint.

Reeves gave considerable satisfaction when he produced standard water-colours. However, the quality and diversity of other materials remained chaotic. Amateurs were ever on the look-out for inks and paper which suited their particular manner, and what suited one person as often as not proved unsatisfactory when used by another. When in 1784 Mason sent Gilpin a sample of his indelible brown ink,[7] the latter replied:

I received your *brown ink*, as you call it: but it was so glutinously stubborn, it would not utter a word. I do not like it half so well as my own. You say, mine blurs; & so would Geminiani's

---

[1] M. Hartley to W. G., 23 Feb. 1783 (W. L. Benson).

[2] Orpiment is yellow sulphide of arsenic.

[3] W. G. to M. Hartley, 7 Mar. 1783 (W. L. Benson). Very similar directions are found in W. G. to W. Lock, 19 Feb. 1783 (Rev. E. G. Benson).

[4] W. G. to W. Mason, 30 Dec. 1784 (W. L. Benson).

[5] See *Kenwood Exhibition Catalogue*, item 81.

[6] B.M. 1923–5–14–35 and 36.

[7] For the recipe see W. Mason to W. G., 29 Mar. 1783 (Rev. E. G. Benson).

fiddle-stick in the hands of a bungler. I do not mean to infer, that you are a bungler; but only that you have not gotten the art of playing with my fiddle-stick. You must move rapidly. If you play de-li-be-rate-ly, every pause is a blot.[1]

A little later Mason was more successful. He considered Gilpin's method of staining paper 'a most unchemical process', for 'Gamboge does not dissolve perfectly in Water & the Acid in Red Ink curdles it'. Instead of red ink he should add a solution of salt of tartar. 'This Salt of Tartar changes its colour into a blood red in the cup, but when laid on paper with a spunge into a good buff which may be lightend at pleasure by added Water.'[2] Gilpin was delighted, 'I shall never again say, you have studied chymistry, thirty years, to no purpose (for I think it is so long, since I first heard you talk on that subject at Sir Robert Hyldyard's table) The solution you have sent me, is a very pretty preparation. As to your oleaginous, & pigmentarian inventions, I did not much value them. But this is really a neat discovery.'

The trouble with his own mixture of gamboge and red ink, was 'that the red ink flies (unless kept from the air) & gives up too much to the yellow'. Mason's recipe was greatly superior, though it too had its limitations. First, it lacked variety: 'Salt of Tartar, unless you mix some other ingredient, gives only one tint'; secondly, 'the salt fixes your wash, whether indian ink, or ombre, too closely; & does not give you the power to graduate so much as you wish.'[3]

From 1786 a general pink or pale-red wash often appeared over his drawings. Experiments with papers continued in the 1780's; after the coarse grey paper (c. 1780), he tried a more spongy one,[4] then in 1786 a brown paper,[5] and after that a smooth stiff one. When in 1790 Mason asked him for the recipe of his own writing ink, which was 'always remarkably Black',[6] Gilpin complied, not without some sly digs at recipe hunters:

It was high entertainment to me, that a man of your chymical abilities, & long experience in the powers of nature, should send to me, a mere natural, for a receipt to make ink. My receipt lies in a very narrow compass. When my ink is gone, I say, Here, Harry, take my ink-bottle, & when you go next to Lymington, desire Jones to fill it. I wrote a note however to Mr. Jones, who is our Lymington stationer, & begged his receipt for a friend, if he did not make a secret of it. Accordingly he sent me the inclosed with a caution, which I trust you will observe: and glad I am that it is in my power to send you one receipt more to 150, which I dare say you have tryed, if you would be candid, & ingenuous to own it. I am acquainted with another clergyman, a very ingenious man, a great philosopher, & an ink-maker. He has tryed all Dr. Lewis's[7] receipts round; & divers others.

[1] W. G. to W. Mason, 12 Feb. 1784 (W. L. Benson). Mason answered: 'If you would have diluted the burnt Umber properly with drying Oyl I am certain you would have found it answer, but only fresh & fresh evry time you draw; for it presently drys & becomes too glutinous. the best thing, to mix it in, is a little earthen cup such as Children play at making tea in.' 13 Mar. 1784 (Rev. E. G. Benson).

[2] W. Mason to W. G., 9 Dec. 1785 (Rev. E. G. Benson).

[3] W. G. to W. Mason, 31 Jan. 1786 (W. L. Benson).

[4] W. Mason to W. G., 20 May 1785 (Rev. E. G. Benson).

[5] 'I have lately been sketching on a kind of brown paper; which I think has a good effect'. W. G. to W. Mason, 31 Jan. 1786 (W. L. Benson).

[6] W. Mason to W. G., 17 Apr. 1790 (Rev. E. G. Benson).

[7] William Lewis's mine of useful information, *Commercium Philosophico-Technicum; or, the Philosophical Commerce*

They had all failed him; as I suppose they have you. When I saw him, he was intent upon a discovery of his own. Before his study-fire, where I found him, stood a large bason of ink, evaporating its aqueous particles. I sat down, but was in constant fear of moving my chair—my foot—or my cane, lest I should overturn the process. I own I often smile at all you philosophical gentlemen, who take such round-about ways to supply the commonest wants. While you are trying all the receipts that ever have been tryed, I get better ink than any of you, by sending, as you might do, to the next stationer.—I must however tell you one improvement I make in Mr. Jones's receipt. I observe he orders you to thin his ink with water. I, self-taught, thin mine with white-wine. My wife often tells me, I know no other use for wine but thinning ink. To say the truth, I make no other use of it.[1]

Little did he realize that for the last six years of his life he was to drink wine daily on doctor's orders! He might laugh at those who were never satisfied with their writing ink, yet for many years he was just as restless about his own drawing inks. He constantly varied the composition and colour of them before he eventually opted for those which characterize the majority of his later drawings. Using a reed pen he employed indian ink, usually diluted to a grey colour, but more often a brown indelible ink, called *iron-water* by the calico-printers.[2] This brown ink mixed satisfactorily with indian ink, which ordinary writing ink tended not to do. He had been partial to a yellowish ink, which was not easily obtained, and tells an amusing story of how he was thwarted in an attempt to procure a supply of this precious ink:

I had money to pay to an old lady, who gave me a receipt, written out of a leaden stand full of it. It was before I had heard of the iron-water, and thinking I had met with a great treasure, I cast about how to get possession of it. I told the old lady, therefore, that I thought her ink was bad, and if she would trust her leaden pot with me, I would fill it with better. She courteously told me, if I did not like her receipt, she would draw me out another. It would have been in vain to have told her, as she was half deaf, and of confused intellect, that her bad ink was to me better than any other, and for what use I wanted it.[3]

Up to 1789 Gilpin drew for his own pleasure. As the drawings accumulated he at first pasted them in large numbers into books, intended as gifts to members of his family.[4] Then in 1785 he started to make books with sets of twelve or twenty-four drawings—these smaller books were destined for his friends. Many of the books were

---

of Arts: designed as an attempt to improve Arts, Trades, and Manufactures, London, 1763.

[1] W. G. to W. Mason, 29 Apr. 1790 (W. L. Benson). After this Mason could hardly be expected not to make a retort, and here it is: 'To revert to Mr Jones & his Ink it is certainly one of the Commonest of the common Receipts. but I like the Idea of your Chemical Clergyman, because it is one I have very lately adopted. I am convinced My Ink writes pale because I have of late usd Wedgwoods Ink standishes, which prevent aqueous Evaporation and have only the merit of keeping the Pen clean. My Curate (I tell you this out of revenge for your sarcasms) says, that your Ink appears black merely because you either dont know how to make a good

Pen, or to use one when it is made. if you have any candour in you you will allow this to be what Shakespeare calls a palpable hit.' W. Mason to W. G., 10 May 1790 (Rev. E. G. Benson).

[2] *Five Essays*, p. 150.   [3] Ibid., p. 151.

[4] 'I send you another book in the same way. They are a number of sketches, which I collected, improved, & pasted in a book. They were chiefly done in the year 1783. Many of them still want improvement—I mean as to the effect, & composition; for I pretend to nothing else.—It must be your book hereafter; for many of the sketches I gave to you, & they have your name behind them.' W. G. to his son William at Cheam, 17 Jan. 1785 (Major J. R. Abbey).

dated on the cover, but as most of them have been broken up, and as Gilpin himself did
not bother to date his drawings after 1768, it is not possible to consider his activity
between 1782 and 1789 on anything but a broad basis.[1] If we consult the 1802 and 1804
sale catalogues we get this picture of his general output:

1782	39 drawings	[1802 sale, lot 130]
1783	73 sketches	[1802 sale, lot 131]
1785	24 drawings	[1802 sale, lots 84–85]
1785–8	216 sketches	[1802 sale, lots 29–43; 1804 sale, lots 87–89]
1786	24 drawings	[1802 sale, lots 86–87]

This total of 376 must be doubled at least, if we take into account the larger drawings
which were sold in loose undated lots, the many gifted, not to mention the semi-topo-
graphical drawings related to the *Tours*.

Their rough chronological sequence can be established by using, as pointers, three dated
books that have survived and a number of individual drawings which W. Thomson secured
in 1789 through his friendship with William Gilpin II.[2] As Gilpin sent these last he wrote
to his son: 'By your account of his esteem for my works, I shall expect, after I am dead (as
an Irishman would say) that he will be a good purchaser.'[3]

The striking feature of the 'Thomson' drawings is their multiple inscriptions. On the
verso of each drawing, either in the top or bottom right-hand corner, William Gilpin II
wrote inscriptions such as, 'WG Lym^n | 1789', 'WG Senr', or 'W.G. *Lym^n 1789*.', before
giving the sketches to Thomson, who in his turn wrote across the lower half of the paper,
either 'By Mr Gilpin of Lymington— | W. Thomson:—', or 'By Mr Gilpin | of Boldre | =
| W Thomson 1786. | — | fr$\underline{m}$ W.G. Junr', or 'By Mr Gilpin—drawn for *W. Thomson*.'
Several of these drawings were subsequently inscribed on the recto by a third hand,
'William Gilpin' or 'W. Gilpin'.[4]

[1] 'As to the book, about which you make such a comment, my only purpose is this. I find I cannot so easily fill a volume with 60 leaves. My purpose therefore is, for the future, to fill smaller books of a dozen, or 20 leaves; which I please myself with the thoughts of leaving as legacies among some of my friends, at my death. I do not think I shall be able to draw many years longer: for my eyes, I think, rather fail.' W. G. to his son William at Cheam, 3 May [17]85 (Major J. R. Abbey). He was to draw regularly for another ten years.

[2] Their friendship may date from undergraduate days at Queen's College, Oxford, for Thomson is probably William Thomson, son of William Thomson of Worcester, who entered Queen's on 20 June 1776 at the age of 15. He became a student of Christ Church in 1779 and took his B.A. in 1780. William Gilpin II matriculated at Queen's on 13 July 1773, and took his B.A. on 3 Mar. 1778.

[3] W. G. to his son William at Cheam, 29 Feb. 1789 (Major J. R. Abbey). When Thomson's direct source of supply stopped, through Gilpin's decision to keep his drawings back for an eventual sale, he had to be satisfied with copies of Gilpin drawings made by others. One of the drawings he thus acquired is now in the Iolo A. Williams Collection. It is a copy made by B. Booth from a drawing in one of the manuscript tours that were circulating. On the verso is the following inscription: 'Ld *Strafford's* Castle, N° 6—of M^r G's MSS. Tour | Copied by B. Booth after Gilpin—1790—*W. Thomson*.' Thomson does not appear as a purchaser at the 1802 or 1804 sales; no doubt by then he possessed all the drawings he wanted.

From the time he was an undergraduate at Oxford, William Gilpin II asked his father for drawings to give his friends. He himself was always a poor draftsman, and several of his clumsy attempts to copy either prints or his father's drawings survive. He was more successful in his later years when drawing trees. Unlike his father who, except for the blind stamp, never signed his work, William Gilpin II often marked his drawings with his initials. There are in the Iolo A. Williams Collection two such early instances inscribed on the verso, 'W Gilpin— of Qu. Coll— | 1777.' and 'WG. Q.C. 1777 | for *CN*.' respectively.

[4] For specific inscriptions see Plate 2. *d*, and *Kenwood Exhibition Catalogue*, items 63, 65, 79, 81, 84.

In 1789, despite the fact that he had no illusions as to the real worth of his drawings, Gilpin realized their commercial potentiality. Hitherto he had met the increasing demand for specimens of his work by giving them away to whoever asked for them; now he wrote to Mason, 'as they have a sort of credit among people, I am desirous of turning them to use'.[1] He would sell his drawings for some charitable purpose. Gradually he evolved a scheme—the proceeds of a posthumous sale were to be used for the endowment of the parish school he founded at Boldre, in 1791, and should the sum realized exceed the requirements of Boldre, the surplus was to assist other institutions in which he had an interest, such as the school at Brokenhurst.

Now that he was drawing for a definite purpose, Gilpin entered on his most prolific period. From 1789 to 1794 he produced the bulk of the drawings which appeared in the 1802 sale, and these are the ones most familiar to collectors. Unlike those of the 1780's which vary considerably in treatment and shape, these are all oblong in shape, and treated with grey washes. Only very occasionally is any colour introduced, and the overall washes range from pale brown to light red. Many of the smaller sketches (approx. $6\frac{1}{2} \times 10$ in.) were gathered together with manuscript instructions into the following books:

24 drawings	*Various circumstances of Lake-scenery*[2] [1802 sale, lot 93]
40 drawings	*A book of Mountain and Lake Scenery* [lot 129]
24 drawings	*'Sketches of Roads—Rivers—Lakes—and Sea-coasts'*[3] [lot 95]
24 drawings	*'Views of buildings, bridges, & aquaducts on the fore-grounds'*[4] [lot 96]
24 drawings	*Landscapes adorned with Buildings at various distances* [lot 97]
24 drawings	*Landscape unadorned with any artificial objects; but depending chiefly upon itself* [lot 98]
24 drawings	*Remarks with corresponding Examples on a few different Modes of Composition in Landscape* [lot 94]
30 drawings	*On sketches, a MS. explaining their composition, and effect; and the amusement derived from them* [lot 135]
10 prints	*The theory of effect illustrated by examples* [lot 115]
32 drawings	*'Instructions for Examining landscape'*[5] [lot 134]
30 drawings	*The idea of roughness as an essential of the picturesque*, 1792[6] [lot 133]

[1] W. G. to William Mason, 25 Aug. 1789 (W. L. Benson).

[2] 'Various circumstances of Lake-scenery'. Bound in half-calf and marbled boards, $12\frac{7}{8} \times 9\frac{7}{8}$ in. Twenty-four drawings and four pages of MS. comment on the drawings which are numbered. Sold at Christie's 6 May 1802 (lot 93) to Sir Robert Harvey for 16 guineas. Peter Bicknell Collection.

[3] 'Sketches of Roads—Rivers—Lakes—and Sea-coasts'. Bound in half-calf and marbled boards, $12\frac{7}{8} \times 9\frac{7}{8}$ in. Twenty-four drawings and three pages of MS. comment on the drawings which are numbered. Sold at Christie's 6 May 1802 (lot 95) to Mr Darby for 14 guineas. Christopher Hussey Collection.

[4] 'Views of buildings, bridges, & aquaducts on the fore-grounds, Vol: I'. Bound in half-calf and marbled boards, $12\frac{15}{16} \times 9\frac{7}{8}$ in. Twenty-four drawings and two pages of MS. comment on the drawings which are all numbered, except 1 to 3. Sold at Christie's 6 May 1802 (lot 96) to Mr. Darby for 13 guineas. Christopher Hussey Collection.

[5] 'Instructions for Examining landscape; illustrated by 32 Drawings'. Bound in half-calf, $8\frac{3}{4} \times 11\frac{5}{8}$ in. Twenty pages of MS. and thirty-two drawings. Inscribed on inside cover: 'T. Bernard | 6 May 1802'. Purchased at Christie's 6 May 1802 (lot 134) by Sir Robert Harvey for Thomas Bernard for 23 guineas. Spencer George Percival Bequest 1922. Fitzwilliam Museum, Cambridge.

[6] A. P. Oppé noted that this MS. book sold for £4, as lot 99B, at the sale of Captain Norcliffe Gilpin, deceased, on 20 Apr. 1915.

In this last book he made drawings from a set of thirty small prints by Paul Sandby, showing views of great country residences. He altered their largely topographical character, to emphasize that 'roughness is the great essential of picturesque beauty'.[1]

In the books of drawings, the sketches are usually so related to a few manuscript remarks as to illustrate various aspects of picturesque theory. As we shall see in the next chapter, the manuscript material can on occasion be sufficiently original and penetrating to contribute something of value to our understanding of the Picturesque; but on the whole, the comments themselves merely repeat ideas more fully expressed at the time in *Remarks on Forest Scenery* (1791) and the *Three Essays* (1792).

In some small drawings the grisaille technique is used to render atmosphere, the misty air of repose, the even, diffused light which brought him in his old age closer to Claude than he was willing to admit in argument. In others he was preoccupied with effects of light and shade at different times of the day:

24 drawings   *Morning, Noon and Evening*, 1795[2] [1802 sale, lot 92]
24 drawings   *'On Sunsets'*, 1791[3] [lot 136]
12 drawings   *Small Sunsets*, 1791 [lot 105]

Others, not related to specific themes, were given individual descriptions:

138 drawings   Sets of 6, with a few remarks under each drawing [1802 sale, lots 50–72]
120 drawings   Sets of 24, with a description of each drawing [lots 73–77]
12 drawings   Sets of 4, with descriptions of the design and composition of each written on the back [lots 89–91]

Here are four specimen descriptions, which reveal the didactic flavour of his analysis. The first is pasted to a sepia paper mount, under a landscape in the collection of Sir Bruce Ingram [10. *d*]:

[1] 'Among other things I have been picturesquing a set of small prints, which Sandby published of gentlemens seats in the several counties of England—that is, I have made little drawings from several of them (about 30) in which by *roughening*, & reducing them to a state of nature, I have shewn how an embellished garden ground may be made picturesque.' W. G. to William Mason, 13 July 1792 (W. L. Benson).

[2] Album bound in marbled boards with green leather spine and corner pieces, $12\frac{3}{4} \times 9\frac{7}{8}$ in. Twenty-four drawings and a four-page index of explanatory notes entitled: 'A few of the innumerable incidents are represented here, which accompany a *morning*, a *noon-tide*, and an *evening* sun.' Gilpin book-plate dated '1795'. Sold at Christie's 6 May 1802 (lot 92) as 'Morning, Noon and Evening' to James Forbes, F.R.S., for £26. 5s. 0d. Probably sometime in collection of Sir Michael Sadler. Sold at Christie's 16 June 1961 (lot 5) to Colnaghi's for £231. Paul Mellon Collection, Washington.

[3] 'On Sunsets'. Bound in dark-blue boards with red leather spine, $14\frac{3}{8} \times 10\frac{1}{8}$ in. Seventeen drawings (originally 24) and five pages o fMS. comment on the drawings. Inscribed on inside cover: 'These Sunsets were drawn by the Revd. William

Gilpin MA Vicar of Boldre Hampshire Prebendary of Sarum (see signature WG in left hand corner (WG) [)] sold at Christies 1802 for the Benefit of the School at Boldre, Hants. Left to me by my Uncle the late Wm Gilpin of East Sheen Cousin of my Grand Father [William Gilpin (1758–1822)] | *Norcliffe Gilpin* | 1913'. A. P. Oppé noted its purchase by Thorpe (lot 96) for £1. 17s. 6d. at the sale of Captain Norcliffe Gilpin, deceased, on 20 Apr. 1915. Dr. T. S. R. Boase Collection.

In a letter to Mason, Gilpin alluded to an early state of this collection of sunsets, when it possessed as yet only twelve drawings: 'In another book I have pasted as many sunsets [twelve]; with a short account of the ways, in which a sunset may be shewn to advantage; all which are exemplifyed. I am informed, that a little bit of writing will shew their authenticity, and add to their value. When I see you here, next summer, if we live so long, I will entertain you, a whole morning, with my contrivances.' 9 Oct. 1791 (W. L. Benson). The reference cannot be to the book of twelve 'Small Sunsets', which contained no manuscript remarks.

The river & the lake have each their characteristics; so that, in many cases, you may easily distinguish one from the other. But some of their characteristics are so much the same, that in large surfaces of water the species may be mistaken. The water represented in the sketch before us, is of this kind. There are many large rivers, which appear in this form; & at the same time, many lakes. This hath however more the appearance of a lake, from the loftiness of its banks, & its smooth, reflecting surface. The grounds about it lye not unpleasantly, & it does not perhaps, in any part, exhibit a more picturesque appearance.

The second is more analytical of the compositional devices used in a landscape seen through a dark foreground screen of trees. The drawing forms part of the same set as the previous one [10. e]:

The spot, from whence this view of an old castle is taken, is not ill-chosen. The foreground, & the background contrast each other. The castle appears to advantage between the trees; all of which have their use. The smaller tree on the right breaks the continuity of the ground, on which the castle stands, at one end: & the great trees, & the little scraggy one, break the continuity of the distance; leaving as much, as the composition requires. The great tree on the left, comes in as a closing frame to the picture.

A third analysis, pasted this time to the back of the drawing itself, uses a musical analogy to describe a line of receding hills [11. a]:

This view was, what might be called, in musical language, a fugue of rocky hills one retreating behind another, from the foreground to the end of the landscape. The rock on the right, joined to a piece of ground, which advances a little nearer the eye, on which a group of cattle, in the shade, were happily opposed to a light ground at the bottom of the rock. The landscape admitted no distance.

The last, like the first description, matches an indeterminate element in the sketch, by means of words such as 'seems', 'probably', or 'loses itself'. This lack of precision in both drawing and language is deliberately suggestive, for the aim is to stimulate the imagination of the onlooker, who in his turn may choose to interpret and complete such details as he sees according to his own fancy [11. b]:

The banks of the river, represented in this sketch, are, on both sides, woody, & adorned; & the whole landscape has a chearful air. Beyond the bridge, the river seems to wind round the projecting ground on the right; & to lose itself in that direction; as the country seems to rise behind the high ground on the left. The distant country is probably a vale, through which the river takes it's course.

In other instances Gilpin projects himself into his own creations, and as traveller and narrator takes the reader on an imaginary journey through the country which they portray:

24 drawings   *'A fragment'*[1] [1802 sale, lot 137]
30 drawings   *Account of a fictitious journey in the form of a fragment* [lot 139]

[1] Album bound in olive morocco, entitled on spine 'Gilpin's Landscapes'. $11\frac{3}{16} \times 8\frac{3}{4}$ in. Contains two separate items purchased by Samuel Rogers: (1) *A fragment* (14 pages of manuscript and 24 drawings) sold as lot 137 in 1802 sale for 18 guineas, and reproduced as Appendix B; (2) twelve drawings sold as lot 88 in 1804 sale for £3. 7s. 0d. S. Rogers sale 1856. Sotherby's July 1921. Family of Sir Michael Sadler. Mrs. Margaret M. Harvey Collection.

This inclination for writing imaginary fragments started in 1791 and continued at least till 1794.[1]

In the 1780's and early 1790's he made a number of larger landscapes (approx. 11×15 in.), and among these are the finest he ever composed. Some can be seen at the Victoria and Albert Museum (Townshend Bequest) and in the Leeds City Art Gallery (Norman Lupton Bequest) [11. c and d], but the majority are still in private hands. Their atmosphere is akin to that of the Italian water-colours of J. R. Cozens. Occasionally he varied the use of indian ink washes with a touch of brown or pink, as, for example, in the complex composition of a lake surrounded by mountainous scenery in the W. L. Benson Collection [10. c], with its central and most effective clump of trees.

Another drawing, of unusual dimensions, epitomizes what Gilpin meant by roughness. The main interest in this mountainous landscape lies in the diagonal foreground, which occupies half the composition. Everything, from the precarious tree at the top of the slope to the nearest undergrowth, contributes to the play of light and shade in this cascade of vegetation and broken rocks.[2]

After 1794 Gilpin drew only very intermittently. He was now seventy and had timed his main effort on the assumption that three score years and ten was the span of life he could expect. As it was, he lived another ten years, and devoted most of these to philanthropic and religious pursuits. The drawings become sketchy and slight, and to judge from a few done in 1796 and 1797, his former expressiveness degenerates into rather loose and vague penwork.[3]

In 1802 he was persuaded to bring forward the sale of his drawings, and the considerable sum it realized encouraged him to draw again. This last effort consisted of some 300 to 400 sketches, including 29 sets of threes, which demonstrated his manner, as outlined in the essay, 'On the mode of executing rough sketches'.

These are all treated in the loose manner of his last years, and only on occasion does he succeed in bringing off a pleasing effect—this is certainly the case with the waterfall in the Mrs. John Perkins Collection.[4]

Gilpin died on 5 May 1804, and a month later his executors arranged a second sale at

[1] 'I have invented several ways of exhibiting my drawings to advantage. I have been amusing myself lately with one in the following manner. I have pasted about a dozen of them into a book. In this book there are a few white leaves; & on these white leaves I have written an account of a journey through the country they describe; referring to each drawing. My motto is, (which will shew the fiction;)

     In nova fert animus mutatos dicere formas
       Corpora'

W. G. to W. Mason, 9 Oct. 1791 (W. L. Benson). The reference may be to lot 139 in the 1802 sale, or to another imaginary journey not yet identified. See also *infra*, p. 138, n. 2.

[2] Reproduced in *Kenwood Exhibition Catalogue*, item 88.

[3] These drawings were dated on the verso in brown ink by Catherine Brisco, in her long and shaky hand. Here are a few examples:

  'Oct 6th 1796' and the initials CB in a circle (George F. Benson)

  'Novr 12,:th 1796 | 2' and the initials CB in a circle (Mrs. John Perkins)

  'Feby 16. 1797 | 2' (George F. Benson)

  'May 19th 1797' (W. L. Benson)

  'May 19th 1797 | 7' (Rev. E. G. Benson)

Although these drawings bear the WG blind stamp, I do not think they were offered for sale in 1802. They were given to various members of the family.

[4] See *Kenwood Exhibition Catalogue*, item 112.

Christie's. Such drawings of his as were offered were inscribed in ink on the verso (left bottom corner) 'Sale 6 June 1804', and bore the usual WG blind stamp.

One last point. It is a mistake to assume that because a drawing bears the WG blind stamp, it went through one of the two sales. Quite a few drawings, so stamped, were either retained by members of the family or given them as mementos by Gilpin shortly before his death.[1]

---

[1] Quite a few of these stamped drawings are to this day among his descendants. There is, for example, a folder, bound in half-morocco and blue boards, $10 \times 13\frac{1}{4}$ in., containing originally twelve drawings (now only four) which it was Gilpin's intention to sell. It has this dedication to his eldest son, John Bernard:

'This book of Drawings
A *Mother* requested of a *Father*
That she might give it to a *son*.

WG
|
MG
|
JBG.

1803'

Lieut.-Col. N. St. Leger Moore Collection.

VIII. Theory of the Picturesque

LARGELY as a result of his travels in the 1760's and 1770's Gilpin turned his attention to a systematic analysis of natural and artificial scenery. With the aid of criteria used for the examination of prints and paintings he was able to evolve and formulate a general aesthetic attitude to landscape, which was to have considerable influence in determining English taste for fifty years or more. This attitude is his theory of the Picturesque, and it was never cogently expounded in any one work. Its various aspects were discussed and elaborated in the *Tours* and *Essays*, in his correspondence with close friends, in his drawings, and in the remarks which accompanied them. His attempt to define it in such theoretical writings as the *Essay on Picturesque Beauty*, has been the despair of some aesthetic writers who have pointed to his contradictions, to his inability to analyse and substantiate a claim for the Picturesque as a subspecies of the Beautiful or as a distinct category from the Beautiful, and to his confusing and hybrid term 'Picturesque Beauty'.[1] Aesthetic speculation was never his strong point, and had it not been for the impact of Burke's *Philosophical Enquiry into the Origin of Our Ideas of the Sublime and Beautiful* (1757), it is doubtful whether he would have even attempted the task. So it was left to Uvedale Price and Payne Knight, when the picturesque ideal had already caught the public imagination, to give an adequate definition to the term.

That it was others who eventually reduced it to a concept with definite attributes, distinguishing it from the already established categories of the Beautiful and the Sublime, in no way affects the fact that the impact Gilpin made on his contemporaries stemmed from the *practical* uses to which the word picturesque was put. The word was taken from the realm of abstraction, was tested against reality, was made to work, to describe real things, real objects in nature, and thereby acquired many meanings, so much so that by 1801 George Mason, in his *Supplement* to Johnson, gave no less than six meanings to the word: what pleases the eye; remarkable for singularity; striking the imagination with the force of painting; to be expressed in painting; affording a good subject for a landscape; proper to take a landscape from. With all these Gilpin would have agreed.

[1] See in particular Walker J. Hipple, *The Beautiful, the Sublime, & the Picturesque in Eighteenth-Century British Aesthetic Theory*, Carbondale, 1957; and J. F. A. Roberts, *William Gilpin on Picturesque Beauty . . .*, Cambridge, Printed for Private Circulation at the University Press, 1944.

For a consideration of the Picturesque in a wider setting consult: Samuel H. Monk, *The Sublime: A Study of Critical Theories in XVIII Century England*, New York, M.L.A., 1935; B. Sprague Allen, *Tides in English Taste (1619–1800)*, New York, 1958; Paul Frankl, *The Gothic*, Princeton University Press, 1960.

This multiplicity of meanings testifies to the success of the word once Gilpin transferred it from the realm of art criticism and made it available as an instrument—admittedly a pictorial instrument—for the analysis, the description, and finally the representation and recording of natural scenery. But the Picturesque is much more than that. It is a frame of mind, an aesthetic attitude involving man in a direct and active relationship with the natural scenery through which he travels.

This active and creative aspect of the Picturesque is all important, for the theory's validity lay in its practice. Here Gilpin, by precept and example, gave the lead. He was able to describe what constituted a picturesque landscape and to show by his writings and drawings what enjoyment could be derived from picturesque practice, that, once the eye had been trained to recognize a picturesque 'object', many pleasures would become accessible through a wide range of associations between individual sensibility and the ever changing panorama of the countryside—for instance the pleasures of seeking, anticipating, finding, examining, comparing, recording, re-creating.

It is very doubtful whether the word Picturesque can be encompassed in a single definition. If we restrict its application to landscape in the latter half of the eighteenth century, we observe that for the term to have any meaning three quite distinct elements are required: art, nature, and a man of sensibility and culture to link the first two in the perennial debate of art versus nature; and according to the way we focus our attention, either on man with his personal aptitudes and inclinations,[1] on nature as seen through art, or on the artistic representation of landscape, we grapple with only one side of the Picturesque. Each of the three elements influences the other two in some degree, and so the various aspects which the Picturesque has assumed depend on the character of these component parts. Thus the way of looking at landscape in the eighteenth century was largely determined by the use of criteria derived from an analysis of landscape painting of the previous century— change these criteria, these standards, and the landscape composes itself in quite a different way. The essential factor without which the Picturesque can find no general acceptance is a society, or at least an effective element in society, which is *actively* interested in art and nature.

The scenery of Britain afforded many varied landscapes, a few of which were 'capable of being illustrated by painting'.[2] The rules of painting, in particular those governing composition and effect, guided the eye to make a choice but were not sufficient in themselves to account for the wide range of subjects which the picturesque school imprisoned within its formula. There was also a large element of personal choice dictated by temperament, predilections, and the physical appearance of the countries one had visited—thus, in any discussion on the beauty of landscape, William Lock's terms of reference were never

[1] Gilpin frequently applies the word to such as share his outlook. Thus he writes of William Lock: 'He is a very picturesque ingenious man; and I expect some good hints from him.' W. G. to E. Forster, 24 July 1781 (Rev. E. G. Benson—Brisco transcript).

[2] *Three Essays*, p. 3.

far away from the Alps and the Italian countryside through which he had travelled; for Mary Hartley they were related to the gentle, rolling, and pastoral scenery of the south of England she knew best; for Gilpin the topography of his native Cumberland cast a dominant shadow over all his thoughts, and as for Sir George Beaumont his enthusiasm was coloured by the latest region visited.

The various qualities which in Gilpin's eyes made a landscape picturesque consisted of an amalgam of personal preferences and aesthetic qualities—roughness or ruggedness of texture, singularity, variety and irregularity, chiaroscuro, and the power to stimulate the imagination. None of these qualities in isolation was picturesque, but where all, or the majority of them, were present in a landscape (real or imaginary), the landscape was said to be picturesque. Contrarywise, a landscape which lacked these qualities—for example, a flat stretch of country devoid of distinctive features—might be termed 'simply beautiful' but certainly not picturesque.

In his effort to find what distinguishes 'objects, as are proper for painting' from the rest, Gilpin singles out the quality of roughness as that which distinguishes 'picturesque beauty' from other kinds of beauty. Though in the preface to his *Essay on Picturesque Beauty* he assured his reader that 'picturesque beauty' is merely one more species of beauty, it becomes quite clear that the 'main body of the essay . . . is devoted to drawing a distinction between the beautiful and the picturesque, which is clearly incompatible with the picturesque being merely one species of the beautiful'.[1] Smoothness, neatness, elegance may be some of the main characteristics of beauty, but Gilpin finds 'that the ideas of *neat* and *smooth*, instead of being picturesque, in reality strip the object, in which they reside, of all pretensions to *picturesque beauty.*—Nay, farther, we do not scruple to assert', he adds, 'that *roughness* forms the most essential point of difference between the *beautiful*, and the *picturesque*; as it seems to be that particular quality, which makes objects chiefly pleasing in painting.'[2]

Thus, in asserting that roughness is both a quality in objects that pleases particularly in painting and one which gives to the Picturesque a distinctive beauty, he was stating a personal preference and no more. He had certainly not substantiated picturesque beauty. By using a term of art to define a quality in nature, he was confusing nature with art, the examination of natural scenery with its artistic representation.

Had Gilpin been content to maintain that roughness or ruggedness was a specific quality 'observable in the smaller, as well as in the larger parts of nature—in the outline, and bark of a tree, as in the rude summit, and craggy sides of a mountain';[3] and that in combination with other qualities it could make a landscape picturesque, he would have met little opposition. As it was, his attempt to make the painterly quality of roughness the *sine qua non* of picturesque beauty met with considerable criticism from both painters and aestheticians. Many rightly saw no difference between picturesque beauty and beauty—

[1] J. F. A. Roberts, op. cit., p. 3.   [2] *Three Essays*, p. 6.   [3] Ibid., pp. 6–7.

Reynolds himself went even further in equating nature, beauty, and picturesque. In his concluding remarks, made in July 1776 after reading the manuscript of the *Essay on Picturesque Beauty,* he stated 'every thing in nature that is beautiful I hold to be picturesque. But beauty in art ought not to be so called; for it is not to art, but to nature which the painter applies, as his object of imitation. Whatever works of art are introduced in a picture, they are there to assist or explain; they make not the bulk or principal of his composition; if they do the work must class among the lowest in the art.'[1] As Reynolds's estimate of landscape painting was pretty low anyhow, the Picturesque, considered as an artistic activity with its considerable borrowing from art, ranks for him as the lowest form of landscape painting. And he insisted that the term picturesque 'should be applied to the beauties of nature only; unless it is so confined, everything may be called picturesque that meets with your approbation, whereas nothing ought to be so called but what makes the subject of the painter's composition, which is, beautiful nature'.[2] On the whole Gilpin agreed with these pronouncements of Sir Joshua's, for he did not make any special claim for the Picturesque beyond that of a legitimate amusement for a man of taste. He had, however, certain reservations which he confided to Mason in August 1776:

> From what sir Joshua told me, I did not expect an intire concurrence. I am far however from thinking, that every opinion of his is an axiom. His considering no *artificial object* as *picturesque,* I think is an abuse of terms: and in his printed essays he makes beauty a mere fancy. It is this, or it is that, or it is any thing, just as you please to make it. The bark of a toad is as beautiful, as the face of a Venus.[3]

On the question of roughness, Reynolds agreed that 'Roughness, or irregularity is certainly more picturesque than smoothness or regularity, because this carries with it the appearance of art, nature being more various and irregular than art generally is', but maintained the general principle that 'beauty and picturesque are . . . synonymous'. In July 1776, after reporting that the young portrait painter, Daniel Gardner,[4] on reading the manuscript of the *Essay,* shared Reynolds's attitude, William Mason suggested to Gilpin a way out of the impasse created by the use of the expression 'picturesque beauty'. He might restate his argument and limit his inquiry to the following problem:

> Q[uestion], what is it that makes Objects *not* absolutely *beautiful* in themselves beautiful in representation, or in other words what quality must these objects have to become Picturesque? Answer. Roughness. instance. a young face is certainly more beautiful than an Old face, but as an old face is rougher than a young one that quality makes it tho *not so beautiful* full as Picturesque. And thus in other instances.

[1] Reynolds's low opinion of picturesque pursuits, already expressed in the *Tenth Discourse* (1780), occurs again in his letter to Gilpin, 19 Apr. 1791 (printed in *Three Essays,* pp. 34–36).

[2] For complete text of Reynolds's remarks on Gilpin's *Essay on Picturesque Beauty* see Leslie and Taylor, *The Life and Times of Sir J. Reynolds,* London, 1865, ii, 606–8. Con-sult also W. D. Templeman, 'Sir Joshua Reynolds on the Picturesque', *MLN,* xlvii (Nov. 1932), 446–8; W. J. Hipple, op. cit., pp. 199–201.

[3] W. G. to W. Mason, 19 Aug. 1776 (W. L. Benson).

[4] For a short account of David Gardner (1750–1805) consult E. K. Waterhouse, *Painting in Britain 1530–1790,* pp. 245–6.

In this manner of stating the Question the objections cannot arise that Sr Joshua & I believe all *Portrait* painters will make. But as they at present will conceive you to mean that Beautiful & Picturesque are synonimous terms (tho for me you have guarded yourself sufficiently) and as they will think that you make *Roughness* the sine quâ non of Beauty, their objections will be endless. With *Landscape* Painters you will find much more credit, they will readily adopt your system evn in its fullest latitude.[1]

Gilpin recognized that the question thus put 'would obviate much cavil',[2] but felt that to accept this suggestion would mutilate his plan by oversimplifying it, for the Picturesque would in effect be separated from the Beautiful, the first applying to art and the other to nature.

Realizing that the ideas expressed in the *Essay on Picturesque Beauty* were not likely to meet with much success, he decided not to proceed with publication, and it was not till 1792, sixteen years later, that he ventured to do so thanks to the help and encouragement of William Lock. During these years before publication he consulted his friends, who as often as not failed to understand his terminology. Edward Forster was one, as may be gathered from Gilpin's reply to him in 1781:

You seem in the beginning of your letter to understand my meaning—that I do not call rough-ness, *picturesque*; but assert only, that it distinguishes beautiful objects as *such*. But as you proceed, you seem to suppose, I assert that roughness itself is picturesque: ask me if the new-ploughed fields &c, are so?—variety, and irregularity, by no means include my idea of roughness.—There must be something more. You must have variety, and irregularity, to make even a piece of [. . .] garden-ground beautiful: but there is nothing picturesque in this.—[3]

At this juncture it may be useful to state Gilpin's position a little more fully. There is no doubt that, although he did not intend the Picturesque to be a rival concept, its advent as a potential theory upset the nice balance which existed between the concepts of the Beautiful and the Sublime, that between them had hitherto shared the aesthetic field; and to confuse matters further the word itself already had for painters a specific meaning;[4] so that it seemed clear to many that this fresh viewpoint, embracing both art and nature, did take unto itself qualities and emotions which had been allocated either to the Sublime or the Beautiful. These various elements he now grouped round a simple definition. In 1768 he had defined the term 'picturesque' as 'expressive of that peculiar kind of beauty, which is agreeable in a picture'.[5] He was then thinking particularly of art. Thirty years later the formula is much the same, though the emphasis is on nature: '*Picturesque beauty* is a phrase but little understood. We precisely mean by it that kind of beauty which *would look well in a picture*.'[6] Picturesque beauty was made up of many attributes none of which

---

[1] W. Mason to W. G., 20 July 1776 (Rev. E. G. Benson).

[2] W. G. to W. Mason, 19 Aug. 1776 (W. L. Benson).

[3] W. G. to E. Forster, 23 Apr. 1781 (Rev. E. G. Benson—Brisco transcript).

[4] William Lock distinguished clearly between Gilpin's

Picturesque and the 'painter's picturesque', that is to say between the general concept and its artistic application. See in particular William Lock to W. G., 21 Dec. 1790 (Major J. R. Abbey).

[5] *Essay on Prints*, p. x.   [6] *Western Tour*, p. 328.

was picturesque by itself, but in combination with each other gave relative degrees of picturesque beauty to the landscape. The chief attribute was the quality of roughness or ruggedness which in conjunction with characteristic and strong delineation, variety and irregularity, light and shade, gave life and meaning to objects:

. . . the wild and rough parts of nature produce the strongest effects on the imagination; and we may add, they are the only objects in landscape, which please the picturesque eye. Every thing trim, and smooth, and neat, affects it coolly. Propriety brings us to acquiesce in the elegant, and well-adapted embellishments of art: but the painter, who should introduce them on canvas, would be characterized as a man void of taste; and utterly unacquainted with the objects of picturesque selection.[1]

Though the man of taste was armed with a selective antenna which enabled him to look at nature in a special manner, when he chose to do so; he was also able to examine her with care for her own sake, untrammelled by questions of picturesque theory—this aspect tends to be overlooked, but it is all important. As Gilpin put it: 'In *arts*, we judge by the *rules of art*. In *nature*, we have no criterion but the *forms of nature*. We criticize a building by the rules of architecture: but in judging of a tree, or a mountain; we judge by the most beautiful forms of each, which nature hath given us.'[2]

By 'beautiful forms' he meant the most usual, the most characteristic ones, and these are endowed with common or simple beauty (a generalized term quite different from the specialized one of picturesque beauty). It is true that his inquiries are never far removed from the avowed purpose of his *Tours*, the search for picturesque beauty, nevertheless the very problem, whether this or that object is suited for representation in a picture, involved him in a systematic analysis of the component parts of nature. At times his examination is quite detailed, as in the *Remarks on Forest Scenery* where trees are subjected to a descriptive analysis, consideration is given to their growth, shape, timber, varieties, roots, trunk, ramification, and even the characteristic spray of their boughs is illustrated by means of diagrams.

Gilpin drew equally from art and nature, and the combination of certain intrinsic qualities he observed in these two fields gave the Picturesque its special characteristics. If art supplied composition and effect, nature provided the subject-matter: 'Nature is always great in design; but unequal in composition. She is an admirable colourist; and can harmonize her tints with infinite variety, and inimitable beauty: but is seldom so correct in composition, as to produce an harmonious whole.'[3]

The fact is, 'the immensity of nature is beyond human comprehension. She works on a *vast scale*; and, no doubt, harmoniously, if her schemes could be comprehended.' Whereas the artist, confined by the limits of his canvas and faced by the complexity of nature, must

---

[1] *Remarks on Forest Scenery*, 2nd ed., 1794, i, 222–3. 'In *nature's works* there is seldom any *deformity*. Rough knolls, and rocks, and broken ground, are of the very essence of beautiful landscape. It is man with his utensils, who prints the mark of *deformity* on Nature's works.' *Scottish Tour*, 2nd ed., 1792, ii, 163.

[2] *Remarks on Forest Scenery*, ii, 262.

[3] *Wye Tour*, p. 18.

make a choice. To do this 'he lays down his little rules . . . , which he calls the *principles of picturesque beauty*, merely to adapt such diminutive parts of nature's surfaces to his own eye, as come within it's scope'.[1]

Nature is the archetype, providing the models for all the objects and passages of a composition.[2] Just as 'in the language of religion, the well-ordered mind acknowledges every thing right in the works of God—so, in the language of painting, the picturesque eye acknowledges every thing beautiful in the works of nature. Some objects indeed may please less than others; and be less accommodated to the rules of painting. But all objects are best as nature made them. Art cannot mend them. Where Art interferes, picturesque beauty vanishes.'[3] This supremacy of nature does not imply slavish copying on the part of the artist—on the contrary, he must respect and understand her features so as to obtain a correct knowledge of them. Beautiful scenes in nature should be appreciated for their own sake, and the same is true for objects of art. As he maintained: 'We pursue beauty in every shape, through nature, through art; and all it's various arrangements in form, and colour; admiring it in the grandest objects, and not rejecting it in the humblest.'[4]

Never far removed from his contemplation of nature is the thought that

> Nature is but a name for an *effect*,
> Whose *cause* is God.[5]

In the last analysis his attitude as a Christian, moralist, and lover of the countryside is akin to Shaftesbury's—nature as a divine work of art is placed above human works of art. Even the man of taste of a picturesque disposition must recognize the primacy of nature as the fountain of picturesque beauty and the great provider of all the ingredients of landscape. It is on this note that he concluded the *Essay on Picturesque Travel:*

The more refined our taste grows from the *study of nature*, the more insipid are the *works of art*. Few of it's efforts please. The idea of the great original is so strong, that the copy must be pure, if it do not disgust. But the varieties of nature's charts are such, that, study them as we can, new varieties will always arise: and let our taste be ever so refined, her works, on which it is formed, at least when we consider them as *objects*, must always go beyond it; and furnish fresh sources both of pleasure and amusement.[6]

W. J. Hipple has ably defined Gilpin's Picturesque as 'a universal complex of properties pervading both nature and art, and acting upon our physical organism or our mental

[1] *Wye Tour*, p. 18. See also *Remarks on Forest Scenery*, ii, 232–6.

[2] To nature the artist must return again and again, if his ideas are not to become stereotyped. See *Five Essays*, pp. 166–7.

[3] *Remarks on Forest Scenery*, ii, 273–4.

[4] *Three Essays*, p. 46.

[5] Ibid., p. 47.

[6] Ibid., p. 58. W. J. Hipple (op. cit., pp. 198–9) after quoting this passage comments: 'There is a paradox here: a system which isolates a certain property of nature for admiration [i.e. picturesque beauty], a property defined by its excellence as a subject for art, comes at last to reject the art for the nature which was at first only its subject.' Paradox there may be, but we should not imprison Gilpin within his theories, as if he had never transcended them.

associations to produce an effect peculiar to itself'.[1] If we relate the theory to its practice, other factors also come into play such as temperament, prejudice, and personal limitations. The quality of roughness provides perhaps the best example of an element whose roots can be traced to most of the components which make up the Picturesque. In nature, Gilpin finds this quality everywhere evident and his enthusiastic advocacy for its wider recognition matches his search for nature's richly varied and intricate features. Roughness allied to wild, uninhabited regions summons his imagination. In art, he uses rough objects as necessary components to form a landscape composition; he needs them for variety, contrast, effects of light and shade, catching lights on prominent features, and even to give variation to colouring.[2] He can also draw such a composition himself, as rough objects come more easily within the competence of the amateur artist. He made himself a master of the bold free touch—his penmanship like his handwriting bears the stamp of a strong personality, and in the best drawings different strokes, each as clear in its meaning as a letter of the alphabet, combine to present a lucid statement. The pen which he handles more proficiently than pencil, brush or colour, conveys nearly the whole expressive quality of the sketch. As he states: 'Of these free touches with a pen the chief characteristic is *expression*; or the art of giving each object that peculiar touch, whether smooth, or rough, which best expresses it's form.'[3]

Instead of the continuous line, which is formal and structural, his pen consistently breaks up the surfaces and seeks their roughness, for therein lies the whole representational value of an object. Even when he treats a fairly smooth surface, such as a rock-face or a gentle slope, the line will be broken up in dots and dashes like a Morse message. Roughness may be the hallmark of his drawings, yet he is fully aware that free and bold strokes must be kept within bounds, if meaning is not to become unintelligible:

The beauty of *execution*, consists in *freedom* [only to be obtained by continuous practice]. But if *freedom* be not accompanied with correctness, or *precision*, the effect is lost. The stroke of the black lead pencil—of the pen—or of the brush, must have *meaning*; or, like a sentiment ambiguously expressed, it only confounds. Happy is that artist, whose execution follows up his ideas; and can readily give life to his conceptions.[4]

There are times, especially in his later drawings, when he carried his predilection to the point of contradicting his own teaching—the reed pen has run riot, loops and sickle-shaped strokes are jumbled together, and the portrayal of rugged nature appears like a country overrun by coils of barbed wire!

He finds that the 'free bold touch is in itself pleasing',[5] thereby the rapid sketch retains the force of the original idea and holds within its small surface great suggestive power,

---

[1] W. J. Hipple, op. cit., p. 199.
[2] *Three Essays*, pp. 19–21.
[3] Ibid., p. 72.

[4] 'Instructions for Examining landscape', p. 12 (MS. in Fitzwilliam Museum, Cambridge).
[5] *Three Essays*, p. 17.

which is often lost in a highly finished drawing, due to the deliberate and largely mechanical process of elaboration, which introduces an air of artificiality.[1]

We shall now examine in some detail aspects of Gilpin's theory as he practised them, to see in effect how mental associations and personal preferences determined the most striking features of the theory, such as his choice of ruins, his rejection of cottages and of the representation of motion near the eye, his notions of composition and effect, his decided views on foregrounds, the role of the imagination, and the part that figures should play in landscape.

If Gilpin were to state the two ideas that were foremost in his mind as he set about his sketches, they would undoubtedly be *composition* and *light and shade*. They are at the very centre of his teaching. Whether we look for his theory of the Picturesque in his drawings, his writings, or his voluminous correspondence, we are brought back to this constant preoccupation with composition and the disposal of light and shade.[2] In the *Essays* he writes mainly for amateurs and consequently gives much the kind of advice that fell to the lot of any drawing-master—showing how to avoid the obvious pitfalls that beset the beginner of landscape drawing. But he also makes it quite plain that his point of departure is *creative* and not *imitative*. By all means copy nature's individual '*objects* & particular *passages*' —these should fill the artist's notebooks—but avoid reproducing the whole landscape as it lies before your eyes, for that will not make a picture, and certainly not a picture that will please. The various parts must be composed into a harmonious WHOLE, as that is the essence that lies behind the often used and badly understood word, PICTURESQUE. When Gilpin defined the term as 'expressive of that peculiar kind of beauty, which is agreeable in a picture' he was also saying that the artist must transform his material by an intellectual and aesthetic effort before he can achieve a satisfactory landscape. 'Nature gives us the material of landscape; woods, rivers, lakes, trees, ground, and mountains: but leaves us to work them up into pictures, as our fancy leads',[3] which means according to the canons of taste of the individual.

Even when gathering material for a future landscape, Gilpin eschews exact likeness— 'we should not copy with that painful exactness, with which Quintin Matsis, for instance, painted a face. This is a sort of plagiarism below the dignity of painting.'[4] Rather should we concentrate on catching the *spirit* and *truth* of the original.

---

[1] 'There is one advantage (if it be an advantage) arising from painting on a small surface, which is painting it *at once*. I have heard painters say, they have been most pleased with such pictures, as they have executed with a wet pencil from beginning to end. I remember, some years ago, Mr. Locke shewed me a portrait of himself, which had been painted at once, & was but just laid in; which he thought so well, that he would not suffer it afterwards to be touched: and I myself remember to have seen pictures in their first colours, which pleased me much: but afterwards, when I saw them finished, the effect was gone. My conclusion is, that *finishing* is one of

the most artificial parts of painting.' W. G. to Sir George Beaumont, 16 June 1802 (Pierpont Morgan Library).

[2] Of the sketches he offered for sale in 1802, he said: 'Few of them will afford more than the *rude conception* of a landscape . . . . They pretend to some degree of *composition* and *effect*; but to little farther.' *Five Essays*, p. 171.

[3] Ibid., p. 159.

[4] Ibid., p. 160. In *Remarks on Forest Scenery* (i, 275–6) he expressed his low opinion of exact still-life and *trompe l'œil* painting.

In this perennial debate he was glad to receive the support of Sir George Beaumont, whom he had at one time suspected of being 'friendly to *exact views*'.[1] Unable himself to find a natural view which might be termed *correct* in every respect, he asked him if in his experience he had met one in the Lake District which quite satisfied him. Sir George replied:

I am always happy to be of the same opinion with you, & on this occasion am perfectly so, there is a servile individuality in mere portrait painting which always displeases me, & is not so interesting to use as a map; it must be full of awkward lines & the artist cramped by given shapes always gives his work the air of a copy. The old masters rarely painted views I believe never, unless commissioned—like poets they did not confine themselves to matter of fact, they chose rather to exhibit what a country suggested than what it really consisted of, & took as it were the essence of things—the servile imitator seems to me to mistake the body for the soul, & will never touch the heart—Moreover every thing looks well in nature; lumpish forms, & counteracting lines touched by her exquisite hand are hardly noticed—but in art they are truly disgusting, & the Artist must avail himself of every advantage if he wishes to cope with her—if he attacks her upon equal terms he is sure to be disgracefully vanquished.[2]

Since most of Gilpin's output consists of imaginary landscapes (variously called by him *fictitious* or *artificial* views) it stands to reason that he can take greater liberties with his material than the representational or topographical artist. And yet Gilpin's predilection for the *sublime* or *grand* manner in landscape imposes upon him several restrictions as soon as he considers design and disposition. What he chooses to accept or reject depends on his personal taste or on his own artistic limitations.

From the moment he considers design, which involves bringing together several elements in such a way as to give a particular *character* to a landscape, we see that in practice, Gilpin's theoretical views of the Picturesque are strictly limited. By nature and upbringing he inclines towards the Grand Manner, and what others tried to do for portrait and history he attempted for landscape. As a churchman and teacher his thoughts naturally turn to God and to the moral welfare of his pupils, so in aesthetics he looks for the sublime rather than the pastoral or rural aspects of nature. This explains why, once his days of travel were over, it was the scenery of the mountains and lakes of Cumberland and Westmorland more than that of any other region of Great Britain that continued to grip his imagination. As he wrote to Mary Hartley on 21 May 1790:

If you had seen as many lakes, and Mountains as I have seen, they would have put every thing else out of your head. For my own part, whenever I sit down with a pencil and paper before me,

[1] W. G. to Sir George Beaumont, 20 June 1801 (Pierpont Morgan Library).

[2] Sir George Beaumont to W. G., 15 June 1801 (Rev. E. G. Benson). With Beaumont's permission these remarks were included in Gilpin's account of his drawings which was attached to the 1802 sale catalogue (see *Five Essays*, pp. 165–6). Sir George returned to the same topic a little later: 'I am heartily glad you mean to touch upon the subject of portrait-painting especially, when treated in a cold & servile manner: for I really think the rage of our worthy countrymen for exact copies of their faces, & their places, is one great cause of the decline of historical & landscape-painting in this country; remarks from such authority as yours may be of essential service.' Postmark 5 January 1802 (Rev. E. G. Benson).

ideas of rocks, and mountains and lakes always crowd into my head. My pencil runs naturally into it; and I conceive no other ideas of landscape, but of this sublime kind, to be worth recording. Indeed no other ideas suggest themselves to me, but these; and such appendages as suit them.[1]

He not only continued to be enthralled by his visit to the Lakes, but with advancing age he also returned in dream to the haunts of his youth and early manhood when he roamed the country round Carlisle or travelled yearly south along the Shap road on his way to Oxford or Cheam. Amidst these mountains, lakes, and rocks he found grandeur and sublimity in a natural setting unspoilt by the civilizing hand of man.[2] It is this *genius loci* which he tried to recapture ideally in the thousands of sketches that he made in the last twenty-five years of his life. Nothing small and insignificant was retained, and what filled the mind with awe was magnified—the mountains became bigger than in reality, the broad river and the wide expanse of lake was preferred to the stream or the narrow inlet, and imposing waterfalls replaced cascades. The scene remained wild and remote.

In these drawings, where the last concession to topographical accuracy has been discarded, Gilpin was able at long last to find a formula which enabled him to express what the Lake District meant and had always meant to him. We speak of the Lakeland poets, the term equally applies to Gilpin; and his brand of the Picturesque, to distinguish it from other kinds, might well be called 'Lakeland' in conception. As an observing traveller and sketcher he forms part of a group of men who nurtured their sensibility and aesthetic conceptions, not by travelling on the Grand Tour in search of the classical ideal but by looking in a new way at the wilder and more mountainous scenery of this island. Christopher Hussey has underlined the part played by the publications of Dr. John Dalton (1709–63) and Dr. John Brown in awakening interest in the Lake District—it was Dalton's poem and Brown's *Letter* to Lord Lyttleton which sent both Arthur Young and Gray to the Lakes. Nor must we forget the role played by the Carlisle group which centred round the home of Captain J. B. Gilpin as from the late 1730's or early 1740'.

It is from this group that we get the earliest critical examinations of romantic scenery (then 'romantic' and 'picturesque' were closely associated). William Gilpin's was the first in 1748 with *A Dialogue upon the Gardens . . . at Stow* (re-edited in 1749 and 1751). As Professor Templeman points out, here occurs the first instance of the word 'picturesque' as applied specifically to landscape. Gilpin was to supply another instance in 1752 in his *Life of Bernard Gilpin*.[3] Dr. John Brown, who was closely associated with W. Gilpin in the 1740's and probably knew all about the *Dialogue*, followed with his own praise of the

---

[1] Rev. E. G. Benson Collection—Brisco transcript.

[2] In this frame of mind he wrote to Thomas Gisborne, then staying at Maryport: 'Your situation near the paradise of England is enviable! Pray, when you see them next, give my respectful compliments to Skiddaw, Helvellin, Grasmire; and the rest of their respectable neighbours, and tell them, I should rather drink a glass of water, drawn out of their cool cellars, and in their company, than eat venison with the Lord Mayor at the Mansion-house, or turtle with the West-Indian merchant at the London tavern.—But I fear they will never meet me again . . . .' 1 July 1793 (W. L. Benson—Brisco transcript).

[3] *Templeman*, p. 199.

vale of Keswick some time before 1756 though the *Letter* addressed to Lord Lyttleton was not printed till 1767.

Many passages could be quoted from Gilpin's writings which underline to what extent his conception of the Picturesque is linked with his native Cumberland and Westmorland, with the idea of the sublime, of rugged and unspoilt landscape, of romantic castles and therefore opposed to what he would term rural or pastoral scenery. An early instance occurs in the *Dialogue*, where Polython praises the country in the north-east of England:

The Place I have in view is upon the Banks of the River *Eden* (which is indeed one of the finest Rivers I ever saw). I scarce know a fitter Place for a Genius in this Way to exert itself in. There is the greatest Variety of garnished Rocks, shattered Precipices, rising Hills, ornamented with the finest Woods, thro' which are opened the most elegant Vales that I have ever met with: Not to mention the most enchanting Views up and down the River, which winds itself in such a manner as to shew its Banks to the Best Advantage, which, together with very charming Prospects into the Country, terminated by the blue Hills at a Distance, make as fine a Piece of Nature, as perhaps can any where be met with.[1]

And nearly sixty years later in Gilpin's posthumous *Dialogues on Various Subjects* (London, 1807) we still meet that same enthusiasm for the Lake District as the ideal picturesque region, with its essential variety, sublimity, and appeal to the imagination. In one passage, Sir Philip Sidney tells Lord Burleigh: 'what first kindled in my breast a love for landscape' and 'the effect, which the wonderful scenes of nature, when considered as pictures, may have on the imagination'. It happened in this way. Sir Philip was staying with the young Earl of Cumberland, who

used often to tell me, that we, inhabitants of the south of England, knew nothing of nature's sublimities. When I talked of the woody scenes of Penhurst, and its delightful meadows, he would laugh, and say they were well enough for shepherds and shepherdesses to dance in; but they were poor scenes compared with those sublime castles, in which the genii of rocks and mountains dwelt. As we were now, therefore, in the neighbourhood of these *sublime castles*, I begged he would introduce me to them; and give me some idea of what he called the *sublimities of nature*. At first he seemed rather backward, as he thought I should scarce be able to travel through such scenes of desolation. In many parts, he told me, we should meet with no appearance of inhabitancy . . . . My curiosity made all difficulties light . . . we travelled over all the mountainous parts of Cumberland, and Westmorland; and I know not, that I ever spent three weeks, in what I may call, so delicious a manner. It was all enchantment; during the whole time I was in a delirium of rapture:—mountains, lakes, rocks, and woods, in an infinite variety of awful combinations, were continually displaying themselves before my eyes in the day—and rising again to my imagination in the visions of the night. I have since, probably, seen as romantic countries among the Alps, Apennines, and the Pyrenees; but, from a first impression, or from the pleasing association of ideas, which my engaging friend has left upon my mind, I certainly never was so much enchanted with any appearances of nature, as with those I have met with here (pp. 393–7).

We could quote many similar passages from the *Tours* to show how Gilpin's love of his

---

[1] 1748, pp. 24–25.

native Cumberland and Westmorland is indissolubly linked with his conception of the Picturesque.

Before returning to our discussion of the theory, we should bear in mind how very early in life Gilpin formulated his ideas. Half a century before Price and Knight were to launch their great debate on the Picturesque, Gilpin was looking at landscape with the eyes of an artist, so that he has every right to be considered our earliest conscious critic of landscape. Take, for example, this humorous description of the view from the old part of Queen's College, Oxford. He is not yet eighteen as he writes to his aunt, Mrs. Griffith (?), on 27 March 1742:

. . . the height of my Room gives me a most noble Prospect. when I consider this, I pitty the poor Fellows pent up beneath me in a ground Apartment: while I can look round me for several Miles, their Prospect is bounded by a dead Wall, or at best confin'd to cross a Street. while they are looking at a dirty Kennel, or a Bed of Nettles, I am entertaining Myself with beautiful Streams, and delightful Groves . . . . The first [objects] which present themselves are two Gardens: In one of them which belongs to New-College you have whatever Art can furnish you with; in the other, pure Nature. The former offers you a fine Variety of Vistas, Shady Walks, and Arbours, and in the open Parts deals mostly in Parterres, in one of which you may discover his Majesty's Arms cut out of Box, in the opposite one they have done as much for the Founder of their College, in a third you have the Figure of a Sun-Dial made of the same Materials, which answers to a fourth clipt out into the Form of a Labyrinth. all this makes a fine Contrast when oppos'd to Beds of Turnips and Carrots, or Rows of Pease and Beans which present themselves in the other Garden. When your Eye is tir'd in one Place with beholding Arches, Pyramids, and Pillars hewn out of Yew-Tree, you may vary your Scene in an Instant, and please yourself with looking at in the other Place sometimes a Cabbage, and sometimes an Apple-Tree. There is as much Variety too in the Inhabitants of these two Gardens. The one daily presents me with pretty Ladies or Gentlemen walking about for their Pleasure; the other as frequently offers me carefull Mothers, or busy-fac'd Matrons hanging out their Linnen, or weeding their Parsnips.

After dwelling on St. Peter's ('an old Gothick Building'), the recent wing of New College, and the old city wall Gilpin completes his description with this capital passage:

As Objects now begin to lessen, you must expect a fainter Description, agreable you know, to the Rules of Painting. Beyond the Gardens then the next Thing is a most beautiful Grove which at once charms both your Eyes and Ears. The one is charm'd by the Linnet the Thrush, and the hoarse Musick of Crows and Rooks, than which no noise is more agreable to one: the other by Deer playing among the Openings of the Trees, and a noble new Building which is so shaded & cover'd with Oaks & Elms that it appears to me like an old romantick Castle rising out of a Wood, or if you please a Scaleby. My V[i]ew is bounded in Front by this Grove; for Variety upon each Side there is an Opening into a most delicious Country, which abounds with Green Fields, Trees, Spires, Villages, and in short wants nothing but a little more Water, and two or three of your Scotch Mountains to make it a most compleat Prospect.[1]

Here we have the imaginative countryman who, though cooped up in a town, makes the

---

[1] Major J. R. Abbey Collection.

best of it by transforming the scene before his eyes into an ideal nearer his heart. The tendency to consider the view in terms of foreground and distances, variety and contrasts is already clearly marked; and what is so striking at this early date is the allusion to those elements (castle, water, mountains) which will become, years later, the subject of his imaginative landscape drawings. It was during the 1740's that he formed his picturesque ideas, and despite changes which succeeding years brought in matters of taste, Gilpin's viewpoint remained substantially unchanged. That he succeeded in capturing the spirit of the Lake District is amply born out by contemporary testimonies, and of these none provides a better confirmation of the validity of his theories and drawings than this extract from a letter written in 1788 by his son William after a visit to the Lakes in the company of his cousin William Farish:

The first day . . . I was very dissatisfied with my studies—we rode up to Borrodale. It was all very magnificent; but the sky was clear—and the distinctness with which we saw so many rocks and mountains, broken into so many parts, and their surfaces again so infinitely varied rendered every attempt I could make to express the same in blacklead altogether vain. I had, however, no idea that the country ever exhibited itself under any other appearance than that in which we saw it. The difference that a cloudy sky might make never entered into my head—I was therefore not only dissatisfied with what I could do; but, likewise, with whatever I had seen of yours. How inadequate, said I, is my father's pencil to express all this! He may substitute what he calls *effect* in the [place] of it—but where is this *effect*? I see such and such parts in shadow; but the variety of the surface even then both in form and colouring is so essential to the beauty of the scene, that it can not be expressed without it. This effect therefore, must be a thing of his own invention—a kind of mantle that he pretends nature is sometimes covered with, which tho' it may conceal some particular beauties, yet amply compensates for that by its great harmonizing power, by which it unites an infinite number of petty beauties (which do indeed almost exceed the utmost efforts of consummate art to express) into one vast stupendous whole: and then he makes his drawing and says, this is some idea of that effect. A fine artifice this, thought I, truely! and so returned home to the inn at Keswick with a sovereign contempt both for your doctrines and drawings—the next morning I opened my curtains and beheld a most dismal prospect for one who had only one day more to stay at Keswick—a steady settled rain, which had all the appearance of continuing thro' the day—after waiting for some hours, we took the first moment of cessation, and mounting our horses, sallied forth, but expecting nothing but rain. We had not gone half a mile before the clouds began to break away; and as if they had assembled on purpose to convince me of the errors of yesterday, after dashing me a little with rain for the sleight I had put upon them, immediately marshalled themselves all around so as to aid the landskip in the most powerful manner. Then what effects of gloom and effulgence—dark mountain forms in all their chaste and corrected colouring—for the most part bosomed in cloud—except over one ragged knoll, where a passage is opened for the light that catches the opposite summits, and melting away the gloom in the richest fringed work broadens as it descends,—but I cant describe—nor need I—for you have only to look into your own store house to take a view of them—It gave me however a very singular pleasure to see your system of effects so compleatly confirmed as it was by the observations of that day—wherever I turned my eyes, I beheld a drawing of yours—and I have no scruple in asserting that your drawings are the most calculated to give an idea of that country of any representations either in *wash, copper*, or *oil*, that ever were made. Nor were these effects transient. They lasted as long as one who had so much to look at could afford time for.[1]

Though the forms with which Gilpin chose to illustrate his picturesque ideas are limited, he is only too willing to admit that had he been fired by other aspects of nature, these could equally well have been expressed in picturesque terms. Landscape can be expressed in *pastoral* or *rural* terms, or a mixed mode can result by using together in a composition features that belong severally to the *rural*, the *pastoral*, and the *sublime* as Poussin and Claude have done. Gilpin's partiality for the sublime led him to reject rural and pastoral subjects which were to be held as inferior, and to dislike mixed modes of landscape as conflicting with the principle that a landscape should have one *leading subject* which 'characterizes the scene'.

Yet when it came to evolving a landscape which measured up to his conception of picturesque beauty, Gilpin himself produced a mixture; a design based on the sublime to which were added some rural embellishments. As he realized, a sublime subject does not easily please because of its austerity, and though it may be termed 'picturesque', it can rarely be called 'beautiful'[2]—the latter quality can only be obtained by the introduction of ornaments ('amenity' as he sometimes calls it) such as trees, shrubs, the ruin and the castle, and these are all rural embellishments. As he says about the sketches drawn from mountain and lake scenery: 'Such scenery affords two great sources of picturesque composition—*sublimity*, or *simple grandeur*; and *grandeur united with beauty*. The former arises from a *uniformity of large parts*, without *ornament*, without *contrast*, and without *variety*. The latter arises from the introduction of *these appendages*, which forms scenery of a *mixed kind*.'[3]

He explains his point still more clearly in the 'Instructions for Examining landscape'. After stating that 'the *grand*, & the *rural* are the two prevailing characters of the landscape' and that sublimity marks the one and amenity the other, he goes on to say:

We seldom however find either of these characters perfectly pure. They are generally intermixed: for little beauty results from sublimity alone: & yet the rural, without a little of the sublime, would be low, & vulgar. The mixture therefore of these two characters forms a third species; which is the character of most of the following drawings [those which illustrate the 'Instructions']: & indeed it is the character of most of the best landscapes we have. We always wish for so much *sublimity*, as to banish every thing low, and trivial; & for so much *amenity*, as to soften the sublime. In this mixed mode of landscape, we hardly admit the cottage. In its room we rather expect the castle. The brook may murmur over pebbles; yet we are better pleased, when it spreads into a river: but as to the appendages of husbandry, and every idea of cultivation, we wish them totally to disappear.

As there are however instances in the grand style of landscape, in which *sublimity alone* is introduced; so there are inferior modes of landscape, in which low vulgarisms may properly make a part—cottages—hay-making—harvesting—and other employments of husbandry.—This low

---

[1] William Gilpin II to his father, W. G., from Carlisle 15 Sept. 1788 (Major J. R. Abbey).

[2] *Remarks on Forest Scenery*, ii, 166.
[3] *Five Essays*, p. 167.

mode of landscape is not however now in question; we are here considering such landscape only, as in part introduces the sublime idea; & in part the rural embellishment.

We may observe farther, that landscape more, or less approaches the *grand* style, as it is more, or less adorned with these embellishments. Thus when rocks are tufted with trees or shrubs, a degree of *amenity* is introduced. As these are increased, the idea improves: as they are removed, it lessens; and in proportion, the *grand* style prevails. If you remove them intirely, as far as the Design goes, it becomes *sublime*.[1]

Having decided it was necessary to his purpose to bring in rural embellishments, Gilpin had the difficult task of deciding which of them he would accept; the choice was bound to be somewhat arbitrary, and his decision to reject many of the most obvious features then in vogue such as peasants and cottages led him into lengthy justifications with his friends. A sublime landscape might be compared to a finely proportioned room stripped of furnishings, but if furnishings are essential these might as well be selected with some care; and as Gilpin is primarily concerned with the portrayal of the natural scene, rather than of man and his activities, he chooses on moral as well as aesthetic grounds features that introduce an element of beauty, and that at the same time cannot be termed vulgar. His rejection of cottages is an example in point. Certain objects were obvious rallying points for the expression of false or cheap sentiments (i.e. sentimentality and sensibility) and the fact that they became so and continue to be so, as, for example, on our Christmas cards and calendars, shows that Gilpin was quite right to reject them as detrimental to his purpose.

The discussion he had with Mary Hartley on the subject of cottages brings out clearly the nature of his conception of the Picturesque, which is austere and idealistic, and runs counter to the general attitude of his age, whose picturesque outlook took account of ordinary emotions and envisaged natural scenery in a direct manner.

Mary Hartley, who advocated a natural approach to landscape and admired the rural scenes of Gainsborough, sent Gilpin, in September 1789, some of her drawings. He, after admiring her efforts, added:

you work best with nature before you; & I, from imagination. Mine is certainly the less pure mode of imitation. You work from the original archytype, I only from its reflected images. My *whole* may sometimes be more picturesque than yours: your *parts* will always be more pleasing, because more truthful, than mine. Your little distances also, where you have now and then given a catch of the country, are very pleasing.—But nothing that you can draw, nor any thing that you can say, can reconcile me to a *cottage*. In nature it pleases me, for reasons I have somewhere given.[2] But when I see it in a picture, I always remove my eye. I mention this however only as an instance of my own squeamishness. I can give no *reason*, why a cottage may not make a pleasing picture. All I can say, is, that my eye is so captivated with sublime subjects, that it will bear no other. Some people have a taste prepared either for the grandeur of Homer, or the elegance of a sonnet. I am inraptured only with the Homerian style in painting.[3]

---

[1] 'Instructions for Examining landscape', pp. 2–4.   [3] W. G. to Mary Hartley, 13 Oct. 1789 (W. L. Benson).
[2] *Remarks on Forest Scenery*, i, 226.

Mary Hartley agreed that their respective talents and preferences were different. 'Your Genius has much more of the *influence of God*. I know not whether my compositions are more *natural* or no; but I am sure they are not so *sublime*.'[1] However, she was greatly surprised he should express such marked dislike to the presence of a cottage in a landscape:

It is not indeed a sublime scene, but few mortal geniuses are capable of being always in the sublime. Our ideas seem to me to want repose sometimes, as well as our bodies; & I shou'd find that after having had my mind raised into the highest enthusiasm, by the sublime views of rocks & torrents, & of all the most wonderful powers of Nature, in her greatest works, I shou'd like afterwards to compose my imagination with a softer scene; where a little straw-roofed cottage shou'd peep out from behind an old hollow oak, with fantastical branches elbowing over it—a little blue smoke coming out from a small chimney, backed by the dark shade of a high & deep wood behind—a young woman at the door, with an innocent unaffected countenance the rose of health on her cheek, & an infant in her arms—on the steps of the door & round about it, 4 & 5 other children, playing with one another, in all the beautiful attitudes of infant sport—at a little distance the father of the family, returning from his work & stooping to embrace two little boys, who run to catch the first kiss—These are what I call Pastorals in painting: such scenes as these I have seen described by the inimitable pencil of Gainsborough; I have thought them interesting & affecting; & I shou'd think that you who *are a father*—& a *beloved* father—& who have seen your *own* little boys run to you to catch the first kiss, must feel it more interesting & more affecting than I do.[2]

This last plea conjures up paintings by Greuze on the other side of the Channel! Gilpin, this time, answered in more conciliatory terms. He was willing to concede that pastoral and rural subjects had their place, but he remained averse to mixed modes of landscape.

I forget what I said about the introduction of cottages in a picture. You seem not quite satisfy'd with it. All I meant to say, was, that my eye, which had been much conversant with the great scenes of nature and had drawn all it['s] favourite images from them, was not fond of rural scenes; in which cottages, and mills, and foot-paths, and foot-bridges are the ingredients. By no means do I depreciate these little simple subjects; I can even conceive them to be picturesque: but I have not a relish for them. I totally however repudiate their *interfering* with grand scenes. If Virgil had introduced his pastorals in his Eneid, he had made a strange jumble. Apart, each has its merit. I cannot say that I am very fond either of rural sports—gambols—and other scenes of pastoral figures. A shepherd, and his flock, I admit even in a grand scene: And the works of Berghem I universally admire. He treats pastoral subjects with dignity, yet simplicity. But all the Dutch masters I dislike; their colouring does not compensate for their subjects.

With Gainsborough's pictures I am little acquainted; He was but coming into vogue, when I left the world; but from two or three things of his, which I have seen, I dare say I should think with you, he treats pastoral subjects very agreably: for it is rather, I believe from seeing these subjects boorishly, or awkwardly represented, that I have taken a dislike to them, than from the nature of the subjects themselves.[3]

And so in his *Remarks on Forest Scenery* Gilpin refused to allow the ubiquitous cottage to appear in representations of the forest. To introduce variety into a picture mainly

[1] Mary Hartley to W. G., 23 Oct. 1789 (W. L. Benson).   [3] W. G. to Mary Hartley, 16 Feb. 1790 (Rev. E. G.
[2] Mary Hartley to W. G., 3 Feb. 1790 (W. L. Benson).   Benson—Brisco transcript).

composed of trees, by all means make use of a sandy bank, an area of rocky ground, a winding path or a pool of water—such features 'are sometimes found in forests; and are always introduced with good effect' (i, 225); but the lowly cottage should be excluded as out of keeping with the dignity of the subject. 'A forest-scene, introduced in picture, is introduced with distinction; and calls for every appendage of grandeur to harmonize with it. The cottage offends. It should be a castle, a bridge, an aquaduct, or some other object that suits it's dignity' (i, 227).

RUINS

Instead of the cottage Gilpin adopted ruins, particularly the ruined castle. Besides providing a suitable focal point, such a choice was in keeping with the imaginative aspect of his drawings. His partiality goes back to his earliest critical writings, and the *Dialogue upon the Gardens . . . at Stow* (1748), where Polypthon says as he looks at the ruin at the head of the artificial lake:

Yes, indeed, I think the Ruin a great Addition to the Beauty of the Lake. There is something so vastly picturesque, and pleasing to the Imagination in such Objects, that they are a great Addition to every Landskip. And yet perhaps it would be hard to assign a reason, why we are more taken with Prospects of this ruinous kind, than with Views of Plenty and Prosperity in their greatest Perfection.

Though he had not yet explained the picturesque value of castles and ruins, his partiality can easily be explained by reference to his upbringing. Born at Scaleby Castle he had spent his early days in this ancestral home which had been a partial ruin since the days of Cromwell. We saw in the letter written from Oxford in 1742 that the idea of 'an old romantick Castle' immediately conjured up the picture of Scaleby. Later, when Gilpin made his tour of the Lakes in 1772, he revisited the Castle now overgrown with weeds and almost entirely abandoned, and allowed his mind to dwell nostalgically on what remained of his former home:

This venerable pile has now undergone a second ruin. The old oaks and elms, the ancient natives of the scene, are felled. Weeds, and spiry grass have taken possession of the courts, and obliterated the very plan of a garden: while the house itself, (whose hospitable roof deserved a better fate,) is now a scene of desolation. Two wretched families, the only inhabitants of the place, occupied the two ends of the vaulted hall, when we saw it, the fragment of a tattered curtain, reaching half way to the top, being the simple boundary of their respective limits. All the rest was waste: no other part of the house was habitable. The chambers unwindowed, and almost unroofed, fluttered with rags of ancient tapestry, were the haunt of daws, and pigeons; which burst out in clouds of dust, when the doors were opened: while the floors, yielding to the tread, made curiosity dangerous. A few pictures, heir-looms of the wall, which have long deserved oblivion, by I know not what fate, were the only appendages of this dissolving pile, which has triumphed over the injuries of time.

Shakespeare's castle of Macbeth could not have been more the haunt of swallows and martins, than this.[1]

Scaleby became the prototype for his ruined castles—it was only necessary to transfer it from the flat country north of Carlisle into a more picturesque setting, on the edge of a lake or perched on a commanding slope. And just as Scaleby was a personal and living link with the past, so when Gilpin, the traditionalist and family historian, expressed his bias for ruins and castles in his landscapes, he sought to stir the imagination, as his had been: we are asked to place ourselves in these buildings, to admire the prospect, and to visualize their former inhabitants and the events that took place—in other words to be possessed of a sense of history.

Gilpin listed the picturesque advantages 'which a castle, or any eminent building, receives from a *state of ruin*':

It gains irregularity in it's *general form*. We judge of beauty in castles, as we do in figures, in mountains, and other objects. The solid, square, heavy form, we dislike; and are pleased with the pyramidal one, which may be infinitely varied; and which ruin contributes to vary.

Secondly, a pile gains from a state of ruin, an irregularity in it's *parts*. The cornice, the window, the arch, and battlement, which in their original form are all regular, receive from ruin a variety of little irregularities, which the eye examines with renewed delight.

Lastly, a pile in a state of ruin receives the richest decorations from the various colours, which it acquires from time. It receives the stains of weather; the incrustations of moss; and the varied tints of flowering weeds. The Gothic window is hung with festoons of ivy; the arch with pendent wreaths streaming from each broken coigne; and the summit of the wall is planted with little twisting bushes, which fill up the square corners; and contribute still more to break the lines.[2]

These are the points which we might expect from his conception of picturesque beauty, yet they would equally have applied to cottages, had he decided to admit them.

Scaleby Castle met the requirements perfectly thanks to Cromwell, for he and Henry VIII gave us the best ruins we have of castles and abbeys. As Gilpin writes: 'I have seen many pieces by' Cromwell, 'executed in a very grand style; but seldom a finer monument of his masterly hand than' Scaleby. 'He has rent the tower, and demolished two of it's sides; the edges of the other two he has shattered into broken lines. The chasm discovers the whole plan of the internal structure—the vestiges of the several stories—the insertion of the arches, which supported them—the windows for speculation; and the breastwork for assault.'[3]

Though ruins are in a sense artificial elements, he welcomes them as rural embellish-

---

[1] *Tour of the Lakes*, 3rd ed., 1792, ii, 124–5. Captain John B. Gilpin had struck a similar note when he visited the ruins of Kentmere Hall, the birthplace of Bernard Gilpin (1517–83), the 'Apostle of the North', and the home of the Gilpins before they moved to Scaleby in the seventeenth century: 'As I stay'd a day or two at Kendal my curiosity led me to see Kentmire Hall, the birth place of Bernard Gilpin—'Tis now an old ruin'd place, at the Foot of a craggy Hill, with a large Lake before it which gives Name to the River Kent which runs by Kendal—The whole has a romantick Appearance—I could not help reflecting upon the Virtues of the good old Man, that had spent his Youth there.' Captain Gilpin to his wife, 18 May [1749] (A. L. Fawcett).

[2] *Eastern Tour*, pp. 121–2.   [3] *Tour of the Lakes*, ii, 123

ments, as they bring into the landscape composition a degree of amenity, and therefore of beauty. As artificial objects in nature ruins are innocuous: through time they have merged into the landscape to form part of our scenery, and the history of our countryside; they are ruins of abbeys and castles peculiar to the English landscape, and as they are 'naturalized to the soil, might indeed, without much impropriety be classed among it's natural beauties'.[1]

The ruined aqueduct, that appears in his drawings of forest scenes, could hardly be classified as one of England's 'natural beauties'; yet its presence is justified on the same grounds of naturalization:

> With regard to aquaducts indeed, the Romans never suffered wood to grow near them, lest it's roots, or seeds, should insinuate themselves into the crannies of the stone, and injure the work. But there can be no impropriety, at this day, in the introduction of a ruined aquaduct amidst a woody scene; as trees of any magnitude may be supposed to have grown up, since it had fallen to decay.[2]

Like most of his contemporaries he was affected by the Gothic revival, but when it came to the use of ruins in landscape gardening he kept both his feet firmly on the ground. Though he wasn't averse to improving an existing ruin,[3] he was far from advocating the building of artificial ones to render the view on an estate more picturesque. What could in imagination be done in a sketch was one thing, but to carry out the idea in reality was quite another. In this matter he found himself in opposition to the current trend of landscape gardening as sponsored by 'Capability' Brown, Thomas Whately, and William Mason, who saw no difficulty in placing ruins into a general conception. And it is to his credit that he constantly showed up their shortcomings, though he could do little to prevent outbuildings being screened as Gothic ruins.

How far he was prepared to go is well illustrated by his clash with Mason, the Gothic landscape gardener. In 1781 Mason brought out the last part of the *English Garden*. Therein he spoke in favour of artificial ruins, as Whately had done, and stressed that they should be put to good use.[4]

Gilpin, who had just expressed some rather different ideas in the manuscript of the *Remarks on Forest Scenery* (ideas which he later expunged in deference to Mason), enjoyed the pathetic tale of Nerina, but objected to a passage such as this, where Alcander, to hide an unsightly ice-house and a dairy,

---

[1] *Tour of the Lakes*, i, 13.

[2] *Remarks on Forest Scenery*, i, 227.

[3] Thus at Tintern Abbey 'a number of gabel-ends hurt the eye with their regularity; and disgust it by the vulgarity of their shape. A mallet judiciously used (but who durst use it?) might be of service in fracturing some of them; particularly those of the cross isles, which are not only disagreeable in themselves, but confound the perspective.' *Wye Tour*, pp. 32–33.

[4] Mason was indebted for some of his ideas, particularly for the description of Alcander's conservatory, to René Louis de Girardin's *De la Composition des Paysages, ou des Moyens d'embellir la Nature autour des Habitations, en joignant l'agréable à l'utile*, Paris, 1777.

> . . . builds of old disjointed moss-grown stone
> A time-struck Abbey. An impending grove
> Screens it behind with reverential shade;
> While bright in front the stream reflecting spreads,
> Which winds a mimic River o'er his Lawn.
> The Fane conventual there is dimly seen,
> The mitred Window, and the Cloister pale,
> With many a mouldering Column; Ivy soon
> Round the rude chinks her net of foliage spreads;
> Its verdant meshes seem to prop the wall.

He expresses his disagreement with 'dressing up out-houses, & offices in fictitious characters' and also with 'fabricating ruins of any kind', adding 'At least I have hardly ever been lucky enough to see any, that were not below contempt'.[1] Mason seems to have been somewhat incensed by this 'argument *ex abusu*' as he chose to call it, especially coming from a friend to whom he had just presented a copy of his book.

I grant you perhaps [he replied] that there are no mock Castles or mock Ruins extant that are what they should be, yet this is no proof but that there *may* be. & if they *may be* it is possible that they *will be* when the rules of Gothic Architecture are ascertained & implicitly followd. certain it is that the modern Improver (or rather let me call him the English Gardener) frequently stands in need of Picturesque forms to mask unpicturesque structures of Utility. & it is as certain that the Castle & Abbey being very picturesque forms are most fitted to this purpose. I do not however recollect that in execution I ever yet saw a fragment of the latter sort imitated which pleased me, yet at Stowe last summer a Castle seen from the Emilian Arch appeard to me to be the best object about the place, & yet this is a farm house & no expensive one either. I do not however say that this was perfect in its kind yet a few more breaks in the plan would have made it so. I conclude therefore that these things are feasible, and if feasible, certainly (on necessary occasions) to be adopted, in scenes where Objects are wanted.[2]

Faced with such intransigence, Gilpin tried to be conciliatory. He said that castles and abbeys were indeed picturesque, but artificial ones were not suitable for the purpose Mason had in mind. He then stressed the financial difficulties involved, and added that if artificial ruins there must be, they must only be perceived at a distance:

I am truly sorry, that you & I differ about this matter of a castle, & an abbey: and yet I do not know, that we do differ. If we *could have the reality* or anything like it, we should *both* wish for it: but I argue not so much ex abusu, as ex impossibili. Such a ruin as Glastenbury abbey, or Fountain's abbey, or as several other abbeys; which I have seen, would cost (even if it could be achieved, which I think impossible) 10, 15, 20, perhaps £30,000. And so likewise of castles. If we *could* make such scenes as these, I grant all you say: but I can never be a friend to a little paltry, affected substitute. If I could see Alcander's (that is, *the picture in your imagination*,) I dare say I should be pleased with it. But I think neither you, nor any body else, could *execute* such a thing *even with*

---

[1] W. G. to William Mason, 8 Nov. 1781 (W. L. Benson).   [2] William Mason to W. G., 23 Nov. 1781 (Rev. E. G. Benson).

30,000 pounds, unless you could call to your aid the picturesque polish of seven centuries. Still if these objects could be seen *only* at a distance, I should be less rigid. Your *castle* I should allow. I speak respectfully of the *distant castle* of a *certain nobleman* in your country. It is *near inspection* which I dread. And indeed I am willing to suppose that in this matter we agree. You have placed your abbey on the side of a piece of water, which forbids all approach in *front*; while

an impending grove
screens it *behind* with reverential shade.

After all, however, I should fear *giving instructions* on this head, lest you should let loose a body of *imitators* who are, you know a *servum pecus*. Less harm, I think, would follow from instructing them to place *unsightly* buildings, *out of sight*.[1]

Anxious for some measure of agreement, Gilpin sought Mason's consent before allowing his views to go abroad in the manuscript of the *Remarks on Forest Scenery*. But when Mason failed to understand his request, he wrote again in stronger terms.[2] Mason, however, was not to be moved from his position. He hit back with a lengthy and well-argued defence of his *English Garden*:

I had said in my first Book that a real Castle & a real Abbey were the happiest Ornaments an English Scene could have, and therefore I advisd a judicious Imitation of these so constructed that each might have its Use, & not be mere things of Parade. I really thought and I still think that the attempt is Feasible, not indeed to build a ruin like Conway Castle or Fountains Abbey, but such a peice of ruin as would have at a given distance a picturesque Effect nay I will venture to say a more picturesque Effect than many large Abbeys & Castles have in real Scenes when seen either at two Great or at an unfavourable distance.

In support of Alcander's embellishments, Mason guaranteed to build ruins which, seen at a distance, would be just as effective as those which Gilpin represented in the landscapes he drew in 1776 on reading the first book of the *English Garden*.[3]

I do not say that either of these [artificial ruins] would give you the precise Idea of that Castle & that Abbey from whence you made the drawings in question, but this I say that you would make as good drawings from them, & that they would look equally well not only on Paper but in the reality. for the Eye in both these matters is not so fastidious as your Critics Judgment, or measures Magnitudes so precisely. consider I beseech you how many advantages a good imitator has in this mode of Imitation, he has his point of sight and distance at his Option, He can chuse what to show & what to conceal by the aid of Plantation He can shew the *Fane Conventual* as *dimly* as he pleases. And if he has necessity, for a *Mitred Window*, it need not be either the East, or the west Window, & his Columns may be as short and as much *moulderd* as he pleases. The Castle in my mind is still a much more easy sport of Imitation and I would wager to execute either at much less expense than a great Man lays out upon a Palladian Bridge a Triumphal Arch or a Corinthian Rotunda and that in many scenes they would have a better effect than these.

---

[1] W. G. to William Mason, 1 Dec. 1781 (W. L. Benson).
[2] W. G. to William Mason, 24 Dec. 1781 (W. L. Benson).
[3] These large drawings were done at Cheam during the Christmas vacation of 1776. Two were sent to the D. Duchess of Portland, one to Mrs. Delany and one or two were kept for Mason. W. G. to William Mason, 24 Feb. 1777 (W. L. Benson).

To the caution against imitators he replied 'that it is right to instruct them to imitate well, and to turn their imitations to some good Use. Objects to their places all improvers must have. and tis more laudable to mask a farm yard with Battlements & make it look like a Castle than to build in its place a thing uselessly ornamental.'[1]

Since no reconciliation was possible, the matter was allowed to rest, each recognizing the other's point of view. 'You are the patron of *improved nature*: my delight is in its *wilder scenes*' wrote Gilpin,[2] while Mason indulged in some good-natured banter, making shrewd digs at the foibles of picturesque artists:

I am well aware that you & I shall never agree in these matters for our two Arts, as much as I have endeavord to bring them into Sisterhood, are but really half blood. Gardening when one has made her as natural and as degagéé as one can, has a certain neatness about her, which makes her chuse always to appear in her starchd Apron, & Ruffles; whereas Landscape Painting loves to have her things rumpled about her, and her hankerchief hardly pinnd to her stomacher. On this account you will not allow one of our tribe to take away a heap of Rubbish from the side of a real Ruin, because Rubbish in Painting has as good an Effect as a building of hewn Stone, & indeed a much better, unless that stone be somewhat mossgrown and Time Eaten and what you proscribe, from taste & feeling, your Critics will proscribe from Axiom. they will tell you that *Ruins are sacred*. that it is impossible to touch a single twig near them without spoiling their effect. tho a Vegitation of ten years or less, left to itself, would in my opinion even restore Fountains Abby to more beauty than it lost by the smoothing hand of Old Aislabey. I say more beauty, because I know that a great part of it was once very much obscured, by too overgrown a foliage.[1]

Mason soon found he had to contend with similar objections from quite another quarter. Jacques Delille in *Les Jardins* (1782) dismissed artificial ruins in no uncertain manner:

> . . . loin ces monumens dont la ruine feinte
> Imite mal du tems l'inimitable empreinte,
> Tous ces temples anciens récemment contrefaits,
> Ces restes d'un château qui n'exista jamais,
> Ces vieux ponts nés d'hier, et cette tour gothique,
> Ayant l'air délabré, sans avoir l'air antique,
> Artifice à la fois impuissant et grossier.[3]

The reply came early in 1783, when Mason's friend, William Burgh, brought out a new edition of the *English Garden*, together with commentary and notes. Gilpin, however, saw no reason to change his attitude, yet he confided to Mason, 'I once was a great friend to fictitious ruins, as you are now. I remember beseeching Tom Whately with great earnestness, to use a heap of old stone & rubbish, of which he had the command, in some-

---

[1] William Mason to W. G., 5 Jan. 1782 (Rev. E. G. Benson).
[2] W. G. to William Mason, 15 Jan. 1782 (W. L. Benson).
[3] *Les Jardins*, 1782, canto IV. The idea that genuine ruins have an evocative power which artificial ruins do not possess was very much in the air in the 1770's, and Delille readily acknowledged his debt to Whately and Chabanon in a footnote. Thomas Whately's *Observations on Modern Gardening* (1770) were translated into French in 1771, and M. de Chabanon's *Epître sur la Manie des Jardins anglais* appeared in 1775.

thing of this kind, when he laid out the garden at Nonsuch. But I had not then seen, what I since have seen, so many awkward, ridiculous, hideous attempts.'[1]

COMPOSITION

Having settled upon the general design of his drawing, Gilpin considers the problem of composition, which is the art of uniting the various parts of a landscape in a pleasing manner. The representational artist may encounter serious difficulties in trying to reconcile the general lines of the country with the exigencies of composition, and if the lines run false or are awkwardly disposed then no good composition is possible. As the natural scene rarely presents a whole where all the lines and objects are disposed in a pleasing manner, even the most topographically minded artist has to make some concession—it may be only the removal of an awkward building or the insertion of a foreground tree; and if the general disposition is unsatisfactory, he must shift his viewpoint till the lie of the land conforms to compositional requirements.

The painter of imaginary views, on the other hand, is not so fettered by his subject, and provided he ensures that all the parts of his composition are founded on natural observation, he has a much better chance of making a good picture—he may, in fact, 'bring together a more *consistent whole*, culled from the *various parts* of nature, than nature herself exhibits in *any one scene*'.[2] And 'nature . . . leaves us to work them up into pictures, as our fancy leads'. Such is the claim of Gilpin the idealist. Whatever may be the individual's choice he must take into account the general rules of composition.

A landscape is commonly divided into three parts: a foreground, a middle distance, and a background, 'tho a good landscape may be formed without either of the latter'.[3] These parts can be sharply defined or blend imperceptibly into each other, as the nature of the subject dictates, always provided they are treated so as to contribute towards the total effect; for, as Gilpin insists, 'in every work of art, . . . it is a breach of the most express picturesque canon, if the *parts* engage the eye more than the *whole*'.[4]

The nature of the country represented should be clearly stated, it should have a unity of character, or, as he puts it, one *'leading subject'* which *'characterizes the scene.* We often see a landscape, which comes under no denomination, Is it the scenery about a ruin? Is it a lake-scene? Is it a river-scene? No: but it is a jumble of all together.'[5]

So if a ruin placed in the foreground forms the subject of a picture, the *distance* introduced must then play a subordinate role. 'But most commonly the scene, or leading subject of the picture, occupies the middle distance. In this case, the *foreground* becomes the appendage; and without any striking object to attract the eye, must plainly shew, that it is intended only to introduce the leading-subject with more advantage.'[6]

[1] W. G. to William Mason, 5 June 1788 (W. L. Benson). Cf. with Gilpin's comments on General Conway's improvements, *supra*, pp. 42–43.   [2] *Five Essays*, p. 128.
[3] 'Instructions for Examining landscape', p. 6.

[4] *Western Tour*, p. 107.   [5] *Five Essays*, p. 126.
[6] Ibid., p. 127. 'It resembles those deep tones in music, which give a value to all the lighter parts; and harmonize the whole.' *Three Essays*, p. 69.

The foreground was that part of the landscape about which Gilpin held very strong views, both with regard to its function in a composition and the way in which it should be treated. All pictures should have foregrounds either considerable in depth or extensive in width, and indeed at times the foreground may provide the whole subject.[1] As an element in the composition it always forms 'the *basis, and foundation of the whole picture*',[2] even when its interest value is quite subordinate. And where such is the case, Gilpin has no compunction, he treats the foreground exactly as he pleases,

restrained only by the analogy of the country. I take up a tree here, and plant it there. I pare a knoll, or make an addition to it. I remove a piece of paling—a cottage—a wall—or any removeable object, which I dislike. In short, I do not so much mean to exact a liberty of introducing what does not exist; as of making a few of those simple variations, of which all ground is easily susceptible, and which time itself indeed is continually making.[3]

The foreground is also required for contrast. In the *Tour of the Lakes* he sums up its treatment in relation to the rest of the picture:

In a *distance* the ruling character is *tenderness*; which on a *foreground* gives way to what the painter calls *force*, and *richness*. *Force* arises from a strong opposition of colour, light, and shade: *richness* consists in a variety of parts and glowing tints. In some degree, *richness* is found in a distance; but never, united with *force*; for in a *distance*, tho the *light* may be strong, and the parts varied; yet the shades and tints will ever be faint and tender.

Moreover, 'this opposition on the foreground, violent as it is, must always be subject to the *ruling masses* of light and shade, and colouring, which harmonize the whole.'

The problem is to reconcile the dictates of harmony with the idea of a strongly contrasted foreground: '*breadth* and *repose*, which consist in uniting the parts, must be made to agree with *force* and *richness*, which consist in violently breaking them' (i, 111–12).

In practice Gilpin treated imaginary views and real scenes in much the same way. The far distance became misty, the middle distance received the main play of light and shade, and the foreground was dark. When criticized by his brother Sawrey and William Lock for not introducing enough variety of lighting in the foreground, Gilpin defended the principles that governed his choice:

A dark foreground makes, I think, a kind of pleasing gradation of tint from the eye to the removed parts of the landscape. It carries off the distance better than any other contrivance. By throwing the light on the foreground all this appears to my eye disagreeably inverted.—Besides, the *foreground* is commonly but a mere *appendage*. The middle, & remote distances, (which include the compass of the landscape) make the *scene*; & therefore require most distinction.—In history-painting it is the reverse. The *principal* part of the subject occupies the *foreground*; & the *distance* is the appendage. Here therefore the force of the light is due. In landscape too, when a building, or

---

[1] *Foregrounds alone* make a better picture than *distances alone* (*Wye Tour*, p. 92).

[2] *Five Essays*, p. 127.
[3] *Three Essays*, p. 68.

other object of consequence occupies the *foreground*, & the *distance* is of little value, on the same principle, the lights should fall upon the foreground.[1]

His views on foregrounds were shared by several of his picturesque friends, though their approach tended on the whole to be more factual and less imaginative. Here is Mary Hartley's attitude:

I often find some pretty object for the fore-ground, by moving (as you say) perhaps only a few yards, if not, I sometimes defer finishing my drawing, till I have met some pretty fore-ground in the country round about, which seems congenial to it; & I think this does rather better than putting in a fore-ground *merely* from imagination. I think a drawing shou'd be A Novel founded on Fact.[2]

In his writings he discussed at length the various elements most suitable for foregrounds. These vary a great deal with the kind of landscape to be depicted. For example, when he sails down the Wye he considers the most effective way of dealing with the screens that rise on either side of this winding river; and when in the New Forest, he finds that the disposition of trees presents special problems.[3] The Lake District offers broken grounds, rocks, valleys, and cascades, these he examines in turn, rejecting the last as unsuitable in the foreground:

(a) Broken grounds

Their accidented outlines and rough shapes are ideal for foregrounds. The variety of material is a great advantage, for 'the painter will easily find some rough knoll, whose parts are ample—the sloping corner of a hill, perhaps worn by a mountain-torrent—a rugged road, winding through the chasm of a rifted promontory'.[4] Though the scenery of the Lake District often lacks large trees, which would give to the foreground 'a grandeur equal to the scene', this deficiency can be overcome by a judicious combination of rocks and smaller trees, or simply by bringing in a large tree from outside. In particular he advocates the use of a great oak

when we want the magnificence of its shadowing form to mantle over the vacant corner of a landscape—when we wish it to hide some heavy promontory; or to scatter a few loose branches over some ill-shaped mountain-line—when it's massy foliage is necessary to give depth to shade—its twisted bole covered with grey moss, to oppose the vivid green in it's neighbourhood—or, lastly, its warm autumnal tint to contrast the colder hues of distance.

(b) Rocks

As might be expected, he prefers rocks which have a fractured surface to smooth ones. 'The fractured parts are larger and sharper; and better adapted to receive either smart, catching lights; or a body of light and shade.' Weeds, mosses, and lychens give touches of

---

[1] W. G. to William Lock, 24 Feb. 1790 (Rev. E. G. Benson).

[2] Mary Hartley to W. G., 14 Feb. 1789 (W. L. Benson).

[3] On foregrounds see *Wye Tour*, pp. 8–9, 12, 18–19; *Scottish Tour*, i, 118; *Remarks on Forest Scenery*, i, 221; *Five Essays*, pp. 68–69, 125.

[4] Quotations on broken grounds, rocks, valleys, and cascades taken from *Tour of the Lakes*, i, 113–24.

colour to the grey rocks in the foreground, and 'the painter, who does not attend to those *minutiae* . . . loses half the beauty of his original'.

(c) Narrow contracted valley

This provides an ideal subject for a foreground, in the same way as the open vale or valley is better placed in the distance. The valley should enter the picture diagonally, so that one of the slopes or side-screens should appear 'a little *removed*'; in this way you 'give your scenery the advantage of perspective', and the eye is carried along the path or stream to the view beyond the contracted valley.[1] Considerable variety is possible: 'The sides of the valley may be high, or low; rocky, or woody; smooth, or full of jutting promontories: and these variations . . . may play into each other with a thousand interchanges.'

When he wishes to represent a much flatter country, he makes a path go through a deep cutting in the foreground; the sides of the cutting then serve the same purpose at the slopes of a contracted valley, they provide the dark framing masses of the picture. Occasionally, he chooses a gill or dell, which differs only from the contracted valley by the absence of a distant vista, the steep rocky slopes closing the view—we have then a subject which is entirely a foreground one.

(d) Cascade or waterfall

This may be a *regular* or a *broken* cascade. The *broken* cascade 'belongs most properly to the rock; whose projecting fragments, impeding the water, break it into pieces—dash it into foam—and give it all the spirit and agitation, which that active element is capable of receiving'. And Gilpin exclaims: 'Happy is the pencil, which can seize the varieties, and brilliancy of water under this circumstance', for he himself was quite incapable of rendering the twists and turns of turbulent water and so eschewed its representation. His sense of frustration is great as he admires the falls of the River Bran, above Dunkeld:

This whole scene, and it's accompaniments, are not only grand; but picturesquely beautiful in the highest degree. The *composition* is perfect: but yet the parts are so intricate, so various, and so complicated, that I never found any piece of nature less obvious to imitation. It would cost the readiest pencil a summer day to bring off a good resemblance. My poor tool was so totally disheartened, that I could not bring it even to make an attempt. The broad features of a mountain, the shape of a country, or the line of a lake, are matters of easy execution. A trifling error escapes notice. But these high finished pieces of nature's more complicated workmanship, in which the beauty, in a great degree, consists in the finishing; and in which every touch is expressive; especially the spirit, activity, clearness, and variety of agitated water, are among the most difficult efforts of the pencil. When a cascade falls in a pure unbroken sheet, it is an object of less beauty indeed, but of much easier imitation.[2]

And so the picturesque artist lacking professional skill must forego animating his landscapes with the more beautiful kinds of waterfalls, and rest content with *regular* cascades, where the water meets with no obstruction as it falls from one level to a lower one.

---

[1] See *Tour of the Lakes*, i, plate facing p. 121.   [2] *Scottish Tour*, i, 122–3.

Proportion is the guiding principle to be observed when drawing a cascade, and on this point Gilpin shows that he has profited from the mistakes of his father, who was very unskilled at representing water. An elegant cascade results if due attention is paid to the ratio between the volume of water and the height of the fall. Though it is impossible to state the exact proportions, the principle may be demonstrated negatively by evident cases of disproportion. 'Thus when a mountain-cascade falls four or five hundred feet, and is perhaps scarce two yards broad; every eye must see the disproportion: as it will also, when the whole breadth of some large river falls only two or three feet.'[1]

While decidedly more at home with the *regular* cascade, Gilpin only occasionally thrusts it into the foreground;[2] he prefers to keep it in the middle distance, with the seething waters at its base hidden from view. If lack of personal skill presented a practical reason for removing cascades from the foreground, there was also a theoretical one—his general dislike of representing movement too near the eye. A waterfall or a torrent is a perfectly valid subject by itself, but in a landscape its movement can only be accepted if the eye is not distracted from considering the picture as a whole. Where a torrent bubbles in the foreground 'I think it fritters the parts too much; & takes the eye from reposing on the grandeur of the whole'; so he writes to William Lock about the lake scene which George Barret was painting at Norbury Park in 1781.[3] Lock too had some second thoughts about the torrent. In 1786, when this large picture, which covered the whole west wall of the drawing room [12. *c*], was near completion, Gilpin repeated his former objections, adding 'that in a picture like this, (which is supposed to possess something more of its archetype, than a common picture in a frame,) you are a little hurt by standing so near a torrent, & not hearing it roar'.[4] From the description of it in the *Western Tour*, it seems that Barret finally managed to fit it into the foreground to Gilpin's satisfaction:

The near ground is composed of bold rocks, and other rough surfaces, with which the banks of lakes commonly abound. Among these a wild torrent, variously broken, pours its waters under the surbase of the room, which intercepts it. This torrent the painter has managed so well, that its spirit and brilliancy produce no lights which interfere with the calm resplendency of the lake, but rather contrast it (p. 16).

DISLIKE OF MOTION NEAR THE EYE

Gilpin's opposition to movement near the eye, particularly rapid movement, is related to his general dislike of falling or moving objects in painting. While he agrees that in the 'art of looking at pictures', the spectator 'must allow himself to be imposed on in *every* thing',[3] he draws the line when it comes to the representation of moving, whirling, and

---

[1] See Captain Gilpin's drawings, as illustrated by Plates 1. *b* and 3. *b*.

[2] Exceptionally a waterfall fills the whole picture, see Plate 11. *e*.

[3] W. G. to William Lock, 13 Sept. 1781 (Rev. E. G. Benson).

[4] W. G. to William Lock, 30 July 1786 (Rev. E. G. Benson).

falling objects. In such instances the spectator cannot be expected to accept the illusion unless the action is continuous or so removed in the distance as not to obtrude upon the eye, which can then concentrate upon its primary function of taking in the whole picture.

He was willing to accept the torrent placed by Barret in the foreground of his large lakeland composition, not simply because it did not distract the eye, but because the artist had captured the idea of a movement that may be said to have started before and to have continued after the instant portrayed. The idea of movement near the eye is therefore acceptable in painting if the 'still' is representative of a continuous action *in situ*. Apart from this dispensation which covered waterfalls and torrents, which might be said to stay in their place in the landscape, he was not at all happy about the actions and movements of animals and human beings, placed in the foreground. In 1783 he aired the problem in his correspondence with Lock:

I dislike all motions & actions brought near the eye, which, in the nature of things, must immediately change into contrary motions or actions. It has something of the air of a *continued* absurdity. A bird flying *at a distance* I object not to: It *appears* to continue long in the same action. A bird flying *at hand*, or a horse galloping, I allow. The action is uniform. I suffer a man to lift up his hand in battle (but not his left hand by the way, on any account;) because, while my eye twinkles, he *repeats* the action. But I am rather hurt with a *horse falling*, because he immediately recovers, & receives a different motion.[1]

Though not '*very fond* of any motion brought near the eye' he had to admit that 'in *some* degree, it *must* always exist, & be tolerated among the imperfections of the art: but I think in general rapid motion should be avoided. I can better endure the slow-rolling wheel of a triumphal car, than the vibrating spokes of an Olympian chariot.' He was also willing to concede Lock's point that action, even violent action can be represented, provided a moment of temporary rest is selected, as in the earlier example of the rapid motion of an uplifted sword.

There is a point, from which the sword returns to it's object. That precise point of rest is the only point perhaps which the eye can endure: Indeed I believe it is, for in any other situation the action would be awkward. Or perhaps it [i.e. the eye] endures the uplifted sword, because it is sometimes held long in a threatening posture. Or perhaps, because in an instant the same motion recurs.[2]

In a similar way 'the eye bears without injury a horse rearing on his hinder legs; because there is a pause'.[3] By 1789 Gilpin only held out against rapid motion near the eye. 'I would not suffer a horse to gallop on the *foreground*; at least I do not like it; tho I should have no objection to see a cow set out [a] leg quietly before another. And yet I like a standing or reposing ground better. As to water running in a sheet, or cascade', the matter

[1] W. G. to William Lock, 25 June 1783 (Rev. E. G. Benson).
[2] W. G. to William Lock, 18 Aug. 1783 (Rev. E. G. Benson).
[3] W. G. to William Lock, 12 Dec. 1783 (Rev. E. G. Benson).

seems to have been settled once and for all: 'I do not call it a moving object. One *part* succeeds another in such perfect continuity, that the whole is at rest. And as to trees in motion, I allow them, wherever you please to place them. The blast *may* continue long enough to take off the absurdity.'[1]

Lock's reaction to all this was a healthy reminder that to exclude the representation of action and movement from painting would be to debase the art:

I agree with you in not adopting from choice subjects which introduce rapid motion into the foreground of a picture, upon the principle of *not loading the spectator with too large a quota*: but not upon that of *the impossibility of expressing rapid motion by what stands still*. Because, the principle unrestrained woud exclude all motion, & make it impracticable to render subjects of action—Care must be taken not to consider Painting wholly as an art of Imitation. It is also, & more particularly in its higher departments, an art of Convention—If it were merely mimetic, exact resemblance wou'd be indispensable: but the exclusion of motion & action wou'd render it an amusement for none but the vulgar—As an art of convention, where only general forms are imitated, & much is supplied by the fancy, exact resemblance is not to be looked for: & the alphabet learnt, becomes an entertainment for men of sense & information.[2]

Gilpin heeded the warning and even inserted parts of it in the explanatory notes to the *Poem on Landscape Painting*.[3] Lock had put his finger on one of the weaknesses or rather limitations of the Picturesque—its tendency to exclude all independent action or motion, save of the slowest kind, such as a man walking or a cow grazing. Yet it is difficult to see how the picture-making principles of the picturesque school could be made to include the representation of any large-scale movement or action, without creating a confusion of aims. The representation of landscape was its real subject. An action in the foreground or middle distance was a foreign element and as such altered the character of the picture. It was no longer a landscape, but a subject in a landscape.

To charge the Picturesque with immobility would, however, be unfair. It sought to animate the landscape and express movement with the material at hand, namely composition and light and shade. In a similar way Robert Adam tried to instil movement into architecture:

Movement is meant to express the rise and fall, the advance and recess with other diversity of form, in the different parts of a building, so as to add greatly to the picturesqueness of the composition, for the rising and falling, advancing and receding, with the convexity and concavity and other forms of the great parts, have the same effect in architecture that hill and dale, foreground and distance, swelling and sinking, have in landscape; that is, they serve to produce an agreeable and diversified contour that groups and contrasts like a picture, and creates a variety of light and shade which gives great spirit, beauty and effect to composition.[4]

Gilpin also disliked the representation in painting of objects moving or falling through

[1] W. G. to William Lock, 4 Dec. 1789 (Rev. E. G. Benson).

[2] William Lock to W. G., 12 Dec. 1789 (Major J. R. Abbey).

[3] *Five Essays*, p. 140.

[4] Quoted by Hussey, op. cit., pp. 189–90, from *The Works in Architecture of Robert and James Adam*, London, 1773, i, introduction to part I.

the air. As a young man he criticized Hogarth for showing a scroll falling from the hands of Felix in the painting of 'Paul before Felix', at Lincoln's Inn.[1] The allegorical figures placed in mid-air, in the seventeenth-century compositions of Lebrun and his Academy, he considered incongruous. 'If Le Brun had sent me home his triumph of Constantine; I should have begged him to be so good as put out the figure of Victory, or Fame, I forget which, flying over his hero.' The intrusion of the allegorical figure in a composition, which tells a story based on fact, destroys all sense of reality. By all means use allegory in a picture which is completely fictitious in subject-matter. 'Fiction is there in character. But when it is mixed with the representation of *fact*, I think, it is as much as to say, *all is fiction*; and the force of truth vanishes'.[2]

This is exactly the kind of advice he gave William Lock II, who in 1782 was working on a composition of Famine, in which the figure of Famine was suspended in the air: 'My objection does not arise from the difficulty of representing an *ideal figure*, (and yet that is a very delicate affair;) but from mixing fact or narration, & allegory together. A famine might be treated either historically, or allegorically; but it is not quite, I think, in the chaste style of composition to blend them.'

The best way to treat the subject is to represent an actual instance. 'I would have him carry the spectator to the banks of the Ganges—add a few Asiatic appendages; & display some of those noble scenes of famine, which our English Nabobs, to their immortal glory, displayed before him.'[2]

HARMONY

We have seen that for the various parts of a composition to be brought successfully together into a harmonious whole many things are required. In particular, attention must be paid to proportion, simplicity, and harmony.

(a) Proportion

Under this head Gilpin offers no fixed rules, for in the representation of landscape it is better not to be tied to exact proportions. In general, one portion of the landscape should not overbalance the others. With an individual object like a cascade, an elegant proportion may be obtained by studying evident cases of disproportion. The rules of perspective will help to adjust the relative size and shape of objects in a composition; after that one's personal taste and intention will determine what features to emphasize. Thus, Gilpin often exaggerates the size of a mountain situated in the distance to underline its particular dominance over the rest of the landscape, which then becomes subservient to that idea.

(b) Simplicity

'Beauty results from a just union of *simplicity, & variety.*' '*Simplicity* arises from the *fewness of parts*', while '*variety*, which is also called *richness*, consists in a *multiplicity of*

---

[1] See *supra*, p. 24.   [2] W. G. to William Lock, 19 Feb. 1782 (Rev. E. G. Benson).

parts.'[1] The problem is to assess the rival claims of these two qualities, for the predominance of the one over the other determines the character of the landscape. Either simplicity or variety will produce a picturesque effect, but it generally takes its tone from one of them:

> When the landscape approaches nearer *simplicity*, it approaches nearer the *sublime*; and when *variety* prevails, it tends more to the *beautiful*. A vast range of mountains, the lines of which are simple; and the surfaces broad, grand, and extensive, is rather *sublime* than *beautiful*. Add trees upon the foreground, tufted woods creeping up the sides of the hills, a castle upon some knoll, and skiffs upon the lake (if there be one) and tho the landscape will still be *sublime*, yet with these additions . . . the *beautiful* will predominate.[2]

We have already noticed that as Gilpin elaborated the theory of the Picturesque his terminology came under fire from those for whom such words as 'picturesque' and 'beauty' already held specific connotations. The words 'sublime' and 'simplicity' were no exception; their range of application to landscape was not the same as to history-painting.

When Gilpin asserted that magnitude and simplicity were the great sources of the sublime, he implied that for a feature, like a mountain, to be sublime it should also contain the idea of *continuation* or *extension*, which is to say that the mountain should convey the impression that, with slight variation of outline and form, it goes on and on, that it is capable of extension beyond the field of visibility. On the other hand, the advocates of the Grand Manner associated sublimity and especially simplicity with finite qualities—with the *repetition* of the same object, with *formality* of parts, and with *regularity* of composition. In trying to show that these qualities were foreign to his conception of sublimity or simple grandeur, Gilpin found himself in disagreement with both Reynolds and Lock.

> Burk[e] says, uniformity is a source of sublimity, because, *if the figures of the parts should be changed, the imagination, at every change, finds a check—you are presented at every alteration with the termination of one idea, & the beginning of another.*[3]
>
> Now if this be just, there must be a continuation—not a repetition, of the same idea. And indeed I think this is the truth. A number of mountains, for instance, ranged one after another, tho exactly of the same form, would never, I think, impress the idea of sublimity, so justly, as the continuation of one large object, ranging uninterruptedly, & uniformly, through a vast space.—In short, I think, the matter is neither more nor less, than this, that simplicity is the principal source of sublimity, as variety is of beauty.[4]

Through the winter of 1782 and much of 1783 he discussed the sources of the sublime with William Lock,[5] their difference of opinion culminating in a disagreement over *simplicity* and the *repetition of ideas:*

---

[1] 'Instructions for Examining landscape', p. 7.

[2] *Scottish Tour*, ii, 121–2.

[3] Burke actually wrote: 'because if the figure [*sic*] of the parts should be changed, . . .' *A Philosophical Enquiry into the Origin of our Ideas of the Sublime and Beautiful*, London, 1757,

part ii, section x, p. 55.

[4] W. G. to William Lock, 29 Oct. [17]82 (Rev. E. **G.** Benson).

[5] The sources of the sublime in history painting are not the same as in landscape: 'When I ventured . . . to assert that

You & I have lately had some little *variation*, rather than *difference*, of opinion, on the subject of *sublimity & grandeur*. You mentioned *simplicity* as being the great source of it: to which I agreed. Afterwards you began to talk of the *repetition of ideas*, which you said, you had been mentioning to sir Joshua Reynolds; & that he and you both resolved *simplicity* into this *repetition*. I think this was the purport of what you said . . . . I did not clearly enter into this idea of *repetition*; yet as a young divine sometimes, overruled by great authority, fancies he discovers truth, where in fact he does not clearly understand it; so I, under the sanction of you two great church-men, was unwilling to have it thought, I did not understand a doctrine, which to you appeared so plain. So I believe I half subscribed, if not wholly, to the doctrine of the *repetition of ideas*.—But now sir Joshua has fully opened his creed. Turn to the 85th page of his notes on Mason's translation of Frenoy;

Here Reynolds, commenting on the arrangement of contrasting figures or groups, recommended 'to the artist, not to destroy the grandeur and simplicity of his design by violent and affected contrasts'. He then proceeded to illustrate his point by a comparison of two paintings of the Virgin and Child, one by Rubens in the Church of St. Augustine at Antwerp, the other by Titian in the Church of the Frari at Venice.[1]

& you will see what he means by the *repetition of ideas* & how far he carries it. The two first paragraphs in the XXVth. note I wholly adopt. He then goes on to illustrate his position by 2 pictures, the works of Reubens, & Titian; & seems greatly to give the preference to the latter in point of sublimity; which, he tells you, *proceeds in a great measure from the regularity of the composition, two of the principal figures being represented kneeling, directly opposite to each other, & nearly in the same attitude.*—If this be your opinion, and you make your *repetition of ideas* to consist in *downright formality*, notwithstanding the high opinion I have, both of you & sir Joshua . . . yet *in this article*, I must beg leave to consider you both as heretics . . . . I will grant almost every thing short of formality itself: but formality I cannot bear.'[2]

(c) Harmony

By 'harmony' he means to achieve an agreement between colours, while 'preserving a contrast among the several parts of the landscape'.[3] It differs from another term he frequently uses, 'keeping', which denotes the relation between near and distant objects 'not only in point of size, but of light and shade'.[4] As he employs colours very sparingly, he

---

magnitude, & simplicity are the great sources of the sublime; I meant only in landscape. In history it is otherwise. The poet, it is true, can, with facility enough, make the figure he would exalt, touch the skies. But the painter cannot. He has only the same dimensions for his hero, & his clown. A man will not admit of plus & minus, like a mountain. If the painter wishes therefore to draw the sublime from magnitude, it is his business to *repeat* his object over & over; & obtain a magnitude in the whole, tho not in the parts. If he cannot produce £20 in one gross sum; he must contrive to produce it in 3 or four. It appears to me there is little more, than this, in the idea of *repetition*. Simplicity is a principle equally with him, & the landscape-painter.—But among all the sources of the sublime in history, I contend with you, totis viribus, that *energy of character, & expression* must take the lead.' W. G. to William Lock, 4 Dec. 1782 (Rev. E. G. Benson).

[1] Note XXV to William Mason's translation of Charles Alphonse Dufresnoy's *Art of Painting* (Sir Joshua Reynolds, *Works*, 4th ed., London, 1809, pp. 126–8).

[2] W. G. to William Lock, 25 June 1783 (Rev. E. G. Benson). See also W. G. to William Lock, 18 Aug. 1783 (Rev. E. G. Benson) for further proof of his intense dislike of formality.

[3] 'Instructions for Examining landscape', p. 7.

[4] Finding that Mason persistently confused the two terms, Gilpin tried once and for all to put him right: 'With *regard to effect* in painting, we must observe 2 things. The first is the agre[e]ment between near & distant obje[c]ts, not only in point of size, but of light & shade. The 2d. is, (a very different thing) the *agreement of colours*.—Now to express these two distinct ideas, I must have 2 words. Keeping will do well to express the former. It is always used & well understood. But

demonstrates harmony by his method of tinting. First, the composition is washed over with a light tint, which takes its colour from the hue of the sky—by this means 'you lay a foundation for harmony'. This wash is then repeated in the distance, 'softening it off into the sky, as you ascend'. Next, with a purplish tint you form your clouds, 'and then spread it, as you did the first tint, over your *whole drawing*, except where you leave the horizon-tint. This still strengthens the idea of harmony. Your sky and distance are now finished.'[1] As you proceed through middle distance to foreground you gradually distinguish between soil and vegetation, till in the very foreground you slightly heighten the colouring of objects.

This method of tinting was certainly helpful to the amateur artist, who through the use of neutralizing washes could avoid the danger of glaring tints. Yet features like the prevailing hue thrown over the whole drawing gave rather a fixed idea of harmony. Nature could be seen and represented in a variety of other ways. William Lock was quick to point out the limitations of this stereotyped treatment of harmony and provoked Gilpin into making a vigorous defence of what he termed his 'doctrine of *harmonizing a picture*':

I cannot allow *the least exception* in my doctrine of *harmonizing a picture*. Nature, you say, is very various; & may not always be in harmony with herself; especially in extensive landscapes. It *may* be so; tho I cannot say, that I ever observed it. In a misty day, one general, hazy veil is thrown over every object. In a grey day, the face of nature wears a sober colouring; in a bright day, a vivid one. However I do not mean to combat this point. In my argument I allow it. I suppose then nature is sometimes not in harmony with herself; you will grant, that this is not often the case— You will grant also, that she appears the most beautiful, when it is otherwise. What does a painter require more? It is his particular business to seek for those effects, which are most usual, & most beautiful. Let nature be out of harmony with herself. In nature, we do not regard it. If one object does not please you, look at another. It is not material. But in artificial landscape the painter confines your eye within a frame of such dimensions. You have a right therefore to expect, that he makes the most of that; & culls out what is most beautiful in nature. If nature's *discords are more pleasing*, represent them: but by no means, if they are not so.—It is thus with the ear. An ear tuned to nature, hears every where harmonious sounds—it hears them in the melody of birds, in the whistling of winds; in the murmuring of brooks; & even in the roaring of torrents, & the crash of storms, & thunder. In my ear the screaming of a jay, or a wood-pecker, when accompanied by the wild scenes of the forest, is harmonious. I readily grant however, that there *may* exist inharmonious notes in nature. But it is of little consequence, because I can range, in nature at large, from one object to another.—Not so in the concert-room. When the master of the band has immured me there; he uses me ill, if he do not treat my ear with his choicest symphonies.—I cannot then allow the least concession in this matter. The painter *must* harmonize his picture; or convince

surely it should not be used to express both. I am as great an enemy, as you are, to far-fetched analogues. I think with you also, that there is very little similitude between sounds & colours: yet there is a unity required in both: & why we may not express in the same terms, what agrees with both, I see not. We naturally fall into the same terms, as most deceptive. We talk of *concord* in both—we say a picture is *in tune*—& I see not why we may not talk of harmony in both. Two words I must have to express these 2 modes of agreement, between objects, & colours. And till you give me a better, I must use *harmony*.' 8 March 1785 (W. L. Benson).

[1] *Three Essays*, pp. 80–81. See also ll. 368–410 of the *Poem on Landscape Painting*; these he sums up as follows: 'In colouring, the sky gives the ruling tint to the landscape: and the hue of the whole, whether rich, or sober, must be harmonious.'

me, that discordant tints are the most agreable.—I need not, I know, to a person of your candid mind, be at the pains of convincing you, that I am no slave to *browns*, or *blues*, or *purples*. I have seen pictures *harmonized with staring colours*, which I thought abominable. All I wish from a prevailing hue is to keep a similarity among the tints; to shew them of one kindred:

facies non omnibus *una*;
Nec *diversa* tamen; qualem decet esse sororum.

But in subjects, you say, *which do not extend beyond a few yards, the imitation of nature lays you under no such necessity. While I am writing, I see none of the harmony in question between the colours of my hand, my pen, my shirt, & the table.* It is very true, that as air is the vehicle of tints, they will be sparingly spread, when you look through a slight medium of it. And here comes in the great difficulty of the landscape-painter. It is a comparatively easy matter to throw the hue of distance over his removed objects. Difficulties begin to arise, as he approaches the eye. But when he arrives at the foreground, (where he cannot have any advantage, or as little as may be, from the tint of his picture,) he must be a ruler of the pallet indeed, who can keep his colours from transgressing.

After all, it is very possible, that this dispute of ours may be a mere logomachy. I have no objection to paint nature, when you cannot observe in her any appearance of what you call *articulated, & emphatic harmony*—even when the air is pure, & diaphanous; but still the landscape, at least the distances, will take a certain hue, of some kind, or other, either gloomy, or vivid, from the reflection of the sky. Grant me *this* in my picture, & I will be satisfyed. I have told you, & I repeat it, that I am no advocate for a staring tint. I remember a painter formerly in the exhibition, whom the sneering artists, as they passed by, would call *blue Wilson*.[1] He was no model of mine: I could call him blue Wilson too. But because some people carry a doctrine into absurdity, are we therefore to settle in no point of orthodoxy?[2]

One colour which Gilpin finds difficult to harmonize with the surrounding landscape is white. Small objects such as 'a white seat at the corner of a wood or a few white cattle grazing in a meadow' are welcome for 'they have meaning and effect'; but large areas painted a raw white, like the country houses of the Welsh gentry, disturb the harmony of the landscape—the glare would be removed if they were painted a stone colour.

He maintains that '*white* is a hue, which nature expunges from all her works, except in the touch of a flower, an animal, a cloud, a wave, or some other diminutive, or transient object', for example nature covers chalky cliffs with plants and stains them with various tints 'so as to remove, in part at least, the disgusting glare'.[3]

Yet, as Lock reminds him, white offers the painter an enormous range. 'No other colour offers so extended a scale of light & shadow, with such a variety of inflections, when near: nor is any so susceptible of the predominant tint of the air, when distant—The transparency of its shadows, which in near objects partake so little of darkness, that they are rather second lights, & without injuring the principal light shew all the details of surfaces.'

---

[1] Richard Wilson (1713–82). Gilpin may be alluding to his pot-boilers. It is clear, however, that he did not appreciate Wilson's transposition of the ideal beauty of the Campagna into his English and Welsh landscapes.
[2] W. G. to William Lock, 7 Jan. 1782 (Rev. E. G. Benson).
[3] *Wye Tour*, pp. 53–55.

Lock shares Gilpin's general dislike for the colour, as he thinks 'it a tint which oftener injures than it improves the scene'. In particular white

disturbs the air in its office of graduating distances: shews objects nearer than they really are; & by pressing them on the eye, often gives them an importance which from their form & situation they are not intitled to—The white of snow is so active & refractory as to resist the discipline of every harmonising principle: & I think I never saw Mont Blanc & the range of snows which run thro' Savoy in union with the rest of the landscape, except when they were tinged by the rays of the rising & setting sun, or participated of some other tint of the surrounding sky—In the clear and colourless days so frequent in that country, the glaciers are always out of tune—[1]

These observations of Gilpin and Lock appeared in the *Wye Tour*, and for years afterwards they summed up the picturesque attitude towards white objects. Wordsworth himself was to share this view and state categorically: 'The objections to white, as a colour, in large spots or masses in landscape, especially in a mountainous country, are insurmountable.'[2]

LIGHT AND SHADE

As we have already seen Gilpin attached the greatest importance to light and shade, and by insisting on its proper handling he guided amateur artists away from the usual monochrome or tinted drawing with its even light cast over all objects, and gave them the machinery for animating their compositions. He accorded to light and shade the same important function as expression occupied in history-painting. This is how Mary Hartley expressed its special role, as she effected a reconciliation between Lock and Gilpin at a time when they were debating 'whether light & shade & *effect in general*, was to be considered as the *first* object in painting, or no'.

You claim it, very properly, as the *first* in landscape, [she wrote to Gilpin,] & yet allow as properly, with him [Lock], that Expression, which is the life & soul of historical painting, is certainly the great object there—the *first* object;—I suppose, for instance, that there is no one who wou'd not prefer the expression of passions in Raphael's cartoons, to the finest effects of local colours, or of light & shade, in the best of Rubens works. But in landscape painting, might I not say that light & shade, & the strong effect that is produced by their judicious disposition, is there the *Life & Soul*? And that the finest trees & the most beautiful prospects, without a pictoresque illumination, wou'd

[1] William Lock to W. G., 7 March 1782 (Major J. R. Abbey).
[2] Wordsworth's *Guide to the Lakes*, ed. by E. de Sélincourt, London, 1926, p. 80. Wordsworth draws on the Gilpin–Lock remarks in the *Wye Tour* (not on the *Tour of the Lakes* as stated by de Sélincourt) and gave additional reasons for his objection to white: 'Five or six white houses, scattered over a valley, by their obtrusiveness, dot the surface, and divide it into triangles, or other mathematical figures, haunting the eye, and disturbing that repose which might otherwise be perfect. I have seen a single white house materially impair the majesty of a mountain; cutting away, by a harsh separation,

the whole of its base, below the point on which the house stood. . . . But, if I may express my own individual feeling, it is after sunset, at the coming on of twilight, that white objects are most to be complained of. The solemnity and quietness of Nature at that time are always marred, and often destroyed by them' (pp. 80–81). For the influence of Gilpin on Wordsworth, see Z. S. Fink, *The Early Wordsworthian Milieu*, Oxford, 1958.

When the poet's library at Rydal Mount was sold in 1859, lot 540 consisted of two books: Gilpin's *Wye Tour* and an interleaved copy of Wordsworth's *Guide to the English Lakes*, . . . 1842 (*Templeman*, p. 285).

have no more effect in moving the imagination, than the most beautiful set of features, without any expression of understanding, sentiments, or passions, wou'd have in engaging the affections?[1]

Light and shade were indeed for Gilpin the life and soul of landscape-painting. Through its effects he could animate the scene and convey a wide range of moods, from the serenity of diffused lighting to the dramatic tension of chiaroscuro.

Generally we can say that he conceives the problem as follows: the landscape is divided into large contrasting areas of light and shade which soften into each other. This gradation adds variety to the broad masses of light and shade, 'by mitigating the glare of the one, and the gloom of the other'.[2] Shaded areas should predominate, and the light which 'is too often scattered on a variety of objects'[3] should in the main be concentrated in the middle distance. In addition, features are blurred by haze or picked out by catching lights to ensure harmony, variety, and contrast.

But for the picturesque artist who deals with sublime subjects, 'mere *light and shade* are not sufficient'.[4] Something more is needed, what Gilpin termed 'effect'. To make his point he draws a literary analogy. 'The tragedian, & the epic poet not only introduce *great characters*; but they find it necessary to introduce them in the *strongest point of light*. It is the *misfortunes* of Oedipus & the *wrath* of Achilles, which point the characters of each hero.'[5] Similarly, if a sublime landscape is to affect, its constituent elements must be given greater force by a dramatic use of chiaroscuro. Ordinary light and shade, what Gilpin calls 'simple illumination', may prove adequate for rural or pastoral subjects; the sublime requires special lighting, such as can be found in nature under certain circumstances and at certain times of the day. Hence his preoccupation with haze and mist, sunrise and sunset, clouds and storms.

'Now among the various modes of producing a picturesque effect, none is equal, in *point of splendor* to a *sunset*.'[5] This point he reiterated in later writings such as the *Poem on Landscape Painting*[6] and the *Remarks on Forest Scenery* (i, section ix), and demonstrated in series of drawings like 'Morning, Noon and Evening' and the 'Sunsets'. It is true that 'the morning-sun, surrounded by vapours, which it tinges with its reddish, or yellowish ray, is always pleasing, & is often grand. It's shadows are deep; & the obscurity in which it involves objects, is a great source of the sublime: but for *rich effect*, it generally falls short of an evening-sun.'[7] Then shadows are deeper, and opposition between light and shade more marked. Also 'the setting sun rests it's glory on the gloom, which often accompanies

[1] Mary Hartley to W. G., 23 Feb. 1783 (W. L. Benson). Of all his correspondents Gilpin recognized that Mary Hartley's picturesque ideas were closest to his own, and on several occasions he told her so: 'I do not know any body whose ideas of composition, & light & shade, are so kindred to mine, as yours.' 4 Sept. 1786 (W. L. Benson); 'I am glad to hear that you like my book [*Tour of the Lakes*]; tho to tell you the truth, I should have been much disap[p]pointed if you had not; for I really do not know any body whose picturesque

ideas I have thought more congenial with my own than yours.' 1 July 1787 (Rev. E. G. Benson—Brisco transcript).

[2] 'Instructions for Examining landscape', pp. 10–11.

[3] Ibid., p. 9.

[4] *Three Essays*, p. 75.

[5] 'On Sunsets', p. 1 (MS. in the collection of Dr. T. S. R. Boase).

[6] *Five Essays*, p. 114, ll. 428–43.

[7] 'On Sunsets', pp. 1–2.

it's parting rays. A depth of shadow, hanging over the eastern hemisphere, gives the beams of the setting-sun such powerful effect, that altho in fact they are by no means equal to the splendor of a meridian sun, yet through force of contrast, they appear superior.'[1]

Sunsets are interesting for their skies alone. Here he foreshadows Constable's *Clouds*,[2] and the preoccupation of many a nineteenth-century painter. 'The sky itself is an endless study for a painter. The forms of the clouds, & the tints, with which they are occasionally overspread,

> as each turns forth
> It's gilded lining to the evening-ray,

are so varied, that he, who can imitate all their hues exactly, has attained a high degree of excellence in his art, tho his pictures have little else to recommend them. The sky, in such landscapes, instead of being an appendage, becomes principal.'[3] On this score, Claude Lorrain, to whom Gilpin was never very partial, is praised for his skies, which are superior to his landscape composition. 'If Claude himself had depended more on his skies, & less on his landscape—that is, if he had preserved his usual brilliancy in the one, & had given more simplicity to the other, his pictures perhaps would have been more valuable.'[3]

A considerable effect is obtained by the use of slanting lights in a clear sky, particularly when the landscape is strongly accidented, yet a more powerful one results when the source of light is partially impeded by mist or heavy clouds. This interference with the sun's rays brings about a tension in the sky area, which dictates the distribution of light and shade on the land in a new way. The whole composition is thereby welded into a single pattern of chiaroscuro, often to such an extent that sky and land will merge into one another. It is this conjunction of light with a disturbed atmosphere which produces the most sublime effects.[4]

When it came to demonstrating the various moods of landscape which he had observed so accurately, Gilpin was severely curtailed by his inability to handle colours and his refusal to represent directly the source of light, be it sun, moon, or lightning.[5] His drawings are only monochromes and his effects restricted to those which could be conveyed by light and shade and an overall tint. He was particularly aware of his limitations when doing the series of 'Sunsets': 'to the humble draughtsman, who deals only in the different shades of *two* colours, all the splendid effects of the pallet are denied. He has nothing to do with gorgeous skies, & the *gilded linings* of clouds. *He* must depend more on his landscape. All he can do, is to produce an effect from the *uniform glow* of an evening-sun: and there are but a few circumstances, of which he can avail himself.'[6] And so Gilpin explored the possibilities open to him. Here are a few. 'A *dark object* against a *glowing light* may often have a

---

[1] *Remarks on Forest Scenery*, i, 254.
[2] K. Badt, *John Constable's Clouds*, London, 1950.
[3] 'On Sunsets', p. 2.
[4] *Remarks on Forest Scenery*, i, 257.
[5] 'You were right in supposing there was no attempt to introduce the sun in person. So far am I from taking that liberty with his highness, that I dare not take it even with the moon.' W. G. to Mary Hartley, 11 July 1792 (Rev. E. G. Benson—Brisco transcript).
[6] 'On Sunsets', pp. 2–3.

good effect.' This object can be a tower or a tree which 'may shew the light through its leaves, and branches, to advantage'. If the object is placed at a distance and low in the landscape, 'it may be right to represent the declension of the sun low likewise, that the object may be seen against the lightest part of the splendor'. The system of lighting can equally be reversed, that is to say, 'the *object* may be *inlightened*, & seen against a *gloomy part* of the sky. This idea may be represented under various forms.' For instance, 'an object *on the foreground* has often a good effect: & it may either receive the illumination full on it's surface, . . . or it may be touched with a catching light'. 'There may be a good effect of illumination also, when a *haziness*, which is sometimes the case, attends the setting sun; & throws a misty obscurity on all the objects between it, & the eye.'

One last circumstance. 'Another mode of beautiful illumination arises from the *splendid appearance* of a sunset, on the *surface of water*. I mean not that brilliant hue, that dazzling of the waves, which Claude often gives his seas, & lakes. This effect can only be produced by colours; & perhaps by no colours, but his own. I mean only that ambiguous splendor, which the setting sun often spreads over the horizon of the ocean: You can hardly, in some parts, distinguish the water from the sky.'[1]

ROLE OF THE IMAGINATION

Though Gilpin rejected many of the elements which would render his sketches 'interesting', he fully realized that 'the chief end of landscape is to please', and that 'in a drama something more is required to give it success, than the bare observance of the unities' (or basic principles applied to landscape composition).[2] The painter should 'endeavour to please the eye. He should aim to make the country he carries us through, such as we should wish to inhabit, or at least to examine.'[3] But what is equally important is to stimulate, to arouse the imagination of the spectator. This Gilpin explains as follows:

When we see a pleasing landscape in *nature*, we not only wish to enjoy it; but we are incited by the beauty of what we see, to proceed in the same direction in search of scenes of the same kind, which we suppose it may lead to. It should be thus in artificial landscape. When we see a pleasing scene, we cannot help supposing, there are other beautiful appendages connected with it, tho' concealed from our view. If therefore we can interest the imagination of the spectator, so as to create in him an idea of some beautiful scenery beyond such a hill, or such a promontory, which intercepts the view, we give a scope to a very pleasing deception. *It is like the landscape of a dream.*[4] The mind naturally runs on with an idea, which had long possessed it. When slumber shuts the senses, after seeing a fine view, the idea often continues—somewhat faded indeed, but strong enough to preserve a very amusing picture.[5]

Here surely by the role he assigns to the imagination Gilpin parts company with a very large group of picturesque artists, in particular with those whom Hussey considers as

---

[1] 'On Sunsets', pp. 3–4.   [3] Ibid., p. 14.   [4] Italics are mine.
[2] 'Instructions for Examining landscape', p. 13.   [5] 'Instructions for Examining landscape', pp. 14–15.

representatives of the painter's ideal of the Picturesque, artists such as George Morland or Barret.[1] By interpreting the Picturesque in purely painterly terms they seek only to please the eye, to evoke a pleasing sensation in the onlooker—all is stated, obvious, and at times anecdotal or sentimental. Gilpin goes further by achieving effects which result in ambiguity and mystery: 'Some people must account for all they see, and hear; they allow mystery in nothing. Now I suppose mystery in every thing; and think that a certain degree of faith, where we *cannot have* compleat knowledge, is as necessary in reading nature, as scripture.'[2]

He also adds an implicit or hidden element to his landscapes, which, while carefully related to the explicit or visible parts, allows the spectator's imagination to run on. In this way he suggests large vistas (often bathed in light) hidden from the spectator's view by intersecting slopes in the middle distance; yet on the crest of those slopes small figures are silhouetted, who, from their privileged viewpoint, contemplate a prospect that must be left to the spectator's imagination. As Gilpin said to William Lock, 'the spectator both in scenical, and picturesque representation, must allow himself to be imposed on in *every* thing'.[3] The spectator is impelled to identify himself with the only figures in the landscape, and thus the artist, by stimulating the imagination, succeeds in opening up his landscape, in suggesting more than he can actually depict within the compass of his frame. It is one way of solving the dilemma of trying to render within a small compass material garnered from the whole of nature. Furthermore, by hinting at vistas seen from a high vantage-point by his banditti, Gilpin solves another problem: he can hint at scenes which may be impressive and even beautiful, but which are not in themselves picturesque, and which cannot be picturesquely represented. As Gray had agreed before him, the picturesque artist nearly always chooses a low vantage-point.[4] William Mason had put it this way: 'The *Picturesque Point* is always thus low in all prospects: A truth, which though the Landscape Painter knows, he cannot always observe; since the Patron who employs him to take a view of his place usually carries him to some elevation for that purpose.'[5]

In other compositions containing only a foreground, Gilpin suggests the chasm that lies just beyond. Figures are made to point at what cannot be seen or at what is only dimly suggested. Others proceed into a cave, the depth of which remains unfathomable to the spectator. And 'even when a figure cannot be supposed to be placed in a situation proper for viewing a scene, yet considering it as a person travelling through a country, we may go along with him, & conceive the view he will have, when he arrives at such a point, or in such a direction'.[6] 'The grey atmosphere, which gives such picturesque indistinctness to objects, . . . the grey, misty air, which rubs off the harsh lines, & corners of objects,

---

[1] *The Picturesque*, pp. 244 sqq.

[2] W. G. to Mary Hartley, 11 June 1792 (Rev. E. G. Benson—Brisco transcript).

[3] W. G. to William Lock, 13 Sept. 1781 (Rev. E. G. Benson).

[4] *The Poems of Mr. Gray. To which are prefixed Memoirs of his Life and Writings by W. Mason, M.A.*, York, 1775, pp. 359–60.

[5] Ibid., p. 360 n.

[6] 'Instructions for Examining landscape', p. 18a.

softening every thing, into one general tint',[1] these are all effects which may give us repose but which also incite the imagination and the chance to dream.

Gilpin not only gave form to his conception of the Picturesque by means of drawings, he also did so in a number of purely imaginary journeys and descriptions. These little known and unpublished pieces epitomize even better than his drawings the ideal landscape of mountain and lake scenery which haunted his thoughts. Two of these pieces of descriptive writing are reproduced as Appendixes A and B. They are necessarily short and fragmentary, for a sustained account of perfection would soon lead to satiety. The first, probably written in the late 1760's, in an imaginary piece of landscape-gardening, entitled *Situation of the house*. The house, ideally placed, is surrounded by a perfect panorama which partakes in turn of lake, woodland, river, and mountain scenery. Years later such perfect scenery was brought indoors and painted on the walls of a room by Barret at Norbury and Sandby at Drakelowe.

The second manuscript dates from his last years. In the guise of *A Fragment*, all that remains of a lost work, Gilpin gives us a picturesque tour of an imaginary country built up from twenty-four of his own drawings, which are made to illustrate the journey like so many chosen 'stills' from a film sequence. He invents place-names and a local history, and fosters a sense of reality by a number of devices. For example, on mentioning the ruins of Groinseg-castle he adds 'I believe I spell the name right', and he decides to gloss over Rocktingen Castle, 'as the gazettes of Europe have been so full of the honour it lately received from an imperial visit'.

He projects himself into this topography and we follow him on his way round Lake Venlis, with its island of Ulmar, its promontory and castle of Bilvers. Around are the mountains of Ooust and Ovedon. Interest is maintained as the scenery unfolds, as features at first only dimly perceived in the distance come more clearly into view. Occasionally the eye is unable to see a distant object, the imagination must then feed on an anecdote:

In a peaceful valley, at the bottom of this mountain, lies a small monastery. It was pointed out to us; but as the eyes of a person acquainted with a spot, see clearer, I suppose, than those of a stranger, we could not even pretend to see it, tho the day was sufficiently bright. In this monastery, we were told, a very extraordinary pennance exists, tho for what particular offences we were not informed. The offender is sentenced to ascend the pinnacle of the mountain; where he waves the flag of St. Anthony, to give notice of his arrival . . . .[2]

At this juncture we may ask ourselves what exactly was Gilpin's conception of the

---

[1] W. G. to William Lock, 24 Jan. 1788 (Rev. E. G. Benson).

[2] *A Fragment*, pp. 2–3 (Mrs. Margaret M. Harvey). Another 'MS account of a fictitious journey in the form of a fragment, illustrated by 30 drawings' was purchased by General Harry Burrard at the 1802 sale (lot 139). A single sheet (wmk: 1794 | J. WHATMAN) until recently in the Gilbert Davis Collection, may be connected with this item. On one side is a drawing of a waterfall [11. *e*], on the other, page '376' of a manuscript account in Gilpin's hand which begins as follows: 'least, for the sake of gain, attempt them. I have seen people in England let themselves down by ropes from frightful cliffs, to gather samphire, & wild-birds eggs.' This sheet may, on the other hand, belong to an unidentified imaginary tour which did not pass through the 1802 and 1804 sales, for the drawing does not bear the usual WG blind stamp.

imagination: was his attitude so different from the general trend of eighteenth-century thought on the subject, and if so, how near did he come to that sincerity of poetic insight we associate with the 'romantic' poets?

If we take our definition of imagination as being that function of the mind which calls up images, having on the one hand the power of recalling in detail experiences already undergone, and, on the other, the power of creating images not previously experienced or merely suggested or hinted at, we find that the eighteenth century did not advance much beyond Hobbes's conception of imagination as 'decaying sense'.[1] We have to wait till Wordsworth before imagination is conceived as a 'power of interpreting the world'. By imagination 'Wordsworth attains something like a mystical vision of the whole world as a living thing, every fragment of the world alive with the life of the whole'.[2] This the picturesque mind could not conceive of, by the very nature of the single-minded inquiry it was engaged upon; in his considerations of landscape the picturesque observer rarely allows ideas which are not pictorial to intrude upon his contemplation of the scene before his eyes or that in his imagination. However, if the picturesque artist's imagination appears limited compared with the all-embracing one of the romantic poets, his grasp of landscape is often all the more profound. As W. P. Ker rightly observed:

> Landscape was, on the whole, better understood in the eighteenth century than it was after the appearance of the 'romantic' authors, because the 'romantic' authors took the mind away from pure landscape to other allied interests, such as the interests of historical association.
>
> Both Cowper and Wordsworth tried to render life. Usually it is life from which the natural landscape is inseparable, life in which landscape has a large share; but what they are interested in is not the scene by itself, not the people by themselves, but the scene as animated by the people, the whole life in which the different elements are inextricable.[3]

The eighteenth-century man of taste tended to remain detached and objective in the pursuit of the several subjects that interested him; each subject studied for its own sake, remaining in its water-tight compartment. Such a person was Gilpin. But what distinguishes him from the majority of his picturesque friends is that he makes much greater use of imagination than they dared to call upon. In fact, one can say that the development shown in his sketches represents a gradual release of imagination from the shackles of objective reason, so that by the time Gilpin settled down at Vicar's Hill in 1777 the last concessions to topographical accuracy had been discarded, and the creative imagination became free to convey the 'spirit' of lake and mountain scenery.[4] How often we find his artist friends

---

[1] *Leviathan*, part i, chap. 2.

[2] W. P. Ker, *On Modern Literature*, Oxford, 1955, p. 102.

[3] Ibid., p. 231.

[4] 'Gilpin's work might be described as a closing of one chapter in the history of the beauties of Nature. It brings the characteristic eighteenth-century regard for nature as near as possible to Wordsworth, without making the transition. Gilpin appreciates the things that Wordsworth appreciates. They would have admired the same landscape, and Wordsworth, if asked to describe it, need not have rejected Gilpin's terms. Gilpin's interpretation of the simple lines of the Border mountains is in no disagreement with Wordsworth's view of the subject. Only Gilpin did not go further; his landscape is distinctly one for the pictorial observer. The imagination and meditative interpretation of Wordsworth are not to be found in him.' W. P. Ker, op. cit., p. 83.

saying to him that his drawings are more 'imaginative', while theirs are more 'natural', more closely wedded to actual observation. Gilpin writing to Mary Hartley recognized this difference: 'You work best with nature before you; and I from imagination. . . . You work from the original archytype, I only from its reflected images.'[1]

His rational attitude, sound common sense, and liking of what appeared normal and natural—all these restricted the field of play of his imagination. The picturesque ideal rejected those weird and curious appearances in nature which could act as such a powerful stimulus: 'Every thing, both here, & among the mountains, was wild, & romantic in the highest degree; *but not fantastic. The shapes were all grand, natural, & noble, & borrowed no affected beauties from odd forms, & lawless singularity.*'[2]

And even where he has deliberately sought to awaken the interest of his reader, Gilpin only allows the fancy to be stirred so far. A good example occurs in the *Fragment*. In a sequestered bay we come upon a strange building, which from the shore appears 'to rise out of the lake'. We take a boat to get a nearer view. The edifice is now seen to stand on an island; it is shaped like an immense roofless church, which however 'seems never to have had any windows'. What can it have been?

The common opinion is, that it was built for a prison; & we heard a romantic story of a prince, who had been confined there, 30 years, with his daughter, a beautiful princess, lest there should be any children to disturb the succession of the usurper. The prince however gave her in marriage to the keeper of the prison, by whom she had a son, who afterwards became a man of great prowess, & cut off the usurper's head.

At this juncture Gilpin calls a halt to what has been for him an enjoyable game of make-believe, and invents a rational explanation: 'I rather believe this strange edifice . . . was built as a repository for . . . goods . . . . On the north side is the appearance of a vast gate, now walled up, opening into the water; which could have been intended, I should think, only to receive barges, & crane up goods.' (pp. 5–6.)

====

By constantly taking the side of observable nature, of what the eye could see, Gilpin's friends exercised a useful restraint, enabling him to test his ideas before trusting them to print. The perennial debate art versus nature provided the ground for another of the debates Gilpin had with William Lock—it concerned the importance which should be attached to the eye and the imagination respectively. The issue was joined when Gilpin, speaking of the superiority of nature compared with art, stated that '*Art*, confined by the rules of picturesque beauty, must keep within the compass of inch, foot & yard. But these slender confines cannot rouse the imagination, like the scenes of nature.' To this Lock replied:

The necessity of *keeping art within the compass of inch, foot, & yard*, is not so evident to me. When

[1] See *supra*, p. 113.   [2] *Situation of the house*, p. 7 (MS. in the W. L. Benson Collection). Italics are mine.

I look through my window, I see an extensive scene confined within the compass of it's frame. If the glass, through which I look, could retain the image it transmits, what would it be but a *picture*, differing in nothing, as to it's effect, from those formed by the pencil? Why then should you call art's limits, *slender confines?* they are the limits, under which we see nature herself. For if I go near enough to my window, the view is wider than I can take in at one glance; & to see *a second scene in nature*, I must move my eye, & take in a *second picture*. The scenes, which surround us, do not exist *for us*, till they are separately made pictures on the retina; & confined within the frame of the iris; just as the landscape now before me, is by the frame of the window. The image is the same, whether transmitted through the body of the glass, or reflected from the surface of a painted canvas.

Gilpin could not accept such reasoning, based on the false assumption that we see with our eyes; for him 'the eye is a mere window', and as such 'is not a medium to be depended on'.

It is the imagination, that sees: it is this, which is impressed by the notices it receives through the eye; which notices, tho sometimes true, are as often false. Through the eye the shape of an object may in great measure be conveyed—the colour—the light, & shade—and, in a degree, the relative situation: but with regard to the size of an object, which is the point we are now considering, no medium can be more deceitful. . . .

If indeed I could be so far deceived, as to believe the landscape painted on the pane of glass, was really a natural view transmitted through it, I might give it credit for being of the dimensions of nature. But unless the imagination be totally laid asleep, tho I see only a piece of ground 10, or 12 inches square, through the glass, I am well assured, that I look at a piece of ground perhaps of the extent of as many miles. I cannot possibly be affected, as I should be with a view of nature, by a trifling object hung against my wall about 2 feet long. If I inlarge it to 2 yards, I am affected more: but if I cover one side of my room with a landscape, I am still more affected, because I see something more proportioned to the size of nature: otherwise I see no reason for giving a large sum of money for a large picture; when, for a small sum I might have a small picture, which would answer the end as well.

On the whole, I cannot allow the eye to be any judge of distance, bulk, & extention. It is the Imagination, aided by it's sage counsellor, Experience, that sees through the eye. If the eye were left to itself, it would be continually involving me in mistakes. I might reach out my hand perhaps to touch the spire of a church, tho at a league's distance. What may be the form of the philosophical eye, I know not. All I assert, is, that the picturesque eye has nothing to do with tunics, irises, & retinas. All things are pictured in it—not on a point, less than a pin's head; but *on an extended plain*, where they *appear of their natural* size. How nature manages this matter, & produces this multum in parvo, I cannot explain to you. All the explanation I can give you, is, that of the sage, who got up & walked, to prove free-will.

Now as the eye is no judge of objects, the imagination must assist us in *painting*, as well as in *looking* at them. When I draw a figure from the life, stationed at a proper distance; & compare it with a notched stick, or an inch-rule, I shall find it to be only a few inches high: & if I looked at it through a pane of glass, it would be just the same. I must either therefore paint a mere miniature; which, according to your hypothesis, is what I see: or I must paint what I know you will expect, the full proportion of a man, on the better intelligence I get from my imagination.

So he concluded that if one conceded 'that we do not receive our notices of things, particularly of the bulk, & extent of objects, from the operation of simple vision', then it followed, *that the slender confines of art cannot rouse the imagination, like the scenes of nature*.[1] Lock's reaction was to come to the defence of the eye:

I have just read your invective against the poor Eye, which of all men it had least reason to expect from you to whom it has furnished so much entertainment, & whom it has enabled to teach others how to find the same. Your pampered Imagination had been starved but for this trusty Purveyor: & whatever may be its skill in made dishes, it woud have cut a sorry figure in furnishing out its entertainments without the stores provided by this honest Agent accused of so much double dealing—You will not be offended, I hope, if I undertake his defence . . . .

Now for my client the Eye, . . . If you looked through it for the first time indeed, you might imagine that the tree which measured one inch on the notched stick held up to it, was only one inch high: but the mind, informed by experience what allowance is to be made for the deceptions of perspective, is led into no error; & the eye is absolved from the charge of being a deceitful medium to those who understand its language—

You think that the construction of that organ has nothing to do with a discussion of this kind, & that I ought not to have brought it forward—Observe, that I am so far from summoning the mechanical agents of vision to a council on the pleasures of the imagination, that I receive their report at the door & dismiss them. It is *you* who let them in, & suffer them to put a negative upon your pleasures, by deposing that the images which they have introduced into the fancy are not the genuine productions of Nature, but the sophistications of Art: & that the light & heat which they there produce, ought neither to illume or warm it—I, on the contrary, maintain, that the Picture in my fancy is the same whether I have derived it from Nature or from Art. If it is Landscape, it consists of a certain combination of hills & plains, woods & water: if well composed it gives me pleasure, & ought to do so without fastidious enquiry from whence it came—You say we derive no right information when looking at Nature without the assistance of experience—Granted—But why may we not expect the same assistance when looking on Art? Why will she not then equally rectify the errors of vision & assign to every thing its true dimensions? She teaches us, that an object seen at a certain distance, tho' shewn by the laws of perspective under an angle of one inch only, is in reality 50 feet high. Will she not apply the same corrective to the report from a Painted Scene? The mind deliberates on an image as offered by the sense of sight, without considering whether it was brought before her by transmission thro' a pane of glass, or by reflection from the surface of a canvas. By whatever means she is put in possession of her ideas, they become her own. The question is not, whether the image she now beholds independent of the giver, be the tribute of Nature or of Art, but whether it be worth the entertaining. Shou'd indeed the mind belong to the man who has read the Paradise Lost, & cou'd not find that it *proved* anything, he might contrive no doubt to defeat all his pleasures; & say, when he saw Garrick in Lear, that the whole being a fiction, it wou'd be childish to be affected by it. But you will confess that neither Art nor Nature work for such a man. The most perfect Poem is such only when it meets a mind made to admit its full effect. It is the joint work of an inspired writer, & of an intelligent reader— The same is true of a picture; & is equally true of Nature. When she works on an obtuse sense, she is neither beautiful, nor sublime: because beauty & sublimity are not qualities in objects, but the effect of qualities on a Mind—

[1] W. G. to William Lock, 24 Dec. 1787 (Rev. E. G. Benson).

A picture covering a wall large enough to admit of things in their natural dimensions, certainly gives more pleasure, than one of a few inches only; & for this reason—that it is a more *perfect* picture, from leaving less to the mind to supply—The question between Art & Nature requires such an one; because it will readily produce illusion: not indeed in a resisting, but in a consenting mind, where the Spectator cooperates with the Artist—

A Rock, or Mountain, of the most stupendous size, loses its magnitude when seen at a distance, & alone. It is only by comparing it with the objects which surround it, or by approaching it, that it ricovers [*sic*] its vast dimensions—The *comparative* magnitude, is as obvious in Painting, as in Nature. The *absolute*, indeed, of which we acquire an idea by the mechanical process of moving the eye & the head with it from part to part till we arrive at its extremities, is not within the competency of practicable art, confined as it is by the limits of a frame or a room. And there, if you will take an unfair advantage, says Art with tears in her eyes, you have it—but give me a canvas of the height of Mont Blanc, & I defy you again—

I retreat then, with poor Art by my side, from this contested bit of ground; & a narrow one it is; for stir but from your mountains foot till the eye can take it in at one glance, & we take the field again—

While waiting for a frank, Lock read his letter over *à tête reposée*, and then added:

something tells me that I ought to add a postscript, to acknowledge candidly, that I think your position taken generally is just, *that 'these slender confines of art cannot rouse the imagination like the scenes of nature'*. But I think that you have occasionally treated art somewhat roughly, in your parallels of her with nature, because she cannot produce in one impression what the other does by successive ones.[1]

And Gilpin answered:

an ecclaircisment has brought us, I think, very nearly together.—But even if the ground of our quarrel had not been well adjusted; you are so open, so candid, so generous an adversary, that I am persuaded my sword would have fallen lifeless to the ground; & my hand would have been presented in its room.[2]

In conclusion, 'though the slender confines of art cannot rouse the imagination like the scenes of nature', it is the function of art so to stimulate the imagination of the spectator that by looking at the landscape depicted, he should thereby recall scenes in nature which have had an even greater effect upon him. For this impressionistic technique to succeed, one must assume that the spectator is like Gilpin, an adept at picturesque travel with many delightful scenes stored in his memory. 'The picture is not so much the *ultimate end*, as it is the *medium*, through which the ravishing scenes of nature are excited in the imagination.'[3]

FIGURES IN LANDSCAPE

Our general understanding of picturesque theory must not be distorted by what Gilpin chose to make of it in his own sketches. It is only too easy, for example, to interpret the

[1] 30 Dec. 1787, and postscript of 7 Jan. 1788 (Major J. R. Abbey).
[2] 24 Jan. 1788 (Rev. E. G. Benson).
[3] *Western Tour*, p. 176. Gilpin published the observations made to Lock in *Remarks on Forest Scenery*, ii, 232–6, and returned to the subject in *Western Tour*, pp. 175–7. For his first lengthy discussion of the role of the imagination see *Tour of the Lakes*, i, 127–40.

function of figures in landscape, solely in terms of the two little banditti walking down a road or the grouped cattle we meet in so many of his drawings.

For him, 'figures of every kind, whether human, or animal, are of great use in landscape'.[1] They serve three purposes: to characterize a scene, to give it life and animation, and lastly they often prove a mechanical necessity.

'They break harsh lines—point out paths over mountains or to castles', they break a piece of foreground and point out the horizon in a sea-view, they give an idea of scale in sublime landscape, and in black and white sketches, 'they are useful in distinguishing roads from rivers'.[2]

'Again, they are useful in *inlivening* a scene. Trees, & lawns, & water are all beautiful: but they are immoveable objects. When figures are introduced, they add *life*, and *animation*.'[1] And we have seen how they can stimulate the imagination of the spectator.

Figures introduced must be in keeping with the character of the landscape:

If we introduce *adorned nature* (which the picturesque eye always resists, when it can) we are under a necessity, as Sandby was, & other draughtsmen in that line, to introduc[e] such modern figures, as inhabit those walks. But when we open scenes of *wild*, or even of *unadorned* nature, we dismiss all these courtly gentry. No *ladies with their parasols*—no *white-robed misses ambling two by two*—no *children* drawn about in *their little coaches*, have admittance here. They would *vulgarize* our scenes. Milk-maids also, ploughmen, reapers, and all peasants *engaged in their several professions*, we disallow. There are modes of landscape, to which they are adapted: but in the scenes we here characterize, they are valued, for what in real life they are despised—loitering idly about, without employment.[3] In wild, & desert scenes, we are best pleased with banditti-soldiers, if not in regimentals, and such figures, as coalesce in idea with the scenes, in which we place them.[4]

The models for Gilpin's banditti-soldiers with their loose cloaks are to be found in Salvator Rosa's landscapes and in the book of models which he drew up. Salvator's banditti are eminently suitable for scenes of wild grandeur for they exhibit traits of greatness, wildness, or ferocity (particularly the latter)—all ideas which touch on the sublime.[5]

If banditti are ideal for wild mountainous landscape, carts, waggons, and horses are equally suitable to mark a road or track; cattle and sheep may be grouped where they can graze, goats are the natural appendages of rocky scenery; the forest may have deer, and the sky may have birds flying at a distance.

---

[1] 'Instructions for Examining landscape', p. 16.

[2] Ibid., p. 16; see also *Three Essays*, p. 77.

[3] Moral and picturesque viewpoints do not always coincide. Thus 'in a moral light, cultivation, in all it's parts, is pleasing; the hedge, and the furrow; the waving corn field, and rows of ripened sheaves. But all these, the picturesque eye, in quest of scenes of grandeur, and beauty, looks at with disgust. It ranges after nature, untamed by art, and bursting wildly into all it's irregular forms. . . . It is thus also in the introduction of figures. In a moral view, the industrious mechanic is a more pleasing object, than the loitering peasant. But in a picturesque light, it is otherwise. The arts of industry are rejected; and even idleness, if I may so speak, adds dignity to a character. Thus the lazy cowherd resting on his pole; or the peasant lolling on a rock, may be allowed in the grandest scenes; while the laborious mechanic, with his implements of labour, would be repulsed.' *Tour of the Lakes*, ii, 44.

[4] 'Instructions for Examining landscape', pp. 17–18.

[5] *Tour of the Lakes*, ii, 45–47.

As we have seen he rejects figures in modern dress because he feels they introduce a note of vulgarity. Though they look well in their natural habitat, be it the town, the village, the country estate, or the farm, they would have a disconcerting effect in his chosen landscape, which is as far removed as possible from civilization and the sophistication of everyday life. His dislike for modern dress in painting is, however, general—he prefers figures clothed in loose drapes and develops the point in a letter to Mary Hartley:

With regard to my dislike to particular figures . . . I am far from establishing my own ideas as dogmas. All I can say is, that I dislike all *vulgarity* of form—modern dresses—modern utensils— any thing, that occurs commonly to the eye. I consider painting as a kind of poetry, which excludes all vulgarisms: & I construe my dislike to vulgar figures, into a profound respect for the art: at the same time I am candid enough to give up all deductions of reasons, which my theory, I doubt, will not stand. I used to have many battles with Miss Crewe on this subject. She drew ladies, with caps, and stays, & gowns, & petticoats, & shoes & stockens. I always reprobated them. Another lady, who sent me one of her drawings, Lady Di: Beauclerk, drew in much better taste. She covers her figures with loose gowns—puts hats, or handkerchiefs upon their heads; & their feet into slippers. *Your* figures however, & those of these 2 ladies, are very different. Their figures are *principal*—*yours* only *appendages*. Of course therefore your petticoated figures do not offend me so much as Miss Crewe's.[1]

He was also out of sympathy with the mythological figures represented in the landscapes of the followers of Poussin and Claude. Their continued presence in painting and poetry had a retarding effect on the true appreciation of nature. Gilpin reacted against their outworn symbolism and considered the intrusion of such history and mythology as anecdotal miniatures out of keeping with the portrayal of landscape:

> Some insert
> A little history. In that nook obscure
> Stands Abraham. Sure 'tis he. Aye: There's the knife,
> The little altar, & the victim son.
> That other landscape, where the river winds,
> Seems to contain the woeful fall
> Of Phaeton. With observation nice
> The eye makes out his sisters weeping oer
> His breathless corpse; & mixing with the clouds
> The car distracted, & the headlong steeds.
> All this I wish not; like the double plots
> Of dramas, it confounds. What Abr'ham there,
> Which any idle figure might not do?
> Is there expression, character, or ought
> That marks the patriarch's firmness, or his faith
> Or brings his story to the heart? Degrade
> Not then his dignity by such

----

[1] 20 Dec. 1791 (W. L. Benson).

Ill-chosen miniatures: but deck thy scenes
With figures to themselves appropriate;
The *landscape* is *thy* object. Figures mere
Appendages, & under-parts?[1]

In keeping with his belief that landscape should have only one leading subject, and that the introduction of subsidiary elements must not create a conflict of interest, figures should be inserted with some care. As appendages they should neither be too large nor too numerous: let them rather be too few and appear insignificant. His own practice was just to indicate his figures, often simply as tiny black silhouettes, with sufficient attention to anatomy as not to offend. When groups are shown, arms and legs are reduced to a minimum. To Mary Hartley, who asked for advice, he said:

I forget indeed the quantity of legs, & arms you allow to 4 people: but I recollect, I thought your allowance very liberal: & I dare say, they will not be the worse for being curtailed. I confess, I think, *figuring a landscape*, as they call it, is a very nice matter. Perhaps my eye is fastidious: it is certain I am seldom pleased. My brother has an excellent knack at touching little figures; & I allow him to put as many legs & arms upon them as he pleases. As for myself, I never attempt it; so I do not allow my figures to be criticized. I wrap up their arms & legs in cloaks, because I am ashamed of them. I mean them only to point out, where figures might be placed.

He then confided:

You are not the only one, who has joked my attachment to the dual number. My brother, turning over my drawings, often says, 'Here come the 2 friends again.' You are both welcome to turn them into moral, or joke, as you like best: I care not. I aim neither at figures, nor at grouping. To *attempt* either, would, *in me*, be affectation.[2]

As an amateur who realized his limitations, he need not have been ashamed of his figures. For what they are they are infinitely better than those of many amateurs, who attempted more than they were capable of expressing correctly. His figures did at least fulfil certain minimum requirements: the proportions of the body and its general balance, whether at rest or in motion, were respected. In his writings he devoted considerable space to giving instruction on the management of figures in landscape, whether human or animal, and drew on his brother's skill to give weight to his demonstrations. In particular, the hints concerning the proportions, balance, size, and grouping of figures in the account, which was appended to the 1802 sale catalogue of his drawings, are Sawrey's. In the *Thames Tour* he examined the role of birds and barges in river scenery; in the *Tour of the Lakes* that of horses, cattle, and sheep, and paid particular attention to problems of grouping; in *Remarks on Forest Scenery*, it was the turn of the animals of the forest to be considered, horses, ponies, asses, mules, stags, and deer; and in the *Western Tour*, he examined the problem of touching small figures.[3]

[1] From Gilpin's first draft of the *Poem on Landscape Painting* (George F. Benson).
[2] 20 Dec. 1791 (W. L. Benson).

[3] *Five Essays*, pp. 176–83; *Thames Tour*, pp. 42–49; *Tour of the Lakes*, ii, 248–57; *Remarks on Forest Scenery*, ii, section xi; *Western Tour*, pp. 297–9.

An admirer of those few deft strokes that succeed in capturing a graceful action (sometimes termed 'picturesque grace'), he recommended as models the small figures of Callot
and Richard Wilson, while those of Claude Lorrain and Samuel Scott were deplored.[1]

[1] For Callot see *Essay on Prints*, p. 76, and *Western Tour*, pp. 73 and 299; for Scott see *Western Tour*, p. 298; for Claude and Wilson see *Five Essays*, pp. 177–8, and especially the exchange of letters between Gilpin and Sir George Beaumont in 1802 (Rev. E. G. Benson and Pierpont Morgan Library).

IX. Drawing-Master

Soon after he settled at Vicar's Hill, Gilpin took on the role of drawing-master on a scale he could hardly have foreseen. True, he had always taught the rudiments of drawing, first to the boys at Cheam, and then to his own children, in particular to his son William till he went to Oxford, and together with Sawrey had helped John Warwick Smith, who was in a sense a family protégé. Now, however, the popularity of his *Tours* and drawings brought about a new state of affairs, as an increasing number of people sought his acquaintance and advice. Some came to his very doorstep hoping to catch a glimpse of his drawings and unpublished manuscripts, others were genuinely interested in picturesque ideas, others still were admirers who wished to be instructed in the art of sketching landscape or to ask for his comments on their own efforts. Faced with this new situation he reacted in the same way as he always did whenever he felt he could answer a need. Having supplied the educational needs of his generation by making Cheam the model preparatory school of the period, at Vicar's Hill he saw to the spiritual and material needs of what was on his arrival a large and lawless parish, and in the matter of educating the taste of the more leisured classes he was always ready to guide and advise. As he wrote in the preface to the *Three Essays*, 'I have practised drawing as an amusement, and relaxation, for many years; and here offer the result of my experience'—that was in 1792, while the *Essays*, like most of his picturesque works, had been written by 1776. Already in 1777 he had begun to give away some of his best drawings to his friends and to those who had been particularly impressed by the manuscript *Tours*; and the voluminous correspondence he undertook from Boldre, peppered as it was with drawing instructions and reflections on the Picturesque, shows to what extent he was willing to give guidance. When considering the impact which he had on his generation and the next, one tends to neglect these private channels which he used to disseminate his ideas—they are just as important as his published works.

Gilpin had a gift for keeping in touch with people of all ages in the most varied walks of life, from artists, country gentlemen, ministers of the Church, to professional men, soldiers, sailors, and politicians. It is true that much of his success was due to his social position and to contacts, built up over the years, as the sons of the great passed through his hands at Cheam—these contacts made it all the more easy for him to spread his picturesque ideas once the fashion had caught on. Nevertheless, that would not be sufficient to explain the enthusiasm with which people quite unknown to him sought his advice, and made sure they called at Vicar's Hill if they happened to be in the vicinity. Gilpin was also by training a teacher, a vulgarizer. Though he could be stern when the occasion demanded, he combined a genial personality with the power to express ideas with conviction—he possessed the knack of getting to the level of his audience, no matter whether he was talking or writing to his uncultured parishioners, his four-year-old grandson William, or to a bishop of the Church. In addition he was able to give voice to the feelings of his age, on subjects as divergent as education, religion, or aesthetics; and he could state clearly what others like himself felt, but unlike him were unable to put into words.

His main correspondents during the late 1770's and 1780's were William Mason, Mrs. Delany, William Lock, William Mitford, Mary Hartley (an artist in her own right), Edward Forster and Henry Bolt Cay—both these being considerable men in the City— and Dr. Barrington the Bishop of Salisbury who, prior to making his acquaintance, had presented him with a stall in his cathedral. Less regular contacts were established with the Earl of Dartmouth, Horace Walpole, and the naturalist, John Lightfoot.

He soon gathered round him a number of lady admirers for which that inveterate bachelor, Mason, continually teased him. No doubt some were driven by curiosity and a general desire to do the fashionable thing, but the majority were genuine enthusiasts eager to sit at the feet of Gamaliel, peruse his manuscripts and emulate his drawings. It is one of the social features peculiar to English society in the eighteenth and nineteenth centuries that one could easily combine the calling of a clergyman with the pastime of an amateur artist. Several of his friends such as Mason and Thomas Gisborne, who was taught by John Warwick Smith,[1] fall into this category. But what made Gilpin more attractive than other clergymen similarly endowed was that he was prepared to be drawing-master and mentor in matters of taste, all this free of charge (no doubt to the annoyance of professional drawing-masters)—for no clergyman, and even less the landed gentry, would think of making money through their artistic skill.

To his more assiduous lady admirers, Gilpin was not content to give advice on picturesque matters, he also saw to their spiritual and religious welfare as befitted his calling.

In 1781 he came into contact with three women who were to affect him in very different ways. One was Barberina Ogle, the precocious daughter of Sir Chaloner Ogle;[2] another was a much older woman, Mary Hartley, the daughter of the philosopher David Hartley, whose theories laid the foundation for the Associationist school of psychology; the third was Emma Crewe, an amateur artist who supplied Bartolozzi and Wedgwood with subjects. As he wrote to Mason in December of that year, 'I have been more honoured by Ladies within these six months than I shall deserve, if I live 60 years'.[3]

---

[1] William Mason to W. G., 5 Aug. 1791 (Rev. E. G. Benson). Iolo A. Williams gives some account of the following clergymen who were amateur artists: Rev. William Bree, Rev. Daniel Finch, Rev. Robert Hurrell Froude, Rev. J. Gardner, and Rev. Joseph Wilkinson (*Early English Water-*

Colours, pp. 230–48).

[2] Sir Chaloner Ogle (d. 27 Aug. 1816, aged 89) was Admiral of the Red.

[3] W. G. to William Mason, 1 Dec. 1781 (W. L. Benson). The letter continues: 'Miss Hartley did me the honour of a

Mary Hartley had done much good drawing and etching in the 1760's—work that was characterized by its graceful delineation. She was cultured, pious, and possessed of a philosophical turn of mind. It was while dining with Mason at Aston in September 1780[1] that she first heard of Gilpin and his manuscripts and borrowed the *Essay on Picturesque Beauty* and two volumes of the *Tour of the Lakes*. As she was to confide much later, 'those works, as well as some drawings that Mr. Mason had of yours, gave me the first inclination to get acquainted with you'.[2]

She copied his drawings and expressed to the Rev. W. U. Wray, whom she met in Derbyshire, a desire to place herself under Gilpin's tuition.[3] The longed-for meeting took place at Vicar's Hill in the summer of 1781, and though it lasted only half an hour and they were never to meet again, the occasion marked the beginning of a spiritual friendship that was to last till her death in 1803. It was the meeting of two people who instantly recognized each other's moral worth as well as the many interests they shared in common. Early in 1782 Gilpin wrote to William Lock: 'I had lately the pleasure of a visit from a Lady of your acquaintance, Miss Hartley, who seems to me to be a Lady of great taste, & genius; & (if it be not tautology) as enthusiastic in the art she loves, as any of us.'[4]

A short while after, she suffered a paralytic stroke, and Gilpin expressed his anxiety to Lock:

I am truly sorry to hear of the complaint in her hand on many accounts. The hand of such an artist belongs to the public. I have seldom seen more agreable landscape; more pleasing forms, and composition, than her drawings exhibit. . . . I thought Miss Hartley, in those views, with whose archetypes I was acquainted, had the happy art of seizing the most beautiful resemblances.[5]

With the years Gilpin grew to rely increasingly on her judgement, to her he confided problems of publication, and with her he discussed very freely all matters religious and picturesque. She, while retaining her own opinions, was able to clarify his ideas, particularly on those points of picturesque theory on which they were at variance.

Patroness of the young Thomas Lawrence,[6] she kept Gilpin informed of what was going on in the artistic world of Bath. In this way we hear of John Warwick Smith, Bampfylde, Serres, Pocock, Sawrey Gilpin, Amos Green, and Miss Harriet Lister. She first broached the subject of Smith in 1788, quite unaware of Gilpin's past association with him:

I have lately seen several drawings of Smith's: an artist lately returned from Italy & very much in fashion now. I dare say you have seen some of his works. What he is most remarkable for, is the

---

visit. She is an acquaintance, I find, of yours. *She* is not surely a coxcomb. And who else, think you, has honoured me? the Queen herself, I assure you; she has desired to see my tour [MS. of the *Tour of the Lakes*] again; & it is set out a 3d. time for St. James's. . . . You will imagine my intelligence about the Queen, came from my good friends at Bulstrode [Dowager Duchess of Portland and Mrs. Delany]. Her majesty told them she had read my Lectures [*Lectures on the Catechism of the Church of England*. 1779], twice over; & was much pleased

with them.'

[1] Mary Hartley to W. G., 25 May 1789 (W. L. Benson).
[2] Mary Hartley to W. G., 14 Feb. 1789 (W. L. Benson).
[3] Rev. W. U. Wray to W. G., 10 Mar. 1781 (W. L. Benson).
[4] 7 Jan. 1782 (Rev. E. G. Benson).
[5] 4 Dec. 1782 (Rev. E. G. Benson).
[6] For Sir Thomas Lawrence and Mary Hartley, see Douglas Goldring, *Regency Portrait Painter*, London, 1951, pp. 47–69.

clearness of his skies, & the tint of air that appears in all his lointains. There is something astonishingly beautiful in all his distant hills. But many of his drawings that I have seen, have too much of a cold blueish tint for my taste; &, if I might venture to say it (tho in truth I only dare *whisper* such a thing) *some* of his drawings that I have seen have been much out of tune, & have not had what you call a Whole. But I wou'd not detract from his merit, for in general, his works are beautiful.[1]

This opening gave Gilpin the chance to say exactly what he thought of Smith as an artist. They diverged on fundamentals. Gilpin stressed the freedom of the artist before his subject and the importance of composition, and made no bones of his dislike of topographical artists or 'literalists' as he termed them:

I am very well acquainted both with Smith, & his drawings. He is an ingenious man: but there is nothing, I think, very free, or spirited in his works. I think there is a littleness in his manner; & a washiness in his colouring. And yet I cannot say, that in those I *have* seen (for I knew him chiefly in the early part of his life, & have not seen *many* of his *latter* works) there is a want of harmony. I have been told he colours much on principle. He takes his first sky tint—we will suppose light orange,—& brushes over with it, not only the sky; but perhaps his whole drawing. His next tint he brushes over in the same way; and so endeavours to make harmony by giving the same hues to the whole drawing: but I cannot say I have been pleased with the effect in such as I have seen; tho I dont think they have that particular deficiency, which you attribute to them. As to any effect of light and shade, I think he never attempts it. But what I have most disliked, is his *composition*. He is a great copyist from nature, with which he will not take the least liberty. . . . On the whole, I think, as to his *mode* of drawing, the taste of the town has spoiled him. He is too smooth. He wants spirit. He makes every thing out too much; & leaves nothing to the imagination. —I say this however only in answer to your letter: for I would not care to speak openly with so much freedom; as it might injure him.

Nevertheless, Gilpin did not hide his personal dislike of the man:

Smith was the son of a gardener of an old aunt of mine: and when my father, on his visits to his sister, used to see the lad employed with his pencil, he took some pains with him & gave him his first instructions in drawing; for which Smith was so grateful, that when my father dyed, he put on mourning; which is the best thing I know of him; for he is not a favourite character with me.[2]

Encouraged by Gilpin's frank opinion of Smith's work, Mary Hartley, in her turn, expressed herself far more freely and explicitly:

I am very sensible of all that you say about Smith's drawings. he has certainly no taste in composition, & very little in the effect of light & shade. I dare say he is a very close copier after nature, (A Literalist, as you expressively call it) by what I hear people say, who know the places that he has drawn. . . . I don't like his fore-grounds at all. there is a *petitesse* in his manner, that gives them the air of a fan mount. The trees are not drawn in a free, bold stile, or in graceful forms; & I cannot say that I like his colouring in any thing but his sky & distance. Those are exquisitely done in most of his works. I never saw any thing so beautiful as the tint of air that he often gives. Yet it is surprizing that I have seen some of his drawings totally without it, the clouds very heavy, very

[1] 29 Dec. 1788 (W. L. Benson).   [2] 26 Jan. 1789 (W. L. Benson).

woolly & the whole composition entirely out of tune. He has lately done a large 5 guinea drawing for a friend of mine, of a building in the Duke of Athol's gardens at Dunkeld: a very fine wild rocky situation. The sky is in itself well done, & the clouds receive strongly the glowing tint of the evening sky; but the building, which is exposed to the same glowing light, is nothing but white paper; so are the rocks that are under it; nothing can possibly be more out of tune than they are, with the tints of the clouds; & then, to produce some effect of light & shade, the continuation of the very same rocks that are white paper in the second distance are made of so dark a grey as to be almost black, in the foreground: No possible difference of light & shade cou'd possibly make such a difference as this, in their colour. . . . I have been told by many people what his method of proceeding is. much as you describe. at least he tells ladies & gentlemen so. they are much delighted with it, & repeat it to one another, like the receipt for soup. 'First, you lay on red, & then you lay on blue, & then you lay in the greys, for the air-tint in the distance, &c, &c, & so, you know, any body may make as good a drawing as Smith's, because, you see, you proceed *exactly* in the same way.' I had these directions the other day from a gentleman who shewed me his own drawings, then mixed some tints for me in Smith's manner, & told me that he thought Pocock's drawings too warm, & Smith's too cold; but that he intended to mix their two different manners & to produce *something*—which I understood we were to conceive wou'd be far *superior* to both.[1]

As regards drawing picturesque landscapes Mary Hartley constituted herself Gilpin's pupil. In December 1781 she summed up in her over-modest way the deficiencies which he could help to remedy:

I shou'd be very glad if I cou'd flatter myself that my ideas in painting are congenial to yours; but mine are crude, & not digested into any regular system; so that if at any time I am lucky enough to hit upon a tollerable effect, I cannot boast of having done it with a regular design; & tho I am so fully sensible of the necessity of tuning, that I do continually sacrifice every part of the manual execution to it, yet I am not always in tune, notwithstanding that I make it my only object. My endeavours are generally to produce large masses of light & shade, & where I can, to place the lights chiefly in the middle of the picture; but I see effects of light & shade in your works that I never shou'd have thought of, nor perhaps have known how to produce if I had, but which equally surprize & delight me; & the principle of this . . . is what I intended to plunder you of, in seeing your works, & conversing with you upon them.[2]

Gilpin was able to help precisely with those aspects of drawing: composition, light and shade, and harmony (or 'tuning' as Mary Hartley called it).

It was in December 1781 that he first heard of Barberina Ogle. Mary Hartley who was staying with the Ogles at Winchester was struck by the precocious talent of this young girl of fourteen, and sent Gilpin a wax model of a horse done by the child. Since Barberina was without any artistic instruction, and her father was 'eager to seize all opportunities of improving her tallents', it was hoped by this means to enlist Gilpin's encouragement

---

[1] 14 Feb. 1789 (W. L. Benson).

[2] Mary Hartley to W. G., 16 Dec. 1781 (W. L. Benson). Towards the end of her life, she summed up the impact of their brief meeting of 1781: 'You and your drawings then took up all my attention. I was then taking a lesson in the art, which has stuck by me ever since.' Mary Hartley to W. G., 4 Oct.

1800 (W. L. Benson).

For further information on Mary Hartley see Richard Warner, *Literary Recollections*, London, 1830, and William Gilpin, 'A short Account of Different people . . .' (J. B. Gilpin-Brown).

and guidance.[1] It was not long before Barberina, to her delight, received a bundle of prints and drawings, carefully chosen to help her with the drawing of horses. In the summer of 1783 Sir Chaloner Ogle and two of his daughters, Barberina and Lady Asgill, paid a visit to Vicar's Hill. On this occasion Barberina borrowed one of Gilpin's illustrated manuscripts, and before long sent him sketches of her own. For years she sought his advice, even after her disastrous marriage to Mr. H. Wilmot. This impetuous, highly strung girl found little satisfaction in landscapes; she had to draw and model cattle and horses, especially horses which were represented either 'scratching & biting or telling some high-flown story'. He did what he could to prevent her from tackling subjects beyond her powers.[2] His brother Sawrey became a close friend of the Wilmot household, and her letters to Gilpin from 1793 to 1795 are full of praise for Sawrey's drawings. He found it at times very trying to deal with the forthright and headstrong Mrs. Wilmot who openly flouted the conventions he respected, and when she finally became separated from her husband (*c.* 1796), he ceased to have any further dealings with her.[3]

Gilpin also took an interest in the drawings of other members of the Ogle family: in particular Lady Asgill, who was later taught by Sawrey,[4] and the 'Revd Mr Ogle', who may have been her brother John.[5]

In the summer of 1781 Gilpin was introduced to Miss Emma Crewe at the house of his neighbours, the Morants of Brockenhurst.[6] Mary Morant, the second wife of Edward Morant, M.P., had taken an interest in Gilpin's drawings soon after coming to reside in Hampshire, and it was no doubt through her initiative that Emma Crewe met the Vicar of Boldre. Little is known about this lady amateur who was probably a sister of John Crewe's (created first Lord Crewe in 1806). She practised allegorical figure compositions which were used by Bartolozzi and Wedgwood, and J. J. Foster records a miniature portrait contributed to the Royal Academy in 1833.[7]

Emma Crewe's letters to Gilpin, from 1781(?) to 1788,[8] show her eagerness to profit from his tuition. She regularly sent him drawings and acted on his advice. He, though not in sympathy with the way she clothed her figures in contemporary dress,[9] encouraged

[1] Mary Hartley to W. G., 29 Nov. and 16 Dec. 1781 (W. L. Benson).

[2] See in particular Mrs. H. Wilmot to W. G., 26 and 29 Jan. and 7 Feb. 1792 (W. L. Benson).

[3] For a biographical sketch of Mrs. H. Wilmot see 'A short Account of Different people . . .' (J. B. Gilpin-Brown).

[4] 'My Sister has taken up the pencil again of late & has made such a surprizing progress that I am sure you wou'd be delighted with some of her sketches. I am perhaps partial—but your Brother [Sawrey] speaks very highly of her taste & genius.' Mrs. H. Wilmot to W. G., 19 Feb. 1795 (W. L. Benson).

[5] A folder 'By Revd Mr Ogle', now in the W. L. Benson Collection, was probably given to William Gilpin. One of the drawings, of a rustic bridge spanning a cutting, is treated

very much in the Gilpin manner.

[6] 'I met with another very ingenious lady this summer, (with whom I was much pleased) at a gentleman's house in this neighbourhood—Miss Crewe. Pray have you any thing to say handsome of her?' W. G. to William Mason, 8 Nov. 1781 (W. L. Benson). Mason replied in typical vein: 'As to your Miss Crew I know her not, & heartily wish I may never more know any more clever & ingenious Misses or Learned Ladies for I have been plagued with one lately most terribly.' 23 Nov. 1781 (Rev. E. G. Benson).

[7] J. J. Foster, *Dictionary of Painters of Miniatures*, London, 1926. Foster and others spell the name 'Crew', yet her letters to Gilpin are signed either 'Emma Crewe' or 'Em Crewe'.

[8] W. L. Benson Collection.

[9] See *supra*, p. 145.

her to draw from casts, to study the human figure, particularly hands and feet, which were her weakness, and to pay more attention to light and shade and the arrangement of drapery. He also lent his manuscripts and gave her and Mary Morant several drawings, which were framed and proudly displayed in their respective homes.[1]

In this way Gilpin parted with many of his best sketches during the 1780's. With lady amateurs this often resulted in an exchange of drawings and a visit to Vicar's Hill. In 1784, for example, he teased Mason with the news that he had sent a drawing to Elizabeth, Countess of Sutherland:[2]

I have just been working for another Lady, whom I have the honour to number among those I have pleased; the young countess of Sutherland. I tell *you* these things, because I know they excite your envy. I am not acquainted with her; but I understand she draws; & is pleased with my manner: and a common acquaintance intervening, I have just sent her a specimen of my art.[3]

She returned the compliment early in 1786 with a large drawing of Appleby Castle,[4] and that summer called on him with Lord Gower, whom she had recently married.[5]

With Lady Diana Beauclerk,[6] it was Gilpin who took the first step to secure a drawing. As he informed Mason:

while my drawings have the honour to please Ladies, the drawings of a Lady have excited great admiration in me—those of Lady Di. Beauclerk. I am never very solicitous about seeing *wonderful works* of art; I feel myself so often disappointed. But a Lady, visiting in this neighbourhood last autumn, Miss Crewe, sent for two of Lady Di's drawings from a friend, on purpose, I believe, to shew them to me. I was indeed greatly surprized at their beauty; they were masterly in a high degree: & I took the liberty to desire Mr. Walpole, if he could by any means, to put me in possession of a sketch of Lady Di's. He gave me a very obliging answer—promised to do his utmost; but told me the extreme difficulty of getting hold of them—not from the value she sets on them; but from the extreme unwillingness, with which she takes up her pencil.[7]

He had to wait four years before his wish was gratified. In September 1788 he heard from Emma Crewe, who was acting as intermediary:

I saw Lady De Beauclerk the day before I left Richmond, & mention'd to her your criticism on

[1] Mrs. M. Morant to W. G., 3 May and 21 July 1790 (W. L. Benson).

[2] Elizabeth, Countess of Sutherland and Baroness of Strathnaver in her own right (1765–1839); daughter of the 17th Earl of Sutherland, she raised a regiment for the defence of Britain in 1779, and married George Granville, Lord Gower, on 4 Sept. 1785. She drew *Views of the Northern and Western Coasts of Sutherland*, engraved by F. C. Lewis; and, in 1808, privately published *Views in Orkney and on the North-Eastern Coast of Scotland*, taken in 1805 (containing forty-three etchings after drawings by herself).

[3] W. G. to William Mason, 22 Apr. 1784 (W. L. Benson).

[4] 'I had a present, the other day, from a young genius, in the landscape way, which surprized me much: especially considering the artist's quality, &, of course, avocations. . . . The drawing is very large; nearly 2 feet long; & a foot & ½

high: & both the mechanical, & theoretic parts are so well managed, that if she had nobody at her elbow, it is a surprizing work.' W. G. to Mary Hartley, 13 Mar. 1786 (W. L. Benson). For Gilpin's reaction to this drawing see also his letter to William Mason, 5 June 1788 (W. L. Benson).

[5] W. G. to Mrs. Delany, 18 July 1786 (see *Autobiography and Correspondence of Mary Granville, Mrs. Delany*, edited by Lady Llanover, London, 1862, 2nd series, vol. iii).

[6] Lady Diana Spencer (1734–1808), daughter of 3rd Duke of Marlborough; married in 1768 Topham Beauclerk, friend of Johnson; some of her drawings engraved by Bartolozzi. See Mrs. Beatrice Steuart Erskine, *Lady Diana Beauclerk— her Life and Work*, London, 1903.

[7] W. G. to William Mason, 22 April 1784 (W. L. Benson). See also Mary Morant to W. G., 14 Jan. [1785] (W. L. Benson).

her drawing, she said she should be very happy to *endeavor* to do one which you would approve, upon conditions, that you would do her the favor to make an exchange, & give her a drawing of yours, she says Mr Walpole has one at Strawberry Hill which she covets & admires beyond expression—I promis'd her to deliver the Message & I shall write to her soon, if you wish to have a drawing of hers, & have a fancy for any particular size or sort (I mean Landscape or figures) if you will inform me I can give her a hint—I *did* venture to say, that you did not lay much stress upon finishing, which seem'd to please her.[1]

Gilpin readily sent his drawing and before the end of the year Lady Di. rewarded him with a visit and four drawings of grouped figures.[2] In retrospect he felt the drawing he had given her was but a poor sketch compared with the ones he received.[3]

With the deaths of the Dowager Duchess of Portland in 1785 and Mrs. Delany in 1788 he lost two old friends who had done much to spread the fame of the manuscript *Tours* in court circles. Through them he corresponded on trees with the botanist John Lightfoot,[4] who, as protégé of the Duchess, assisted her at Bulstrode in making a hortus siccus of all English grasses. Mrs. Delany had many talents. Interested in music and landscape-gardening, she was taught drawing by Joseph Goupy in the 1740's and took to painting oils in the 1750's, mainly picturesque landscapes and copies of old masters.[5] But what Gilpin and his contemporaries admired most were her albums of artificial flowers. This is how he describes her way of combining artistic skill with a botanical interest:

Her method was, first to pull the leaves off the flower she meant to imitate; & cut pieces of coloured paper of the size, & tint of each leaf. Her coloured paper[s], which she had of all hues, were her pallet. She then laid a *perfect* flower, of the *same kind*, before her; & put all the leaves together again with such nicety, pasting them on black paper, that the flowers had a very beautiful effect. She gave Mr. G[ilpin] a wild strawberry, executed in this manner, which he values much.[6]

Her albums are now in the British Museum. Mrs. Delany was also skilled in shell-work and embroidery, and to her Gilpin recommended his niece Sarah Matilda Farish in 1781. For a time Sarah taught embroidery to the children of the nobility, using perforated working patterns evolved from her own drawings of natural flowers.[7]

Gilpin's own interest in botany took a different line. He did not draw plants, but in collaboration with his wife made a number of leaf impressions. Some of these were collected

---

[1] Emma Crewe to W. G., 29 Sept. 1788 (W. L. Benson).

[2] These drawings are in the W. L. Benson Collection.

[3] Mary Hartley to W. G., 3 Jan. 1789 (W. L. Benson).

[4] John Lightfoot (1735–88), F.R.S., librarian and chaplain to the Dowager Duchess of Portland. In 1772 he joined Pennant in a tour through Scotland and the Hebrides, collecting material for his *Flora Scotica* (1778).

[5] A number of her sketches were in 1927 in the possession of Lord Treowen (Hussey, *The Picturesque*, p. 95). Her most ambitious composition, The Raising of Lazarus, was given to her friend Lady Bute.

[6] 'A short Account of Different people . . .' (J. B. Gilpin-Brown). See also W. G. to Mary Hartley, 21 July 1788

(W. L. Benson).

[7] Sarah Matilda Farish (b. 1 Dec. 1759), daughter of Elizabeth Gilpin and Rev. James Farish. For instruction she charged £1 per person in the family. Worked for the Duchess of Atholl, probably also for the Duchess of Argyle. Embroidered eight chairs for Mrs. Delany for £20. Several of her flower drawings, dated 1777, and a considerable number of her embroidery patterns are in the A. L. Fawcett Collection. See also W. G.'s letters to Mrs. Delany in 1781 and 1782 (*Delany Correspondence*, 1862) and the long letter of Sarah Matilda Farish to her aunt Margaret Gilpin at Vicar's Hill, 6 Mar. 1782 (A. L. Fawcett).

into a folio volume entitled 'On the Variety of the *forms*, And in the *internal tracery*, of *Leaves*', 1794,[1] which may be considered as an appendix to his *Remarks on Forest Scenery*. The impressions, all taken from the leaves of trees in the neighbourhood of Vicar's Hill, are arranged as to form, shape, and internal tracery, showing nature's infinite variety within this narrow field of study. The introduction concludes with a

Method of taking off the impressions of leaves

Oil a piece of paper of the size you wish; & when it is thoroughly dry, black one side of it over the flame of a thick candle. If you black several pieces at the same time, it may be worth while to tye 2 or 3 candles together: they will produce a more oily smoke, & give the blacking more uniformly. On this black paper lay your leaf (the veined side generally gives the better impression) & covering it with a piece of paper, lay a weight over all to flatten the leaf. After it has been thus pressed an hour, or two, more or less, as the leaf is more or less stubborn, rub it hard with your finger, that it may imbibe the soot. Then taking it off lightly, lay the blacked side on the clean paper, on which you wish to have the impression taken; & covering it with another piece of paper, rub it again with your finger, that it may give the impression it had just received. But take care you do not let it slip from its place, as a little alteration will occasion double lines. It may be necessary perhaps to touch the stems, or any part, which has not received the impression, with a pencil, & Indian ink.

Gilpin and his wife contented themselves with single impressions, but others, notably Mrs. Lock of Norbury Park, combined the impressions of different plants into compositions, which were then coloured [12. *a*].

As was inevitable, Gilpin was at times approached by ladies whose skill did not match their enthusiasm. Thus, for example, early in 1788 he had to deal with a delicate situation when Caroline Yorke, a young lady of fashion, sent him a couple of her etchings for his approval, and offered to etch a plate for his next tour, if he would send her the drawing. He tells Mason of his diplomatic reply:

I answered her, whether politely or not, you shall tell me, that I would not class her among artists, & professional men; but if she would favour me with her interest among 2 or 3 of her friends, who could etch as well as herself, I would turn one of my little journeys into an exhibition-room for gentlemen, & ladies, without the intrusion of any artist. A few gentlemen I could procure, I believed, myself: but I could not presume to ask a lady. Her I should task at 3. But I fear I have offended her; for I have heard nothing more from her; & it is 4 or 5 months ago.[2]

We have seen that almost from the start of their friendship, Gilpin acquainted Mason

[1] Alan de Gylpyn Benson Collection. Dedicated on verso of title-page: 'To their beloved daughter Elizabeth Gilpin [Elizabeth Farish who married W. G.'s second son William on 24 Apr. 1782] this joint-work of her father, and mother, is given by them as a token of remembrance. *Will: Gilpin Margaret Gilpin*'. The introduction is dated: 'Vicar's hill June 2. 1794.' Other leaf impressions on loose sheets are in the possession of George F. Benson and W. L. Benson.

[2] 5 June 1788 (W. L. Benson). Miss Yorke eventually replied and Gilpin sent her and her brother Charles two of his drawings. However, the scheme he had outlined came to naught, for as Caroline Yorke confessed: 'I was discourag'd on the first proposal, by failing in my Application to two Gentlemen whom I knew to be draughtsmen, & who either from Modesty or Indolence, refus'd to take any Part, in an Undertaking that would have handed down their Names to Posterity in Conjunction with Mr. Gilpins—We will therefore leave them to enjoy the Obscurity they have chosen, and I will release you from the dull Employment, you are now engag'd in'. 7 Nov. [1788] (W. L. Benson).

with his sketching techniques. The Rev. William Mason was a versatile person. He is perhaps best remembered for his literary works, but he also made incursions into musical composition, and tried his hand at painting,[1] drawing, and landscape-gardening. Though only a mediocre artist himself, he brought up and helped to train two painters, first his servant Charles Carter,[2] and later in 1794 a young lad of fifteen who remains unidentified.[3] Outside his own home he occasionally took on the role of drawing-master, for we hear of him in 1783 teaching Mrs. William Harcourt at Nuneham to paint with a new medium of his own invention.[4]

With him Gilpin exchanged information about drawing materials and techniques—their letters show a constant preoccupation with ink recipes, glazing,[5] the search for suitable paper, the use of water-colours, and with various etching and tinting methods. The very first day they met, they discussed the advantages of carrying pen, ink, and a memorandum book, when going on a solitary walk.[6] Though Mason can hardly be called a pupil of

[1] Among the subjects which Mason is known to have treated in oils are a *Holy Family*, a *Cure of Saul*, and a *Good Samaritan*. This last was the altar-piece in the church at Nuneham, much admired by Horace Walpole (Horace Walpole to Mason, 22 Sept. 1783, in *Horace Walpole's Correspondence*, Yale edition, vol. xxix, p. 312). Mason writing to Gilpin on 31 Jan. 1785, says of these three paintings: 'My Samaritan had for two years a kind of pu[r]ple *vest* under a Crimson Mantle he chang[e]d it last summer for a chastised Yellow, which harmonized better with the pale carnation of the wounded Man to which it was in junction . . . But my Theological studies have made me drop the Pencil for some time. My Holy Family tho much improv[e]d wants its last touches, & then My Cure of Saul, that chef doeuvre, is at present in a miserable Condition. much the worse for the last sitting but far from irrecoverable.' (Rev. E. G. Benson.)

[2] Charles Carter (living 1788). As Mason's servant he was taught drawing and engraving. He etched rather indifferently the portraits of Mason (after Lewis Vaslet 1771), Gray (after Mason and Benjamin Wilson 1773), and Mrs. Pope (after J. Richardson 1774). In 1778 Mason left him in London 'to perfect himself in drawing at the Academy' (Mason to Horace Walpole, 13 Mar. 1778, in *H. W.'s Correspondence*, vol. xxviii, p. 369). After leaving his master's employ, Carter's career as a copyist does not appear to have been particularly successful. We find Mason recommending him to Walpole: 'He is a good copyist in oil and if you could recommend him to anybody who wants a picture cheaply and faithfully copied, he would answer their purpose and be an act of charity' (4 May 1783, in *H. W.'s Correspondence*, vol. xxix, p. 291).

[3] In June 1794 Mason visited Vicar's Hill attended by 'a young Lad of 15 whom (out of Charity) I am bringing up as a Painter' (Mason to W. G., 30 May 1794). On that occasion Gilpin gave the boy lessons, and the following summer he received further instruction in landscape-drawing from Thomas Gisborne (Mason to W. G., 18 June 1795). The last we hear of the young man is in Mason's penultimate letter to Gilpin: 'My Young Painter makes great strides towards Excellence. He has lately painted from his own design entirely a History

peice with four figures, the subject *ecce agnus Dei* which I think you would at least think very promising.' 19 Jan. 1797 (all three letters in the Rev. E. G. Benson Collection).

[4] Horace Walpole to W. Mason, 22 Sept. 1783 (*H. W.'s Correspondence*, vol. xxix, p. 311 and footnotes). Mason tried to obtain the qualities of miniature and oil painting by adding red lead (minium) to his oil-colours.

[5] See in particular W. Mason to W. G., 29 Mar. 1783 (Rev. E. G. Benson) for Mason's recipe for a brown indelible ink in answer to Gilpin's advice to use gum espaltum (see *supra*, p. 88); also W. Mason to W. G., 5 Aug. 1791 (Rev. E. G. Benson) for Mason's method for glazing prints and drawings with oil.

[6] Gilpin was to recall the incident in his portrait of Mason: 'Mr. William Mason was among Mr. G[ilpin]'s earliest acquaintance. Their first interview was accidental. Mr. M[ason] was going on a visit to Nonsuch, about half a mile from Cheam; & for some reason, I know not what, called on Mr. G[ilpin] in his way; and they went to Nonsuch together. Mr. M[ason] used afterwards to laugh, & mention a circumstance, which he said first prejudiced him in favour of Mr. G[ilpin]. As they walked to Nonsuch-park, the conversation turned on the advantage of taking pen & ink, & a memorandum-book, in a solitary walk. They both practised it; but Mr. G[ilpin] said, his great difficulty was in getting an accommodating mode of carrying ink; & mentioned several methods he had tryed; none of which pleased him. Some years afterwards, when the same subject happened to come up again, Mr. M[ason] alluding to the conversation they had formerly had in Nonsuch-park, told Mr. G[ilpin] how much pleased he was with the candid simplicity he shewed in entering into the various experiments he had tryed in procuring a portable ink-bottle. There is not a man in England, said Mr. M[ason], who has spent more time & attention on this very subject, than I have done: but I was ashamed to mention it to you in the same open manner, you mentioned it to me. From the time of this walk in Nonsuch-park, their acquaintance, which began then, continued till it afterwards grew into a friendship . . . .' 'A short Account of Different people . . .' (J. B. Gilpin-Brown).

Gilpin's, we find him sufficiently captivated by the picturesque formula to try out his hand at landscapes. In 1785 he confessed he had been making landscapes for five years,[1] without much success, for working rather slowly he could not reproduce the effects Gilpin achieved with a freely moving pen. Here is Gilpin's criticism of four of his early landscapes:

I transmit your drawings by the hands of Mr. Fraser; & now I will tell you what I have done, & I have not done. I have numbered them on the back, for the sake of reference. No. 1 has suffered little, but in the alteration of the light, & shade; & in the touching of the trees on the foreground. But here I must remark, that you should never touch your distances, (objects especially so distan as mountains,) with any warm tint, which belongs only to foregrounds. The sky, & distances will have a better effect, if they are touched with the colder tint of Indian ink. You are apt I think to make your wooded hills too regular.—In No. 2 I have made nearly the same alteration; but the distance is too strong: & I durst not apply my sponge too much, least I should disfigure the likeness. I have endeavoured to introduce a little variety into the valley in front, by the application of a more confined light: but I know you will think I have done mischief. For I know 2 things: the one is, that you will think I have spoiled your drawings; & the other is, that you will be so civil, as not to tell me so.—No. 3 I have not touched; & the reason is, I think you have mistaken the water-line, & I did not understand it. Besides, I never dare attempt water in motion. I do not think *you* are very great in your attempts of that kind: but I think you are greatly superior to *me*. Your hill on the foreground is too regular; & so are your rocks on the edge of the bank.—No. 4 is untouched likewise; & for a similar reason. Your agitated water is not well expressed; but it is not in my power to amend it. Besides, there is something wrong, which I cannot set right, in the perspective of your rocks; those beyond the wheel; & those beyond the river. And here I cannot help lamenting that proneness to self-deceit which is so inherent in human nature. You can tell half a dozen files [?] in perspective, & go to bed with an easy conscience. Whereas if I happen to make a slip only of a straw-breadth in a water-line, your wrath is up, & I am branded with all the opprobrious names you can invent. For shame! for shame! Have more candour, & fellow-feeling.[2]

He sweetened the pill with a gift of three of his own drawings.[3] During the 1780's, the person whose talent Gilpin tried to foster most was William, the eldest son of William Lock.[4] From a very early age he showed an astonishing gift for drawing, and his precociousness may be judged from the portraits of two schoolfellows he etched in 1780, when only a schoolboy of thirteen at Cheam.[5] Under the influence of Fuseli, who stayed

---

[1] W. Mason to W. G., 28 Feb. 1785 (Rev. E. G. Benson).

[2] W. G. to W. Mason, 9 Aug. 1779 (W. L. Benson).

[3] Mason thanked Gilpin for 'the pains which you have bestowd on my miserable Drawings which had you thrown into the fire I should have been full as thankful, had not they been the cause of my receiving three beautiful ones of your own in the Pacquet'. 12 Jan. 1780 (Rev. E. G. Benson).

[4] William Lock II (1767–1847). See Duchess of Sermoneta, *The Locks of Norbury*, London, 1940; and I. A. Williams, *Early English Water-Colours*, p. 232. Judging from the number of Lock drawings still in the hands of the Benson family, Gilpin must have had a large collection of them. There are eight folders, including juvenalia, in the possession of George F. Benson. Other drawings are in the collections of Rev. E. G. Benson and W. L. Benson. The British Museum

has a few, and the Victoria and Albert Museum received a number in 1947, through the gift of Dr. Annette M. Benson. Lock's work is often confused with that of Fuseli and Blake. For example, 'The Ancient of Days' in the Thomas Lowinsky Collection has wrongly been attributed to Blake (see Michael Ayrton, 'British Drawings', *Aspects of British Art*, London, 1947, p. 37).

[5] George F. Benson Collection. They are portraits of 'N. Vansittart', later Lord Bexley, and 'S. M. Godschall'. On the verso of this second etching Lock II wrote 'June 1780. This & its partner are the two first portraits & etchings the author of them ever made, being then in his 13th. year. They are taken of two of his school-fellows. The lines are too black & strong, which was occasioned by the badness of the plates; & has given the portraits an older look than they should

at Norbury Park, he continued to progress; then in about 1786, as the indolent side of his nature asserted itself, the spark of genius left him, and for the rest of his long life he hardly drew anything worthy of notice. There is a world of difference between the charming but rather insipid prints done after William Lock II by Bartolozzi, and others between 1796 and 1799 and the vitality and dynamic quality to be found in the drawings executed between 1780 and 1786 [12. *b*].

From the time he was a boy of ten, Gilpin followed William's development with as much wonder and anxiety as his fond father. He early sensed his instability and did all he could to encourage him to concentrate on and finish the particular project in hand.

> What shall we call his genius? [he wrote to his father.] I protest, I think it is something of what the ancients called an *afflatus*. I dare say, if you would watch him narrowly, when the fit is on him, you would see the signs of it: *Non comptae mansere comae—pectus anhelum*, &c—When he is not under this influence, he can do nothing.—When I saw him, last summer, I gave him a very noble subject, the death of Cardinal Woolsey in the abbey of Leicester; & desired he would put together a few figures on that subject for me. I am sure, he would have wished to gratify his old master: nay I know he tryed earnestly to do it.—It would not do.—The fit was not on him—nothing was produced, that pleased either himself, or me.—I went a step farther. I told him, how I thought the figures might be combined—how employed—& what appendages would be proper.—It was all one. Neither monk, nor cardinal appeared with any effect. So that you see plainly his powers are not under his own controul.[1]

Instead of persevering with the death of Cardinal Woolsey, William Lock II started on a study of Famine, which prompted Gilpin to exclaim: 'It is a happy thing for him however, that he has not his bread to get by his art. It would never do, if a person should employ him to paint the death of Woolsey; & he should send him home a picture of famine.'[1] The death of Woolsey begun in 1781 was not completed till 1787.[2]

From the correspondence and parcels of drawings which passed between Cheam, Norbury Park, and Vicar's Hill, we gather that until 1785–6, Gilpin saw and commented on nearly everything that William tackled. He mixed praise with honest criticism. His observations were taken seriously at least by Lock I, and often provided the springboard for discussions on wider artistic issues in which, as we have seen in the previous chapter, Lock shows himself an extremely capable exponent of picturesque theory.

As William's indolence became the despair of all who wished him well, Gilpin decided to make one last effort to shake him out of his lethargy. As all the normal ways of encouraging the young man had failed to produce the desired effect, he hit on the drastic measure of writing William's obituary notice as it might appear in some future work of

have had: but they are, otherwise, both very striking liknesses.—'

[1] W. G. to William Lock, 19 Feb. 1782 (Rev. E. G. Benson).

[2] The painting of 'The Death of Cardinal Woolsey' was engraved by C. Knight, 1 Mar. 1797. See B.M. 1917-12-8-3194.

reference. The mock obituary notice was sent to his father on 22 February 1786, with this injunction: 'You will shew it to him, or not, as you think it may affect him.' Here it is:

Lock (William) flourished, if I may use the expression, in the reign of George III. He was born with the full genius of a painter. His ideas, & conceptions were sublime & energetic in a great degree; & classically pure. His observations on nature, & the works of the best masters, had been made with so much precision; that not only all his faces were varied (for he had as many different molds to cast them in, as nature herself) but the same passion, in different characters, was distinguished by something peculiar to itself. Besides the knowledge of real forms, he had the happiest invention in conceiving such as never existed. If he did not give you truth, he gave you that verisimilitude, which corresponded with your own happiest ideas. Indeed he was the only artist I know, whom I should have allowed to deal in (that very delicate species of composition,) ideal forms.

But all this variety of knowledge, to which was added a great accuracy in execution, did little more than furnish amusement to his own thoughts. His magic lanthorn was rarely exhibited. Mere thinking—that is, employing his imagination on agreable subjects—was an amusement to him. When he could call up, like a magician, with a glance of thought, or a few careless strokes of his pen, some noble figure, it amused him: but to draw into action the grand conceptions he had formed, to combine them in some noble whole—to pay an attention to grouping attitudes, & contrast—to consult the most beautiful disposition of light—in a word to study the arrangement of a whole picture, was an exertion, he could not easily prevail on himself to make. It is said, he attempted colours; & from the little he did, it was very evident, he might soon have made himself master of their powers, both simple, & combined: but it was too great an exertion to study them; & I cannot hear, that any cabinet can produce a specimen of his labours. All that remains of this master's works are the outlines of a few heads, characters, & slight detached figures, which were collected with some pains, & etched in a masterly manner, by signr. Stampozzi, who published them in a book, consisting of about 50 pages. At the same time, I must needs say, for the sake of truth, that Stampozzi's account of him, at the beginning of his book, in which he speaks so largly of his application & industry, is not sufficiently founded. The fact is, he was a born gentleman; & lay under the misfortune of not being obliged to use his pencil for his maintenance. If his father had been so kind as to have disinherited him; & bequeathed him only a pot of oil—a few bladders of paint—a pallet, & a dozen brushes, it is thought he would have made one of the greatest masters in the art of painting, the world ever saw.[1]

The 'prophetic' notice was shown by William Lock to his son, but it also failed to elicit the desired response.[2] For the next few years Lock II made several intermittent efforts at painting, and, in the autumn of 1789, set out full of good resolutions on a Continental Tour. However, when he realized his inability to compete with the great masters of Italy, he admitted final defeat. Gilpin for a time kept hoping for a miracle, and as late as 1791 read Lock II's observations on his travels for some sign.[3] Of the young man's studies of the works in Rome he wrote:

[1] Rev. E. G. Benson Collection.

[2] William Lock to W. G., 19 Mar. 1786 (Major J. R. Abbey).

[3] W. G. to William Lock, 14 and 30 Mar. 1791. (Rev. E. G. Benson). The Gilpins never quite gave up trying. In 1816 William Gilpin's son tried on behalf of a friend to secure drawings from William Lock II. His reply to his old headmaster was: 'With regard to your friend's wish to have some disigns of mine in the work he is going to publish, I must avail myself of the permission which you gave me & at once decline it—You have most considerately made this quite easy to me: & I do it the rather because there is at this time

He will probably improve his ideas of *form*: but as to *expression*, & *grand conceptions*, I know not where he will get any superior to his own. The great mischief is, he keeps his camera to himself. As young artists however are in general, I believe, more afraid of transgressions in *form* (as scholars are in grammar) than in any other part of their art, I hope Rome will give him a confidence in his lines, of which we shall see the effect.[1]

———————

Now that his picturesque works had made him a public figure, his opinions on architecture and landscape-gardening came under scrutiny. Those particularly interested were the nobility and country gentlemen, whose seats and estates he had described in the course of his travels. Some pointed to the inaccuracies of his observations or complained that he had not done justice to their latest improvements; others accepted his censure and carried out alterations. That Gilpin conscientiously took notice of these various reactions, is amply borne out by the numerous alterations and additions that appeared in subsequent editions of the *Tours*.

He himself was never able to indulge in building or landscape-gardening on anything but a very modest scale. This is a pity, for had he been able to lay out the grounds of an estate, it would have been interesting to see what practical form he would have given to his principles. As it was, the little money available was largely swallowed up in necessary repairs. At Cheam he eventually adapted the school to allow for a larger intake of boys, and his friend Whately laid out the grounds of his small garden. When he retired to the New Forest, he was faced with a vicarage and a church in dilapidated condition. At Vicar's Hill there was much to be done before he could take up residence, and for three or four years afterwards, as he told a friend of Oxford days, the Rev. W. Clarke, he was spending more than he could afford, 'by about 60, or £70: but I do not despair to get within compass. I have laid out more upon my house and garden, than what a prudent man would say was right: but I *resolved* to *live at home*; and therefore I thought it right to make my house comfortable; that my resolution might not be misled.'[2]

When he turned his energies to the garden, he certainly shocked the local residents with his innovations. 'In the midst of pick-axes, & wheelbarrows', he wrote to Mason, who was expected on a visit: 'I have begun my wonders; to the no small astonishment of my parishioners; who see the green walks of their late vicar rolled up, & laid aside; his gravel shovelled into heaps, & a thousand comical things, which they cannot account for. I am only afraid they will account for them by thinking their new vicar turned in his head.'[3]

To repair Boldre Church he displayed the same drive and initiative. Unable to get money

an artist of the name of Stothard whose labours in that way are preeminently successful tho his circumstances I fear bear no proportion to them.' W. Lock II to William Gilpin II, 6 Feb. [1816] (Rev. E. G. Benson).

[1] W. G. to William Lock, 20 Dec. 1790 (Rev. E. G.

Benson).

[2] W. G. to W. Clarke, 7 May 1781 (Rev. E. G. Benson— Brisco transcript).

[3] W. G. to W. Mason, 1 Oct. 1778 (W. L. Benson).

from the parish, he raised £70 by selling two of the church bells, one of which was useless, and met the rest of the cost out of his own pocket, with the result that 'I added two windows to the church gothizised a 3d—made a neat cornice, gave capitals to my pillars—tinted the whole a light leaden hue, and turned a very ugly, deformed thing, into a very decent parish church; I know not whether I have given intire satisfaction, for there is not the least red, or blue, nor yellow,—nor the least flourished ornament on the walls'.[1]

A great champion of Gothic architecture, he was fond of vistas and simplicity of colour and decoration. Though he disliked medieval paintings in churches and did not appreciate the Grotesque element in Gothic architecture, his viewpoint is nearer that of today than that of the nineteenth century. He would have been horrified at the elaborate ornamentation, the filigree ironwork, and the stained glass the Victorians introduced into churches and cathedrals.

His Gothic outlook, conditioned by picturesque ideas, is well illustrated by his reactions to James Wyatt's plans for 'improving' Salisbury Cathedral. In general, he approved of Wyatt's schemes: to remove the choir-screen and the massive beam above it, and to paint the whole church 'one uniform stone-colour', thus obliterating the decoration of the nave and aisles, as well as the 'circles containing ugly figures of legendary saints'[2] which covered the vault. On two points, however, he expressed reservations to Dr. Barrington,[3] with whom he had become acquainted in 1783. First, he objected successfully to Wyatt's proposal to fill with traceries the three arches leading into St. Mary's Chapel, at the eastern end of the Cathedral. Writing to his friend Clarke he told him in confidence what had happened:

The Bishop gave me Wyatt's plan[s] in my hand, and desired I would go into the Cathedral alone, and examine them at my leisure; which I did. To one capital part of the intended improvement, I ventured to object; and gave the Bishop my reasons in writing; which he sent to Wyatt: and I have reason to believe, Wyatt had the candour to be convinced: for the Bishop tells me in a letter, he is persuaded I will now object to nothing.—The case was this. At the east end of the church are three grand Gothic arches; beyond which is St. Mary's Chappel. Mr Wyatt, proposed to fill these three arches with tracery-work in the manner of the great window at Carlisle. I said I thought it was introducing a nugatory ornament; as no kind of use could be obtained by it.—And likewise, an inharmonious ornament, as there was *nothing* in the Cathedral of that mode, and age.—and lastly, it was destroying a great beauty; for the view of the pillars &c, of St. Mary's Chappel through the great arch, was both a very beautiful piece of perspective; and gave space to the Choir. I only tell you this to amuse you; but would not have you mention it; as there is great appearance of vanity in setting my opinion against the architect of the Pantheon.—But Mr Wyatt was probably never engaged in any Gothic work before; whereas I have in a degree studied it.[4]

---

[1] W. G. to W. Clarke, 9 July 1787 (Rev. E. G. Benson—Brisco transcript) and Catherine Brisco's footnote.

[2] *Western Tour*, pp. 56–57.

[3] Shute Barrington (1734–1826), an ardent champion of the protestant establishment, was successively Bishop of Llandaff (1769), Salisbury (1782), and Durham (1791). He spent large sums upon the repairs of Salisbury Cathedral and its episcopal palace.

[4] W. G. to W. Clarke, 3 July 1788 (Rev. E. G. Benson—Brisco transcript).

Next, he objected when Wyatt went so far as to leave the vista into St. Mary's Chapel entirely unobstructed, thus providing no natural break between church and chapel. Wyatt removed the communion-table from its original place (it was to be brought forward into the choir only when needed) and placed the low altar-screen at the far end of St. Mary's Chapel. Gilpin, on the other hand, wanted the table to remain in its original position, and the altar-screen to go immediately behind it, thus hiding from view the floor of the chapel and the bases of the pillars to the three arches, while at the same time ensuring a view into the chapel over the screen.[1]

Though these suggestions were overruled, Gilpin's attitude seems sound on aesthetic as well as liturgical grounds. The view right up the long nave of Salisbury requires some features to check the eye if only momentarily before it passes on, enabling the mind to register scale, proportions, and distances; these features are also needed to mark the separate functions of nave, chancel, and chapel.[2]

In the 1790's Gilpin continued to advise much in the same way as he had done in the 1780's, but his interests gradually changed. After 1794 drawing ceased to occupy him seriously. He felt he had lived his span of three-score years and ten, and such time as remained to him should be devoted to moral and religious works. Topics of a picturesque character still formed part of his exchanges with Mason, Mary Hartley, and Lock, and these are referred to in other chapters, while religious and philanthropic questions brought him in touch with new correspondents: Thomas Gisborne,[3] Dr. J. Sturges, the Chancellor of

[1] 'Tho I was always against closing the arches with tracery; I am doubtful, whether the effect was not better, before they were thrown so *intirely* open.—If that beautiful screen your Lordship shewed me, together with the communion-table, were fixed, where they stood before, the *base only* of the pillars of St Mary's-Chappel would be hid, while all the beautiful perspective would be seen through the open part of the arches. The eye then not having so good a criterion to judge of distance, as the base, and ground-plot of those pillars offered, will imagine the distance greater than it really is; and the idea by being in part curtailed, will in fact be enlarged.—In the theory of painting, I know it an undoubted rule, that an *exact-delineation*, of a grand object, often injures it's sublimity, whatever is discreatly left to the imagination, is always better compleated,—so much for the learned eye—for the unlearned, the Choir will then retain it's natural form, which many perhaps will think too bold so intirely to reject.—If Your Lordship thinks these hints worth communicating to Mr Wiat, and he should repudiate the idea, he has done all things so well, that I should be apt to repudiate it also.' W. G. to Dr. Shute Barrington, 11 Oct. 1790 (Rev. E. G. Benson—Brisco transcript).

Before publishing the *Western Tour* (1798), Gilpin added a whole chapter on Salisbury to his original manuscript.

[2] Would that those who recently advised the Dean and Chapter of Salisbury Cathedral to remove the Skidmore screen and the Gilbert Scott reredos, were imbued with Gilpin's picturesque attitude! Those features were erected in the nineteenth century to counteract Wyatt's uninterrupted vista. Gilpin's outlook is echoed in Mr. Richard Mount's article, 'Screens or Vistas in Cathedrals?' (*Country Life*, 29 Sept. 1960, pp. 672–3), which aptly calls the present bare roodless vista up the nave, 'an elementary exercise in perspective that has to do with telegraph poles and railway lines'.

[3] Thomas Gisborne (1758–1846), divine and philanthropist, who preferred the quiet life of a country squire at Yoxall Lodge in Needwood Forest to the bustle of a political career. He took an early stand against slavery and was an intimate friend of Wilberforce, Dr. Barrington, and Hannah More. His poems include *Walks in a Forest* (1794), and his ethical writings *An Inquiry into the Duties of Men in the Higher Ranks and Middle Classes* (1794) and an *Inquiry into the Duties of the Female Sex* (1797).

Gisborne became one of Gilpin's particular friends from the time of their first acquaintance in the summer of 1792. See in particular 'A short Account of Different people . . .' (J. B. Gilpin-Brown), and W. G. to Mary Hartley, 11 Oct. 1792 (Rev. E. G. Benson—Brisco transcript).

Winchester,[1] the Rev. William Green,[2] and Thomas Bernard.[3] His house continued a centre of pilgrimage for the curious and the genuinely interested, and among the most fruitful contacts he established in this way were firstly with Sir George Beaumont, who came with Sawrey Gilpin to stay for a week in 1795, and secondly with the poet Samuel Rogers the following year.[4]

Mary Hartley remained his most diligent pupil, consulting him at every turn whenever a problem of etching, aquatint, or colouring presented itself.[5] She was never very happy with the aquatint process and would on occasion get another artist to finish her etchings in that manner. With her he exchanged views on the work of a number of artists. There was the amateur Lord George Townshend,[6] of whom he possessed a sketch. Gilpin felt his caricatures were overpraised, as 'the likeness is not made out with a few free strokes, but by several unmasterly scratches', then added this anecdote which showed that Lord Townshend could on occasion use his skill to good purpose:

The late Mr. Glover told me, he was dining once with Lord T[ownshend], when in the evening a bonfire was made near the house, on the account of some naval victory. They had in the room an American savage, who was in the greatest distress at the thought of being roasted, & eaten at the fire, which he concluded was made for him. They all tryed to remove his fears; but in vain. They had no medium of language. At last Lord T[ownshend] took a piece of paper, & gave him a representation of a naval engagement—some ships sinking, & others running away. In short, he made him understand, that the bonfire was a rejoicing for a naval victory.[7]

Mary Hartley remembered staying at Raynham in 1779, when Lord Townshend gave her a number of his 'slight etchings' and drawings. While in general agreement with Gilpin's criticism, she recognized his gift for caricature, for as Sir Joshua Reynolds used to say, 'Lord Townshend cou'd draw the *soul* without the *body*'.[8]

Another artist was Miss Harriet Lister of York. This accomplished amateur was a person of education and means, who yearly travelled in the company of her mother into

---

[1] John Sturges (*c.* 1736–1807), L.L.D., author of sermons and religious pamphlets. From 1791 to 1803 he corresponded with Gilpin, and gave him useful advice on his *Exposition of the New Testament* and on the art of writing dialogues. See in particular the manuscript, 'On the Essay on Dialogue' (Dec. 1796) in the W. L. Benson Collection.

[2] William Green (1715–94), rector of Hardingham. Early education at Newark under David Hartley who became his friend. Fellow of Clare, Cambridge, for twenty years. Hebrew scholar, he assisted Gilpin with revisions to his *Exposition of the New Testament*. Gilpin wrote 'An account of the Revd. Mr. William Green, Rector of Hardingham in Norfolk, 1795' (W. L. Benson).

[3] Sir Thomas Bernard (1750–1818), Chancellor of Durham, barrister, treasurer, and vice-president of the Foundling Hospital and of the Royal Institution. Succeeded as third baronet in 1809. Took a great interest in Gilpin's charitable schemes and became a trustee of his school. Purchased drawings at the 1802 sale (lot 134).

[4] See *Samuel Rogers and William Gilpin*, 1959.

[5] In 1797 Mary Hartley etched a plate to illustrate 'The Graves of Glamorganshire', a poem by Miss Coxe (sister of William Coxe), which formed part of the *Female Mentor*. The following year she sent Gilpin a proof with this comment: 'I have lately been busy with aqua-tinta again; & perhaps hurt my eyes a little with too much employment; tho this has been only repairing the little plate that I did some time ago, for Miss Coxe's female mentor. I hope you will think I have improved it, by giving more strength & opposition to the lights & shades, than it had at first. 300 impressions are now striking off, but as I find there will be no less than 1000 wanted, for the second edition of the book, I imagine it will want repairing again. The soft tints of the distances wear out very fast. If you see any faults that I can rectify, it will be kind to tell me of them.' 9 June 1798 (W. L. Benson).

[6] George Townshend (1734–1807), 4th Viscount and 1st Marquis Townshend. A son of his, Lord Frederick, was at Cheam under Gilpin.

[7] W. G. to Mary Hartley, 13 Nov. 1794 (W. L. Benson).

[8] Mary Hartley to W. G., 8 Dec. 1794 (W. L. Benson).

different parts of Great Britain sketching landscape and setting down her impressions. In 1792 she called on Gilpin, and was greatly encouraged by his comments on her drawings of the Lake District and the Yorkshire coast.[1] She, at some time, had lessons from John Warwick Smith, and in 1793 we find her in Bath renewing acquaintance with Mary Hartley and discussing Smith's *'neutral tint'*, which, as Mary Hartley told Gilpin, 'she shewed me how to compose, with Prussian blue, Lake and light Okre. I think this mixture has an excellent effect in the distance & in the clouds; but I can hardly think it necessary, as I find Smith does, to cover the whole drawing *all over* with it, before he puts in the coloured tints.'[2]

In 1796 Harriet Lister made a late marriage[3] with Amos Green (1735–1807), a professional artist settled in Bath. Mary Hartley's letters tell us of Harriet Lister's sketching tours in Devonshire (1793), Cumberland and Dorset (1795), then with her husband in Derbyshire (1797), North Wales, Lancashire, and East Yorkshire (1801).[4] After his marriage Green left Bath for his wife's property in Yorkshire. He was known for his flower pieces, but by 1789 had become a picturesque convert, who frequently expressed his admiration for Gilpin's *Tours*.[5] His last years were devoted exclusively to landscape, in which he combined picturesque principles with an admiration for Claude. As the Greens worked side by side, their drawings took on a similarity, which makes it difficult to tell their work apart.[6] Actuated by a real love for natural scenery, they sought it in their old age in a far more dedicated manner than the majority of their younger contemporaries. As Mary Hartley reported in 1801, 'they travel in pursuit of picturesque beauty; they take sketches whenever they come, pursuing the course of rivers, & riding upon ponies, or climbing on foot, where carriages cannot pass'.[7] Furthermore, in her letters and diaries, Mrs. Green was able to give direct expression to her feelings for nature; the impact of colour and atmosphere is conveyed without the use of clichés or stilted imagery.[8]

[1] 'I had the honour of a call lately from a lady of your acquaintance—Miss Lister of York. She shewed me some of her drawings, which I admired much. Two of them, I thought excellent—one was taken from Windermere, or some other (I am not sure which) of the Cumberland lakes: the other was a corner of a cliff at Scarborough, with an opening in the second distance to a corner of the frothy tide coming in. The composition was picturesque, & the execution masterly.' W. G. to Mary Hartley, 17 Sept. 1792 (W. L. Benson).

[2] Mary Hartley to W. G., 9 Aug. 1798 (W. L. Benson).

[3] Harriet Lister's dates are uncertain. She was probably a little younger than Amos Green, and 'survived him some years' (*Gentleman's Mag.* xciii (1823), 124).

[4] See in particular Mary Hartley's letters to W. G., 3 Aug. and 8 Sept. 1793, 6 July 1795, 4 Aug. 1798, and 12 Nov. 1801 (W. L. Benson).

[5] 'Mr. Green . . . draws & paints better than any gentleman that I know; & he is so enthusiastic about all these effects that you speak of, from mists, clouds, streams of light, & other accidental causes of light & shade, that I wish you cou'd have some conversation together. I have lent him all your picturesque works, & he is so charmed with them, that he is determined to buy them all, but I am afraid that he will not now be able to get any editions of the Welsh Tour or the Cumberland Tour with good impressions of the prints.' Mary Hartley to W. G., 15 Aug. 1789 (W. L. Benson).

[6] It has been suggested, I think wrongly, that Harriet Lister 'must have been an amateur pupil of Amos Green's', and that her subsequent work illustrates the contention 'that the talented amateur was quite often the equal of the average professional' (I. A. Williams, *Early English Water-Colours*, pp. 240–1). The evidence of available drawings and of the Hartley letters makes it clear that Harriet Lister had been a skilled landscapist long before she met Green, that he never quite matched his wife's competence in this field, and that he probably learnt far more from her than she ever did from him.

[7] Mary Hartley to W. G., 12 Nov. 1801 (W. L. Benson).

[8] See in particular the 'Extract from Mrs. Green's account of her journey Nov. 1797', which Mary Hartley copied for Gilpin's benefit (W. L. Benson).

The letters from Bath brought Gilpin news of other artists: C. A. Bampfylde (1720–91), the elder Dominic Serres (1722–93), and especially Nicholas Pocock (1740–1821).[1] He knew little of their work, though in 1795 he was given a Pocock drawing by Sir John Blaquiere.[2]

Among other young ladies he encouraged there was Miss Sunderland of Lymington, who came to Vicar's Hill for drawing lessons,[3] Kitty Fanshaw of Reigate, who, after he had taken notice of her work, sent him an etching of chess players,[4] and Maria Pixell, who painted landscapes in the New Forest in 1799 and 1800. Early in 1799 she called on him to use his good offices with his brother, Sawrey, to get her four entries placed to advantage at the Academy exhibition,[5] and the following year she brought him two landscapes to examine—he found their foregrounds deficient.[6]

One of his parishioners was to make his mark as a humorist and amateur artist of Indian scenes; he was Charles D'Oyly,[7] the son of Sir John D'Oyly. When his father was forced to return to India after squandering away a fortune in England, his son went with him, though not before Gilpin had taken considerable interest in the young man and given him a love for drawing. In a letter which, posted in Calcutta on 3 September 1803, only reached England after Gilpin's death, Charles D'Oyly reassures him that 'I continue to amuse my vacant hours with Landscapes & sketches of figures. I own with shame a little in the Caricature. I endeavor to keep this latter talent within the bounds of Moderation & I think I succeed as I have not yet found the objects of my pencil in anyways affronted by it.'[8]

During his last years Gilpin had numerous contacts with the members of the Burrard family, who all practised drawing. There was General Harry Burrard,[9] who found sketching

[1] For Bamfylde see Mary Hartley to W. G., 29 Dec. 1788 and 14 Feb. 1789; for Serres, 4 Jan., 14 Feb., and 28 July 1789; for Pocock, 29 Dec. 1788, 14 Feb. 1789, 28 Oct. and 6 Nov. 1791, 10 Feb. 1796, and 31 Oct. 1799 (all letters in the W. L. Benson Collection).

[2] 'It represents the St George of 98 guns, coming out of Portsmouth harbour.' W. G. to Mary Hartley, 23 Jan. 1796 (Rev. E. G. Benson—Brisco transcript).

[3] W. G. to Mary Hartley, 11 Nov. 1796 (Rev. E. G. Benson—Brisco transcript). Miss Sunderland became Mrs. Neufville.

[4] 'Your friend Baron Maseres, and General Hyde are represented at the board. I never saw either of these gentlemen; but the former is represented rather an undersized, fat man,—the latter tall, and rather thin. But the expression of both, especially of the general, and of the young man leaning over the board, is admirable. If you never saw this etching, and have any means of getting a sight of it, I desire you will, as it will entertain you.' W. G. to Edward Forster, 12 Jan. 1798 (Rev. E. G. Benson—Brisco transcript).

[5] 'I have been employed these last three weeks in arranging the pictures for exhibition at the Royal Academy, & from the various claims I have found it a most troublesome office. I received your last whilst I was engaged in it, & gave two out of four of Miss Pixel's pictures conspicuous places; it was the best I could do for her. I have not seen her, nor do I know where she is to be met with in London. If she calls on me I shall be glad to see her, & will do her any service in my power.' Sawrey Gilpin to his brother W. G., 3 May 1799 (Rev. E. G. Benson).

Redgrave says of Miss Pixell: 'She was probably a pupil of S. Gilpin. She practised both in oil and water-colours, painting views and compositions. From 1796 to 1811 her works occasionally found a place in the Academy exhibitions, and were extravagantly praised by the press in her day.' She could only have become a very late pupil of Sawrey Gilpin's.

[6] W. G. to Lady Neale, 2 Apr. 1800 (Rev. E. G. Benson—Brisco transcript).

[7] Sir Charles D'Oyly, Bart. (1781–1840), married his cousin Marian Greer, who painted miniatures. See M. H. Grant's article on 'Notable Amateur Artists', *Country Life*, 18 Oct. 1956, pp. 840–1.

[8] Letter reached England on 26 Apr. 1804 (W. L. Benson).

[9] Sir Harry Burrard (1755–1813), lieut.-gen. in the army, commanded 1st Guards, and commanded the British forces at the victory of Vimeira, 1808; created a baronet, 12 Nov. 1807, for services at Copenhagen. He purchased many of Gilpin's drawings at the 1804 sale.

a useful accomplishment during bouts of enforced inactivity, as a prisoner of war of the French at Lille. His manner was close to William Sawrey Gilpin's, from whom he probably received instruction.[1] Gilpin himself encouraged the general's very limited skill with his usual tact. In 1799 he commented favourably on the Lille drawings, finding them superior to earlier efforts,[2] and on another occasion returned a drawing of a tree with these remarks: 'I think it is a master-piece; the bole is particularly well touched, and the whole management of it gives an excellent idea of what it is intended to represent.'[3]

Admiral Sir Charles Burrard (1793–1870) attained much greater proficiency than his father. He drew marine subjects and landscapes with equal facility,[4] and his choice of colour was similar to William Sawrey Gilpin's.

Caroline Bowles (1786–1854), a niece of General Burrard's, received her first drawing lessons from Gilpin. She drew very picturesque landscapes, as can be seen from a sketchbook of a tour in the Lakes (1823), now in the Library of MacGill University, Montreal.[5] She was to become a poetess and later the second wife of Robert Southey. Much of her life was spent at Buckland Cottage by the New Forest, and there she cherished the memory of her 'old friend', whom she was to recall in her narrative poem, *The Birth-Day* (1836). Therein she recaptured the feelings of the young girl who walked eagerly to Vicar's Hill, where a kind reception awaited her when she intruded upon the old man's privacy. There, in the calm of the small study, filled with pictures, books, and papers, she found Gilpin 'busy with his pen' or with

> grave tome, or lighter work of taste
> (His no ascetic, harsh, soul-narrowing creed),
> Or that unrivalled pencil, with few strokes,
> And sober tinting slight, that wrought effects
> Most magical—the poetry of art!
> Lovely simplicity! (true wisdom's grace)
> That condescending to a simple child,
> Spread out before me hoards of graphic treasures;

[1] W. G. to General Harry Burrard, 8 Jan. 1799 (W. L. Benson—Brisco transcript).

[2] 'Your servant was gone yesterday before I had time to acknowledge the receipt of your drawings—I now acknowledge them with many thanks for the great entertainment you have given me.—I remember, many years ago, when you were in America, your good Mother shewed me some of your drawings which hung in her parlor. She pointed out their beauties to me; but as I did not entirely agree with her, I was obliged with all my art, to parry what she said: and for my own credit's sake, I do not recollect once inspiring my conscience in that business. To say the truth, your *first manner*, (to speak of your works, as we do of Raphael's) was certainly not excellent.—Your present manner I assure you pleases me very much: and when we please other people, we should not talk of *spoiling paper*; we have a right to be pleased ourselves. Those drawings you made at Lisle (which I pre-

sume are intirely your own), must have contributed greatly to amuse during your imprisonment.' W. G. to General Harry Burrard, 8 Jan. 1799 (W. L. Benson—Brisco transcript).

[3] W. G. to General Harry Burrard, n.d. [c. 1799] (W. L. Benson—Brisco transcript).

[4] See Oliver Warner's articles: 'The Sketch-Book of a 19th century country gentleman', *Country Life*, 27 Feb. 1948, pp. 439–40; and 'Admiral Burrard's Red Book', ibid., 19 June 1948, pp. 1239–40.

[5] See Oliver Warner's article, 'Miss Bowles visits Southey' (*Country Life*, 2 May 1947, pp. 808–9), which reproduces two of her landscapes. The album is entitled 'Sketches from Nature Illustrative of the Picturesque and Beautiful'. Caroline Anne Bowles was the daughter of Captain Charles Bowles and Anne Burrard, sister of General Harry Burrard. She married Southey in 1839.

> Smiling encouragement, as I expressed
> Delight or censure (for in full good faith
> I played the critic), and vouchsafing mild
> T'explain or vindicate; in seeming sport
> Instructing ever; and on graver themes
> Winning my heart to listen, as he taught
> Things that pertain to life.[1]

Other young ladies who came to him were Harriet and Mary Anne, daughters of Colonel William Burrard. It was Harriet Burrard, the elder of the two, whom Gilpin knew best. He first met her as a very beautiful and playful girl of fifteen 'running about with her hair dishevelled over her face; & turning every thing into mirth'. She would then 'run up to Vicar's hill with her little sketches; & he was glad to overlook, & correct them, as he always found her diffident of herself; and ready to take advice'. As she grew up, she gave him some uneasy moments. Harriet was fond of riding at speed on horseback, but unlike Barberina Ogle, was prepared 'to listen to his advice with all gentleness; and always followed it,— till she was fairly out of sight'! After her marriage to Sir Giles Rooke, she settled down to raise a large family and continued to practise drawing. Sometimes she accompanied her husband, who was a judge, 'in his summer-circuit; & brought home her memorandum-book filled with sketches. These, at her leisure she formed into finished drawings; & touched her trees, & distances particularly with great skill, & a great readiness of execution.' Lady Rooke's willingness to learn gave Gilpin much pleasure—it also enabled her to achieve with some degree of competence those effects that lie within the compass of amateur dilletanti.[2]

Her brother, Sir Harry Burrard Neale, and Lady Neale became his neighbours at Walhampton after their marriage in 1795. Soon there developed between the old people at Vicar's Hill and the Neales a great intimacy. Whenever they were in residence, 'sir Harry, and his Lady, generally spent one or two evenings in the week at Vicar's hill. If the evening was fair, they generally walked down their own lawn; which brought them to Mr. G[ilpin]'s garden, the gate of which was left open. A dish of tea was their only repast; & about 9 or 10 their carriage came for them.'[2]

Lady Neale[3] drew figures and painted historical subjects before she met Gilpin. He soon advised her to study landscape, in which he felt 'she might *really* excell'.[4] In this he was not mistaken. For a time she made copies after Gilpin,[5] and took lessons from John Laporte,[6] in London in 1800. She converted her husband to drawing, and in the summer

[1] *Templeman*, pp. 203–6, reproduces in full that final section of the poem devoted to Gilpin.

[2] 'A short Account of Different people . . .' (J. B. Gilpin-Brown).

[3] Grace Elizabeth Neale (d. 31 Dec. 1855, aged 83), daughter and coheir of Robert Neale, Esq., of Shaw House, Wilts.; married Sir Harry Burrard on 15 Apr. 1795. For Gilpin's portrait of Lady Neale see 'A short Account of Different people . . .' (J. B. Gilpin-Brown).

[4] W. G. to Mary Hartley, 13 Sept. 1800 (W. L. Benson); W. G. to Lady Neale, 2 Apr. 1800 (Rev. E. G. Benson—Brisco transcript).

[5] Lady Neale to W. G., 18 July 1799 (Major J. R. Abbey).

[6] John Laporte (1761–1839). See Basil S. Long, 'John Laporte', *Walker's Quarterly*, no. 8, July 1922; and I. A. Williams, *Early English Water-Colours*, pp. 61–62. From

of that year the Neales brought Laporte with them to Walhampton.[1] Gilpin was delighted with some landscapes done in body-colours, and for a time was fascinated with the possibilities of the Laporte gouache technique, which Lady Neale handled with some skill. Here was 'a most beautiful mode of colouring landscape . . . more forcible than water-colours; & . . . without the glare of oyl'.[2] There was one snag: 'unless you can handle your brush notably, the colour dries so quickly that you cannot soften your tints.'[3]

His enthusiasm for body-colours was short-lived. He sounded Thomas Gisborne and Mary Hartley, but their reactions were not at all encouraging.[4] At the beginning of 1801 he was forced to agree with Gisborne that gouache was best left to the competent artist, and so advised the Neales 'to leave off body-colours for a while at least, and study more, in black & white, the *theory* of composition, and light in landscape. Colours, I know, are very fascinating to young eyes: but to old, and practiced eyes, like mine, they are very disgusting, unless very harmonious.'[5] And here is a sample of the instructions he forwarded to Sir Harry Neale,[6] to whom he had become attached as if he were his own son:

In the first leaf of the book, you will find a rough sketch. It is in that way I would wish you to study the *theory of landscape*, and refresh your mind only *now and then* with *colours*, which I know are very fascinating.—If you will bring half a dozen compositions in this way, merely in black-lead, when I have next the pleasure to see you, I will, in the room of a better master, correct your compositions.—It would not be a bad way to *examine closely* some *composition*, if it were even of mine, and then laying it aside make it out from your memory, and then correct it by the original.[7]

1794 to 1800 Laporte's London address is given as 34 Thornhaugh Street, Bedford Square. Lady Neale to W. G., 29 Mar. [1800] (Major J. R. Abbey).

[1] W. G. to Thomas Gisborne, 29 Aug. 1800 (W. L. Benson—Brisco transcript).

[2] W. G. to Mary Hartley, 13 Sept. 1800 (W. L. Benson).

[3] W. G. to Thomas Gisborne, 29 Aug. 1800 (W. L. Benson—Brisco transcript).

[4] 'Now for drawings in body-colours. I am not at present a convert to your opinion of the superiority of that method; but I am willing to listen to reason. I admit that I have not been in the way of seeing many good drawings in body-colours. In those which I have seen, I have admired the spirit & effects of parts. But the very circumstances which produced these merits seemed accompanied with great & uniform defects. Lights, & half-lights, lay in *patches* on the mass of shadow, without blending with it anywhere. Surfaces which shou'd have been horizontal stood perpendicular like walls. The general effect was dry & chalky. In short there was such a want of due softening & gradation, that the mode seemed fit for bold rough sketches, but for little else. I must add too, that I may bring together the whole body of my accusations, that I have been making (in conjunction with a very able Painter, whom at first I found strongly attached to your opinion), some experiments to put the powers of water-colours used liquid, & of body-colours, to the proof. And we find that in brilliancy of tone & colour in light, & in force & depth of shadow, the latter mode, in our hands, will not bear any comparison with the former. I say in *our* hands: for we neither of us profess to be skilled in using body-colours. I shou'd therefore like to know what vehicle Mr. Laporte uses to mix up his colours, on what substance he draws, what white he employs, & in short any particulars you please to communicate.' Thomas Gisborne to W. G., 29 Dec. 1800 (W. L. Benson).

'I am surprized that you like the style of painting in Body Colours; but I suppose you have seen better works of that kind than I have. All that I have seen have been detestable; neither having the clearness of watercolours, nor the force of oils. In some the colours have been glaring & tawdry; in others cold & dry. In all of them the shades have been lurid & without force.'—Mary Hartley to W. G., 4 Oct. 1800 (W. L. Benson).

[5] W. G. to Thomas Gisborne, 20 Jan. 1801 (W. L. Benson—Brisco transcript).

[6] Sir Harry Burrard Neale (1765–1840). Admiral of the White, Lord of the Admiralty, Groom of the Bedchamber to George III and William IV, M.P. for Lymington for forty-six years, commanded the St. Fiorenzo at the Mutiny of the Nore, 1797, and received the thanks of the city of London for sailing out under the fire of the fleet and escaping. George III visited him at Walhampton in 1801 and 1804. Commanded the Mediterranean fleet in 1825. On his marriage to Grace E. Neale, assumed surname of Neale. See 'A short Account of Different people . . .' (J. B. Gilpin-Brown) for Gilpin's eulogy of this man's exemplary life, written in 1801.

[7] W. G. to Sir Harry Burrard Neale, n.d. [prob. Dec. 1800] (Rev. E. G. Benson—Brisco transcript).

Sir Harry was never very proficient, though he sketched with pleasure, and made a number of drawings in Italy in 1802.[1] What he quickly acquired was a picturesque outlook that made him very critical of his surroundings. Stationed at Weymouth in the summer of 1801 he found nothing to excite his curiosity, the hills in the vicinity were hardly worth climbing for the view,

> & now you have open'd my understanding a little to the principles & Beauty of Composition, [he wrote to Gilpin,] I very frankly confess that I scarcely meet with any Scenery that meets my Bold imagination. I look for mountains & I see Mole-hills; lakes & I see Puddles, Trees & I see long Poles nicely trim'd by some dextrous Gardener. In short one would suppose that my late Gardener had planned all this part of the County, & yet some of the Promontories that present themselves to the Sea are very fine & would make good Pictures.[2]

Over the years the Royal family had shown an interest in his drawings. True the King had not always been very appreciative, preferring drawings that were neat and finished,[3] but the Queen had several times favoured him with direct requests to see his manuscript *Tours*, and latterly had expressed her appreciation of his religious works.[4] During 1799 the Princesses made several inquiries after his health, and early in 1801 he sent Princess Amelia two drawings of sunsets through Lady Neale who was her particular friend.[5] That summer their Majesties proposed to call on him at Vicar's Hill, but the visit never materialized, and although the King stayed with Sir Harry Burrard Neale at Walhampton, Gilpin was too old and infirm to make the journey. He recounted the whole incident to Gisborne and swallowed his disappointment philosophically:

> Sometime ago, my friend Mr Lock at Norbury-park, delivered me a message from the king, or queen or both, that when they came near Vicars hill, they would call upon me.—I concluded this was the time. So I consulted Lady Neale, my great oracle, in matter of etiquette, how I was to manage this arduous business? She told me, if I received them as an invalid, in my silk night gown, and slippers it would be well. 'But I cannot stand without my hat'—'You need only just raise it when you speak to them, or they to you'—Thus instructed I waited patiently; only practicing now

[1] Sir Harry Burrard Neale to W. G., Naples, 27 Nov. 1802 (Major J. R. Abbey); Lady Neale to W. G., n.d. [*c*. May 1803] (W. L. Benson).

[2] Sir Harry Burrard Neale to W. G., 5 Aug. [1801] (W. L. Benson).

[3] 'The poor king, who had seen several of my drawings, was speaking of them lately to a friend of mine, only a little time before he was taken ill; Well, said he, I must confess, I like to see something more neat: & I believe nine in ten are of his Majesty's opinion.' W. G. to Mary Hartley, 19 Dec. 1788 (W. L. Benson).

[4] 'I have this day written to Cadell at the Queen's desire for your serious Books & likewise those published particularly for the poor which she wishes to have to distribute about Windsor.'—Lady Neale to W. G., 30 Sept. 1799 (Major J. R. Abbey).

[5] Initially Gilpin sent two rough sketches, then wrote to Lady Neale: 'Mrs. Gilpin, who reads unuttered sentiments much better, than I can, tells me, she saw, you did not think the drawings you took home, such as you thought would please. Indeed they are only very rough sketches, fit only to be exhibited before such a judge as sir Harry, who sees in them, what alone they aim at, a little spirit, composition, and effect. If Mrs. G. has read your Ladyship right, I will instead of the 2 drawings you took, make 2 glowing sunsets, which perhaps may please better.' 22 Jan. 1801 (Rev. E. G. Benson—Brisco transcript). Lady Neale replied: 'I am of your opinion and Mrs. Gilpins, that *two glowing Sunsets* will more probably dazzle the Eyes of our young Princess.— Sir H[arry] will not let me return both the drawings, as he fancies he has more *taste* than the noble family in question & admires the Composition of one so much that he wishes you to allow him to copy it.' N.d. [prob. end of Jan. 1801] (Major J. R. Abbey).

and then a respectful bow: but not to the point of adulation, which I detest.—I was very desirous to have a little conversation with the king, and to make my own observations upon him.—But now, my dear sir, how do you think all this matter ended?—I did not see one of them, I was a little huffed at first, but humbler ideas soon arose: & I easily acknowledged the object not of consequence to arrest a cavalcade of forty horse; and carry such a body, tho but a little out of their way. The next morning Lady Neale told me they had desired to see me, at Walhampton; But she excused me, as she knew it would be inconvenient—Indeed I should never have thought about it. I must have dressed, which would have been one of the labours of Hercules.[1]

[1] W. G. to Thomas Gisborne, 8 July 1801 (W. L. Benson—Brisco transcript).

X. Sales of Drawings

In keeping with everything he undertook, Gilpin assured the success of the 1802 sale by careful planning. Nothing was left to chance. He started to advertise his charitable projects in 1791–2, by arranging for sets of his drawings to be displayed at the London residences of the Speaker and of the Bishop of Durham. This is how he approached Henry Addington, the Speaker of the House:

> I told him, that as he entertains, all the world, during the sitting of parliament, I thought it would benefit my scheme, if he would take half a dozen of my drawings (not as a *gift*; but to be *paid for hereafter*, as such drawings sell) and hang them up in one of his entertaining rooms; which would both introduce them into a good shew-room; & give him an opportunity to descant handsomly upon them. I owned, I was treating him too much on a footing with Langford, & Christie; but I hoped his dignity would accede to my request. He has promised all I could wish . . . .[1]

A similar request was made to Dr. Barrington through his wife.[2] Other friends received their drawings before the sale, on the same understanding that when the day came they would give their sale value for them. In this way Sir Harry Burrard Neale paid sixty guineas.[3]

In 1798 Gilpin considered selling his drawings through the Repository at Bath. This organization, presided by Mrs. Hannah More and a committee of ladies, periodically received works of 'ingenuity and industry', which were sold for charitable purposes.[4] Mary Hartley had herself supplied the committee with painted boxes and etchings. On learning that drawings sold at Bath were 'in general . . . but poor things; the works of Misses & petit maitres',[5] disposed of for very low prices, Gilpin did not proceed; as he confided to Mary Hartley, it would be bad salesmanship:

> Tho I have really a very moderate opinion of them myself, yet I should not wish other people to hold that opinion; & I rather think it would be degrading them to send them among the drawings of boys, & misses. When they come to the hammer, if they ever do come to it, it might be said, *that cart-loads of them* (as stories never lose in telling) *had been sent to the Bath-repository, where they were sold for eighteen pence, and half a crown apiece.* In earnest, as you tell me, very little

---

[1] W. G. to William Mason, 6 Sept. 1791 (W. L. Benson).

[2] W. G. to Mrs. Barrington, 20 July 1792 (Rev. E. G. Benson—Brisco transcript).

[3] '[Sir Harry Neale] had several of my drawings before the sale, which he was to pay for at the price such drawings sold for. I was sorry he was taken in for sixty guineas. He had particularly a book; a fellow to which was bought by an old pupil of mine, Sir Harry Mildmay [probably lot 129]', W. G. to Sir George Beaumont, 3 Nov. 1802 (Pierpont Morgan Library).

[4] On 12 Mar. 1798 Mary Hartley sent Gilpin the Repository's printed sheet for the previous season (W. L. Benson).

[5] Mary Hartley to W. G., 12 Mar. 1798 (W. L. Benson).

prices are given, I fear it might tend to fix a small price upon them; & I have too much modesty to fix a large one myself.[1]

In 1801 he decided to test the value of his drawings on the London market, and offered those of the *Scottish Tour* at White's in Fleet Street. Highly gratified at the sixty guineas they realized, Gilpin agreed to bring forward the sale of his work. The catalogue was ready, and his publishers, Cadell & Davies, printed free of charge an explanatory essay to be sold with the catalogue. He informed his friends of the impending sale and gathered a list of official sponsors. The main ones were the Earls of Dartmouth and Harcourt, the Bishop of Durham, Lord Redesdale and his brother Col. William Mitford, the Right Hon. Henry Addington, the Right Hon. Charles Yorke, Sir H. Burrard Neale, and Sir George Beaumont. The last was by far the most willing and active of his 'puffers', as he called them. Sir George increasingly took charge of the final arrangements. He favoured Christie as the most suitable auctioneer:

If you wish for a good flourish; according to the present state of that sort of pulpit-eloquence I believe Christie is the best *orator*. even Mr Philipps, as I was informed, after exhausting his power of description on a China utensil of a pea-green patern, confessed his want of ability to do justice to it, without he could be endowed with the stupendous talents of *Pall Mall*.[2]

He saw to the advertising, read through the catalogue, and was consulted on the order of presentation of the various lots.[3]

Prior to the sale Gilpin had already collected together £500 towards his school fund, mainly from the proceeds of the *Western Tour* and from the *Scottish Tour* drawings. The main sale of his drawings, on 6 May 1802, brought him the considerable sum of £1,625. 11*s*. 6*d*. (less £67. 15*s*. 6*d*. duty), and when James Christie waived his commission, 'I thought it right to return him my thanks in an inscription on a bit of plate'.[4] By August, with some 'picturesque debts' still to come in, the fund stood at £2,350.[5] Gilpin sought to increase it further, and to this end published the *Two Essays* and arranged for another sale of drawings, which took place two months after his death, on 6 June 1804, and realized about £200.[6] Through the efforts of his trustees the endowment finally reached the sum of £2,900.

His end was quick and not unexpected. Dropsy had gradually turned him into a near invalid.

[1] W. G. to Mary Hartley, 28 Mar. 1798 (W. L. Benson).

[2] Sir George Beaumont to W. G., 7 Dec. 1801 (Rev. E. G. Benson).

[3] In the draft of the catalogue, Gilpin had entered his drawings '*as* they were executed; which is not perhaps the best way of exhibiting them to the public. There is an art, I suppose, in classing them, either the best, first; or the reverse.' W. G. to Sir George Beaumont, 16 Feb. 1802 (Pierpont Morgan Library).

Christie's final order differed considerably from Gilpin's. Inside the cover of his folders and books of drawings, Gilpin had inserted his bookplate, and on the scroll surrounding the shield he indicated a lot number, which does not correspond to the one used in the 1802 sale. For example, lot 40 bears the number 23 on the scroll, 93 has 68, 95 (67), 96 (59), 122 (100), 134 (26), and 136 (12).

[4] W. G. to Mary Hartley, 5 Nov. 1802 (W. L. Benson).

[5] W. G. to Mary Hartley, 14 Aug. 1802 (W. L. Benson).

[6] For details of the two sales, consult Christie's marked catalogues. For additional information on the 1802 sale, see Gilpin's own catalogue (Rev. E. G. Benson) and another in the W. Frank Perkins Collection.

By early 1804 he found it increasingly difficult to go upstairs to see his ailing and bedridden wife. One evening he sent her this message:

My dearest Love, I was coming up in the morning, when you prevented me. In the evening I found my leg so stiff, that it rather wishes repose: yet I am not happy, when I do not see you at least once a day.—May the Almighty, who lays his hand upon you, lay it easy, is the affectionate prayer of your ever, ever faithful, W. G.[1]

Henceforth they communicated regularly by such little notes. On 4 April Gilpin seemed as well as could be expected, if not a little better. That afternoon he rested as usual on his couch. Shortly before dinner he got up walked over to the window and threw up the sash, when he was seized with a shivering fit, which, however, soon passed off. His nephew and curate, John Gilpin, was with him at the time. At dinner he ate little, then experienced another violent fit which greatly alarmed Catherine Brisco. He asked her for a glass of beer, followed this with his usual prescription for dropsy, a little wine, and fell asleep in his chair. Catherine Brisco, leaving him with John, went upstairs to look after Mrs. Gilpin. On coming down she found him unconscious on his couch, and breathing with great difficulty. Mr. Beckley was summoned. It was thought that something he had eaten disagreed with him, but as no remedy could be applied in his present state, he was with difficulty put to bed. He passed a relatively quiet night without regaining consciousness. By six in the morning his condition grew worse. Mr. Beckley came again only to say the end was at hand. It came between eleven and twelve. Only John was at his bedside during 'his last struggle', which 'was of short duration, after which he breathed easy for a few minutes and expired with out a groan'.

The funeral was as simple as he had always wished. The hearse driven by his own servant was followed by a carriage containing his son, William, and three nephews—they were his only attendants save for twelve of his poor parishioners who were his bearers. At Boldre Church the small procession was joined by the master, mistress, and children of his school.[2]

---

[1] In the possession of Mrs. Gwen C. Mellis.

[2] Based on Catherine Brisco's account of the death of William Gilpin (Rev. E. G. Benson) which complements that given by *Templeman* (pp. 215–17) and differs from it on points of detail.

APPENDIX A

William Gilpin: *Situation of the House*[1]

THE house stood upon a gentle eminence, fronting the setting sun. Before it, at the distance of half a mile of sloping lawn, diversified only with a few gentle swellings was spread a noble lake, at least 20 miles in circumference. Nature had traced along it's margin the most beautiful line; which it had ornamented with a great variety of enchanting scenes. The view from the house was very fine. The lawn descended to the water, which was spread at least three leagues before the eye. The shore, on the right was level, ornamented with clumps of trees, & scattered oaks: on the left it was hilly with close groves, which descended to the very edge of the water. At the distance of 2 miles a bold projection of wood shot half a league into the lake, & gave a noble turn to the water. Behind this promontory lay a considerable market town, of which very little more was visible than the spire & the ruins of a monastery among the trees. This village was a sort of port-town on the lake, & supplied all the country, on the other side with corn: so that little winged skiffs were continually traversing the lake in various directions; & gave great life to the scene. The full extent of the lake, which wound to the left, about a league beyond the promontory, was not discoverable from the house; the limit which appeared, about the distance of six miles from the house, was closed by a thick forest, which seemed at that distance only an hazy mass of wood. Beyond this limit, an extensive prospect of a rich, & woody country, with scattered towns, & villages, closed the scene.—Such was the appearance which the lake made from the house. But this is only a single view; to see it in perfection, you should sail round it. It exhibits a thousand beautiful scenes in its various bays & windings, perhaps none so grand as this; but many of them more picturesque.— Such was the view from the house in front.—Behind, it was more majestic. The rising ground, on which it stood, fell gently about ½ a mile on this side, as in the front: but was rather more abrupt, & uneven. On the south, the lawn was confined by a river, not deep, but rapid, forcing its way through rocks, which every where opposed it's passage in the mid channel. This river fed the lake, which it entered with a broad, & full current, having now gotten clear of the opposition which had fretted it.—Beyond the lawn rose a noble wood, which circled the house on the north, the east, & the south; but circled it irregularly, sometimes coming forward in bold clumps, in other places receeding into woody bays: Here leaving the lawn quite vacant, & letting in the river; & there detatching single trees, or 3 or 4 in a body, boldly into the middle of the lawn. On the south particularly the wood advanced nearly to the house; & some of the noblest oaks of the forest mantled it, on that side, with their shade.—Beyond the wood, on the north, & east, at a mile's distance from the house, rose a noble chain of mountains. On that which was nearest the eye, the wood seemed to struggle to get footing upon its shaggy sides, but was every where dispossessed, by bold projections of rocks, which reared themselves up, not in minute patches; but in grand masses, and beautiful strata. These mountains ran many leagues into the country; & afforded an endless variety of those grandest of all the scenes of nature. Many of them were rich with wood: some almost

---

[1] W. L. Benson Collection. From Gilpin's handwriting, this fragment was probably written in the late 1760's.

entirely covered with it: others lifted up their scathed, & weather-bleached bosoms, the skeletons of nature, & made a beautiful contrast with that variety of tints, which [. . .] the rest. But the most picturesque, tho not the noblest scenes, were afforded by following the course of the river, which ran through a winding valley formed by the chain. There you had rocky banks, water-falls, lakes in miniature encompassed with craggy precipices, & all that endless variety of scenery, which is produced by the association of rocks, wood, & water. Every thing, both here, & among the mountains, was wild, & romantic in the highest degree; but not fantastic. The shapes were all grand, natural, & noble, & borrowed no affected beauties from odd forms, & lawless singularity.— The view from the house received additional beauty from a setting sun, which threw such a glow over the chearful part of the landskip, the lake & country, while a solemn gloom took possession of the mountains, that the contrast was very pleasing. One evening I saw the contrast in great perfection, when a storm rising from the north spread itself, in the majesty of darkness, over half the hemisphere, & mingling with the mountains, produced one vast whole; while a bright sun, setting at the extremity of the lake, threw a thousand resplendent tints over that part of the landskip; & at the same time gave the storm it's full grandeur. A rising sun too appears with great beauty over the tops of the mountains. The indistinct haziness, & the various hues are often fine. The catching lights are beautiful; & the shades,

which, from rock to rock
irregularly thrown, with solemn gloom
Diversify the whole.————————

alps   a poem

William Gilpin: *A Fragment*[1]

—————————As imagination bodies forth
The forms of things unknown, the *painter's* art
Turns them to shape, & gives to aiery nothing
A local habitation, & a name.
                                        Midsummer night's dream

* * * * * * Having left this wild, & romantic country with regret, we came in view of lake Venlis; which being contiguous to the grand scenes we had just parted with, would, in a degree, we conceived, participate of their grandeur. As we had heard much of the beauty of this lake, we resolved to incircle the whole, tho it's circumference is estimated at 13 leagues.

I. Our first view of the lake displayed an extensive portion of it. On the left, in the 2d. distance arose the promontory, & castle of Bilvers. The island, & castle of Ulmer occupied the middle of the lake. Beyond them appeared the mountains of Ooust. The whole view was pleasing from various stands: but to make it particularly picturesque by gaining a good foreground, we were obliged to change our station backward & forward, till we had obtained a good one. Two large plane trees, which we met with, were of great assistance to us. The peak of Ooust is supposed to be the highest land within a hundred leagues of this place. In a peaceful valley, at the bottom of this mountain, lies a small monastery. It was pointed out to us; but as the eyes of a person acquainted with a spot, see clearer, I suppose, than those of a stranger, we could not even pretend to see it, tho the day was sufficiently bright. In this monastery, we were told, a very extraordinary pennance exists, tho for what particular offences we were not informed. The offender is sentenced to ascend the pinnacle of the mountain; where he waves the flag of St. Anthony, to give notice of his arrival; as a chimney-sweeper is obliged to shout, when he gets to the top of his chimney. But the flag of st. Anthony, it seems, has not lately been waved; whether the pennance is now connived at; or the house is become more regular.

II. As we moved a little to the left, we had another, and a better view of the promontory of Bilvers. It stood boldly out into the lake; & made the capital feature of the scene. The mountains of Ooust did not appear in this view. They were removed far to the left: & the distance was composed of the northern part of the lake, which consists of low ground. But tho the promontory of Bilvers appeared to more advantage in this view, the castle appeared to less, as part of it was concealed by rising ground. We got a very good foreground to examine this view composed of a rocky knoll.

III. We had still a nearer view, soon afterwards, of the castle of Bilvers; in which *it* appeared to more advantage, & the promontory lost much of its shape. None but persons used to examine the scenes of nature, can easily conceive what changes in the features of a country a little variation

[1] Mrs. Margaret M. Harvey Collection. Roman numerals placed beside the text refer the reader to illustrating sketches (see plates 13 to 16).

of position occasions. Nobody could have conceived the promontory, as we now saw it, to be the same, which ran out into the lake, in the last view. We saw this landscape to great advantage through the skirts of a grove.

IV.   We had also a different view of the island, and castle of Ulmer, which we had seen at a distance in our first view of the lake. The castle appeared in a very pleasing manner, united with a promontory, under which it seemed to stand; tho, in fact, it is half a league from it. The evening was hazy, which gave an indistinctness to the view, blotting out all the little parts of the promontory. But by giving an indistinctness to it, it gave it also a simplicity; & consequently a degree of grandeur.

V.   Here we took a boat, to get a nearer view of a strange building, which appeared from the shore to rise out of the lake; tho in fact it stood on an island in a sequestered bay, where it is not easily seen, except by those, who go in quest of it. It's form was that of the body of an immense church; but if any light was introduced, it must have been introduced from the top; for it seems never to have had any windows. For what use this strange edifice was originally constructed, we could not learn. The common opinion is, that it was built for a prison; & we heard a romantic story of a prince, who had been confined there, 30 years, with his daughter, a beautiful princess, lest there should be any children to disturb the succession of the usurper. The prince however gave her in marriage to the keeper of the prison, by whom she had a son, who afterwards became a man of great prowess, & cut off the usurper's head. But we could neither learn the name of the prince, nor of the usurper; nor in what period of time they lived. For myself, tho my opinion is unsupported, I rather believe this strange edifice, instead of a prison, was built as a repository for the goods, which were brought from all parts of the lake to the great fair at Vazner; which tho now decayed, was, 2 centuries ago, the greatest mart in the country. On the north side is the appearance of a vast gate, now walled up, opening into the water; which could have been intended, I should think, only to receive barges, & crane up goods.—In a picturesque light, the form of this building is simple; and makes a pleasing picture, as it breaks the lines of the promontory, that falls into the water beyond it.

VI.   Here we were driven from the shores of the lake by an immense bog; & traversing the higher grounds, had a very pleasing view of the water, in a 2d. distance. The lake here forms a narrow pass by the jutting out of 2 promontories. At the bottom of that on the right stands the tower of Herensaw, the only remaining part of the famous castle of that name; where the dukes of Wenmar lived in regal splendor.

VII.   Of this tower we had a nearer view soon after, where the lake appeared winding round it; the other promontory, which we saw in the last view, being removed out of sight.

VIII.   We saw it afterwards on the spot, where seated among its own ruins, & on a rocky knoll, it made a picturesque appearance. Yet in *itself*, it is merely curious, as the only remains of a celebrated edifice. We could just trace the great hall, where that definitive sentence passed, which gave the last blow to the liberties of the country. As the states were no longer assembled, this hall (as the Abbè [*sic*] Reynac informed us) was purposely demolished, that the people might no longer have before their eyes this palladium of their liberty.

IX.   The next form, in which the lake appeared, was a very contracted one. The ground, on the right, rose very high; & on the left, high enough to hide the extremity of the lake; so that only a small portion of it was seen. The distance consisted of flat country; in which we saw a castle on an eminence; but we could not learn it's name. The whole made a good composition, assisted by 2 or 3 trees on the foreground.

X. In the next view a portion of Liscomb-castle (or a name very similar) seated on a rock, formed an excellent foreground. The great hall here hath had a better fate, than the hall of Herensaw. It's massy ruins still exist, & shew it to have been a noble room, not less than 53, or 53, & a half of my paces in length, & about 35 in breadth. It is supported with buttresses, on one side, & inlightened with 6 noble Gothic windows on the other; which survey a very grand expanse of the lake; every where beautifully broken by promontories, & woody peninsulas running into it; with mountains rising beyond them. I scarce indeed know any place, which commands in all respects, a grander, or more beautiful view; tho it is greatly too extensive for the use of the pencil.

XI. The last view we saw on the lake, was a noble opening towards the mountains of Ovedon. The form of the landscape was (something like what we had just seen) a contracted portion of the lake. It is a form indeed, in which lakes, confined within lofty boundaries, frequently appear. But the Ovedon mountains made the grand part of this view; which were indeed very formidable. In these mountains, it is commonly believed, there are rich gold-mines: but they have never been wrought; & as nobody has disturbed them, they have disturbed nobody.

XII. We come now to the point, where this grand lake issues into the country in a noble stream. We crossed it by a bridge of 3 arches, where the river is contracted by high rocky banks. We then wound round a hill, on the other side, along a kind of precipitous road; & had a view of a

XIII. very noble curve of the river, near a broken arch on the foreground, which set it off to great advantage. The ruin is evidently of Roman architecture; & I should suppose a portion of an aquæduct: but we had no antiquarian at hand; & were no antiquarians ourselves.

XIV. We had afterwards another pleasing view, where the ruins of Groinseg-castle (I believe I spell the name right) in the 2d. distance made a conspicuous appearance. We only see a small curve of the river: but the imagination easily traces it's course. It first winds round a skreen on the right. Then it takes another turn round the promontory of the castle; & is afterwards lost among the mountains in the distance.

XV. We were presented, soon after, with another pleasing view of the river, in which it winds round the abbey of Stolpingen. The great church, with it's lofty spire, is the only part, which appears.

XVI. From hence we were introduced into a wild country, where we again met our old acquaintance, the peak of Ooust, which now took a station on the right. This was the best view of that celebrated mountain, we had ever had. It appeared here to be of the biceps family; & channelled with large fractures of rock. In the 2d. distance we had a beautiful bend of the river round a rocky promontory on the left. On the other side, the lights fell beautifully on a hill, covered with wood; under which, on a projecting knoll, stands a monastery. I inquired its name; but having been negligent in not minuting it on the spot, it has escaped me. And here we could not help remarking how beautifully every curve of this river is adorned with some particular object, either a castle or an abbey. If picturesque beauty had been the thing attended to, it could not have been better ordered. We were surprized at seeing, in several parts of this neighbourhood, a number of stone-pines; & almost imagined ourselves in Italy: but we were informed, that some years ago, an Italian monk, belonging to the monastery, who was fond of trees, had introduced this species of pine into the country, where they throve exceedingly.

XVII. The next reach of the river was a very pleasing one; but it was rather of the pastoral kind. The banks were low, & woody. The country beyond the river was flat; & the mountains very distant.

XVIII. Having passed through a thick wood, we emerged into a plain, which gave us a distant view of the magnificent ruins of Rocktingen castle. They are seated on the point of a rocky hill; & descending gently down the declivity, cover 9 acres. But I shall say no more of this old castle, as the gazettes of Europe have been so full of the honour it lately received from an imperial visit. I shall only add, that notwithstanding this honour, it would not, at the distance, at which we saw it, have afforded a picturesque view, if we had not been obliged to an old gateway, which occupied the foreground.

XIX. After riding a dreary league, we had a beautiful catch into an extended vale. On our right stood a rocky hill of a conic form; to which we were led through a woody foreground. A road, hewn out of the rock, was carried round the point of the hill. As we descended the other side,

XX. the vale opened beautifully. It consisted of much varied ground; the woody hills receding one behind another, in pleasing perspective. A river ran through the vale; but in this view we could but just see it, far to the left, under a woody hill. The rocky foreground, on the left, was

XXI. a part of the conic hill we had descended.—Behind a few trees, on the right, we were carried to see a cascade, which from the form of the ground, the woody recess, in which it stood, & the vapoury surge, which spread the light around it, made, all together a pleasing picture.

The vale became now so extensive, that we could take a view only of one side at a time.—On the

XXII. right, we had a very rich scene. A rock, rudely broken, arose as a side-skreen; & the river of the vale now appeared to more advantage, adorned with it's woody banks. I cannot however say much for the composition. The mountains rise too high on the left; unless there had been a skreen also on the left, somewhat higher. The composition would have been improved, if the highest part of the mountain had been nearer the rocky hill; & the lower part had gone off in perspective towards the left; but we must consider this as the part only of a scene. The vale is here bisected. If the left skreen had been added, the mountains on the left, would have united with it. But 2 reasons forbad. In the first place, the left skreen was not picturesque: & in the 2d. place, if it had been so, it would have made the scene too vast.

XXIII. A little below, we took a view of the skreen on the left hand side of the vale. It presented the simplest idea, that can possibly be conceived—a perfect contrast to the right hand side. It consisted of one plain declivity of a lofty hill; with all the detail about it, plain, & simple likewise; & unadorned even by a tree. Yet such simplicity, where the lines fall happily, is pleasing.

XXIV. We had the same simplicity, but in a grander stile, when the vale opened, as it did a little below, to the sea. We had only the simple view of a promontory running out into the water: but it's parts were so large, & indistinct; & it's form, connected with the sky, & the sea, so obscure, that the idea was not only pleasing, but sublime.

In a sheltered cove hard by, we found our little bark waiting for us, as we had directed: and going on board, we made towards the island of * * * * *

Desunt cætera.

Summary of William Gilpin Manuscripts

On Gilpin's death, the bulk of his large collection of manuscripts, letters, drawings, and prints passed intact to his second son William Gilpin, of Pulverbatch, and then to his grandson, Charles Bernard Gilpin, of Edinburgh (1801–91). On the latter's death the collection was divided among several Benson nephews, and to this day the contents of what was known as the 'Gilpin chest' are scattered among numerous descendants. The main sections of this collection are in the hands of Mr. Willoughby Lockwood Benson (W. L. B.) and his brother Rev. E. G. Benson (E. G. B.), Mr. George F. Benson, and Mr. Alan de Gylpyn Benson. One section formerly in the hands of Mr. Francis Alan G. Benson is now in the possession of Major J. R. Abbey (Abbey). Of the material which was sent to Gilpin's eldest son in America, John Bernard, what has survived is now shared by Lieut.-Col. N. St. Leger Moore and his brother Lieut.-Col. D. St. Leger Moore. Gilpin's nephew and curate, Rev. John Gilpin, who on marriage changed his name to Brown, inherited several papers and drawings: these are in the hands of his descendant, Dr. John Bernard Gilpin-Brown. Another collection, owned by Mr. Archibald L. Fawcett (A. L. F.), contains documents, letters, and family portraits, relating to the Gilpins and Scaleby Castle. This particular collection passed into the hands of the Farish family who lived in Carlisle, and in the nineteenth century the papers and paintings returned to Scaleby Castle, where they remained till the Fawcetts left the Castle in 1904.

A. MANUSCRIPTS

Poems

'Mors per Christum triumphata', 1740's	W. L. B.
'Upon a Shadow', 1740's	W. L. B.
'The Epicure & the worm, an epigrammatic fable'	W. L. B.
Epitaph on Mrs. Barwell, *c.* 1760	E. G. B.
Epitaph to his Father and Mother, *c.* 1776	E. G. B.—B. transcript
114th Psalm, a transcription, 1795 (in a letter to W. Mason, 27 Oct. 1795)	W. L. B.

On Animals

On the character of Horses, written by another hand with corrections by W. G., *c.* 1760	W. L. B.
Observations on Horses and Domestic Fowls:	Miss Anne Benson
(*a*) Observations on Horses	
(*b*) Account of Dingo, a dog from Botany Bay	
(*c*) Observations on Domestic Poultry	
Observations on Domestic Poultry (same as previous item)	Abbey—B. transcript
Observations on Turkies, Ducks, and Bees	W. L. B.
On the Character, and Expression of Animals written by Catherine Brisco with corrections and additions by W. G.	E. G. B.

Picturesque Works

Situation of the House, late 1760's	W. L. B.

A Fragment, containing a Description of the Thames, between Windsor and London, 1764	Victoria and Albert Museum

Kent Tour, 1768

3 small notebooks	W. L. B.

Eastern Tour, 1769

8 small notebooks	W. L. B.

Wye Tour, 1770

8 small notebooks with sketches	E. G. B.
Leather-bound volume of early draft with sketches, written by John W. Smith with corrections and additions by W. G.	A. L. F.
Beginning of a later draft, written by another hand	A. L. F.
MS. in author's hand	W. L. B.
Draft of dedication to Mason	W. L. B.

Tour of the Lakes, 1772

15 small notebooks of 'Particular Thoughts', 'Rough Thoughts', &c.	W. L. B.
8 leather-bound volumes of 'Tour thro' England'	
	W. L. B. (4), Abbey (3), Charles Traylen (1)
Mr. Hamilton's gardens at Painshill near Cobham, small notebook, 1772	G. F. Benson

North Wales Tour 1773

8 small notebooks	E. G. B.
5 small notebooks of sketches	W. L. B. (2), E. G. B. (3)
Leather-bound volume written by his son John Bernard, with corrections by W. G.	Abbey

South Coast Tour, 1774

3 small notebooks of sketches	W. L. B.

Western Tour, 1775

15 small notebooks	W. L. B.
2 leather-bound volumes of early draft	J. B. Gilpin-Brown
Bound volume of later draft written by his son John Bernard, with corrections by W. G.	Abbey
2 MSS. in another hand corrected by W. G.	W. L. B.
Fragments in the author's hand	W. L. B.

Scottish Tour, 1776

14 small notebooks	W. L. B.
2 small notebooks of sketches	E. G. B.

Remarks on Forest Scenery

38 small notebooks	W. L. B.
Bound volume, containing Book I only	W. L. B.
Treatise on an Oak Tree	W. L. B.
'Cadenem Oak', small notebook in another hand with corrections by author	A. L. F.

Three Essays

3 small notebooks (Three Essays)	W. L. B.
1 small notebook (First Essay)	W. L. B.
1 small notebook (Third Essay)	W. L. B.
1 small notebook (Third Essay incomplete) (see also catalogue of 1802 sale, items 127 and 128)	W. L. B.

Poem on Landscape Painting

Gilpin's first draft with Mason's transposition	G. F. Benson
Criticism of Mason's first draft	W. L. B.
2 drafts of Poem	W. L. B.
1 further draft in another hand?	W. L. B.
Remarks by Mason on Poem	E. G. B.
Drafts of Dedication to Lock by Gilpin and Mason (see also Mason–Gilpin correspondence)	W. L. B.

Two Essays

Drawings and Principles on which they are executed	W. L. B.
Draft of Essay II	W. L. B.

Religious Works

Morning, Noon and Evening, 3 personal prayers	E. G. B.—B. transcript
Noon and Evening, rough draft	E. G. B.
Distress, and Recovery collected from the Psalms	W. L. B.—B. transcript
A State of Trial and its Consequences, bound volume	W. L. B.
Psalm 19, a metrical version	W. L. B.

Exposition of N. Testament

Bound volume of Preface to Revelations	W. L. B.

Sermons

Wages of Sin, 5 volumes?	W. L. B.

School Work and Notes

The Cheam Promise Book, 1759–66	Abbey
Remarks upon shield of Aeneas, 1772, transcribed by Mr. Kinersley	W. L. B.
Commentary on Virgil (*Aeneid* viii, ix, x), 6 notebooks	W. L. B.
Commentary on Sallust, 1 notebook	W. L. B.
Notes on Plato, Epicurus, &c.	W. L. B.
Of Grammar	W. L. B.
Story of Niobe	W. L. B.
Notes on Virgil, as artist and historian	W. L. B.

Biographical Works

Life of Wycliff	W. L. B.
Life of Cranmer, incomplete	W. L. B.

Account of Mr. George Potter — E. G. B.
An Account of the Rev. Mr. William Green, 1795 — W. L. B.
Memoirs of Joseph Rogers, R.N., corrected by W. G. — W. L. B.

Memoirs

Memoirs of Dr. Richard Gilpin, 1791, written in another hand — Abbey
Another copy — Hesketh Hubbard
An Account of the Rev. Mr. Gilpin, rough draft — J. B. Gilpin-Brown
A short Account of Different people with whom Mr. G[ilpin] was more — J. B. Gilpin-Brown
or less intimate in the several periods of his life. (Containing short
biographies of Osborne Barwell, Thomas Bowen, Henry Bolt Cay,
Lord & Lady Dartmouth, John Davenport (pseud. Charles Thompson),
Mrs. Delany, Thomas Denton, Charles Etty, Edward Forster, Thomas
Gisborne, Mary Hartley, Dr. Jacob Jefferson, Richard Johnson, Mrs.
Leveson-Gower, William Lock, Mr. Long, William Mason, William
Mitford, Mrs. Morant, Sir Harry & Lady Neale, D. Duchess of
Portland, Lady Rooke, Mrs. William Rooke, Peter Waldo, John
Wilmot, Mrs. H. Wilmot, Thomas & Joseph Whately, William
Wray, and Sir Joseph Yates)
Sir Henry St. John, with copy of a letter apologizing to Sir H. St. John for — W. L. B.
writing his life

Moral Contrasts

Naimbana, 1 small notebook in another hand — W. L. B.
            2 MSS. in another's hand — W. L. B.
Lord Rochester — W. L. B.
Jonas Hobson, a poor day labourer — W. L. B.
Richard Philipson, incomplete — W. L. B.
Captain Savage and his Crew — W. L. B.
Blackbeard the pirate — W. L. B.

Various Works

Plan of Scaleby Castle, hand coloured — A. L. F.
Utopia, incomplete, 1740's — W. L. B.
Three Letters of Advice to an Undergraduate at Oxford, *c.* 1749 — W. L. B.
An Historical Account of the Weather during twenty years, from 1763 to 1785 — Abbey
Analysis of Mason's 3rd Book of the *English Garden* — W. L. B.
On the Variety of the Forms, and in the Internal Tracery, of Leaves, 1794 — A. de Gylpyn-Benson

Three Dialogues on the Amusements of Clergymen

1 MS. in small notebooks — W. L. B.
Another, on larger sheets, incomplete — W. L. B.

Dialogues

Preface on Modern Dialogue — W. L. B.
On Polite Arts, between Burleigh and Sidney, in another hand, corrected by — W. L. B.
the author

On Duelling W. L. B.
On Equality, in another hand, corrected by the author W. L. B.

Account of Boldre Parish School, in another hand, but corrected by the author W. L. B.
Contemporary MSS. on William Gilpin

Account of the Death of William Gilpin, by Catherine Brisco E. G. B.
Catherine Brisco's Letter to W. G. III, handing over her transcripts of
W. G.'s letters A. de Gylpyn-Benson and E. G. B.
Elevation, and Ground Plan of Boldre Poorhouse, 1801 J. B. Gilpin-Brown
Notes on Scaleby Castle and the Fawcett Family, 3 vols. A. L. F.

Personalia

7 documents relating to W. G.'s collation & induction to the Vicarage of A. L. F.
    Aspatrick in Cumberland in 1771, and to his preaching there in 1772
Drinking cup, horn lined with silver W. L. B.
Landscape glass George F. Benson
Silver watch Lieut.-Col. D. St. Leger Moore

B. LETTERS

Thanks to the piety and diligence of Catherine Brisco we possess the text of many letters which would otherwise be lost. After Gilpin's death she borrowed from their owners such letters of her cousin as she could find, and these she transcribed into notebooks. Later she made partial copies of her transcripts for members of the family. In the following summary of letters, Brisco transcripts and printed sources are only quoted where the originals have not been traced, and Catherine Brisco's second copies where her original transcripts are not available. The relationship to William Gilpin is indicated with round brackets after the correspondent's name.

I. *Early letters, 1739–1751*

3   to an aunt [Mrs. Griffiths?], 1742–5   Abbey (2), W. L. B.—B. transcript (1)
2   to Brown, Dr. John, 1744, 1745   A. L. F.
18 from „   „   1741–7?   W. L. B.
1   from Farish, James (future brother-in-law), 1745   W. L. B.
5   Gilpin, Elizabeth (*née* Langstaffe—aunt) to Gilpin, Matilda (mother),   A. L. F.
        1744–60
4   to Gilpin, Elizabeth (sister), 1742–4 (see also Section III)
                            Abbey (3), W. L. B.—B. transcript (1)
1   to Gilpin, Captain John Bernard (father), 1743 (see also Section II)   A. L. F.
1   from Gilpin, Captain John Bernard (father), 1744 (see also Section II)   A. L. F.
19 Gilpin, Captain John Bernard (father) to Gilpin, Matilda (mother),   A. L. F.
        1749–55
18 to Gilpin, Matilda (mother), 1739–47 (incl. one in part to his sister
        Elizabeth)   A. L. F. (16), Abbey (2)
10 Gilpin, Matilda (mother) to Gilpin, Captain J. B. (father), 1732?–55
                            A. L. F. incl. 2 transcripts
1   Gilpin, Matilda (mother) to Gilpin, Richard (uncle), 1730   A. L. F.—transcript

1	Gilpin, Matilda (mother) to Griffith, Dorothy (aunt), 1743	A. L. F.
5	to Griffith, Rev. Thomas of Houghton, 1749–52	Bodleian Gough MS. Durham 10.
42	from Potter, George 1745–55, (incl. 7 to Thomas Denton)	W. L. B.

II. *Cheam, 1752–77*

Letters written when Gilpin was at Cheam include a number of transcripts. Catherine Brisco explained how she secured these transcripts (indicated by an asterisk): 'I think it *incumbent* upon me to account by *what means* I have been able to insert the copys of the 53 [really 54] following letters, which were never intended to have been preserved.—When Mr Gilpin left Cheam in the year 1778; among several things committed to my care, were a great number of papers, and MSS, some to return when called for, others to amuse myself, other[s] to destroy or do what I would with,—among the latter, were several *copy-books*, filled with *copys* of letter[s], by way of *exercise* for his *eldest* son during the latter years of his being with him, for as it was necessary for *him* to emprove his *hand*,—his *stile*; and *readiness in writing*, his father when he used to fall in his way out of school hours, or holidays, used to bid him take copys of any letters that *happened* to be lying *unseald* on his table.—of course numbers of them were very *uninteresting*; but seeing among them others, that deserved a better fate, I never could bring myself to destroy them unlooked over, I have distroyed the whole of them; after merely taking a few; as a *testimony* to his *grandson*, how *strongly* they further *tend to characterize, every sentiment*, and every *action* of his *invaluable* Grandfathers life!—for *candour open dealing—care of his young folks*, while *under* it; and *solicitude* for their well-doing, after they *left him*.—I only lament that I cannot get hold of, the *large numbers* of *much more valuable letters*, that I *know* have been *variously* written, and on *various occasions*. Cath: Brisco.'

2	to Addington, Dr. Antony, a parent, 1762, 1768	printed in G. Pellew, *The Life and Corr. of the Right Hon. Henry Addington, First Viscount Sidmouth*, London 1847, i, 12; and in *Notes & Queries*, clv (1928), 313. Pellew also refers to two further letters.
*1	to Bardieu, [or Bourdieu] Mr., 1770	E. G. B.
*1	to Blackstone, a parent, 1770	E. G. B.
1	to Blackstone, Sir William, 1771	E. G. B.
1	to Brisco [brother of Catherine Brisco], 1765	E. G. B.
*1	to Clavering, General, a parent, 1769	E. G. B.
*1	to Clayton, William, 1773	E. G. B.
*1	to Collet, Mr., 1769	E. G. B.
*1	to Cranmer, Mr., a former pupil, 1771	E. G. B.
*2	to Farish, [Rev. James, his brother-in-law?], 1770	E. G. B.
*1	to Foot, Rev. Mr., a parent, 1770	E. G. B.
*1	to Ford, John, a former pupil, 1769	E. G. B.
*1	to Fowke, Mr., a parent, 1765	E. G. B.
*3	to Fowke, Frank, a former pupil, 1769–70	E. G. B.
*1	to Fraser, [William?], a parent, 1778	E. G. B.
*2	to Gale, Mr., 1770	E. G. B.
1	to Gilpin, Captain John Bernard (father), 1773	E. G. B.—B. transcript
3	from „ „ „ „ „ 1769–73	Abbey
1	Gilpin, Matilda (mother) to Gilpin, Margaret (wife), 1770	A. L. F.
3	to Gilpin, Margaret (wife), 1763–8	Abbey

1	to Gilpin, Thomas (uncle), 1760	E. G. B.—B. transcript
*1	to Glover, Richard, poet, 1769	E. G. B.
*3	to Greme, Mrs., a parent, 1769–70	E. G. B.
14	to Grimston, John, a parent, 1762–71	Lady Waechter de Grimston
*1	to Henley, Mr., 1769	E. G. B.
1	to Horton, [a brother-in-law?], 1771	E. G. B.
*1	to Jefferson, Dr., 1765	E. G. B.
*1	to Jennings, Mr., 1769	E. G. B.
*1	to Kelner, T., a former pupil, 1767	E. G. B.
*1	to Lloyd, Mr., a parent, 1766	E. G. B.
*1	to Lowth, Dr. Robert, Bishop of Oxford, 1769	E. G. B.
*3	to Mitford, William, 1770	E. G. B.
*1	to Moss, Dr. Charles, Bishop of St. David's, 1769	E. G. B.
*1	to Newton, Thomas, Bishop of Bristol, 1769	E. G. B.
*2	to Ord, [W.?], a former pupil, 1770	E. G .B.
*1	to Roebuck, Benjamin, a former pupil, 1770	E. G. B.
*1	to Sanxey, Robert, 1770	E. G. B.
*1	to Stamford, Earl of, 1774	E. G. B.
*1	to Steel, Mr., a parent, 1766	E. G. B.
*1	to Tappenden, Mr., a parent, 1770	E. G. B.
1	to Waldo, Peter, 1768	B.M. Add. MS. 38457, f. 250
*1	to Wall, Mr., 1769	E. G. B.
*6	to Ward, Mr., a parent, 1767–70	E. G. B.
*1	to Ward, J., a former pupil, 1770	E. G. B.
1	from Whately, Thomas, 1769	W. L. B.
*5	to Willes, Mr. Justice, 1767–70	E. G. B.
*2	to Yates, Lady, a parent, 1770	E. G. B.

III. *Vicar's Hill, 1778–1804*

1	to Anon. [a young officer], 1802	E. G. B.—B. transcript
1	from Anon. [prob. convict in N.S. Wales], 1797	W. L. B.
1	from Addington, Henry [later Viscount Sidmouth], 1801	W. L. B.
1	from Addington, John H., 1802	W. L. B.
1	from Antrobus, William, 1800	W. L. B.
2	to B., Rev., curate at Lymington, 1784	W. L. B.—B. transcripts
26	to Barrington, Dr. Shute, Bishop of Salisbury and later of Durham, 1783–1803 (incl. 2 to Mrs. Barrington)	E. G. B.—B. transcripts
8	from Barrington, Dr. Shute, 1798–1802	Abbey
1	from Beaulieu, Ch. (?) Baron de, n.d.	W. L. B.
11	to Beaumont, Sir George Howland, 1801–2	Pierpont Morgan Library
12	from „ „ „ „ 1801–2	E. G. B.
14	to Bernard, Thomas, 1798–1803	E. G. B.—B. transcripts
1	to Blaquiere, Sir John, 1795	Tullie House, Carlisle
2	from Bowen, Geoffrey, 1802–4	W. L. B.
3	from Brunskill, M., Mason's curate, 1797	E. G. B.

2	to Burrard, General Harry, 1799	W. L. B.—B. transcripts
7	to Cay, Henry Bolt, 1777–90	E. G. B.—B. transcripts
2	from Chamberlain, Mason, 1802	W. L. B.
1	from Chelsum, Dr. James, 1799	W. L. B.
13	to Clarke, Rev. Wilfrid, 1771–90	E. G. B.—B. transcripts
1	from 'Clericus', n.d.	W. L. B.
1	from Coram, Thomas, 1799	W. L. B.
6	from Crewe, Miss Emma, 1781?–88	W. L. B.
4	to Dartmouth, Earl of, 1776–90	}printed in *Historical MSS. Commission*, 15th
1	from ,, ,, ,, [a draft], 1790	}Report, Appendix, Part I: *The Manuscripts of the Earl of Dartmouth, iii*, 1896.
1	from Davies, Henry, 1802	W. L. B.
14	to Delany, Mrs., 1781–6	printed in *Autobiography and Correspondence of Mary Granville, Mrs. Delany*, edit. by Lady Llanover, London, 1862, 2nd series, vol. iii
1	from D'Oyly, Charles, 1804	W. L. B.
3	from Drummond, Andrew Berkeley, 1800	Abbey (1), W. L. B. (2)
1	to a Farish (?), 1781	A. L. F.
1	to Farish, Elizabeth (sister) & Moseley, Mrs. (sister), 1802	A. L. F.
1	to Farish, Miss Fanny (?), 1794	A. L. F.
1	to Farish, Rev. James (brother-in-law), 1789	A. L. F.
1	Farish, Miss Sarah Matilda (niece) to Gilpin, Margaret (wife), 1782	A. L. F.
89	to Forster, Edward, 1779–1803	E. G. B.—B. transcripts
10	from ,, ,, 1798–1803	W. L. B.
1	to Gilpin, John Bernard (son), 1798	W. L. B.—B. transcript
1	from Gilpin, Joseph, of America, 1800	E. G. B.
1	to Gilpin, Joseph Dacre Appleby (brother), 1795	E. G. B.
46	from ,, ,, ,, ,, ,, 1782–1803	E. G. B.
1	Gilpin, Joseph Dacre Appleby (brother) to his niece Mrs. Fawcett, 1799	A. L. F.
1	to Gilpin, Mrs. Joseph Dacre Appleby, 1802	W. L. B.
2	to Gilpin, Margaret (wife), *c.* 1803–4	Mrs. Gwen C. Mellis
2	Gilpin, Margaret (wife) to Farish, Elizabeth (sister), 1776, 1805	A. L. F.
1	Gilpin, Margaret (wife) to Fawcett, Frances Mercy (niece), 1794	A. L. F.
1	Gilpin, Margaret (wife) to her 5 sisters, 1803	A. L. F.
1	Gilpin, Margaret (wife) to Gilpin, John Bernard (son), 1803	E. G. B.—B. transcript
1	from Gilpin, Robert (nephew), 1800	A. de Gylpyn Benson
12	to Gilpin, Sawrey, R.A. (brother), 1789–1803	E. G. B.—B. transcripts
6	from ,, ,, ,, ,, 1795–1804	E. G. B. (4), W. L. B. (2)
54	to Gilpin, William II (son), 1782–1804	Abbey
100	from ,, ,, ,, 1772–1805, (incl. to his mother Margaret Gilpin, brother John Bernard & sister)	Abbey (99), E. G. B. (1)
33	to Gilpin, William III (grandson), 1794–1803	Abbey
23	from ,, ,, ,, 1794–1803	W. L. B.
31	to Gisborne, Thomas, 1792–1804	W. L. B.—B. transcripts
27	from ,, ,, 1793–1804	W. L. B.

2	from Goodenough, A., 1803(?)–4	W. L. B.
6	to Green, Rev. William, 1792–4	
	printed in *Gentleman's Mag.* lxxxix (1819), 503–4 and 606–8.	
8	from Green, Rev. William 1792–4	W. L. B.
1	from Grimston, Henry, 1800	W. L. B.
1	from Grinfield, Thomas, 1803	W. L. B.
2	from Guybon, Anne, 1794–5	W. L. B.
1	Hamilton, Dr. James to Gilpin, Joseph D. A. (brother), 1798	W. L. B.
1	from Hamond, Sir Andrew Snape, 1803	W. L. B.
1	to Hansard, Mr., printer, 1800	Hyde Collection, Somerville, N. Jersey
2	from Harnett, Henry, 1803–4	W. L. B.
3	to Hartley, David, 1783–5	E. G. B.—B. transcripts
2	from Hartley, David, 1785, 1801	W. L. B.
98	to Hartley, Mary, 1782–1802 (incl. 29 B. transcripts)	W. L. B. (64), E. G. B. (30), 4 printed in Rebecca Warner, *Original Letters*, London, 1817
109	from Hartley, Mary, 1781–1803	W. L. B. (105), 3 printed in R. Warner, *Original Letters*, 1 printed in Richard Warner, *Lit. Recollections*, London, 1830 (material from Warner sources most unreliable)
1	from Hatsell, William, 1803(?)	W. L. B.
1	from Holden, J., 1803	W. L. B.
20	to Holden, Rev. R., 1786–95	E. G. B.—B. transcripts
1	from Inglis, John, 1801	W. L. B.
2	from Johnson, Richard, Bishop of Botany Bay, 1798–1802	W. L. B.
1	from Knox, John, 1789	W. L. B.
1	from Lambert, Catherine, 1803	W. L. B.
3	from Lancaster, Daniel, 1800–3	W. L. B.
1	from Latham, William, 1800	W. L. B.
1	from Leveson-Gower, Mrs. Frances, 1799	W. L. B.
1	Anon. to Lewis, Rev. Dr., n.d.	W. L. B.
1	from Lewisham, Viscount, 1801	W. L. B.
7	from Lightfoot, John, botanist, 1782–7	W. L. B.
49	to Lock, William, 1781–96	E. G. B.
18	from ,, ,, 1782–1802	Abbey (16), W. L. B. (2)
1	from Marsh, Charles, n.d.	W. L. B.
117	to Mason, William, 1772–97	W. L. B.
107	from ,, ,, 1772–97	E. G. B.
12	from Mitford, John [Lord Redesdale], 1784–1803	W. L. B. (11), A. L. F. (1)
18	from Mitford, William, 1798–1802	W. L. B.
20	from Morant, Mrs. Mary, 1785–1801	W. L. B.
2	from Morant-Gale, E., 1799	W. L. B.
	Moseley, Mrs. (sister), see under Farish, Elizabeth	
16	to Neale, Sir Harry Burrard, *c.* 1800–4	E. G. B.—B. transcripts
23	from ,, ,, ,, ,, 1799–1804	Abbey (15), W. L. B. (8)

3	to Neale, Lady, 1799–1801	E. G. B.—B. transcripts
7	from „ „ 1799–1803 (incl. one to Mrs. Margt. Gilpin)	Abbey (5), W. L. B. (1), E. G. B. (1)
1	to Osborne, J., 1802	B.M. Add. MS. 42575
3	from Parkhurst, John, 1782–4	W. L. B.
1	from Pepys, Sir Lucas, 1795	E. G. B.
1	to Plumtre, Rev. James, 1801	Cambridge Univ. Libr., Add. MS. 5864. 220
1	from „ „ „ 1801	W. L. B.
1	from Polhill, Charles, 1800	W. L. B.
1	from Raches (?), Rev., 1802	W. L. B.
1	from Raikes, Richard, 1802	W. L. B.
1	to Reynolds, Sir Joshua, 1791 }printed in *Three Essays*, 1792	
1	from „ „ „ 1791	
1	from Richards, George, 1803	W. L. B.
9	to Roberts, Mrs. Eliza, 1789(?)–1803, (including one from Mrs. Margt. Gilpin)	W. L. B.—B. transcripts
2	from Roberts, Mrs. Eliza, 1792 and later	W. L. B.
12	to Rogers, Samuel, poet, 1796–1805 (including one from Mrs. Margt. Gilpin, 1805)	Professor E. S. Pearson
10	from Rogers, Samuel, 1796–1803	E. G. B.
1	from Rooke, H. S., *c.* 1801	W. L. B.
2	from Salter, Thomas, 1800	W. L. B.
	(also T. Salter to Dr. S. Barrington, 1800 W. L. B.)	
1	from Sanxay, William, 1798	W. L. B.
1	from Seward, William, 1796	W. L. B.
2	from Sharp, Richard, 1797	W. L. B.
1	from Somerset, A. M., 1800	W. L. B.
15	to Sturges, Dr. J., 1791–1803	W. L. B.—B. transcripts
6	from „ „ „ 1799–1803	W. L. B.
1	from Thomas, John, Bishop of Rochester, 1784	W. L. B.
1	from Vialls, Thomas, 1802	W. L. B.
5	to Warner, Rev. Richard, 1794–1802	printed in Rebecca Warner, *Original Letters*, 1817
1	to Weld, Thomas, 1802	W. L. B.—B. transcript
1	from „ „ 1801	W. L. B.
1	to White, Mr., 1801	Hyde Collection, Somerville, N. Jersey
1	to Wilmot, Mrs. H., *née* Barberina Ogle, 1796	E. G. B.—B. transcript
16	from „ „ „ „ „ 1784–96(?)	W. L. B.
13	to Wilmot, John, 1793–1803	W. L. B.—B. transcripts
20	from „ „ 1793–1803	W. L. B. (19), Abbey (1)
17	from Wray, Rev. William Ullithorne, 1763–94	W. L. B.
4	from Yorke, A., 1781–1801	W. L. B.
1	from Yorke, Mrs. A., n.d.	W. L. B.
2	from Yorke, Miss Caroline, 1788–9	W. L. B.

Addenda

SINCE the present work was completed the important collections of Gilpin family papers, which were in the hands of Mr. W. L. Benson and the late Rev. E. G. Benson, have been deposited in the Bodleian Library. The same library has also received the whole of Major J. R. Abbey's collection of Gilpiniana, except for three manuscript volumes of the *Tour of the Lakes* now in the Paul Mellon Collection, Washington. Major Abbey's gift contains several items I would have consulted had I known of their existence in time:

(*a*) Sketchbook of faces depicting various human emotions signed by Captain John Bernard Gilpin with his monogram (MS. Eng. misc. f. 198).

(*b*) Catherine Brisco's copy of the *Wye Tour*, from which the plates have been removed, tinted in wash, remounted and bound in (MS. Eng. misc. d. 557).

(*c*) *Scottish Tour*, three small notebooks of sketches (MSS. Eng. misc. e. 491–3).

(*d*) Draft of *Remarks on Forest Scenery*, volumes II–IV (MSS. Eng. misc. e. 499–501).

(*e*) 'The character of a good school-boy' (MS. Eng. misc. c. 338, fols. 94–105).

(*f*) 'The character of a bad school-boy' (MS. Eng. misc. c. 388, fols. 106–15).

(*g*) Copy of William Gilpin's will, accounts and letters of his executors, &c. (MS. Eng. misc. b. 73, fols. 275–338).

Mention should also be made of an interesting collection of William Gilpin drawings which recently appeared in the saleroom. This is an album of forty-six drawings, bound in half-calf and green linen cloth, $18\frac{1}{2} \times 14\frac{3}{4}$ in., inscribed on the outside cover 'Drawings by W. Gilpin.' Made up of several lots purchased by Sir Robert Harvey at the 1802 sale, it was bound together in the nineteenth century, each drawing mounted on buff paper with the watermark '1820'. Formerly in the H. C. Green Collection, it was sold at Sotheby's on 10 October 1962 (lot 92) to Colnaghi's for £360, and now rests in the Paul Mellon Collection, Washington. The volume contains: (1) eight large drawings *c*. $10\frac{3}{4} \times 14\frac{1}{2}$ in., (2) fourteen drawings *c*. $6\frac{1}{4} \times 10$ in., (3) twenty-four drawings *c*. $5 \times 7\frac{1}{2}$ in. Twelve drawings in the *second group* are provided with descriptive texts similar to those reproduced on page 95. In one of these texts Gilpin vindicates in picturesque practice Hogarth's 'line of beauty':

'The *waving line* was, no doubt, always more pleasing to an eye formed on the principles of beauty, than a *straight*, or *crooked* one; tho I know not that any one ever examined it scientifically, under the denomination of the *line of beauty*, before Hogarth. According to him (& he exemplifies, in his Analysis, all his positions) it pervades almost every thing beautiful both in art, or nature. In landscape, it's grand objects are *roads*, & *rivers*. It adds a beauty often to *trees*— to *surfaces of land*—& other forms, are often used by way of contrast. But in *roads*, & *rivers*, unless the reach be very short, the line of beauty is essential.—All these remarks may, in a degree, be exemplifyed in this sketch.'

Index

PLATE 1

a. Captain Gilpin: 'An emblem of the impotent effects of malice and envy'

b. Captain Gilpin: Ambleside Force

PLATE 2

a. Captain Gilpin: Lake scenery

b. Sawrey Gilpin: Lake scenery

c. Captain Gilpin: Lake scenery with boat and jutting rocks

d. William or Sawrey Gilpin: Mountain and lake composition

e. Captain Gilpin: Rocky landscape with waterfall

f. John Bernard Farish: Rocky landscape with waterfalls

PLATE 3

a. Captain Gilpin: Ideal landscape

b. Captain Gilpin: Pool in rocky scenery

c. Captain Gilpin: Entrance to a cave

PLATE 4

a. Joseph Goupy after Rubens: Diana and nymphs hunting a stag

b. Abraham Hondius: Hunters and their dogs

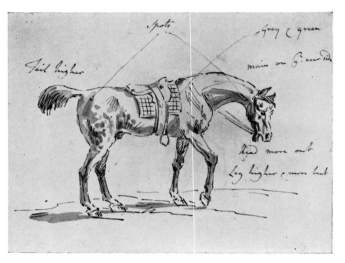

c. Sawrey Gilpin after James Seymour: Saddled horse

d. William Gilpin: Cockermouth Castle

e. William Gilpin: Rocky landscape

f. William Gilpin: Open landscape

PLATE 5

William Gilpin: Forest scene

PLATE 6

b. Genoese School: The blind Belisarius receiving alms

a. Salvator Rosa: Democritus

c. Rubens: Jesus at the house of Simon the Pharisee

d. Salvator Rosa: Belisarius

PLATE 7

a. Rembrandt: The sacrifice of Isaac

b. William Gilpin: 'Krickhowel-
castle' and 'Tratower-castle'

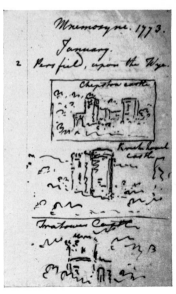

c. John Warwick Smith: Sheet
from a notebook

d. Sawrey Gilpin: 'Near Levens'

e. William Gilpin: 'View in Newton Park'

f. William Gilpin: 'An intersection . . .'

PLATE 8

a. John Warwick Smith: Carlisle 'From the Race-ground near the starting post'

b. John Warwick Smith: 'A view of Carlisle from the Raceground'

c. William Marlow: 'Scaleby-castle'

d. William Gilpin: 'A view in the vale of Lanercost . . .'

e. John Warwick Smith: 'Rose-castle'

PLATE 9

a. William Gilpin: Sketch No. 6 of Glastonbury Abbey

b. John Warwick Smith: View of Glastonbury Abbey

c. William Gilpin: 'Tintern-abbey from the land-side'

d. William Gilpin: 'View of Tintern-abbey from the road'

e. William Sawrey Gilpin: View of Tintern Abbey from
the road

f. Francis Jukes: View of Tintern Abbey from the road

PLATE 10

a. William Gilpin: Mountainous lake scene

b. William Gilpin: Figures in a cave

c. William Gilpin: Lake surrounded by mountainous scenery

d. William Gilpin: Mountainous lake scene

e. William Gilpin: Landscape seen through a screen of trees

PLATE 11

a. William Gilpin: Lake set in mountainous scenery

b. William Gilpin: Landscape with a winding river

c. William Gilpin: Looking up a narrow lake set in mountain scenery

d. William Gilpin: A view into a winding valley

e. William Gilpin: The waterfall

PLATE 12

a. Mrs. William Lock I (Frederica A. Schaub): Composition
of plant impressions

b. William Lock II: The conspirators

c. George Barret: Mountain and lake scene with a torrent in the foreground

PLATE 13

I

II

III

IV

V

VI

William Gilpin: Sketches illustrating the manuscript of *A Fragment* (see pp. 177–8)

PLATE 14

VII

VIII

IX

X

XI

XII

William Gilpin: Sketches illustrating the manuscript of *A Fragment* (see pp. 178–9)

PLATE 15

XIII

XIV

XV

XVI

XVII

XVIII

William Gilpin: Sketches illustrating the manuscript of *A Fragment* (see pp. 179–80)

PLATE 16

XIX

XX

XXI

XXII

XXIII

XXIV

William Gilpin: Sketches illustrating the manuscript of *A Fragment* (see p. 180)